M000315642

Post-Islamism

Post-Islamism

*The Changing Faces of
Political Islam*

Edited by

ASEF BAYAT

OXFORD
UNIVERSITY PRESS

OXFORD
UNIVERSITY PRESS

Oxford University Press is a department of the University of Oxford.
It furthers the University's objective of excellence in research, scholarship,
and education by publishing worldwide.

Oxford   New York
Auckland   Cape Town   Dar es Salaam   Hong Kong   Karachi
Kuala Lumpur   Madrid   Melbourne   Mexico City   Nairobi
New Delhi   Shanghai   Taipei   Toronto

With offices in
Argentina   Austria   Brazil   Chile   Czech Republic   France   Greece
Guatemala   Hungary   Italy   Japan   Poland   Portugal   Singapore
South Korea   Switzerland   Thailand   Turkey   Ukraine   Vietnam

Oxford is a registered trademark of Oxford University Press
in the UK and certain other
countries.

Published in the United States of America by
Oxford University Press
198 Madison Avenue, New York, NY 10016

© Oxford University Press 2013

All rights reserved. No part of this publication may be reproduced, stored in a
retrieval system, or transmitted, in any form or by any means, without the prior
permission in writing of Oxford University Press, or as expressly permitted by law,
by license, or under terms agreed with the appropriate reproduction rights organization.
Inquiries concerning reproduction outside the scope of the above should be sent to the Rights
Department, Oxford University Press, at the address above.

You must not circulate this work in any other form
and you must impose this same condition on any acquirer.

Library of Congress Cataloging-in-Publication Data

Post-Islamism : the changing faces of political Islam / edited by Asef Bayat.
p. cm.
ISBN 978-0-19-976607-9 — ISBN 978-0-19-976606-2
1. Islam and politics.   2. Islam–20th century.   3. Islam–21st century.   I. Bayat, Asef.
BP173.7.P67 2013
320.55'7–dc23
2012042888

3 5 7 9 8 6 4
Printed in the United States of America
on acid-free paper

In memory of Nasr Hamed Abu-Zaid, scholar and friend.

Contents

Preface

Currently a growing anxiety is expressed in the belief that the "Arab Spring" has turned into an "Islamist winter." Are we then on the verge of yet another wave of religious radicalism in the Muslim world? Has the forward march of Islamism beginning with Iran's revolution of 1979 assumed a new momentum with the Arab revolutions of 2011? This book, drawing on the historical studies of ten Muslim-majority countries extending from Indonesia to Morocco, suggests that the Muslim world may, in fact, be on the verge of a "post-Islamist" path, as political Islam is undergoing a significant transformation pushed by forces from within and without. Surely many religious parties in the Muslim world, as in Tunisia, Turkey, or Morocco, have indeed scored significant electoral victories and moved to the helm of governmental power. But is every "Islamic" party or movement necessarily "Islamist"?

It is striking that while so much is said about Islamism as a political and moral project, scant attention is paid to its shifting trajectories, especially if we exclude those who have suggested that political Islam has failed altogether. Even though there is now growing acknowledgment within the scholarly and policy communities that Islamism is in the throes of transformation, little is actually known about the nature, direction, or variations of change. Nor is there an adequate comparative framework to gauge the diversity of Islamist trajectories and investigate its implications for democratic order in Muslim-majority societies.

To explore the differentiations within Islamic politics and highlight their implications for a democratic polity, a few years ago I conducted a comparative study of religious politics in Iran and Egypt covering the period between the 1970s and 2005. The central preoccupation of that study, *Making Islam Democratic* (2007), was to interrogate the infamous question of whether Islam is compatible with democracy. I concluded that whereas Islamism understood as the deployment of Islam for the political project of establishing an Islamic state was unlikely to embrace democratic order, post-Islamism could and did. For unlike an Islamist politics that stresses citizens' obligations, "post-Islamism" is characterized by the fusion of religiosity and rights, faith and freedom, Islam and liberty. It is an attempt to transcend Islamism by building a pious society within a civil nonreligious state.

My early formulation of post-Islamism was based primarily on the experience of the Islamic Republic of Iran in the late 1990s, even though the transformation of Turkish Islamism embodied in the Justice and Development Party could readily invoke this trend. But a fundamental question remained as to the extent to which the post-Islamist trend had found meaningful resonance in other societies of the Muslim world and how much this early conceptualization could explain the diverse patterns of shifts found among different Islamist movements. I was already aware that the concept of "post-Islamism" had instigated some lively debate in both scholarly and political circles in Europe as well as in Turkey, Sudan, Indonesia, and other countries. To investigate the possibility of post-Islamism at large in the Muslim world, I convened an international conference in the International Institute for the Study of Islam in the Modern World (ISIM), Leiden, the Netherlands, in 2009, bringing together a dozen scholars of religious politics to discuss and highlight the traces of post-Islamism in multiple Muslim settings that ranged from Indonesia to Morocco.

That conference resulted in the studies compiled in this volume, which examine the historical trajectories of Islamist movements and regimes, bringing to light how they have shifted in the past three decades, in what directions, for what reasons, and what alternative trends they have engendered. The conclusions alert us that we should not look at Islamism as a static phenomenon but, rather, as comprising dynamic entities, which have been shifting as a result of their own internal dynamics as well as external and international exigencies. In addition, we learn how Islamism by its very operation has caused robust critical spin-offs expressing themselves in alternative trends of thought and action.

While the book offers fresh and comparative interpretations of the historical transformation of Islamism in individual countries of the Muslim world, it is particularly adamant to conceptualize such shifts with the aim of building a broad analytical perspective that can make sense of the general trends of Islamism in contemporary times. Drawing on the rich studies of individual Muslim societies offered by the contributors, I attempt to reengage with and revisit the notion of "post-Islamism," a notion that represents a critical break from and an alternative to "Islamist politics" and promises to make Islam compatible with democracy.

A number of individuals and colleagues have helped bring this project to its successful conclusion. Dennis Janssen, Marlous Willemsen, and the staff of ISIM assisted in organizing the Leiden conference; contributors came mostly from distant places to partake in the deliberations, while others served as discussants or assisted in logistical matters. Cynthia Read, my editor at Oxford University Press, appreciated the project and encouraged me to pursue its publication. I am grateful to them all. My greatest debt goes to the colleagues whose contributions constitute the bulk of this book: those who participated in the conference and those whose studies were solicited later. Their well-crafted works have enriched the debate about and our understanding of Post-Islamism. I wish to dedicate this volume to the memory of Nasr Hamed Abu-Zaid, a friend and an astute scholar of Islam, whose "untimely" departure has left many of us with a real void. His voice and wisdom are acutely missed in these unsettled times.

Contributors

Joseph Alagha teaches political science at Haigazian University, Beirut, Lebanon. His publications include *Hizbullah's DNA and the Arab Spring* (2012), *Hizbullah's Identity Construction* (2011), *Hizbullah's Documents* (2011), and *The Shifts in Hizbullah's Ideology* (2006).

Asef Bayat is the Catherin and Bruce Bastian Professor of Global and Transnational Studies and a professor of sociology at the University of Illinois, Urbana-Champaign. His interests range from religion and politics to social movements and urban space and politics. His latest books include *Being Young and Muslim* (2010) and *Life as Politics: How Ordinary People Change the Middle East* (2013).

Ihsan Dagi is a professor of international relations at Middle East Technical University, Ankara, Turkey. He has published widely on the topics of human rights, human rights and world politics, democratization in Turkey, and Islam and politics.

Abdelwahab El-Affendi, FRSA, is a Reader in Politics at the Centre for the Study of Democracy, University of Westminster (London), and coordinator of the Democracy and Islam Programme at the centre. He is also an AHRC/ESRC Fellow in the Research Council (UK) Global Uncertainties Programme, working on a research project titled "Narratives of Insecurity, Democracy and Mass Violence." He is the author of *Who Needs an Islamic State* (2008) and *About Muhammad: The Other Western Perspective on the Prophet of Islam* (2010).

Noorhaidi Hasan is a researcher on political Islam and associate professor of Islam and politics at Sunan Kalijaga State Islamic University of Yogyakarta, Indonesia. Currently he is the dean of the School of Law at the university. He has published books and articles on political Islam in Indonesia and other Muslim-populated countries in Southeast Asia.

Humeira Iqtidar is a lecturer in the Department of Political Economy at King's College London. She is the author of *Secularizing Islamists? Jamaat-e-Islami and Jamaat-ud-Dawa in Urban Pakistan* (University of Chicago, 2011).

Stéphane Lacroix is an assistant professor of political science at the Paris School of International Affairs of Sciences Po and a visiting researcher at the Centre d'Études et de Documentation Économiques, Juridiques et Sociales, in Cairo. His research focuses on Islamic politics in Saudi Arabia and Egypt. His most recent book is *Awakening Islam: The Politics of Religious Dissent in Contemporary Saudi Arabia* (Harvard University Press, 2011).

Thomas Pierret is a lecturer in contemporary Islam at the University of Edinburgh. He is the author of *Religion and State in Syria: The Sunni Ulama from Coup to Revolution* (Cambridge University Press, forthcoming) and the coeditor of *Ethnographies of Islam: Ritual Performances and Everyday Practices* (Edinburgh University Press, 2012).

Cihan Tuğal is an associate professor of sociology at the University of California, Berkeley. His book *Passive Revolution: Absorbing the Islamic Challenge to Capitalism* was published by Stanford University Press in 2009. He now works on welfare and Islamic charity in Turkey and Egypt.

Sami Zemni is a professor of political and social sciences at the Center for Conflict and Development Studies, Ghent University (Belgium), where he coordinates and leads the Middle East and North Africa Research Group. He currently holds the Francqui research chair (2012–2015). His area of expertise is politics within the Middle East and North Africa region, with special reference to political Islam. He has also written on issues of migration, integration, racism, and Islamophobia.

Post-Islamism

PART ONE

Introduction

I

Post-Islamism at Large

Asef Bayat

DESPITE THE CIVIL and secular thrust of the Arab Spring, many have expressed serious concerns about an impending revival of Islamic fundamentalism in the region. Supporters of the fallen regimes and right-wing U.S. and Israeli politicians as well as segments within the "expert community" in the West tend to view in the current uprisings the seeds of a creeping Islamist resurgence. Thus, the well-known Orientalist scholar Bernard Lewis, just weeks into the monumental popular revolutions that deposed Arab dictators, insisted that Muslims in the Middle East "are simply not ready for free and fair elections," for democracy, and that the best they could hope for would be a shari'a-inspired practice of *shura*.[1] The panic over a "resurgent Islamism" in the revolutionary Arab region was further bolstered when religious parties—Hizb al-Nahda in Tunisia, the Muslim Brotherhood and the Salafi Hizb al-Nour in Egypt, and the Justice and Development Party in Morocco—scored impressive victories in the general elections during fall 2011.

One should not rule out, at least in the short run, the possibility of religious resurgence by social forces that for years had been suppressed by secular undemocratic regimes. In fact, the removal of autocracies opens the social and political fields for all sorts of ideas and movements—regressive, progressive, religious, or secular—to emerge. The unexpected visibility of Salafi groups in the societies involved in the Arab Spring has caused genuine concern about the erosion of individual liberties, artistic expression, and gender rights. In such volatile times of realliance and renewal, there is no guarantee that a democratic order will come to life. It all depends on the intense and incessant struggles for hegemony among the innumerable political forces—known and unknown, old and new—that revolutions tend to release; it depends also on how the remnants of the defeated regimes and their domestic and foreign allies will behave.

However, the anxiety over "religious rule" associated with the Arab revolts is partly to do with a long-standing habit of equating anything "Islamic" with intolerance, misogyny, and authoritarianism. This frame of mind tends to connect, in one way or another, any type of "Islamic move-ment" with Khomeini-type clerical regimes or the Taliban's totalitarian rule, overlooking the fact that there are very different trends within such catego-ries as "Islamic movements" and "Islamic politics." The other part of the problem is conceptual. There is an unfortunate tendency to lump together quite different kinds of religiously inspired trends as "Islamist" while avoiding articulating any definition of the term,[2] as if any Muslim man with a beard and galabia, or woman with a *hijab*, or volunteer in a religious association is Islamist. I would suggest that, in fact, many of the religious parties (such as Hizb al-Nahda in Tunisia, Justice and Development in Morocco, and the ruling Justice and Development Party in Turkey) that seem to cause anxiety in the mainstream media are not actually Islamist, strictly speaking; they are arguably "post-Islamist," even though they all self-consciously remain Islamic. This essay is devoted to a discussion of "post-Islamism" at the global level. Here I examine the transformation of Islamism in the past three decades and highlight the implications of its multiple discursive and strategic shifts for democratic polities in Muslim societies. Particularly, I would like to revisit and sharpen the notion of post-Islamism with reference to the historical analyses offered in this book by eleven studies that cover Muslim-majority countries stretching from Indonesia to Morocco.

Islamism

But how do we understand "Islamism"? I take *Islamism* to refer to those ideologies and movements that strive to establish some kind of an "Islamic order"—a religious state, shari'a law, and moral codes in Muslim societies and communities. Association with the state is a key feature of Islamist politics—one that differentiates it from such reli-giously inspired but apolitical collectives as the Jama'at-i Tabliq-i Islami, a broad transnational movement that is not interested in holding gov-ernmental power but is involved in a missionary movement of spiri-tual awakening among Muslims. The primary concern of Islamism is to forge an ideological community; concerns such as establishing social justice and improving the lives of the poor are to follow only from this strategic objective.[3]

The Islamists' insistence on holding state power derives from the doctrinal principle of "command right, forbid wrong." This broad Quranic dictum remains vague, with varied interpretations about what constitutes "right" and "wrong," who is to command or forbid them, and how. Historically, it was largely the Islamic jurists or Muslim zealots who took it upon themselves to command right and forbid wrong, as in prohibiting wine, prostitution, or singing. But in contemporary times, modern movements and states (such as those in Iran and Saudi Arabia) have increasingly assumed that role. Islamists, then, are adamant to control state power not only because it ensures their rule but also because they consider the state the most powerful and efficient institution that is able to enforce "good" and eradicate "evil" in Muslim societies. As a consequence, the Islamists' normative and legal perspective places more emphasis on people's *obligations* than on their *rights*; in this frame, people are perceived more as dutiful subjects than as rightful citizens.

But Islamist movements vary in terms of the different ways in which they are to achieve their strategic goals. The *reformist* trend aspires ultimately to establish an Islamic state but wishes to do so gradually, peacefully, and within existing constitutional frameworks. These are the "electoral Islamists," as Humeira Iqtidar puts it. This strand rejects the use of violence and hopes to operate within the nation-state by invoking many democratic procedures; it focuses on mobilizing civil society through work in professional associations, NGOs, local mosques, and charities. The original Muslim Brothers in Egypt and its offshoots in Algeria, Sudan, Kuwait, and Jordan represent this trend; so does the Jama'at-e Islami in Pakistan and the Melli Gorus (National Order) movement in Turkey. Many groups associated with the Muslim Brotherhood seem to adopt a somewhat Gramscian strategy of establishing moral and political hegemony in civil society, expecting that the state will turn Islamic in the long run following the Islamization of society. Yet their actual co-optation within legal political structures may entail what Olivier Roy calls the "social democratization" of these movements, referring to how the European Socialist parties opted to work within rather than against capitalism. The Islamist parties in Jordan, Morocco, and Indonesia are argued to have paved a reformist path similar to that of European Social Democracy.[4]

The *revolutionary* or *militant* trends, such as the Jama'a al-Islamiya in Egypt, the Algerian Front Islamique du Salut, Lashkar Jihad in Indonesia, and Hizb al-Tahrir and Lashkar-e-Tayyaba in Pakistan, resort to violence and terrorism against state agencies, Western targets, and non-Muslim civilians, hoping to cause a Leninist-type insurrection to seize state power, which would then unleash the Islamization of the social order from above. Still, such militant Islamism differs from the prevailing *Jihadi* trends, such as the groups associated with al-Qaeda. Whereas militant Islamism represents political movements operating within their given nation-states and targeting primarily the secular national state, most Jihadies are transnational in their ideas and operations and often represent apocalyptic "ethical movements" involved in "civilizational" struggles, with the aim of combating such highly abstract targets as the "corrupt West" or societies of "nonbelievers."[5] For many Jihadies, the very struggle itself, or jihad, becomes an end in itself. And on this path, they invariably resort to extreme violence against both their targets and themselves (suicide bombing).

Global events since the late 1990s (the Balkan ethnic wars, the Russian domination of Chechnya, the Israeli reoccupation of the West Bank and Gaza under Likud, and the post-9/11 anti-Islamic sentiments in the West) created among Muslims a sense of insecurity and feeling of siege. This in turn heightened their sense of religious identity and communal bonds, generating a new trend of "active piety," a sort of missionary tendency quite distinct from the highly organized "apolitical" Islam of the Tablighi movement in being quite individualized, diffused, and inclined toward quietist *Salafism*. The adherents of such piety, which Olivier Roy calls "neo-fundamentalist," aim not to establish an Islamic state but to reclaim and enhance the self while striving to implant the same mission in others. As such, this trend is not "Islamist" by definition but may in practice lend support to Islamist moral sensibilities.

Modernist interpretations view Islamism as a movement of "traditional" Muslims (e.g., the ulema or clerical class, merchants, and the urban poor) who forge an alliance to resist Western-type modernization. Evidence, however, suggests that Islamism has received support from different social groups—traditional and modern, young and old, men and women, the better-off and the lower classes. But the core constituency of Islamist movements comes from the modern, educated, but often impoverished middle classes—professionals, state employees, college students, and graduates. The fairly popular idea that the urban poor and slum dwellers become the natural allies of Islamism—because of their "intrinsic religiosity," social dislocation, and need for community—is exaggerated. Indeed, the relationship between the Islamist movements and the urban poor remains mutually utilitarian. The urban poor lend pragmatic support to Islamists in exchange for tangible gains (services, aid, or social protection) in more or less the same way that they forge alliances with secular and leftist groups.[6] On the other hand, although some leaders come from the clerical class (like Ayatollah Khomeini in Iran, Hasan Nasrullah in Lebanon, or the militant Jebha ulema within the Egyptian al-Azhar), the bulk of the Islamist leadership in the Muslim world remains lay activists rooted in modern education and professions. In fact, the majority of the traditional and quietist clerics oppose Islamism for its politicization and secularization of the "spiritual realm" and the ulema's place in it. It is in this sense that El-Affendi describes Islamism essentially in terms of its "this-worldliness," which distinguishes it from the "otherworldly" Islam of the traditional ulema.

Notwithstanding their variation, Islamists in general deploy a religious language and conceptual frame, favor conservative social mores and an exclusive social order, espouse a patriarchal disposition, and adopt broadly intolerant attitudes toward different ideas and lifestyles. Theirs, then, has been an ideology and a movement that rests on a blend of religiosity and obligation, with little commitment to a language of rights—something that distinguishes it from a post-Islamist worldview.

What Is Post-Islamism?

In 1995, I happened to write an essay entitled "The Coming of a Post-Islamist Society" (published in 1996)[7] in which I discussed the articulation of the remarkable social trends, political perspectives, and religious thought that post-Khomeini Iran had begun to witness—a trend that eventually came to embody the "reform movement" of the late 1990s. My tentative essay dealt only with societal trends, for there was little at the governmental level that I could consider "post-Islamist." Indeed, as originally used, post-Islamism pertained only to the realities of the Islamic Republic of Iran and not to other settings and societies. Yet the core spirit of the term referred to the metamorphosis of Islamism (in ideas, approaches, and practices) from within and without.

Since then, a number of prominent observers in European and other countries have deployed the term, even though often descriptively, to refer primarily to what they considered a general shift in the attitudes and strategies of Islamist militants in the Muslim world.[8] In this early usage, post-Islamism was deployed primarily as a historical, rather than analytical, category, representing a "particular era" or the "end of a historical phase." Olivier Roy's well-known book *The Failure of Political Islam* implicitly heralded the conclusion of one historical period and the beginning of a new one. Thus, partly due to its poor conceptualization and partly for its misperception, the term initially attracted some unwelcome reactions. Some critics correctly disputed the premature generalization about the end of Islamism,[9] arguing that what seemed to be changing was not political Islam (i.e., doing politics in an Islamic frame) but only a particular, "revolutionary," version.[10] Others went on proclaiming, incorrectly, that post-Islamism signified not a distinct reality but simply one variant of Islamist politics.[11]

In my original formulation, post-Islamism represented both a *condition* and a *project*. In the first instance, post-Islamism referred to a political and social condition where, following a phase of experimentation, the appeal, energy, and sources of legitimacy of Islamism are exhausted even among its once-ardent supporters. Islamists become aware of their discourse's anomalies and inadequacies as they attempt to institutionalize or imagine their rule. The continuous trial and error, pushed by global factors or national realities, would make the framework susceptible to questions and criticisms. Eventually, pragmatic attempts to maintain the system would reinforce the abandonment of certain of its underlying principles. Islamism becomes compelled, both by its own internal contradictions and by societal pressure, to reinvent itself, but it does so at the cost of a qualitative shift. The tremendous transformation in religious and political discourse in Iran during the 1990s exemplified this tendency.

I saw post-Islamism not only as a condition but also as a project, a conscious attempt to conceptualize and strategize the rationale and modalities of transcending Islamism in social, political, and intellectual domains. Yet, in this sense, post-Islamism is neither anti-Islamic nor un-Islamic or secular. Rather, it represents an endeavor to fuse religiosity and rights, faith and freedom, Islam and liberty. It is an attempt to turn the underlying principles of Islamism on their head by emphasizing rights instead of duties, plurality in place of a singular authoritative voice, historicity rather than fixed scriptures, and the future instead of the past. It wants to marry Islam with individual choice and freedom (albeit at varying degrees), with democracy and modernity, to achieve what some have termed an "alternative modernity." Post-Islamism is expressed in acknowledging secular exigencies, in freedom from rigidity, in breaking down the monopoly of religious truth. I concluded that, whereas Islamism is defined by the fusion of religion and responsibility, post-Islamism emphasizes religiosity and rights. Yet, while it favors a civil and nonreligious state, it accords an active role for religion in the public sphere.

In Iran, the end of the war with Iraq (1988), the death of Ayatollah Khomeini (1989), and the program of postwar reconstruction under President Rafsanjani marked the onset of what I have called "post-Islamism." As a master movement, Iran's post-Islamism was embodied in remarkable social and intellectual trends and movements—expressed in religiously innovative discourses by youths, students, women, and religious intellectuals, who demanded democracy, individual rights, tolerance, and gender equality as well as the separation of religion from the state. Yet they refused to throw away religious sensibilities altogether. The daily resistance and struggles of ordinary actors compelled religious thinkers, spiritual elites, and political actors to undertake a crucial paradigmatic shift. Scores of old Islamist revolutionaries renounced their earlier ideas, lamenting the danger of a religious state to both religion and the state. In a sense, the Islamic state generated adversaries from both without and within, who called for the secularization of the state but stressed maintaining religious ethics in society.

Clearly this formulation of post-Islamism has an Iranian genealogy. But how extensive is the post-Islamist trend in other Muslim countries? And to what extent is the concept applicable to other settings? The studies in this volume offer detailed narratives on the ways in which Islamist politics in ten Muslim-majority countries (Iran, Egypt, Indonesia, Turkey, Sudan, Lebanon, Morocco, Saudi Arabia, Syria, and Pakistan) has been transformed over the past three decades. The outcome involves complex, multifaceted, and heterogeneous histories that nevertheless attest to the shifting dynamics of Islamism in varied forms, degrees, and directions. While the Islamic Revolution acted in the 1980s as the demonstration effect to bolster similar movements in other Muslim countries, Iran's post-Islamist experience has also contributed to an ideological shift among some Islamist movements. But how much have internal dynamics and global forces since the early 1990s contributed to instigating a post-Islamist turn among individual movements in the Muslim world? And what can these multiple histories tell us about how to conceptualize post-Islamism?

Critique from Within

Surely the Islamic Republic of Iran, the primary case upon which my earlier notion of post-Islamism rested, possessed its own particularities: Iran has been governed by a full-fledged Islamic state; and its top-down

Islamization has instigated much dissent from diverse constituencies, while the state's "developmental" policies have unintentionally generated modern subjects who aspire and push for a democratic polity within a post-Islamist frame. But post-Islamism is not unique to Iran. Numerous Muslim societies have experienced varied forms, degrees, and trajectories of the post-Islamist path. In the 1980s Turkish Islamists considered Islam a form of ideology that should regulate social, political, cultural, and economic domains through an Islamic state; and they believed that Muslims should be liberated from such Western notions of modernity as democracy, secularism, nationalism, progress, and individual liberties. But by the late 1990s, the Islamists abandoned these ideas. Instead they searched for a kind of modern polity that could secure a place for pious subjects. Thus, instead of forging an Islamic state, they opted to deepen democracy, pluralism, and secularism against the authoritarian Kemalist state. Not surprisingly, the prime beneficiaries of what the Islamists fiercely advocated—human rights, pluralism, and democracy—were themselves (see chapter 3).

Turkish Islamism had been embodied in the Melli Gorus led by Necmettin Erbakan, who established the National Order Party in 1970. The party opposed bank interest and membership in the European Economic Community and favored a "civilization inspired by Islam." Banned for being "antisecular," Melli Gorus established the National Salvation Party, with more populist and anti-West postures, which rose to prominence in the 1980s elections. Clamped down by a military coup, the party was resurrected in 1983 under a different name, "Refah," or Welfare, Party, with further radical stands. In the 1991 parliamentary elections, it captured 17 percent of the total votes and sixty-five seats. This remarkable victory marked the beginning of a steady process of "social-democratization." The Refah began to collaborate with non-religious groups focusing on nonreligious matters like poverty. Yet it caused a shockwave in the secular establishment when it seized in 1994 most of the municipal governments, including Istanbul and Ankara, and then defeated all secular parties in the 1995 general elections. Led by the military, the media, and the judiciary, secular forces unleashed a relentless campaign against the Islamic trend. They banned head scarves in government offices, cracked down on Imam-Hatip Islamic schools, and placed heavy surveillance on religious activities. The Refah was disbanded, and the popular mayor of Istanbul, Tayyib Erdogan, was arrested.

It was this secular opposition that, according to Ihsan Dagi, compelled the Islamists to "moderate" their positions. So, the Fezilat, or Virtue, Party, which replaced Refah, adopted from the beginning a pro-democracy and pro-Europe discourse. But the breakthrough came at the 2001 party congress, when the reformist Abdullah Gul challenged the traditional leadership of Erbakan and obtained the support of the rank and file to become the party's leader. Upon yet another military crackdown on Virtue, the Islamists gradually dissipated, while the reformists, organized in the Justice and Development Party (Adalet ve Kalkinma Partisi or AKP), thrived, winning 47 percent of the total votes in the 2007 general elections. The AKP has ruled the Turkish Republic until today. During its rule, the AKP extended the democratic space in Turkey; it restricted the military's interference in politics, abolished the death penalty, authorized Kurdish-language broadcasting, and eased the tension between Turkey and Greece. With steady economic growth over the past decade, Turkey became a model of democratic governance in the Middle East, and Erdogan became a hero of the Arab revolutionaries. When visiting Egypt in September 2011, Prime Minister Erdogan urged the Muslim Brothers to embrace not a religious but a secular democratic state.

This trajectory, for Ihsan Dagi, represents the Turkish path to post-Islamism. Or does it? Taking a political economy approach, Cihan Tuğal argues in this book that the AKP does not represent a shift to post-Islamism but, rather, a retrenchment of Turkish conservatism—that is, a mix of development, democracy, and Turkish nationalism as well as the piety of citizens and rulers. Islamism in Turkey, according to Tuğal, reflected the ideology of the declining provincial small entrepreneurs who stood against both state industrial policies and labor militancy. This ideology, couched in religious language and anti-Western sentiments, found appeal among conservative peasant farmers and artisans, many of whom had ended up in the slums and informal settlements (*gcekondu*) of large cities. Erbakan embodied that ideology. In view of Tuğal, what the AKP represents is not post-Islamism (marked by a blend of religiosity and rights, faith and freedom) but, rather, the rise of conservative religious communities, notably the Nurcu Gulen movement, against both the Islamism of the Melli Gorus and the peculiar Turkish secularism or state control of religion. Religious ideology apart, the AKP in essence has embodied Turkish "passive revolution," in that it has absorbed the challenge of Islamism into a neoliberal governmentality—one that is marked by national conservatism, free market globalization, limited pluralism, and the instrumentalization of religion.

Clearly both accounts on Turkey attest to a fundamental shift in and departure from Islamism. What they diverge on pertains to the degree to which the Islamic AKP really embraces democracy. While Dagi shows AKP embodying the democratic and post-Islamist shift in Turkish Islamism, Cihan Tuğal stresses its authoritarian thrust. Indeed, reports on the incarceration of journalists for publishing oppositional articles, intolerance toward Kurdish nationalism, and growing restrictions on secular behavior and lifestyles in public spaces have caused serious concerns about AKP's increasingly authoritarian behavior.[12] But repressive behavior of this sort is not necessarily related to AKP's religious sensibilities. Secular governments may also indulge in such undemocratic conduct, particularly when their self-confidence is boosted, as is the case with AKP, by economic success, regional power, and a feeble opposition. Yet, as I will discuss later, the post-Islamist extension of democratic space comes into conflict with its ambivalence toward the value of individual rights and liberties. In short, the AKP's extension of democratic space constricted the military's control over the polity and facilitated its own growth. But that same democratic space also fostered forces, like the more vocal Kurdish voices, to challenge AKP rule.

The course of Morocco's religious politics shows some similarities. Radical Islam in Morocco, similar to many other cases, had a partly Cold War origin—it was encouraged by the state as a way to counter the secular Left, which was identified with the Soviet Union and communism in general. Thus, in the 1970s, as Sami Zemni discusses here, King Hassan II courted the ulema to thwart the growing leftist movement. More importantly, the regime bolstered the Chebiba Islamiyya (Islamic Youth) of Abdelkarim Mouti'i, a Qotbian Islamist movement that spread its activities largely in the universities. But the activism of such groups often goes beyond what the regime intends; it also targets the regime itself. As the Moroccan state began to round up the militants in response, the leadership of the movement fled the country and planned in vain to ignite a revolution. But many of those who stayed behind began a course of reflection, questioning the merits of their violent strategy and radical views. Out of a final split in the movement emerged a "reformist" trend, which eventually moved toward legal party politics. "We went from a project of establishing an Islamic state [in the early 1980s]...to the establishment of a new mentality that has now a more positive relationship with reality," stated an ex-militant leader. Ex-Islamists such as Ben Kirane managed to overcome the regime's obstacles to set up the Movement for Unity and Reform

(Harakat al-Tawhid wa Islah) and later, in a coalition with older parties, the Justice and Development Party (Parti de la justice et du développement or PJD). The PJD rejected violence and recognized the constitution and the king as the Commander of the Faithful. With growing popularity, the PJD became the third largest party in the parliament by capturing forty-two seats in the 2002 elections, moving to first place in the 2011 elections making Ben Kirane the prime minister. Officially, the PJD does not identify itself as a religious party with "Islamic reference" but, rather, as a part of the "Islamic current."

Certainly the transformation of Islamism in Morocco has had its own particular course—not least because Islamists in Morocco, as in Turkey, had to modify their religious project in order to "make it work" within the constraints of state opposition and political exigencies. Yet, in the process, they undertook a paradigmatic shift in their perspective. Having embodied this shift, PJD then represented the Moroccan path toward post-Islamism. As Sami Zemni shows, the PJD has transcended the idea of an "Islamic state"; instead it aims to create a social order where justice is guaranteed through respect for Islamic values. In this process, it recognizes the people's "rights" and choices rather than merely stressing their "obligations." Even though the Movement for Unity and Reform, an illegal but tolerated Islamist party, continues to operate as an association, uttering at times the language of shari'a and even an "elected khalifa" within a democratic system, its discourse remains notoriously vague and thus subject to varied interpretations. It has announced its commitment to Moroccan constitutional monarchy. Some pragmatism seems to have permeated into even Sheikh Yassin's powerful—and illegal—al-Adle wal-Ehsan movement, as it has recently begun to train activists, prepare programs, and work with Moroccan political actors.

Unlike in Turkey and Morocco, where Islamist movements encountered hostile opposition, especially from governments, to pursuing their projects (which then forced them to change course), radical Islam in Indonesia thrived under the political openness that the overthrow of Suharto unleashed. Yet the outcome has been somewhat similar to the Turkish and Moroccan experience. The downfall of Suharto's New Order regime in May 1998, as Noorhaidi Hasan discusses in his essay, unleashed a new era of relative openness and democratization in the largest Muslim country in the world. The subsequent Reformasi—the far-reaching social and political reforms—paved the way for both democratization and decentralization, which then facilitated the public activism of radical Islamists who were vying to establish an Islamic state in Indonesia. The Muslim Brotherhood (MB), the Salafies, and the Hizb al-Tahrir increased their public profiles, and newly emerged violent groups such as the Indonesian Mujahedin, Holy Warrior Council, Defendants of Islam Front, Lashkar Jihad, and Jama'a Islamiya exhibited at times spectacular drama in public. While the MB and Salafi groups opted to implement shari'a peacefully, the militants resorted to violence—attacking cafés, casinos, and brothels and calling for jihad in Maluccas. Hizb al-Tahrir favored establishing an Islamic khalifa in Indonesia.

However, failing to deliver, the violent strategy of militant Islamists gave way after a decade to peaceful *da'wa* to promote the shari'a at the personal level, rather than wanting a national state to enforce it. In fact, Indonesian decentralization policies facilitated the integration of militant Islamists into the political structure, where they managed to put into practice some tenets of Islamic laws at the local level after winning local elections. This was the beginning of a process of Islamic "moderation" in general, to which the critical campaign of mostly post-Islamist advocates contributed significantly.

Militant Islamism in Indonesia had alarmed many Muslim activists and thinkers because of what they saw as the considerable harm that radicalism had inflicted on Islam, society, and politics. They were thus compelled to come forward to redress the situation by offering a different, post-Islamist, agenda. Outspoken groups such as the Liberal Islamic Network, the Wahid Institute, and the Ma'arif Institute for Culture and Humanity took up the banner of a critical campaign to present "true" Islam as opposed to that of the militants. These critical groups were alarmed that radical Islam had rejected democracy, distorted politics by bringing faith into it, and marred faith by politicizing it. While they yearned to remain Muslim and promote Islamic faith, they equally wished to maintain a secular democratic state where the affairs of religion are separate from those of the state.

One outcome of this ideological contestation has been the development of the Prosperous Justice Party (Partai Keadilan Sejahtera or PKS). The PKS originated from an Islamist past marked by a paradigm that saw Islam as a complete system of life as well as a political ideology with the Islamic state as its core. Failing to garner much support in the 1999 elections, the party went through a major rethinking and renovation. In the process it adopted a national and democratic discourse, focusing more on moral reform than on political gains. Just like the People's Justice Party in

Malaysia, PKS shifted its doctrinal attention from establishing an Islamic state to focusing on *maqasid al-Shari'a* as the real objective of Islam, which it defined in terms of justice, good governance, and human rights.[13] The party went on to acknowledge the principle of a secular political state as a prerequisite of liberal democracy; it accepted the secular design of the Indonesian state and advocated the compatibility of Islam with democracy. With this new vision, PKS increased its support considerably, from just over 1 percent in 1990 to nearly 8 percent of the national vote in the 2009 general elections, establishing itself as the fourth largest party after the Democratic Party and two secular counterparts.

Electoral democracy certainly opened space for the growth of Islamism in Indonesia after 1998. However, with the deepening of democracy, Islamism was pushed to the sidelines, primarily through the democratic process. Those who advocated shari'a have moved to pursue personal da'wa, and those religious parties following electoral politics have become an integral part of the Indonesian democracy, even though they remain marginal. They participate in elections; sometimes they win, and other times they lose—and carry on campaigning for future elections. This, in Hasan's account, represents the Indonesian pattern of post-Islamism.

Change in Ambivalence

In some ways, postrevolutionary Egypt after Mubarak resembles post-Suharto Indonesia. As in Indonesia, Islamic parties in Egypt have become more visible and vocal, already controlling the first post-Mubarak parliament. Does the Indonesian path reflect the possible future for Egypt's Islamism, especially its Muslim Brothers, now that electoral democracy may facilitate its ascendancy? The trajectory of Egypt's Islamism might give us some clue. When in September 2011 in Cairo Tayyib Erdogan wished that Egypt would adopt not a religious but a secular state, some Muslim Brothers leaders showed disquiet, while others, notably the youth, expressed enthusiasm. Such duality in views reflects both the ideological continuity and the discursive shift in Egypt's Islamism in general. At its height in the 1980s, as I elaborate here, Egyptian Islamism consisted of a vast sector composed of organizations, activities, and sympathies. At the core stood the reformist MB, surrounded by militant Jihadies and al-Jama'a al-Islamiya, as well as Islamist students, women, and professional associations. This Islamism espoused a conservative moral vision, populist language, a patriarchal disposition, and adherence to scripture.

By the early 1990s, through da'wa and associational work, the movement had captured a large segment of the civil society and was moving to claim space in state institutions. Although it failed to dislodge Egypt's secular regime, the Islamist movement left an enduring mark on society and the state. Overwhelmed by the pervasive "Islamic mode," major actors in Egyptian society, including the intelligentsia, the new rich, al-Azhar, and the ruling elites, converged around a language of nativism and conservative moral ethos, severely marginalizing critical voices, innovative religious thought, and demands for democratic transformation.

However, pushed by global and regional dynamics, the end of the Cold War, and the escalating language of democracy and civil society, as well as the rise to power of the post-Islamist Khatami, Egypt's Islamist movement experienced some important modifications. The militant and violent al-Gama'a al-Islamiya put down arms, denounced violence, and opted to work as a legal political party to pursue peaceful da'wa, even though its Islamist ideology remained. MB leader Mustafa Mashur spoke of "pluralism" for the first time in 1997, and "young leaders" uttered the language of democracy, civil society, and accountability, favoring Mohammad Khatami's concept of "Islamic democracy." Some even spoke of women's and minority rights. The new discourse was to deepen in the years after the 2005 Kifaya movement, most notably after the Egyptian revolution of 2011, when an internal debate and discord between the old guard and the "young" leadership engulfed the movement. While the old guard, led by Mohammed Badie and Mahmoud Ezzat, remained conservative Islamists, the young leadership, represented by such figures as Abdel Moneim Abou el-Fotouh, leaned more toward the Turkish AKP, a position that brought them closer to the Hizb al-Wasat, which had already defected from the Muslim Brothers' ranks in the late 1990s. Al-Wasat privileged modern democracy over Islamic *shura*, embraced pluralism in religion, welcomed gender mixing, and supported women's high public roles and ideological diversity. A Christian activist, Rafiq Habib, served as the group's key ideologue.[14] In the aftermath of the Egyptian revolution, many young MB activists leaned toward post-Islamist outlooks, resulting in their expulsion or collective exit from the organization.

The crisis of Islamism worldwide (spearheaded by Iran, the Taliban, and al-Qaeda) in the post-9/11 aftermath, the failure of Arab nationalist politics to help tackle Palestinian self-determination, and then the rapid expansion of new communication technologies and social media had given rise to a new public in Egypt with a broadly postideological and post-Islamist orientation. The revolution of January 2011, with its call for "freedom, justice, and dignity," embodied this new vision.[15] Even though in such circumstances the MB organization was compelled to take account of these new sensibilities, it failed to undertake a systematic reevaluation of its past outlook. Consequently, its new positions were largely pushed by events rather than by a deliberate rethinking of past ideas. Thus, pragmatism and a piecemeal approach characterized the unsystematic course of change in the MB's religious politics. But working within an electoral democracy might condition the Muslim Brothers to experience a more orderly metamorphosis, perhaps similar to the AKP in Turkey, PKS in Indonesia, and PJD in Morocco. Otherwise the likely splits and erosion would diminish the ideological edifice of the MB. In either situation, debates about freedoms, individual rights, gender equality, or the protection of minorities might find fertile ground.

Whereas secular sensibilities and a hostile environment in Turkey and Morocco and a generational shift together with new sensibilities in Egypt pushed Islamist movements there to undertake a new course, the confessional division in Lebanon played a key part in Hizbullah's shifting ideology. Joseph Alagha's study shows how Hizbullah has evolved from a movement strictly adhering to Khomeini's doctrine of *wilayat al-faqih* since the 1980s into a political party fully integrated into the Lebanese political structure. Its early idea of establishing an Islamic state in Lebanon has in practice been abandoned in favor of the concept of *muwatana*, or citizenship, which recognizes the full rights of non-Muslims. Thus Hizbullah has moved from an exclusivist movement considering Lebanon's Christians as minorities subject to a poll tax into a political entity that has forged partnerships with and garnered support from Christian counterparts in recent years. This change in Hizbullah's political ideology angered such hard-liners as Subhi al-Tufayli, who as a consequence formed a dissenting faction to maintain orthodoxy, but it has enjoyed little support among the Shia community.

It is true that Hizbullah has forged strong alliances with the Islamist state in Iran and the Ba'thist regime in Syria; self-interest has largely guided such alliances. In fact the party has supported Iran's rulers irrespective of whether they were hard-liners or reformists. In the late 1990s, Hizbullah favored Khatami when he was in power, but it sided with hard-liners even when the latter rounded up reformists and post-Islamists after the fraudulent 2009 elections. Hizbullah did not even shy away from supporting Bishar al-Asad's regime when it was brutally cracking down on the Syrian revolutionary opposition in 2011. These political postures derive less from some ideological principles of the party and more from the realpolitik of survival and self-interest.

So, what kind of "post-Islamist" is Hizbullah, if at all? At best, Hizbullah may represent an aspect of post-Islamism that is geared more toward practice than toward rhetoric, a shift in policy that is pushed by the complex reality of Lebanese society and history. While Hizbullah actually abandoned the idea of an Islamic state by opting to work in and come to terms with a multiconfessional and multiethnic country, the rhetoric of wilayat al-faqih has lingered. In fact Hasan Nasrullah has tried to tackle this duality by distinguishing between *al-fikr al-siyasi* (political ideology), which Hizbullah has maintained, and *al-barnamaj al-siyasi* (political program), which it has modified. Simply put, the multiconfessional reality of Lebanon would make the idea of an Islamic state untenable, even if it was desired. Thus it is not surprising that when I asked Ayatollah Muhammad Hussein Fadlullah, the "spiritual mentor" of Hizbullah, in 2004 what he imagined to be the best form of government for Lebanon, he made a categorical disclaimer—"Certainly not the wilayat al-faqih." In reality, as Alagha concludes, Hizbullah's 2009 manifesto came to attest to its complete Lebanization, without any reference to wilayat al-faqih or any form of Islamic state.

Critique from Without

In the experiences of Iran, Turkey, Morocco, Egypt, and Lebanon, it was the Islamist movements themselves that experienced change (in thought and/or practice) as they encountered their own paradigmatic limitations, external pressure, and the realities of their societies. In the cases of Pakistan and Saudi Arabia, certain post-Islamist strands emerged to redress and neutralize what they saw as the alarming consequences to society and faith of a militant and exclusivist Islamism. Many of them did not have an Islamist past. Theirs, then, was not simply an immanent critique of self but mostly a critique of their discursive family, that is, a critique of other Islamists with whom they shared a broadly religious language.

Humeira Iqtidar's careful study sheds much-needed light on the complex landscape of religious politics in Pakistan, where the long-standing Jama'at Islami (JI) has given rise to both more militant and more inclusive trends. Among the many strands of Islamism in Pakistan, JI remains the most established and powerful group. Founded by the legendary Abul-alaa Maududi, JI became the significant partner in General Zia's Islamization project and has continued to wield power since. But JI is not a Jihadi, violent, or revolutionary movement; it represents, just like the Muslim Brotherhood, Pakistan's "electoral Islamism." Yet it is committed to taking governmental power to Islamize the society and the state. In this sense, it remains Islamist. Even though very little has changed in the core constitution of the JI, a number of "spin-off" individuals and groups have broken off from the JI, creating their own ideas and entities. The derivatives have developed in two opposite directions. The first trend includes a number of radicalized and militarized factions, notably Jama'at-ud-Da'wa and its militant wing, Lashkar-e-Tayyaba, which are active in Kashmir and have moved closer to "al-Qaeda." Even though Jama'at-ud-Da'wa began by pursuing nonviolent activism around da'wa and welfare/charity, it moved toward militancy and violence primarily in response to U.S. involvement in Pakistan. The militant Salafies had already risen up in the context of the Afghan War but have reportedly been courted by Pakistani Inter-services Intelligence.

Precisely because of growing religious radicalization, very different spin-offs from JI have promoted, on the one hand, a modernist anti-Islamist line represented by Javad Ghamidi and, on the other, a more pietistic trend close to Tablighi Jama'at Islami. Ghamidi, a Quran scholar and ex-colleague of Maududi, broke away from JI in the late 1970s because of his critique of Maududi's theology, which focused on obligations. For some time, he was associated with President Musharraf's program of secularization through "enlightened moderation," vehemently combating against Jihadi ideology and the idea of a state run by Islamists. In somewhat similar terrain, al-Huda, founded by the female preacher Farhat Hashimi, has taken up the banner of personal piety, prescribing change in individual ideas and behavior as the basis of transformation in society at large. Having earned tremendous popularity mostly among women and the well-to-do, al-Huda has grown to become a global movement, with branches spreading in Canada, Australia, and the United States. Altogether, the "liberal" Islamic trends preach inclusive Islam and ethical conduct combining rational thinking and faith. This trend, largely disengaged from conventional politics, finds appeal among the educated, urban, and well-to-do classes who wish to keep their Islam and yet distance themselves from the debilitating politics of radical Islamism with respect to their everyday life and the well-being of their nation.

Even though on the rise, these inclusive and modernist Islamic currents remain frail before the hegemonic position of the radicals, whose growth is vindicated primarily by Pakistan's geopolitical position—its relations with Afghanistan, the Taliban, the "War on Terror," and the intrusive U.S. presence. Indeed, it is precisely this imperial intrusion that hinders the growth of inclusive Islam, including ideas of freedom, choice, and tolerance, because they are easily framed and rejected as imported values associated with the West, the United States, and imperialism.

Similar conservative discourse pushed by the Saudi state and the ulema hindered in part the growth of a budding "Islamo-liberal" trend in Saudi Arabia in the past decade. This current, discussed cogently by Stéphane Lacroix in this book, came to life in the early 1990s as an offshoot of the suppressed Sahwa movement—a mix of ideas from both Wahabism and the Muslim Brotherhood—in the context of an intellectual *infitah*, openness, that Crown Prince Abdallah was promoting. Members of this current—including professors, judges, journalists, professionals, and NGO activists, among others—followed one another's activities on the Internet, in the traditional press, and at NGOs, organizing weekly salons and discussions in Burayda, Riyadh, and Jeddah. Some were ex-Islamists who had called for Islamic revolution in Arabia but later opted to promote democracy, human rights, and a pluralistic system. The group especially called for reforming the Wahabi ideology, which was seen as responsible for Saudi's "political backwardness." In its manifesto of April 2002, published in the critical post-9/11 aftermath, the group worked for peaceful coexistence with the West. A year later it asked for political reform, an elected parliament, a constitution, separation of powers, and fundamental freedoms. A nascent post-Islamist movement was in the making on the Arabian Peninsula.

Such ideas and demands, however, proved to be far too radical from the perspective of the Saudi authorities and their Wahabi ideologues, who, as a result, charged the "Islamo-liberals" with "terrorism," sending several of them behind bars. Yet, in their open trials, the accused turned the courthouses into public forums for free speech and advocacy; and once out of jail, they resumed their activities, by holding meetings, releasing pro-reform statements, and issuing manifestos. A few activists went so far as to create the Saudi Civil and Political Rights Association, and later, during the Arab Spring in 2011, they formed Saudi Arabia's first political party—the Islamic Umma Party. But as Lacroix demonstrates, one should not exaggerate the power of this nascent movement. It suffered from serious limitations, which eventually came to undermine it. As early as 2004, widespread arrests and surveillance had already diminished the group's advocacy capabilities. The group's call for democracy was far less likely to capture popular imagination than the king's immediate offer of a $36 billion welfare package (wage increases, benefits, and subsidies) to Saudi citizens to buy off political dissent in the midst of Arab uprisings. The nascent movement also suffered from internal ideological and strategic disagreements—such as whether to give priority to political or religious reform—and failed to garner support from or at least neutralize the powerful Saudi ulema, who showed little sympathy for what the group stood for. Finally, the trend's opportunity also proved to be its handicap. The current had benefited from the political space that the rivalry within the royal authority—between Crown Prince Abdallah and Sudayri Prince Salman—had created. However, once Prince Abdallah dropped his support—because the group proved to be too radical to his taste—the "Islamo-liberals" were pushed to the sidelines.

This may not be the end, however. The advent of the Arab Spring, and the great excitement it triggered among Saudi citizens and the fear it triggered among the rulers, revealed the fragility of the Kingdom's political theology. Indeed, the news of Saudi youths, women, intellectuals, and social activists expressing their discontent in public forums, on social media, and in the streets reminds one of the Iran of the early 1990s, where the everyday expressions of discontent and unorthodox lifestyles spearheaded Iran's post-Islamist turn. A values survey conducted in summer 2011 revealed that 71 percent of the Saudi respondents agreed that "democracy is the best form of government," up from 58 percent in 2003. While some 70 percent of respondents in 2003 believed that "shari'a is important," only 30 percent did so by 2011.[16] As Saudi scholar Madawi al-Rasheed reminded her readers in February 2011, with the underside of society changing rapidly, Saudis can indeed cause big surprises.[17]

Post-Islamist Always?

The post-Islamist movements and trends I have discussed so far have historically been born out of a transformation and/or critique of some preexisting Islamist politics that dominated Muslim societies in recent years. However, the experiences of Sudan and Syria show that post-Islamism is not simply a phenomenon of the new millennium. It seems to have a longer history. In his intriguing discussion (chapter 11), Abdelwahab

El-Affendi shows the development of certain post-Islamist trends in Sudan long before the dominance of global Islamism in the 1980s and 1990s. In fact, in Sudan the modern Islamist movements (such as one led by Hasan al-Turabi) emerged into an already existing "post-Islamist condition." El-Affendi traces the history of Islamism in Sudan to the late nineteenth century, when the anticolonial Mahdi movement declared that all *tariqas* and *madhahib*, or schools of law such as Hanafi or Shafei or Shi'i, were redundant because Mahdi as the manifestation of divine authority could be readily accessed. In El-Affendi's view, this movement, which mobilized the struggle against British colonial power, represented Sudan's Islamist revolution a century before what took place in 1979 Iran. Mahdism, then, signified Sudan's first full-fledged Islamist movement. Despite its drama, the movement, however, declined after the death of Mahdi, when his revolutionary excess and false prophecies were exposed. The aftermath brought disillusionment to wide segments of the population, generating conditions in which Islam was tamed and harnessed in favor of a more quietist and spiritual orientation, one that rejected political theology. These post-Mahdi conditions also caused a serious "rethinking and remolding of revolutionary Islamic ideology so as to keep up with the challenges posed by the colonial order and modernization." Thus "Mahdism" was resurrected by his last son, Sayyid Abd el-Rahman, but in a very different "post-Islamist" constitution. This "neo-Mahdism," according to El-Affendi, was the "post-Islamist movement par excellence."

So, twentieth-century Sudan saw a series of post-Islamist discourses and movements that at times operated alongside an Islamist movement from which they had separated. For instance, in 1953 the Islamic Group, later named the Islamic Socialist Party, came to life out of a defection from the Islamic Liberation Movement. More influential was the "new Islamism" of the Republican Brothers, whose message consisted of a "fusion of Sufi principles and the notions of political freedoms, economic justice and social equality."[18] This trend was led by the legendary Mahmoud Mohamed Taha, whose death sentence for an apostasy charge in 1985 triggered a popular revolution that toppled the military dictator, Jafar Numeiri. Taha promoted the Islam of Mecca and its message of freedom, equality, and human rights. Taha's ideas remained, and they were reinforced in recent years by the pragmatic and modernist approach of political and religious leader Hasan al-Turabi. Even though General Bashir's military coup of 1989 ejected such ethos, the very repressive conduct of the regime has given a new life to them, causing a lively debate about a "post-Islamist" Sudan.[19]

While Sudan's early post-Islamism emerged as a critique of a preexisting Mahdi tradition, which then evolved intermittently through Mahmoud Taha and others, the Syrian Muslim Brothers, according to Thomas Pierret in this volume, have "always" been "post-Islamist." Formed in 1949 after the French withdrawal, the MB remained an integral component of the Syrian liberal polity, which ended with the Ba'thist coup in 1963. In the pre-Ba'thist period, MB members joined all elected parliaments and served in the governments as ministers. Their program emphasized respecting the constitution, safeguarding the republican system, and upholding civil rights and free elections and viewed the "people" as the "supreme authority." The group did not shy away from embracing socialist ideas, naming its political wing the "Islamic Socialist Front." Even though the MB tried—but failed—to convince other political forces to stipulate "Islam as the religion of the state," it remained ideologically flexible, compromising on "*fiqh* as the main source of law"—a common clause in many "secular" constitutions in the Middle East.

This unique "moderation" seems intriguing, for it distinguishes Syrian Muslim Brothers markedly from their counterparts in the Arab countries. Pierret offers a combination of factors. The MB was a relatively small group (garnering less than 10 percent of the electorate) that was informed by the "moderate" sensibilities of its urban, bourgeois, and educated constituency. More importantly, the members' integration into the Syrian political structure socialized them into the norms of political negotiation and flexibility, and this at a time when activists valued the parliament as a bastion of anticolonial struggle. Yet it is important to see if the group adhered ideologically to the family of Muslim Brothers, especially to the ideas of Hasan al-Banna that lay at the foundation of this transnational movement. Did the MB formally reject the idea of establishing an Islamic state or implementing shari'a? Or perhaps the group kept the idea of an "Islamic state," but as in the case of the Lebanese Hizbullah, the idea was sidelined as members became integrated into the liberal Syrian polity of the time. At any rate, things changed after the Ba'thist coup of 1963. The outlawing of the MB in 1964 augmented a prolonged campaign against the regime, culminating in the "Islamic uprising" of 1979–1982, in which a radicalized MB played the key role. In the brutal repression that ensued in Hama in 1982, the MB was completely crushed. There remained only a network of dispersed activists mostly in exile, who began to adopt a more explicit reformist and pluralistic vision. So, after the death of Hafiz al-Asad, the MB supported a peaceful democratic transition in Syria. In a

January 2006 interview in London, MB leader Ali Sadreddin Bayanouni called for "the establishment of a 'civil, democratic state,' not an Islamic republic."[20]

Instead of the MB, it was the ulema, the guardians of the spiritual sector, who took up the banner of "Islamizing" society and politics—and fighting against secular values. To this end, they set up religious schools, charity associations, and mosque networks. The ulema openly called for the establishment of an Islamic state and the rule of shari'a—objectives that were to materialize through Islamization from below. This remarkable contrast between the "moderate Muslim Brothers" and the "radical conservative ulema" seems to have persisted to this day. In the political climate following the assassination of Lebanese prime minister Rafiq Hariri in 2005, the remnants of the MB sided with the secular and liberal opposition to push for openness. But the ulema kept on their conservative agenda, implicitly supporting the regime. Only grave crises, such as the regime's excessive violence against civilians in the 1980s and 2011, would compel the ulema to take sides, often leading to a split between the critical ulema and loyalists who would usually strike a deal with the regime to get some concession in exchange for support.

In fact, some threads of post-Islamist thought have emerged in recent years. They are expressed in the writings of such religious intellectuals as Muhammad Shahrur, who believed that truth should be sought not in Islam's basic texts but in the progress of human reason. In a similar frame, parliamentarian Muhammad Habash rejected Islam's monopoly of salvation, in an attempt to build a theological argument to protect the rights of religious minorities. Habash became a key advocate of democratization among religious activists during the short-lived "Damascus Spring" following the death of Hafiz al-Asad in 2000. Finally, unorthodox clerics such as Sheikh al-Saqqa brought liberal values into their sermons to blend them with their Islamic teachings to extend women's rights within Islam. But these reformist views were harshly attacked by the ulema as well as the regime, which has exploited conservative religiosity to shield itself against the democratic space that critical religious thought might open. Thus a renewal of the post-Islamist turn in Syria may be possible, argues Pierret, only by weakening the ulema, because as the strategic allies of the Ba'thist regime, they stand against any expressions of a democratic and inclusive Islam. A new post-Islamism, a religious reform, may come to fruition only on the ruins of the Ba'thist regime.

Revisiting Post-Islamism

These diverse narratives suggest that there is not one but many different trajectories of change that Islamist movements may experience. Iran's
post-Islamism developed on the perceived failure of the ruling Islamist
politics to address fundamental citizen needs. Turkish Islamism "adapted"
itself to meet the political realities of the country as well as its position
vis Europe. While in Morocco and Indonesia (as in Iran and Turkey) the
Islamist parties self-consciously departed from an Islamist past to act
as players in the nations' polities, the Egyptian Muslim Brothers and
Lebanese Hizbullah pursued somewhat ambivalent courses of change.
They were pushed largely by the events and geopolitical realities of their
own settings and the region, without, however, undertaking a systematic
reevaluation of their ideologies. In Egypt, the old guard of Muslim Brothers
continued to pursue an "Islamizing" agenda, while its "youths" leaned
toward a post-Islamist perspective; and in Lebanon the Hizbullah changed
more in practice than in rhetoric. In Saudi Arabia and Pakistan, strands
of post-Islamist outlooks emerged to redress what was seen as the harm
that Islamism had inflicted on society and faith. Finally, the experiences
of Sudan and Syria reflect the presence of some forms of post-Islamist
trends long before the global rise of Islamist movements since the 1970s.
Most of these trends and movements came to life in and were informed by
the post–Cold War political climate, in which the language of civil society,
democracy, and reform had assumed unprecedented global currency.

The narratives also show that the forms, depth, and spread of
post-Islamist experiences may vary. Yet they all point to some shift in
vision. In each of these cases, post-Islamism denotes a critical discursive
departure or pragmatic exit, albeit in diverse degrees, from an Islamist
ideological package characterized broadly by monopoly of religious truth,
exclusivism, and emphasis on obligations, toward acknowledging ambiguity, multiplicity, inclusion, and flexibility in principles and practice.

Clearly, then, post-Islamism represents a discursive and/or pragmatic *break*, a break from an Islamist paradigm. But the direction is not
"post-Islam*ic*," as some erroneously call it; it is post-Islam*ist*. In other
words, I am not speaking about a shift away from Islamic faith toward
secularism, even though post-Islamism does denote a process of secularization in the sense of favoring the separation of religious affairs from
the affairs of the state. Rather, I am speaking about post-Islamization as
a complex process of breaking from an Islamist ideological package by

adhering to a different, more inclusive, kind of religious project in which Islam nevertheless continues to remain important both as faith and as a player in the public sphere.

Thus, the claim by some observers that this new type of religious politics differs only in form and is simply a variant of the broad Islamist paradigm remains unwarranted.[21] For, as I have tried to show, Islamist movements in the past three or so decades have, more or less, experienced change into or instigated a qualitatively different religious project. Consequently, lumping these rather dissimilar discursive bodies and movements together as "Islamist" points to a conceptual sloppiness, to say the least. Even a notion like "adaptation," as suggested by Ihsan Dagi to describe the Turkish transformation of Islamism, fails to do justice to the process, for it implies some kind of continuity rather than a break. Like a number of observers who do not subscribe to the "failure of Islamism," Dagi suggests that in the Turkish case, post-Islamism emerged not because of the "failure" of Islamism but because of its adaptation. If *adaptation* here means giving up certain underlying principles and policies in favor of adopting new ones in order to fit in and face existing realities, then this in effect means that the old paradigm has failed to apply and had to change. The fact is that the AKP represents a qualitative departure from Melli Gorus, just as Iranian "reformists" such as Mir-Hussain Mousavi are a departure from Islamists such as Ayatollah Khomeini and the post-Islamism of the Sudanese Mahmoud Taha is a departure from the exclusivist Islamism of the Mahdi movement.

This means that we should not confuse "electoral Islamism" with post-Islamism. "Electoral Islamism" refers to the reformist Islamist movements (such as the Muslim Brotherhood, the current Gama'a al-Islamiyya in Egypt, and Jama'at-e Islami in Pakistan) that, instead of resorting to violence and revolution, join the electoral structure, follow legal procedures, and remain part of the system, to pursue a gradualist strategy of Islamizing the society and the state. The exigencies of integration may, depending on the political climate, condition "electoral Islamists" to practically transcend their Islamist outlook. While the Syrian Muslim Brothers in reality left their Islamist ideas on the back burner, Jama'at Islami of Pakistan did not. Electoral Islamism might be "moderate," but it is not post-Islamist per se. Post-Islamism is more than simply legal status or participating in elections.

And this, perhaps, is one reason why understanding post-Islamism in terms of simply "moderation" would conceal its distinct markers. The problem with the term *moderation* lies in its descriptive nature. Lacking analytical power, the term would be unable to ascertain the dynamics and direction of change. As such, it signifies the degree (rather than the kind) of departure from "radicalism" and thus remains highly relative. In such a relative frame, one's "moderate" can be another's "extremist."

The more analytical observers tend to equate post-Islamism with "liberal Islam" or "Islamic liberalism." If "liberal Islam" means an interpretation of Islam that accommodates modern democracy, a civil nonreligious state, freedom of thought, and human progress, then certainly this shares considerably with post-Islamist thought.[22] But "post-Islamism" is more than simply what it projects; it is also about what it transcends: it is, in other words, a critique of something else. So, beyond the kinds of ideas that it projects, post-Islamism also concerns the roots, development, and relations of such ideas with Islamist politics. If, on the other hand, "liberal Islam" implies the "privatization" of Islam, then this is not what the post-Islamists aspire to. For they want religion to be present in the public arena and wish to promote piety in society even though they favor a nonreligious civil state. And finally, if liberal Islam is taken to signify an Islam that respects individual rights and freedoms, then we need to consider the relationship between the post-Islamist polity and liberalism. This interaction remains an untested terrain; the post-Islamist project is yet to determine how much individual freedom is compatible with the public religion that it so passionately promotes. So far only Iran under the reformists (1997–2004), Turkey under AKP, and Tunisia under the Islamic al-Nahda Party have experienced some forms of post-Islamist rule. In these cases the record of handling individual liberties (minority rights, gender rights, and freedom of thought, religion, and lifestyle) remains a mixed bag. Although Iranians felt by far "freer" under the post-Islamist government of Mohammad Khatami, nonetheless restrictions on women's attire, choice of lifestyle, and freedom of thought and religion (e.g., for the Baha'i faith) largely remained, even though these were all beginning to be debated. The AKP in Turkey fared much better, yet reports of increasing surveillance over public morality (like consuming alcohol outdoors or serving food in public during the fasting month of Ramadan), "cultural production," Internet use, and scientific institutions point to some conflict between the AKP's ethical standings and liberal values.[23] It is too early to judge about the ruling al-Nahda Party in Tunisia, but indications so far are that the leadership stays alert about protecting individual rights. Yet, as the party's spokesman conceded in January 2012 over a controversy, "the line between freedom of expression and religious sensitivity would not be drawn very soon."[24] As for Morocco, Sami Zemni's account uncovers the quandary of the ruling PJD about how to resolve the contradiction between "liberties" and "Islamic values," between the demands of citizens and the proclaimed goals of creating a moral polity. In sum, the likely clash between post-Islamist ethics and liberal values might (depending on the extent of the clash) settle in some kind of "illiberal democracy," where electoral democracy may proceed with some variable curb on liberties. Of course, this tension is not restricted to the post-Islamist polity. Western democracies have also experienced at some points in their development certain restrictions on individual and civil liberties (as in gay marriage, gender equality, and civil rights). However, electoral democracy, if it persists, can open the space for debate over, and possibly extend the scope of, these very liberties.

The association of Islamism with exclusion and authoritarianism and post-Islamism with inclusion and democracy has prompted some critiques to charge my formulation of post-Islamism with normativity.[25] Two arguments are advanced. The first argument is that my concept of post-Islamism focuses on the views of "progressive Muslims" and excludes the conservative Islamic outlook; the second is that Islamism is presented as a "problem," and post-Islamism, as a "solution." These commentaries appear plausible, particularly with respect to my earlier formulation that drew primarily—though not exclusively—on the experience of the Islamic Republic of Iran, but rest on some misunderstandings of the concept. Indeed, the wide-ranging data on multiple countries presented in this book help construct a clearer concept of post-Islamism that can address such concerns. To begin with, I have taken "post-Islamism" as an outlook that critically transcends duty-centered Islamist politics. Therefore, the kind of individual conservative and Salafi-type piety that has spread in recent years does not represent a post-Islamist shift. For this individualized piety is neither a *critical* departure from nor an alternative stand to redress the consequences of Islamist politics. Rather, its preoccupation lies with the construction of an ethical self in a highly conservative direction, one that can accommodate an authoritarian religious order. In fact, the designation "neo-fundamentalism," proposed by Olivier Roy, serves as a more appropriate description of this kind of religious trend than rights-centered "post-Islamism."[26]

On the other hand, it was, admittedly, this emancipatory potential of the post-Islamist project—that is, the possibility that Muslims may confidently adhere to their faith and yet embrace inclusive and democratic ideals—that inspired me to reflect on this trend in the first place. But post-Islamism, it turns out, is not a coherent religious and inclusive project. Although it is too early to judge, nevertheless, there are signs that the model espouses its own tensions, chiefly the tension between post-Islamist religious ethics and liberal social values such as the extent of individual liberties, even though it seems to go well with economic liberalism and the free market.

At any rate, "Islamism" and "post-Islamism" constructed in this fashion serve primarily as conceptual categories to signify change, difference, and the root of change. In the real world, however, many Muslim individuals or groups may adhere eclectically and simultaneously to aspects of both discourses. The advent of post-Islamism, as a real trend, should not be seen necessarily as the historical end of Islamism. It should be seen as the birth, out of a critical departure from Islamist experience, of a qualitatively different discourse and politics. In reality we may witness the simultaneous operation of both Islamism and post-Islamism. This implies that we should perhaps rethink the *historical* connotation of *post-* in post-Islamism and, instead, attribute to it a more analytical substance. For the term needs to take account of nonevolutionary processes, simultaneity, mixture, and historical retrospection. As I noted earlier, even though we are witness to the rise of post-Islamism at the global level in current times, certain post-Islamist movements, such as neo-Mahdism in the Sudan in the early twentieth century, had come to life prior to the worldwide hegemony of Islamism in the 1980s and 1990s. Some observers have even spoken of such movements as that associated with Mohammad Abdou as resembling post-Islamism of a sort. In addition, while only a few movements, such as the Iranian one, emerged directly out of experimentation with an Islamic state, many others developed in a critical departure from Islamist activism and discourse in society, and still others emerged to redress the effects of existing Islamist trends on religion and politics. Therefore, I deploy the prefix *post-* in post-Islamism not simply as a marker of historicity but primarily to signify a *critique* from within, a "critical departure." Thus, post-Islamism may be understood as a critical departure from Islamist politics. It describes transcending from the duty-centered and exclusive Islamist politics toward a more rights-centered and inclusive outlook that favors a civil/secular state operating within a pious society. Post-Islamism may take the form of a critique of the Islamist self or of the Islamism that others embrace; it may historically come after Islamism or may operate simultaneously alongside of it; it may be observed in contemporary times or in the past.

Yet, independent of the analytical inference of the *post-*, we cannot overlook the historical embeddedness of post-Islamist experience. For doing so would take us to the slippery ground of subjectivism. Simply put, post-Islamism does not emerge out of nowhere; it builds against a historical backdrop. The fact is that even though neo-Mahdist post-Islamism emerged, as El-Affendi contends, long before the recent (1980s and 1990s) wave of Islamist movements, it was built on the experience of, and critically departed from, the earlier Islamism of the Mahdi in the 1880s. Around the same time, Mohammad Abdou, a stretch to be labeled as post-Islamist, launched his "Islamic reformism" not only to fight against Western colonialism but also to construct an Islam that could accommodate and meet the challenge of Western modernity, against which the Muslim traditionalists had little to offer. And today, in a radically different age of globalization, we seem to be entering a new era in the Muslim world where Islamism—stricken by a legitimacy crisis for ignoring and violating people's democratic rights—is giving way to a different kind of religious polity that takes democracy seriously while wishing to promote pious sensibilities in society. Ours seems to herald the coming of a post-Islamist Muslim world, in which the prevailing popular movements assume a postideological, civil, and democratic character. Iran's Green Movement and the Arab uprisings represent popular movements of these post-Islamist times.

Notes

1. Bernard Lewis, interview by David Horovitz, *Jerusalem Post*, February 25, 2011.
2. See, for instance, John M. Owen, "Why Islamism Is Winning," *New York Times*, January 6, 2012, in which there is nothing about what "Islamism" really is.
3. This section draws heavily on Asef Bayat, "Islamic Movements," in *The Wiley-Blackwell Encyclopedia of Social and Political Movements*, ed. David Snow, Donatella della Porta, Bert Klandermans, and Doug McAdam (New York: Wiley-Blackwell, 2013).
4. Olivier Roy, *The Failure of Political Islam* (Cambridge: Harvard University Press, 1998).
5. Faisal Devji, *Landscapes of Jihad: Militancy, Morality, Modernity* (Ithaca: Cornell University Press, 2005).
6. Asef Bayat, *Life as Politics: How Ordinary People Change the Middle East* (Palo Alto: Stanford University Press, 2010), 171–184.
7. Asef Bayat, "The Coming of a Post-Islamist Society," *Critique: Critical Middle East Studies* (Hamline University, Saint Paul) 9 (Fall 1996): 43–52.

8. Olivier Roy's "Le Post-Islamisme" (*Revue du Mondes Musulmans et de la Méditerranée* 85–86 [1999]: 9–30) is an introduction to a number of essays that Roy considers to speak of a post-Islamist trend. Reinhard Schulze uses *post-Islamism* to describe "postmodern Islamism" as an increasingly fragmented and "ethnized" worldview due to growing reinterpretations and localizations of Islamism; see Reinhard Schulze, "The Ethnization of Islamic Cultures in the Late 20th Century or From Political Islam to Post-Islamism," in "Islam: Motor or Challenge of Modernity," ed. George Stauth, *Yearbook of the Sociology of Islam* 1 (1998): 187–198. In turn, for Gilles Kepel, in his *Jihad: The Trial of Political Islam* (2nd ed. [London: I. B. Tauris, 2002], 368), the term describes the new orientation of some Islamists who in the name of democracy and human rights have departed from radical, Jihadi, and Salafi doctrines. Others fall short of conceptualizing the term altogether. One exception is Farhad Khosrokhavar's treatment of the term when assessing the views of some "post-Islamist intellectuals in Iran" such as Abdul Karim Soroush. See Farhad Khosrokhavar, "The Islamic Revolution in Iran: Retrospect after a Quarter Century," *Thesis Eleven* 76, no. 1 (2004).

9. For instance, see Diaa Rashwan, "Wishful Thinking, Present and Future," *Al-Ahram Weekly*, February 7–13, 2002.

10. See Alain Roussillon, "Decline of Islamism or the Failure of Neo-Orientalism?" [in Persian], *Goft-o-gu* (Tehran) 29 (Fall 2000): 163–185.

11. See, for instance, Salwa Ismail, "The Paradox of Islamist Politics," *Middle East Report* 221 (Winter 2001): 34–39. See also Francois Burgat, *Face to Face with Political Islam* (London: I. B. Tauris, 2003), 180–181. Only very recently, Olivier Roy came up with a definition of *post-Islamism* as the "privatization of re-Islamization." It refers to individualized "neo-fundamentalism." See O. Roy, *Globalised Islam: The Search for a New Ummah* (London: Hurst and Co., 2004), 97. The way I use the term is fundamentally different.

12. See, for instance, Berna Turam, "Turkey under the AKP: Are Rights and Liberties Safe?" *Journal of Democracy* 23, no. 1 (January 2012): 109–118.

13. Halim Rane, "The Political Sociology of Maqasid in Contemporary Islamic Thought" (paper presented at the annual meeting for the Middle East Studies Association, San Diego, November 20, 2010).

14. Just after the Egyptian revolution, when Egyptian politics were polarized between the Islamist and non-Islamist camps, Hizb al-Wasat moved away from the middle ground, becoming closer to the Muslim Brothers in exchange for political gains (it was given eight seats in Majlis al-Shura). It is yet to be seen if this political alignment will affect al-Wasat's ideological stands.

15. Asef Bayat, "The Post-Islamist Revolutions," *Foreign Affairs*, April 26, 2011. An opinion poll in November 2011 showed that 75 percent of Egyptian respondents favored a "civil state" as opposed to a "religious state," and only 1 percent wanted a "military regime"; *Al-Masry al-Youm*, November 12, 2011.

16. Mansoor Moaddel, Arland Thornton, Stuart Karabenick, Linda Youg-DeMarco, and Julie de Jong, "The Arab Spring: What It Represents and Implications for National Security," unpublished survey results (data from Egypt, Lebanon, Iraq, and Saudi Arabia), January 2012, a summary of which appears in Mansoor Moaddel, "What Do Arabs Want?" at http://mevs.org/files/tmp/ArabSpring.pdf.

17. Madawi al-Rasheed, "Yes, It Could Happen Here," *Foreign Policy*, February 28, 2011.

18. Muhammad Mahmud, "Sufism and Islamism in the Sudan," in *African Islam and Islam in Africa: Encounters between Sufis and Islamists*, ed. Eva Evers Rosander and David Westerlund (London: C. Hurst and Co. Publishers, 1997), 182.

19. See, for instance, a debate among scholars on "post-Islamism in Sudan" at http://africanarguments.org/2008/06/26/post-islamism-questioning-the-question/.

20. Roy McCarthy, "We Would Share Power, Says Exiled Leader of Syrian Islamist Group," *Guardian*, January 26, 2006.

21. See, for example, Graham Fuller, *The Future of Political Islam* (London: Palgrave Macmillan, 2004); Ismail, "Paradox of Islamist Politics."

22. For an articulation of "liberal Islam," see Charles Kurzman, "Liberal Islam: Prospects and Challenges," *Middle East Review of International Affairs* 3, no. 3 (September 1999): 11–19.

23. Howard Eissenstat, "Turkey: A Repressive Model for the Middle East?" *Human Rights Now* (blog), December 19, 2011, http://blog.amnestyusa.org/middle-east/turkey-a-repressive-model-for-the-middle-east/.

24. Quoted in Anthony Shadid, "Tunisia Faces Balancing Act of Democracy and Religion," *New York Times*, January 30, 2012.

25. See, for example, El-Affendi, this volume; and Ben Soares and Filippo Osella, "Islam, Politics, Anthropology," in special issue, *Journal of the Royal Anthropological Society* 15 (May 2009): 9.

26. For a fine elaboration of this trend, see Roy, *Globalised Islam*.

PART TWO

Critique from Within

2

The Making of Post-Islamist Iran

Asef Bayat

An irony of Iran's recent history is that its Islamic Revolution of 1979 emerged not out of a strong Islamist movement but in spite of the absence of one, so that by the mid-1990s the revolution that had so intensified a process of Islamization from above led to one of the most remarkable post-Islamist movements in the Muslim world.[1] Here I discuss the logic behind the contours of sociopolitical change in Iran since the revolution, highlighting the emergence of post-Islamism as both the engine and the embodiment of this change, one that culminated in the rise of the Green Movement, which shook the moral and political foundations of the Islamist regime. Driven primarily by students, women, youths, and religious intellectuals, as well as state employees and the professional class, post-Islamism heralded a new vision of society and polity that was expressed in a new outlook on public space, youth culture, student politics, gender relations, the state, and religious thought. At the heart of the post-Islamist project lay a blend of republican ideals and religious ethics, with "democracy" as its political mission. Post-Islamist republicanism was a response to the popular disenchantment with a revolution that had come to recognize its own deficits and discrepancies. It embodied widely held dissent against a religious polity that had denied many citizens their individual rights, gender equality, and meaningful participation in public life. Reform (*eslahaat*) became the strategy sought out by emerging popular forces and social movements to realize the post-Islamist goals of democratizing the polity and religious thought, separating religious affairs from the state.

Islamization

On February 11, 1979, Tehran radio announced the victory of the Iranian Revolution with feverish jubilation, thus heralding the end of a 2,500-year-old monarchy. The victory day was the culmination of over eighteen months of mass demonstrations, violent confrontations, massive industrial actions, a general strike, and many political maneuverings. Yet the genesis of the revolution went far back; indeed it was rooted in the structural changes that had been under way since the 1930s, when the country began undergoing a process of modernization. It was accelerated after the CIA-engineered coup in 1953 that had toppled nationalist prime minister Muhammad Mossadeq and reinstated the shah's autocratic rule, until it was dismantled by the revolution of 1979. These structural changes engendered many conflicts, the chief among them being the tension between socioeconomic development and political autocracy. In the midst of this, state inefficiency, corruption, and a sense of injustice among many sectors of Iranian society accelerated political conflict in the country.

The opportunity for popular mobilization arrived with President Carter's human rights policy in the late 1970s, which forced the shah to offer a political space for a limited degree of expression. This expression, in the process, built up cumulatively and in the course of less than two years swept aside the monarchy. But why did the clergy in particular lead the revolution? For over twenty-five years of autocratic rule, since the 1953 coup, all the effective secular political parties and nongovernmental organizations had been removed or destroyed. The main organized political dissent came from underground guerrilla organizations, the Marxist Fedaian and the radical Islamic Mujahedin, whose activities were limited to isolated armed operations. Student activism also remained restricted either to campus politics inside the country or to those carried out by Iranian students abroad. In short, the secular groupings, while extremely dissatisfied, were organizationally decapitated.

Unlike the secular forces, however, the ulema had the comparative advantage of possessing invaluable institutional capacity, including its own hierarchical order, with over ten thousand mosques, *husseiniehs* (informal and ad hoc religious gatherings), *hawzehs* (theological seminaries), and associations that served as vital means of communication among the revolutionary contenders. Beyond the lack of a credible alternative, this *institutional capacity* and a remarkable generality and thus *ambiguity* in the message of the clergy guaranteed the ulema's leadership. What maintained that leadership was the relatively rapid conclusion of revolutionary events—there was little time for debate and dissent or for a social movement and a possible alternative leadership to develop. Thus, the nascent Islamic movement of the 1970s rapidly transformed into a parallel state. "Islamization," then, unfolded largely *after* the victory of the revolution and was enforced primarily from above by the new Islamic state. It was manifested in the establishment of clerical rule, the Islamic legal system, new cultural practices and institutions, and the moral surveillance of public space.

The Islamist order was expressed immediately in urban public space. In the early 1980s, the regime launched a "cultural revolution" to transform the nation's education system. It shut down the universities for three years to reorganize them around "religious" values. Aiming to produce an "Islamic man," it abolished prerevolution youth centers, turning them into headquarters for Revolutionary Guards or police stations. Workplaces, factories, offices, banks, and hospitals became the sites of moral prescriptions; sex segregation and daily collective prayers were imposed by law and enforced by hard-line Islamic associations established within most public institutions. Revolutionary posters and slogans adorned all public spaces, and the constant blaring of religious recitation from loudspeakers reminded citizens of the new social order.

The urban social scene and street culture went through a dramatic transformation. Western names, logos, and symbols were drastically diminished, and cinemas and theaters ceased to attract audiences. Bars, cabarets, and nightclubs had already been shut down during the revolutionary turmoil. The red-light district in south Tehran was deliberately set ablaze, forcing sex workers, now literally undercover, to spread in the streets. The visual legacy of the revolution—political graffiti, gigantic murals, posters, and placards—embellished every urban street and back alley. The old street corner culture, or *sar-e kuche*, where young men would assemble, socialize, form gangs, and ogle young women, faded away rapidly, demonized by revolutionaries as breeding vanity and idleness. In their place the *pasdaran*, or Revolutionary Guards, and the dozen or so groups of male vigilantes, or *hizbullahies*, wielded clubs and guns and patrolled the streets to enforce the new moral order. The escalation of the war with Iraq further militarized the mood in the public sphere. The dramatic increase of street names beginning with *shahid* (martyr) became a testimony to this new geography of violence. But no other sight was more jarring in the new public space than the sudden disappearance of bright colors. Black and gray, reflected most spectacularly in women's veils and men's facial hair, dominated the urban visual scene, mirroring an aspect of Islamists' draconian control of body, color, and taste.

Compulsory veiling signified the most severe measure to give religious identity to postrevolutionary Iranian women. Indeed, many liberal laws that had favored women under the shah, such as the Family Protection Act, were annulled. The legal age of maturity declined (to nine for girls and fourteen for boys). Day-care centers and family-planning programs were devalued; polygamy and temporary marriage assumed renewed legitimacy, and men lawfully received custody of children and the automatic right to divorce. The imposition of a quota system effectively barred many women from studying in a number of colleges and restricted their enrollment in others.

Central to Iran's Islamism was the establishment of an Islamic state based on *wilayat al-faqih*, or the supreme rule of jurists. The constitution, written for the most part by the ulema, granted the *faqih*, or supreme jurist, the power to govern the nation according to "Islamic principles." Although the "people's sovereignty," which God had transferred to them, was institutionalized in the Western-style parliament, parliamentary deputies and their decisions were subject to the approval of a Council of Guardians, a twelve-member jury appointed by the faqih and the head of the judiciary. Although Shari'a was the law of the land, much of the prerevolution legal code continued unaltered, and only eighteen articles of the civil code changed, with the penal code going through the most drastic transformation. Labor law was altered considerably but not necessarily in an "Islamic" direction, and commercial law remained almost intact. Islamism proved to be compatible with capitalism.

Ideologically, however, Islamism represented a reading of Islam that interpreted it as a complete social, political, economic, and moral system that had answers to all human problems. It was up to the "true" Muslims, through resiliency and commitment, to discover them. The Islamists' monopolization of truth meant that there was little room for the coexistence of competing worldviews. Islamism appeared exclusionary, monovocal, and intolerant to pluralism, representing an absolutist and totalitarian ideology that placed a disproportionate emphasis on people's obligations, enforced by draconian social and moral surveillance. It is simplistic, however, to assume that Islamism was fully internalized by the populace or even by the "true Muslims." Scores of ordinary people, and even some grand ayatollahs, resisted authoritarian Islamism, especially Khomeini's concept of wilayat al-faqih. Many Muslim women contested forced veiling, while the secular-leftist and liberal-religious opposition vehemently fought religious rule. But this early opposition was soon repressed. The war with Iraq, where Islamic symbols were fully utilized, contributed to the Islamist vision.

However, with the end of the war (1988) and the death of Ayatollah Khomeini (1989), a new phase began. The program of postwar reconstruction under President Rafsanjani marked the beginning of what I have called "post-Islamism." As both a condition and a project, post-Islamism characterized a series of remarkable social and intellectual movements driven by younger generations, students, women, religious intellectuals, and a new perception of urban space that would shape Iran's political and social course in the years to come. By embracing a fusion of faith and freedom, religion and rights, post-Islamism transcended the Islamist polity. It called for individual choice, pluralism, and democracy, as well as religious ethics.

Toward a Post-Islamist Society

An early and more visible sign of the post-Islamist trend appeared in urban public spaces, beginning first in Tehran in 1992 and spreading to other cities. By the late 1980s, Tehran reflected a general crisis of governance in the nation as a whole. The city had become overgrown, overpopulated, polluted, unregulated, mismanaged, and exhausted by war. Its Islamist (exclusionary, masculine, harsh, segregating, and highly regimented) spatiality had alienated the majority of youth, women, and the modern middle classes. In 1989, the pragmatist President Rafsanjani appointed Gholamhussein Karbaschi, an ex-theology student turned urban planner, to fix the capital city. In the course of eight years (1990–1998), Tehran assumed a new character that had little to do with the image of an "Islamic city." Its new aesthetic, spatial configuration, symbolism, freeways, huge commercial billboards, and shopping malls emulated Madrid or even Los Angeles more than they did Karbala or Qom.

Revolutionary graffiti was replaced gradually by commercial billboards; Bahman cultural complexes were established in south Tehran to cater to arts, music (including Western classical genres), and modern technology; the spread of shopping malls made them an element of urban culture while breaking the monopoly of the "traditional" bazaar over retail commerce. While forced use of head scarves and gender segregation were still enforced by the state, the municipality's newly constructed six hundred public parks brought men and women, boys and girls, together in public places. Recreational activities, including mountain climbing, skiing in north Tehran, and bike riding in the forest plantations on the city outskirts, facilitated a less restricted mingling of the sexes. City dwellers who previously spent their leisure time in the seclusion of their homes or those of relatives and friends, or attending religious gatherings, now flocked to public places. Whereas the urban space of the 1980s fostered domesticity, kinship, and worship, the new spatial logic embraced civility, citizenry, and secular pursuits. It was a space of relative inclusion, dialogue, and agonistic interactions. The municipal leadership did not want to "Westernize" youth but, rather, to protect them from unregulated and "corrupting" behavior, aiming for an alternative, hybrid modernity—efficient but responsive to certain ethical sensibilities. The effect created an urban individual and habitus that angered many Islamists, who lashed out against "Western-style urbanization" that, in their view, undermined "Islamic values and identity." Although conservative Islamists took their revenge in 1998 by putting the popular mayor behind bars on charges of embezzlement, the drive for post-Islamist spatiality continued, as other cities followed Tehran's lead.

Muslim youths and women were clearly the integral players in this new urbanity. Indeed, the post-Islamist urban space was both a product and a producer of new post-Islamist youths. For more than any other social category, as agents of movements and cultural politics, youths were shaped by and expressed themselves primarily from within urban public places. Under the Islamic Republic, where moral and political authority converged, draconian social control gave rise to a unique youth identity and collective defiance. The assertion of youthful aspirations, the defense of their habitus, lay at the heart of their conflict with the Islamist moral and political authority. The struggle to reclaim youthfulness melded with the struggle to attain democratic ideals—a process through which youth experimented with how to be simultaneously young and Muslim. Thus, in their everyday life, urban youth expressed the kinds of behavior and subculture that challenged the moral and political precepts of Islamism. Young people got involved in underground music, illicit sex and dating games, drug use and fashion, laxity in observing *hijab* (veil), and an aversion to official religious and moral edicts. Yet these youths did not abandon their Islam altogether. Most of them exhibited strong "religious belief" and "religious feeling," even if they neglected religious practice.[2] Their Islam seemed to have little impact on their daily lives; God existed but did not prevent them from drinking alcohol or dating. Few attended mosques, but most filled the lecture halls of "religious intellectuals" who preached a more inclusive Islam. The young were forging new religious subcultures that embraced the sacred and the secular, faith and fun, the divine and diversion.

The authorities remained deeply divided as to what to do about such subversive behaviors. Hard-liners repeatedly called for those taking to the streets to fight against "cultural invasion," "hooliganism," and "anti-Islamic sentiments."[3] They punished people whom they saw as promoting immorality, "depravity," and "indecency," closing down boutiques, cafés, and restaurants.[4] In July 2002, for instance, some sixty "special units," including several hundred men wearing green uniforms and toting machine guns and hand grenades, drove up and down the streets of Tehran chasing young drivers listening to loud music, women wearing makeup or loose veils, partygoers, and alcohol drinkers.[5] Yet the crackdown did little to change behavior. Instead, it caused a public uproar in which the fundamentals of the Islamic penal code came under attack, as scores of reform-minded clerics questioned its application in this modern age.

At the core of post-Islamist youth lay Iran's student population, including one million college-goers. Students' activism of the late 1990s, which reflected their triple identities of being young, schooled, and increasingly female, had come a long way to become the backbone of the post-Islamist reform movement. Things were different earlier on. Immediately post-revolution, the student movement retained much of its ideological character (political radicalism, a revolutionary strategy, nationalism, Third Worldism, and an anti-imperialist orientation) but was overwhelmingly Islamist and male. University campuses virtually turned into headquarters of radical Islamist and leftist groups, whose radicalism often disrupted academic life. The student movement was deeply divided between pro-regime Islamist students gathered around the Daftar-e Tahkim va Vahdat-e Anjoman-haaye Eslami (Office of Consolidation and Unity of Islamic Associations), or DTV, and secularists, nationalists, leftists, and regime opponents—in a word, nonconformists. Reopened in 1983, universities were now dominated by the DTV, which along with members of the pasdaran and *basijis* acted on campuses as agents of the regime, mobilizing for war efforts or the Construction Crusade (an institution of rural development), using surveillance to drive nonconformists into hiding, jail, or apathy and demoralization.[6]

Between the early 1980s and mid-1990s, the official student organization, DTV, remained an extension of the state, allied with the Islamic/ Left factions, with student leaders acting like state officials. For Islamists, student activism was an obligation, not a right, and was meant to solidify the Islamic state's legitimacy.[7] The DTV's exclusivist ideological approach, Islamist rhetoric, populist disposition, and patriarchal propensity deeply alienated the vast majority of students, who were not only increasing in number but also increasingly female and coming from provincial backgrounds.[8] And unlike students of the 1970s, who had prolonged their studies because they cherished free and fun campus life, the 1990s generation had no interest in college except for the degrees it offered. Compared with my student experience in the late 1970s, the highly repressive feel at universities in the Iran of the mid-1990s was shocking. The campus's previous centrality in student life, its prestige, exclusivity, vitality, and vigor, had gone—no more was it a place of socializing, fun, and freedom or of cultural, athletic, and political life. Instead, draconian social control had pushed students to spend much of their time off-campus.

So 1990s student activism concerned itself not with conventional politics and ideological squabbles, as in the 1970s or just after the revolution, but, rather, with economic and social issues that immediately affected the students themselves. The student body was a potential social force, but one whose desire for a better material life and political participation had been dashed by the sluggish economy and the clergy's tight control over political institutions and everyday life. They were ready for mobilization; but what ideological inclinations would these Iranian youngsters pursue when they were already experiencing Islamism? Far from being anti-West radicals, ideological, or at least Islamist, this new generation of students became pragmatist and nonideological, with a clear dislike of violence and distrust of officials. They praised the West for its openness, advances, and comforts; internalized its affordable cultural imports (fashion, music, cinema, dating games); and aspired to become as much a part of it as millions of their compatriots had become. In short, students of the 1990s had departed from radicalism and ideological orientations, Marxist and Islamist alike. The older generation had demanded social justice; the younger generation yearned for individual liberty.[9]

It was this newer rank and file, their political apathy and noncompliance, that compelled DTV, the official student leadership, to call for a gradual revision of its outlook. Islamist students who had accepted the charismatic Khomeini as a supreme faqih (who stood above the law) now began, in this post-Khomeini era, to view the law as being above the faqih and favored a more open and democratic polity.[10] In addition, the "defeat" of the war and of its early utopian ideal ("to establish a world Islamic government")[11] had pushed many committed students toward pragmatism and political rationality. Some abandoned politics altogether, but many joined the Islamic Left, and still others, such as leaders of the

1980s, pursued academic studies to become what came to be known as the "religious intellectuals" highly critical of the Islamist polity.

By 1997, DTV mobilized its members not in the name of Islamization, anti-imperialism, or class disparity but, rather, in the name of the centrality of liberty, democratic participation, and the intrinsic dignity of student and teacher.[12] While there had emerged a new subjectivity among both the mass of students and DTV leaders, student mobilization remained sporadic, localized, and small scale, until the presidential election of 1997 pushed the student population into a spectacular return to national politics. Their participation had more to do with them being long-suppressed youths and students suddenly unleashed than it did with an organized pursuit of a political goal. Mohammad Khatami's victory and reform government provided a new structure in which a novel student movement with a post-Islamist identity, reformist outlook, and pluralistic orientation was born. With its focus on "democracy," the movement developed an elaborate organization and network structure. In May 2000, the first national student paper, *Azar*, was published, and by summer 2001, the number of college student newspapers topped seven hundred. By that same year 1,437 scientific, cultural, artistic, and professional organizations had been established in the universities. They were the movement's grassroots.[13]

The presence of female students in the movement contributed to this new "democratic" orientation. Women, who made up half the total student population, linked student concerns with those of young women, who were suffering more than their male counterparts owing to gender inequality that inflicted even more draconian social controls and moral patronizing. Nevertheless, the student movement remained overwhelmingly male in disposition and policy. Women needed to express their claims and concerns in their own, feminist, circles. A "post-Islamist" vision articulated Iran's women's orientation of the 1990s.

Post-Islamist Women

Perhaps no social group felt so immediately and pervasively the brunt of the Islamic Revolution as middle-class women. Only months into the life of the Islamic regime, new misogynist policies enraged women who only recently had marched against the monarchy. The new regime overturned the family protection laws of 1967, and overnight women lost their right to be judges, to initiate divorce, to assume child custody, and to travel abroad without permission from a male guardian. Polygamy was reintroduced, and all women, irrespective of faith, were forced to wear the hijab in pub-lic.[14] In the early years, social control and discriminatory quotas against women in education and employment compelled many women to stay at home, seek early retirement, or go into informal or family businesses.[15] Many sought life in exile. But many more resisted.

The initial reaction to these drastic policies came from secular women. They set up dozens of albeit desperate organizations mostly affiliated with sectarian leftist trends. But these groups were soon put down by the Islamic regime once the war with Iraq began in 1980. Then there emerged a spectrum of "Muslim women activists" such as Zahra Rahnavard who, inspired by the writings of Ali Shariati and Morteza Mutahhari, set out to offer an endogenous "model of Muslim women" (*olgu-ye zan-e Mosalman*)[16] in the image of the Prophet's daughter Fatima and his granddaughter Zeinab, who were simultaneously "true" homemakers and public per-sons.[17] Instead of equality, these activists advocated the complementary nature of men and women. Some justified polygamy on the grounds that it protected widows and orphans. Most refused to acknowledge, let alone communicate with, secular Western feminists, whom they saw as "pro-voking women against men" and questioning religious principles and the sanctity of Shari'a.[18] Instead, they placed emphasis on the "family as the heart of the society, and women as the heart of family."[19] Thus, day-care centers became "harmful for children,"[20] even though their closure would throw many women out of work. Muslim women activists accepted the Islamic "tradition" (Quran, Hadith, Shari'a, and *ijtihad*) as an adequate guide to ensure women's dignity and well-being.[21]

With the onset of the war with Iraq (1980–1988) debate about women's status was suppressed. The authorities continued to project women pri-marily as mothers and wives, who were to produce manpower for the war, for the glory of Islam and the nation. But by the late 1980s dissent sim-mered in women's "politics of nagging." Women complained in public daily, in taxis, buses, bakery queues, grocery shops, or government offices, about repression, the war economy, and the war itself. In so doing, they formed a court of irrepressible public opinion that could not be ignored. Mobilization for the war effort had already placed them in the public arena as "model Muslim women," making them conscious of their power. Beyond illusions imposed by men, there were also facts. In a mere twenty years, women's unprecedented interest in education had more than doubled their literacy rate: in 1997 it stood at 74 percent. By 1998, more girls than boys were entering into universities. For young women college offered not only education but a place to socialize, gain status, and develop a better chance for jobs and more desirable partners.

While for some sheer financial necessity left them no choice but to seek employment in the cash economy, most middle-class and well-to-do women chose working outside the home in order to be present in the public realm. By the mid-1990s, half of the positions in the government sector and over 40 percent in education were held by women. Professional women, notably writers and artists, reemerged from domestic exile. Over a dozen female filmmakers were regularly engaged in their highly competitive field, and more women than men won awards at the 1995 Iranian Film Festival.[22] In fact, the economic conditions of families made housewives more publicly visible than ever before. Growing economic hardship since the late 1980s forced middle-class men to take multiple jobs and work longer hours, so that "they're never home." Consequently, all domestic and outside chores shifted exclusively to women.[23] In addition, in this new moral order, traditional men felt at ease allowing their daughters or wives to attend schools or appear at public events. Friday prayer sermons dramatically increased the public presence of women from traditional families who would have otherwise remained in the confines of their unyielding dwellings. This public presence gave women self-confidence, new social skills, and city knowledge and encouraged many to return to school or to volunteer for NGOs or charities.

Women's daily routines and resistance to the Islamic government, especially its forced hijab, did not mean their departure from religiosity. Indeed, most displayed religious devotion.[24] Yet they insisted on exerting individual choice and entitlement, which challenged both the egalitarian claims of the Islamic state and the premises of orthodox Islam. Women wanted to play sports, work in desirable jobs, study, listen to or play music, marry whom they wished, have a choice on wearing hijab, and reject the grave gender inequality. The hardship of sweating under a long dress and veil did not deter many women from jogging, cycling, or target shooting or from speed racing, playing tennis or basketball, or climbing Mount Everest. Nor did they avoid participating in national and international tournaments.[25] These seemingly mundane desires and demands, however, were deemed as redefining the status of women under the Islamic Republic, because each step forward would encourage demands to remove more restrictions. The effect could snowball. How could this general dilemma be resolved? Post-Islamist feminism emerged to take up the challenge.

In a departure from the Islamist women activists, post-Islamist feminism articulated a blend of piety and choice, religiosity and rights. It set
out a strategy for change through discussion, education, and mobilization in a discursive frame that combined religious and secular idioms.
Post-Islamist feminists valued women's autonomy and choice, emphasizing gender equality in all domains. For them, feminism, irrespective of its
origin (secular, religious, or Western), dealt with women's subordination
in general. As feminists, they utilized Islamic discourse to push for gender
equality within the constraints of the Islamic Republic. But they also benefited from secular feminism.[26] The women's magazines *Farzaneh, Zan,*
and *Zanan* spearheaded this trend by running articles on, for instance,
how to improve one's sex life, cooking, women's arts in feminist critical discourse, deconstruction of patriarchal Persian literature, and legal
religious discussions, written by Muslim, secular, Iranian, and Western
authors including Virginia Woolf, Gilman, de Beauvoir, and Faludi.[27]

The major challenge for post-Islamist feminists was to demonstrate
that claims for women's rights were not necessarily alien to Iranian culture or Islam. To this end, they undertook women-centered interpretations
of the sacred texts, in a fashion similar to how early European feminists
such as Hildegard of Bingen (1098–1179), Christine de Pizan (1365–1430),
Isotta Nogarola (1418–1466), and Anna Maria van Schurman (1607–1678)
deconstructed Bible-driven perceptions about the "sinful" and "inferior"
disposition of Eve/women.[28] Within this emerging "feminist theology,"
interpreters questioned misogynist legislation and the literal reading of
Quranic verse; they emphasized instead the "general spirit" of Islam,
which, they argued, is in favor of women. Methodologically grounded
on hermeneutics, philology, and historicism, women interpreters transcended literal meanings in favor of tangential deductions. For instance,
to refute the "innate superiority of men" that orthodox readings deduced
from Quranic verses (such as Surah 4:34 Nisa, where men seem to be
favored over women), *Zanan* writers shifted the basis of hierarchy from sex
to piety by invoking the gender-free verse: "The noblest among you in the
sight of God is the most God-fearing of you" (S. 49:13). Accordingly, child
custody was not automatically the right of men (as the Shari'a authorizes)
but, rather, determined by the well-being of children, which Islam stresses
highly.[29] Consequently, the Quran does not give the right to divorce to men
alone or deny such a right from a woman.[30] Indeed, the gender-neutrality
of the Persian language offered much discursive opportunity for women
to campaign for equal rights.[31] The major novelty of these gender-sensitive

theological debates was that, beyond a few enlightened clerics,[32] women were waging them—and they were doing so on the pages of the popular daily press.

The new women's activism alarmed the clerical establishment, ordinary men, and conservative women. Some ayatollahs warned the activists "not to question Islam's principles by your intellectualism": "Who are you to express opinions…before God and his Prophet?"[33] They denounced women who "questioned religious authorities on hijab and Shari'a." Islamist women in Majlis joined in. Such attacks became intellectual justifications for hard-line mobs and the media to harass "bad-hijab" women on the streets, denounce women's sports and recreation, and fight against the return of "decadence, fashion, and individual taste."[34] *Zanan* was taken to court and eventually banned, and, among others, Mohsen Saidzadeh, a cleric whose women-centered essays on theology and Islamic law had dismayed the conservative clergy, was jailed in June 1998.

Despite all this pressure, the struggles made considerable inroads, empowering women through education, employment, family law, and raised self-esteem. The opportunity for equal education with men made a comeback following the official restrictive quotas that favored men. Polygamy was seriously curtailed, men's right to divorce was restricted, and religiously sanctioned *mut'a* (temporary marriage) was demonized. New laws authorized benefits for working women and obliged the government to provide women's sport facilities.[35] In 1998, a pilot project to prevent wife abuse was launched.[36] Child custody was intensely debated, while the fight for women to be judges led to their appointment as judicial counselors in lower courts and co-judges in high courts. In 1997, fifteen female deputies sat on the Women's Affairs Commission of parliament.[37] These struggles, meanwhile, led to changes in power relations between women and men within the family and society. Opinion polls on women's public role showed that 80 percent of respondents (men and women) were in favor of female government ministers, while 62 percent did not oppose a female president.[38] The Western perception of Iranian women as helpless subjects trapped in the solitude of domesticity and hidden under the long black chador proved to be an oversimplification.

This is not to overstate the status of Iranian women in the Islamic Republic. Flagrant gender inequalities persisted in, for instance, men's right to divorce, child custody, polygamy, and sexual submission, and the amount of a man's blood money was still twice that of a woman. Yet it is also true that the daily struggles of women subverted the conventional gender divide of "public men" and "private women." Against much hostility, Iranian women imposed themselves as public players. Thus, by the late 1990s women's groups were involved in hundreds of women's NGOs and solidarity networks; they held rallies, participated in international women's meetings, lobbied politicians and clerical leaders, and campaigned in the Majlis. Women's weeks, book fairs, film festivals, and sporting events were sites of their public mobilization. Over two dozen women's magazines communicated ideas, advertised events, and established solidarity networks. Feminist ideas permeated universities, with female student groups publishing newsletters on gender issues, and by the late 1990s four Iranian universities had established Women's Studies programs.

Yet institutional activities of this sort made up only an insignificant aspect of women's struggles. The more enduring ones pertained to the practices of daily life that challenged the religious state and its doctrinal foundations. Women pursued education and sports, jogged and cycled, and participated in world championships; they worked as professionals, novelists, filmmakers, or bus or taxi drivers and ran for high public office. And these very public roles beset the social and legal imperatives that had to be addressed—restrictive laws and customs needed to be altered to accommodate the requisites of public women within the prevailing patriarchal system. College education, for example, often required young women to live independently from their families, something that would otherwise be deemed inappropriate. If women could act as high officials, would they still need to obtain their husbands' permission to attend a foreign conference? Thus, such daily practices and persistence by women, students, youth, and other subaltern groups deepened contention within religious discourse and enforced a different, post-Islamist, interpretation of the sacred texts. "Religious intellectuals" articulated this new vision in a more systematic fashion.

The Post-Islamist Intellectuals

At the height of religious control of the state and society, a group of clerics and religious-minded intellectuals raised the flag of a discursive campaign against orthodox interpretations, opening the way for a significant rethinking of sacred texts. The attempt was to secure both the sanctity of religion and the rationality of the state. Somewhat reminiscent of the European Reformation against the Catholic Church, the post-Islamists' ideas navigated through theology, jurisprudence, clerical institutions, and the fusion of religion and state. As in the Reformation, dissent came from both within and, more significant, outside the religious establishment.[39]

The term *rowshanfekran-e dini*, or "religious intellectuals," first appeared in a speech by Mohammad Khatami in 1993, long before he became president, in which he deplored the fact that Islam and Muslim revolutionaries suffered from a "vacuum of theory."[40] He felt that a new type of intellectual was needed to replace both the "religious fanatics who were preoccupied with God but neglected humans" and "secular intellectuals" who focused on man alone and ignored God. The religious intellectual "respects reason and appreciates freedom" but perceives the body as more than mere matter and man as greater than mere nature.[41] Thus, reason, rights, and religion became fundamental elements in the discourse of these thinkers. The core of the group came from a middle-class, revolutionary, Third Worldist, and, above all, Islamist background. They had been invariably influenced by the thoughts of Muslim modernists Ali Shariati, Morteza Mutahhari, and Ayatollah Khomeini. During the 1980s, most of them were functionaries of the Islamic state, having been appointed to sensitive positions or having worked in revolutionary institutions, such as Sepah-i Pasdaran, or in theological seminaries.

Over the course of more than a decade, these individuals "matured," transforming intellectually and expressing ideas that radically distinguished them from their own past and their predecessors such as Ali Shariati. First, the religious intellectuals self-consciously embraced modernity, emphasizing such notions as "critical reason [*aqlaniyyat-e intiqadi*] as the essence of modern life," rationality, human rights, liberty, plurality, science, and free market economics. But they also espoused faith, spirituality, and religious ethics. Of course, many of the earlier "Muslim reformers," notably al-Afghani, Abdul-Rahman al-Kawakibi, and Muhammad Abdu, and even their conservative opponents, also considered science and reason as compatible with Islam. However, for the post-Islamists modernity required embracing not only science and technology (hardware) but also a new mentality, new attitudes, and new concepts (software).[42] In addition, post-Islamist intellectuals departed from older Muslim reformers in their nationalist, anticolonial, and Third World persuasions.

Second, the religious intellectuals espoused generally "postnationalist" orientations. They no longer blamed the nation's problems exclusively on foreign powers and Western imperialism. Iran's underdevelopment, they believed, originated in its own historical despotism.[43] Therefore, focus should not have been on some abstract Western conspiracy but, rather, on institutionalizing the ideals of freedom and democracy within society. Third, religious intellectuals were "postrevolutionaries," post-idea-of-revolution, that is. They had experienced and transcended the revolutionary discourse of martyrdom, bravery, discipline, militancy, war, and especially violence,[44] the kinds of idioms that conservative Islamists continued to embrace. The absence of a populist language markedly distinguished religious intellectuals from the Islamists. Instead, they emphasized reform, tolerance, acknowledging differences, and peaceful coexistence. Finally, religious intellectuals were "postideological." Ideology was seen as rigid, the antithesis of free critical thinking, and as needing to create "enemies." "Ideologizing religion," something commonly practiced by Ali Shariati and Morteza Mutahhari, was fiercely critiqued by the post-Islamist intellectuals.[45] Thus, they read and were inspired by Marx, Popper, Giddens, David Held, Homa Katouzian, and Hussein Bashiriyeh, but they made little attempt to establish dialogue with marginalized Iranian secular intellectuals whose ideas on politics, culture, and society, which circulated in several journals, contributed considerably to this intellectual shift.

The religious intellectuals represented perhaps the first significant postcolonial intellectuals in the Muslim world. Postcolonial intellectuals discarded "orientalism in reverse," refusing to view either the Muslim world or the West as an undifferentiated, unitary, and unchangeable entity or to view the two in binary opposition. Rather, they discerned differentiation, change, and hybridity within, and flow and dialogue between, these worlds. According to *Kiyan*, "the West is not just a place of 'nightlife' but also the locus of intellectual, technical precision. It is in here that fundamental human questions are raised and addressed."[46] In cleric Mohsen Kadivar's view, the notion of the "dialogue of civilization" was nothing but an exchange between the Islamic world and the West. "We give something, and take something else." We take industry, modernization, philosophical, and social science categories, and we offer concepts in ethics and mysticism.[47]

Deeply influenced by social and political conditions in the 1990s, the post-Islamist intellectuals sought to redefine the capabilities of religion in the modern age in order to address complex human needs. Thus their intellectual efforts centered on constructing a *republican theology* by blending the ideals of modernity, democracy, and religiosity. Fundamental to their thinking on religion was the role of reason and rationality (*aqlaniyyat-e dini*). The Quran, according to the cleric Abdullah Nouri, frequently invites humans to think, reason, and discover, rather than to imitate.[48]

Thus, religious texts are to be understood only through reasoning and deliberation. Indeed, faith and freedom are two sides of one coin: "People are free to choose a religion and free to leave it."[49] Religious faith cannot be forced on people; compulsion produces hypocrites. Deliberately hostile apostates may have to respond to God only in the hereafter; otherwise "apostasy does not have punishment in this world."[50]

Epistemologically, the "religious intellectuals" called for a hermeneutic reading of the religious texts, including the Quran, rejecting a single "true reading" or, for that matter, an exclusive "expert reading" by the ulema.[51] In fact, many wished to end the professionalization of religious interpretation by the clergy, who faultily subsist on religion and who monopolize religious knowledge and spiritual property.[52] In a devastating critique of the "clerical establishment," Hashem Aghajari, a war veteran, dismissed the ulema's role not only in politics but also in religion. Proposing an "Islamic Protestantism," he called for individual Muslims to seek their own religious truths without the medium of clerics.

The question of religious or divine truth is a fundamental issue in the philosophy of religion. How could post-Islamist intellectuals justify the different truths of different religions? Does this mean that religious truth is relative? The cleric Abdullah Nouri was confronted with precisely such questions during his prosecution in a religious tribunal in 1999. "Relativity of truth is one thing, and epistemological error is something else," he replied: "Simply, truth is not obvious." As far as Islam is concerned, "except God, there is nothing absolute."[53] In sum, "the idea of religion is complete, truthful, and sacred, but our perception of it is not. The idea of religion is not subject to change, but our perception of it is."[54] In the view of post-Islamists, the significance of religion, notably Islam, lay neither in fiqh (the lowest order) nor in rituals but, rather, in its ethics and moralities. Instructions based upon fiqh should not be mandatory unless they become law. And laws should reflect social necessities that may conflict with Shari'a.

Indeed, as their ideas evolved, many post-Islamist intellectuals discarded the idea of wilayat al-faqih as an "undesirable" and "undemocratic" and thus unacceptable model of government. Abdulkarim Soroush explicitly argued that the management of modern societies was both possible and desirable not through religion but through scientific rationality in a democratic structure.[55] Not only are Islam and democracy compatible; their association is inevitable. In fact, religious intellectuals called for the establishment of a secular democratic state that was compatible with "religious society." Some of the "religious intellectuals," such as the cleric Sayyed Mohsen Saidzadeh, offered a "women-centered" reading of Islamic sacred texts and equipped the post-Islamist feminists with the conceptual resources necessary to sustain their struggles. The feminist monthly *Zanan* was in essence the sister publication of *Kiyan*, the journal of the religious intellectuals.

These thinkers, in sum, explicitly rejected "Islam huwa al-hall" ("Islam is the solution"), the popular slogan among Islamist movements in the Arab world. For Iran's religious intellectuals, Islam had limitations in answering all of humanity's problems. In fact, religion was in essence seen not as the domain of mundane concerns but, rather, of meaning, mystery, love, and devotion. In that spirit, religious faith must be encouraged, not only because it makes life tolerable by enabling humans to cope with the harsh realities of life but also because it can provide mechanisms for internal control against individual abuse of others, just as democracy facilitates external control.[56]

The new religious thinking found currency not simply among the literate public but also in seminaries, or hawzehs, and not among the established ulema but primarily among younger clerics. The monthly *Kiyan* established a substantial following in Qom, the city of Islamic seminaries.[57] The younger ulema began to critique the cultural and epistemological legacy of their hawzeh.[58] Religious knowledge ceased to draw merely on the traditional texts and increasingly relied on literature from outside the seminary, including Western philosophers. Fiqh lost its authority to theology and philosophy, while the scripturist method gave way to the centrality of reason and hermeneutics.

The ideas expressed by the religious intellectuals were neither flawless nor utterly original. They also had little to say about economics. Indeed, the ongoing debates and differences within the group, disclosed in the monthly *Kiyan*, chronicled the community's intellectual evolution. The epistemology adopted by religious intellectuals could be found among other Islamic modernists in the Muslim world such as Algerian Muhammad Arkoun, Egyptian Hasan Hanafi, Syrian Shahrur, and secular Egyptian Nasr Abu-Zeid, not to mention in the rich scholarship on religious pluralism.[59] Yet the significance of these ideas in the Iranian context lay not in their originality but in their popular appeal under a self-conscious Islamic state. Not only did these views shake up the conceptual foundation of the traditional clergy and theological seminaries; their convergence with the people's political grievances rendered them a social force. These ideas gathered support primarily among the young, educated, largely religious-minded, but also secular, Iranians, especially the modern middle classes, many of whom had been politically marginalized.[60] Forums with mass audiences, such as lecture halls, mosques, and the daily press, spread the ideas across other segments of the population. Remarkably, they secured a significant following among theology students, including those of the conservative Ayatollah Mesbah-Yazdi.[61]

The formation of the group, as the nucleus of a trend, went back to 1991, when Mohammad Khatami, just out of the Ministry of Culture, had called for the necessity of creating "religious intellectuals." The group was involved in reading circles, publishing, study projects, and lecturing at homes or religious locations. The Tehran headquarters of *Kiyan* virtually turned into an intellectual salon of post-Islamist thought, while new intellectual circles were identified and linked to a network of religious intellectuals. Liberal-religious activists (*melli-mazhabiha*) rallied around the monthly *Iran-e Farda*, while intellectual circles in the Qom Seminary, such as those around Mustafa Malekian and students of Ayatollah Montazeri, worked through *Naqd-o-Nazar*; and the secular intellectuals established *Goft-o-gu* and a number of literary social publications.

The religious intellectuals were soon to encounter a strategic question: Where to go from here? Some believed that they should disseminate their ideas to a broader segment of the population by establishing daily papers and a political party. However, the early pressure from conservative Islamists confirmed the concern of others within the group who thought that it was premature to engage in such radical activities, for they could provoke a backlash. To spread its discursive project on a mass scale, members of the group felt that it needed to wait for a more open political climate. They needed to create such a climate.

At the same time that youths, Muslim women, student activists, intellectuals, and state employees were mobilizing their constituencies for social and ideational change, "religious intellectuals" began to ponder how such civil society movements could be sustained and how this tremendous energy could be translated into political change at the state level. Thus, "political development" became the group's preoccupation, and their ultimate objective was democratizing the patrimonial Islamic state, hoping to realize a new model of "religious democracy." The idea of political development originated in the early 1990s from religious intellectuals' reexamination of Iran's closed political structure. It was formulated in a systematic fashion by a research team headed by Saiid Hajjarian located in the Political Bureau of the president's Center for Strategic Studies. Launched under President Rafsanjani, the Center for Strategic Studies became the organizational and intellectual hub for political reformers. Hajjarian brought together the most talented post-Islamist political strategists, assigning to each a particular project, such as "cultural studies," "Islamic political thought," and others covering Iran's political culture, the nature of the state, modernization, political and strategic theory, and theories of revolution.[62]

Political development was crucial, Hajjarian concluded, first, because it was a precondition for economic development (similar to the notion that democracy is good for economic growth)[63] and, second, because it could contain the repercussions of new economic restructuring—inequality and social unrest.[64] In addition to conceptual work, the team was also concerned with practical matters, beginning with establishing a college to train intellectuals and cadres, promoting civil society organizations, and launching the daily *Salâm*. Study findings were covered in the monthly *Rahbord* and later in *Asr-e Maa*.

The group unleashed an unprecedented debate on the nature of the religious state in Iran, often questioning the relevance of the concept of wilayat al-faqih. In this new reading, a "religious state" should receive its legitimacy from the will of the people, who are God's vice-regents on earth,[65] with a plurality of views, orientations, and lifestyles. The separation of the institutions of religion and the state was advocated as a precondition for an ideal religious republic.[66] To begin a process of modification, they favored the election of the supreme leader—serving as the spiritual, not political, leader—to a limited term by direct popular vote.[67] In this fashion, Iran's Islamic Republic could be as democratic as the British monarchical democracy. A post-Islamist polity called for "secularization" (institutional separation of religion and state) but not "secularism," which meant diminishing the significance of religion in society. This vision was reflected in Khatami's notion of "religious democracy" (*mardom-sâlâri-ye dini*), which was to guide national policies on culture, economics, and international relations. Khatami's "dialogue of civilization" and subsequent improvement of relations with many Arab, Asian, and European countries represented the international dimension of this project.

Notwithstanding much talk about "religious democracy" for over a decade, the exact meaning of the term remained ambiguous.[68] In general, it referred to the quest to democratize the patrimonial Islamist system without losing sight of religious ethics. For, in addition to their intrinsic value, the post-Islamists argued, religious sensibilities needed to be respected were modernity and democracy to succeed in Muslim societies like Iran.[69] Yet the precise place of religion within their projected democratic system remained contested, and with the changing political circumstances perspectives evolved. Whereas it was enough for some that their ideal democratic state not be hostile to religion, others, such as Soroush, perceived a religious state as one that responded to the sensibilities and interests of a religious population. For the cleric Mojtahed Shabastari, "religious canons" regulate the relationship between individuals and God, but democracy grounded on human rights would be sufficient to organize the relationships between individuals in an Islamic society. Later on most wished to take out the adjective *religious* from "religious democracy," not only because democracy alone would fulfill the desires of a religious society but because the conservative Islamists might appropriate the term and make it meaningless.[70] This vision was to be achieved through a nonviolent strategy, "mobilization from below and negotiation at the top." Mobilization from below was already well under way. Negotiation at the top had to win over elements of state power. To this end, a post-Islamist intellectual, Mohammad Khatami, was nominated to run for president in 1997. Saiid Hajjarian led the campaign strategy and ensured a decisive victory.

Explaining the Shift

Why did post-Islamism, as a condition, project, and movement, come into existence? At least three general factors were responsible: first, the failures and contradictions of the Islamist project that entailed a rethinking of Islamism from within; second, social changes (increasing literacy, urbanization, and an economic shift) that generated actors (educated middle classes, the young, increasingly literate women, and a collective urban consciousness) who pushed for social and political transformation; and third, the global post–Cold War context within which these changes were taking place.

The Islamist project unleashed by the Islamic state was bound to eventually generate dissent. The system of wilayat al-faqih was opposed from the start by the majority of Shi'i grand clergy.[71] Although the faqih ruled alongside an elected parliament, restrictions on forming political parties and the Council of Guardians' veto power marginalized other political tendencies. Consequently, even some of the ardent supporters of the system became disenchanted with the government's excessive political control and factional infighting. Former allies turned into enemies, while secular leftist groups and ethnic political organizations were harshly repressed.

Meanwhile, the economy did not deliver. "Islamic economics" remained a "disputed utopia"[72] and in the end settled for an often disrupted and distorted capitalist economy. Income distribution improved slightly compared with before the revolution, but during the same period per capita income dropped by half. Economic blockades, the devastating cost of war (some $90 billion),[73] mismanagement, and a lack of security for capital accumulation played debilitating roles. Subsequently, idealistic and still young Islamic war veterans, disenchanted by the populist rhetoric of the Islamic state, rioted in Islamshahr, Shiraz, Mashahd, Arak, and Khoramabd.[74] Industrial workers barely managed through strikes to maintain their purchasing power, while professionals and the salaried middle classes—the privileged prerevolution groups—were ravaged by inflation and recession. State control of individual behavior and leisure, and the moral regulation of females in particular, frustrated middle-class women and urban youth. In the universities, the "cultural revolution" dismissed 180,000 students and two out of every three faculty members.[75] An estimated three million Iranians left the country,[76] working and investing billions of dollars outside Iran.

By the early 1990s, social problems associated with crime, divorce, deviance, exclusion, apathy, a growing population, and women's daily quarrels with the morals police had confronted Iranian Muslims with a sobering question: "Is this the kind of Islamic society we are building?" Those in authority had sensed the mood. "By our wrongdoings," admitted the prominent Ayatollah Mousavi Ardabili, "we have alienated three-fourths of the people.... We are responsible for creating a violent, detestable, terrifying, inflexible, irrational, anti-science, unethical, and inhuman image of Islam."[77] A survey by the Tehran Municipality painted a grim picture of private religiosity under the Islamic state: 73 percent of Tehranies did not recite their daily prayers, and 17 percent did so only occasionally. Drug use and divorce were sharply rising, with vices increased by 635 percent in 1999.[78] Up to two million Iranians were reportedly addicted to narcotics. In 1996 half of all Iranian households filed over three million criminal and legal suits in the courts of a nation that promised social peace and harmony.[79] "Islamic solidarity" was no more than a mere myth.

Youth, the children of the revolution, caused the most concern. The regime's control of leisure and suppression of youthful desires alienated them from the Islamist authorities. Officials panicked when surveys unveiled the growing indifference and hostility of the young toward religion, the clergy, and the religious state. How could the state integrate youth into religious politics from which they were exiting en masse? What ideological alternative was there to offer the young who were departing from Islamism?

Post-Islamism emerged as a way out. "Today more than any other time," *Kiyan*'s editorial proclaimed in 1993, "the Islamic revolution needs to formulate a new vision in order to rescue our current generation from mental disorder, nihilism, and degeneration."[80] The paradoxes of the Islamic state facilitated the growth of this new vision. The very Islamization of the state had led to a growing secularization of Shari'a, because the latter largely failed to respond to the demands of complex modern life. Khomeini's ruling in 1987 to "absolutize" the wilayat al-faqih—whereby the faqih was authorized to change or disregard any law, precept, or religious injunction if such an action was deemed to be in the interest of the state—subordinated religious sanctity to secular concerns and encroached on the clergy's prerogative of an autonomous interpretation of Shari'a. To their further dismay, the ulema's fatwas, or verdicts, on public affairs became subject to approval by the supreme faqih, and their access to *haq-i imam*, or donations from the faithful, was conditional on the faqih's permission. Because the state (Assembly of Experts) took charge of disbursing *khums* and *zakat*, the *mujtahids* lost their power of distributing stipends to their student clientele. Still further, the Special Clerical Courts, in which a number of clerics have been prosecuted for expressing unorthodox ideas, eroded the clerics' intellectual immunity. And all these emerged in conditions where the fusion of the state and religion had stained the spiritual and social legitimacy of the clergy, as many Iranians tended to equate the failures of the state with those of the ulema.

For the first time in their modern history, the mainstream Shi'i ulema were losing their independence and much of their traditional power, and this was happening, ironically, under a self-conscious Islamic state. Increasing ulema dependency on the state, itself ruled by a few powerful clergy, worried many younger clerics about their future and that of the institution of the ulema. Many expressed their worries publicly. "If we tie religion to politics," one said, "all the mundane and everyday troubles will be identified with religion, degenerating religion from its sacred plain of spirituality into the everyday political games. Religion should be saved for the days when politics fail."[81] In a sense, post-Islamism sought to save Islam as a faith by undoing Islamism as politics.

Although post-Islamism had indigenous roots, it developed within a particular global context: the collapse of the USSR and its allies, the "triumph" of liberalism, and the globalization of the languages of civil society, pluralism, and human rights. Post-Islamist activists adopted many of the popular idioms of the day (civil society, rule of law, transparency, democracy, accountability) and blended them with religious ethics to generate their own hybrid alternative for a society that was yearning for change.[82]

But how was the social foundation of the movement built? Spectacular social changes since the 1980s had produced social actors, notably educated but impoverished middle classes, urban youth, and women, who aspired to social and political transformation. First, a high fertility rate (3.2 percent) during the 1980s created one of the world's youngest populations.[83] At the same time, the population had emerged from a semiliterate state (48 percent in 1976) to become a literate society. Within that same twenty-year period the student population had increased 266 percent to a staggering twenty million, or one-third of the population. College students tripled; one out of every five households produced a college student or graduate, including young women and people from rural areas.[84]

Second, Iran was rapidly becoming an urban society. In 1996 over 60 percent of its people were living in cities, compared with 47 percent twenty years earlier. Mass urbanization spawned urban individuality, self-expression, diverse lifestyles, media exposure, and demands for urban citizenship. In the meantime, urbanity crept into rural areas, changing occupational structures, the division of labor, literacy rates, and consumption patterns, while new means of communication, expanding electronic and print media, and college education drew the rural world into the urban trajectory.

One key outcome of all this has been the decline of traditional sources of authority and the emergence of new ones. The rural *mulla*, or clergyman, is no longer a dominant village figure. Ageism, it seemed, was finally giving way to an appreciation of competence. This trend at the national level was reflected in the declining authority of parents over children, fathers over sons, teachers over students, religious experts over laypeople, and husbands over wives.[85] The prevailing hierarchical dichotomies were subverted, giving rise to new social divisions and conflicts, and the structure of the family at the national level had begun to transform. Compared with youth in the Muslim Middle East, Iran's were undergoing a notable trend of individualism.[86] The expansion of new urban lifestyles and "apartment settlement" both reflected and intensified this process of new individuation.

Finally, the class structure experienced a profound change character-ized by a relative de-proletarianization, informalization, and the predomi-nance of middle-class occupations.[87] From 1976 to 1996, when the total private labor force increased only 37 percent, the number of small busi-ness entrepreneurs tripled, and public-sector employees expanded by a startling 254 percent. In the meantime, while the number of private wage earners remained virtually stagnant (6.5 percent), self-employed workers in the informal sector increased by 190 percent. In general, then, more people were employed in more flexible work conditions and middle-class occupations, displaying a wide range of choices in consumption. Yet the economic downturn and low income frustrated the realization of middle-class lifestyles.[88]

Thus by the mid-1990s, a new type of middle class was in the mak-ing—one characterized by enormous size, educational capital, global dreams, and yet an economic condition far inferior to that of its affluent prerevolution counterparts. Frustrated and morally outraged, the middle class constituted the core of the social base for the post-Islamist move-ments, pushing the "reformist" Mohammad Khatami to the presidential office. Post-Islamism ascended to governmental power. Could it spearhead a democratic transformation?

Post-Islamism in Power?

Khatami's triumph on May 23, 1997, described as the "second revolu-tion," was to implement the basic tenets of a post-Islamist polity, which informed the ideological foundation of what came to be known as the "reform movement." Once in power, he drew many of the post-Islamist intellectuals into the new government as ministers, deputy ministers, advisers, and parliamentary deputies. The government's strategy was to empower civil society from below and negotiate legal and institutional change at the top, where conservative Islamists still wielded real power, controlling the judiciary and nonelected but powerful bodies (such as state-run television, the security forces, the Guardian Council, the Council of Expediency, and the influential Friday prayer leaders). Khatami put to task a number of ministries (Interior, Foreign Affairs, Intelligence, Higher Education, and Culture) to facilitate reform strategies from above. Leaders in the local grassroots networks that helped Khatami's electoral campaign came to make up the bulk of the new governors, mayors, and local officials.

At the base, meanwhile, civil society institutions expanded, and free press, associational life, and social movement activism (among students, youth, women, NGOs) assumed unprecedented energy; the somber and repressed mood in the streets and in government offices relaxed. The post-Islamists in power managed to establish the language of reform and the necessity of converging Islam with democratic ideals. Never before in Iranian political history did such fundamental concepts as democracy, pluralism, accountability, the rule of law, and tolerance become so pervasive, and all this in a political culture that nurtured seniority and patronage. This was an extraordinary time for a society reborn, where an immense sense of vitality and energy animated every sector of society to stand up and assert itself.

Thus, after years of exclusion and intimidation by the Ansar-e Hizbullah, youths regained their presence in the public space—in streets, parks, cafés, shopping malls, cultural centers, concerts, and stadiums. Most young people were students, who blended youthful dispositions with student aspirations to create a spectacular student movement with a new identity and vigor. With an organization (DTV) already in place and new support from the reform government, the student movement grew rapidly, expanding its nationwide networks, publishing a national student paper (*Azar*) and seven hundred local student magazines, and instituting 1,437 cultural, scientific, and social associations.[89] Now with a new generation of students at its helm, the movement experienced a striking ideological shift away from utopian Islamist and Third Worldist revolutionary politics and toward a pragmatist post-Islamist paradigm based on democracy and civil liberties. At the same time, female students bonded through growing feminist circles, contributing to an already flourishing Muslim women's activism.[90] Women expanded their networks, created publications and organizations, and voiced both feminist and political aspirations. Women's organizations reached 230 by 2000 and 330 by 2003.[91] Meanwhile, marginalized groups both in exile and at home returned to the political scene. In 2000, ninety-five new political parties and organizations had registered, including eighteen reformist political groups, compared with thirty-five in 1997.[92] A year later there were 110 employers' guilds and 120 workers' associations,[93] while one out of three workers belonged to Labor House, the main workers' organization.[94]

Nothing was more visible than the energy around newsstands. Reform sparked an explosion of relatively free and independent print media unprecedented in the previous one hundred years. The reform era would spawn 2,228 new titles, including 174 dailies.[95] Women and students initiated their own specialized press: Women's publications reached forty by 2002, and the students' reached 286 by 2000.[96] These periodicals sparked debate about taboo subjects and gave rise to a political glasnost that not only embodied unfolding social struggles but made people aware of factional conflicts within the state.

Within this vibrant public sphere, the mobilized public delivered resounding electoral victories to the reformists at the top. In the first nationwide polls for city and village councils in February 1999, reform candidates won 90 percent of the 200,000 seats.[97] Many city councils became both a support base for reformists and institutions of grassroots social development.[98] In January 2000, control of parliament fell in a landslide to the reformists. By the reelection of Khatami in the following year, the reform movement had gained control of almost all elected institutions. As a result of a détente, in less than four years, relations with the West and pro-West Arab states improved, while the democratic thrust of the reform movement had alarmed authoritarian Arab regimes. With its "model of democracy," Arab headlines warned, "Iran this time is exporting free elections instead of Islamic Revolution."[99]

As the reform process unfolded, the movement experienced signs of differentiation. Many of the earlier critical ideas on wilayat al-faqih or the religious state became explicit. Known post-Islamists moved toward more liberal and secular ideals in political domains. In August 2003, Hussein Khomeini, the grandson of Ayatollah Khomeini, went into exile in Iraq and launched a political campaign to dismantle the religious state in Iran. To him, Iran's religious state was the "worst dictatorship in the world." While the tendency toward secularization facilitated a broader coalition for secular republicanism (such as the new Front for Republicanism, which linked exiled and homegrown republicans), the more religious-minded reformists were dismayed. With its religious but also democratic idioms, the reform movement posed perhaps the most serious challenge to the conservative Islamists. It demolished their moral and political legitimacy. The discursive onslaught of post-Islamism was so devastating that in the view of many Islamists, "the assault that our sacred principles have endured [since Khatami] is far more than during the Pahlavies."[100]

Beaten and bewildered by their crushing electoral defeat, the conservative Islamists sought every opportunity to regain confidence and fight back. If the reform movement focused on "mobilization from below and negotiation from above," the conservative backlash aimed to subvert just that, to impair the reformist mobilization in society, and to paralyze the reform government at the top. To this end, the hard-liners combined a discursive campaign with everyday violence, instigating crises and using legal channels to suppress dissent and decapitate reformist-controlled institutions.

As early as 1996, a conference organized by conservative clerics in Qom Seminary had already attempted to confront the "ideological crisis" and head off the post-Islamist challenge. Participants had called on the grand clergy and supreme leader to articulate and disseminate through textbooks rebuttals to post-Islamist theological "flaws" (shubihaat).[101] The opponents targeted the elements of post-Islamist discourse—religious pluralism, secularization, tolerance, and above all democracy—that were wrecking the Islamist paradigm. Both the theological and the social status of Islam (e.g., religious truth, Shari'a, religious freedom, the clergy, and religious politics) became matters of intense verbal struggle. With Khatami's election, however, the reaction turned hostile. "Nothing is dirtier than [the idea of] a pluralist reading of religion," declared Ayatollah Khaz'ali of the Guardian Council, warning Khatami to avoid using such terms in public.[102] For Rahim Sawafi, the commander in chief of the pasdaran, these ideas were "produced by our enemies to cause uncertainty among Muslims."[103] The Society of Combatant Clergy of Tehran warned, "We must not permit the sacred principles of Islam to become the subject of diverse interpretations of this or that individual."[104] And Ayatollah Mesbah-Yazdi declared, "We must shut the mouth of those who call for a new reading of Islam."[105] He went as far as declaring the "wilayat al-faqih as the continuation of divine rule; opposing it would be equal to apostasy and the negation of Islam."[106] And the Ansar-e Hizbullah blatantly warned, "We will chop the pens of those who unknowingly write against the wilayat al-faqih; and will shed their blood if they do so deliberately."[107]

Indeed, for Islamist hard-liners, the use of everyday violence in the name of "safeguarding Islam and the revolution" became an effective way of doing politics. Through repression by proxy—"ordinary people" used as pawns—hard-liners aimed to recapture the public sphere. Hundreds of semiclandestine "cultural" groups associated with the Ansar-e Hizbullah and basije vigilantes found fertile ground for activism after the reformists had come to power. Reminiscent of Fascist vigilantes, the Ansar-e Hizbullah violently disrupted scores of reformist and secularist rallies, lectures, and events, ravaging offices and university dorms, beating up individuals, and committing murders and assassinations (of reformists, secular intellectuals, students, and activists). In almost all of these assaults, police stood aside and watched. Those who were arrested were set free later by the judiciary.[108]

To stifle alternative thought, the hard-line judiciary closed down 108 major dailies between 1997 and 2002, putting thousands of reformist journalists, publishers, and writers in detention or out of work. The student movement was seriously curtailed by the harsh violence of the Ansar-e Hizbullah or the pure and simple dismissal of activists. The hard-line faction effectively neutralized many parts of the government that were controlled by the reformists; at times they created alternative institutions to those of the government (e.g., the pasdaran created a different intelligence service). More importantly, the Guardian Council's veto power, often blessed by the supreme leader, rendered the reformist-controlled parliament virtually powerless. Even its parliamentary deputies were barred from running for upcoming elections, with the result that the parliament fell back to the hard-line Islamists. So, little changed in the conservatives' institutional power—namely, in nonelected bodies, the army, the police, the pasdaran, the *basij*, institutions of propaganda, and numerous violent pressure groups. Instead, popular disenchantment with the reform project allowed the conservatives to complete their *coup de force* and finish off the reform process when the presidential office passed on to the hard-line Ahmadinejad in 2004. With the grassroots demoralized, the gradual indifference of the urban middle classes, students, youths, and women diminished the reformists' social power. What particularly contributed to this process were the fragmentation of the reform camp and the lack of a common strategy among partners who held diverging visions about what kind of Iran they wanted.

Although it failed to dislodge the Islamists, the major triumph of the post-Islamist movement lay in fundamentally undermining the moral and political legitimacy of Islamism. It hegemonized the ideals of democracy and political (if not social) pluralism to heights never before reached in Iran or, Turkey aside, in the Muslim Middle East. Reformists clearly demonstrated that one could be both Muslim and democrat. But the reform government, with its feeble leadership, middle-class constituency, focus on discursive change, and reluctance to mobilize popular classes (notably the poor, working people, teachers), was unable to tackle the coercive power and clientelistic networks of its conservative rivals. Instead, the revengeful conservatives embarked on a massive operation—political, legal, and blatantly violent—to win back what they had lost throughout the reform years. Ahmadinejad and his government embodied an urge for restoration, specifically a return to the revolutionism of the early 1980s, by forging new sources of legitimacy—that is to say, populism, radicalism, and messianic discourse. They were determined to offset any possibility of yet another reform government. The hard-liners sought adamantly to consolidate the conservative Islamists' power in line with the visions of Ayatollah Mesbah-Yazdi—Ahmadinejad's doctrinal mentor—by stripping the Islamic Republic of its republican component and turning it into an Islamic *government*, in which elections would serve not as a venue for the free expression of ideas and dissent but simply to confirm allegiance to the supreme faqih, as the true essence of the "Islamic system."[109]

Thus, under Ahmadinejad, scores of NGOs were closed down; hundreds of dissident students, faculty, women, and civil society activists were incarcerated, and the mass protests of teachers, bus drivers, and other workers were suppressed. Subsidies were cut, privatization reached a new height (eighteen times more than that in 2001–2003), and a 25 percent inflation rate drastically diminished the purchasing power of the wage earners. Ahmadinejad's electoral campaign in 2005 focused on fighting corruption, generating jobs, and a generous redistribution of oil money. But under his government, cronyism and corruption reached a new level, and people living below the poverty line increased by 13 percent, with nine million–ten million falling below it (according to the Islamic Works Council).

In this light, the "nightmare" of yet another term for Mahmoud Ahmadinejad caused unprecedented enthusiasm for the reformist candidates. Indeed, the 2009 presidential election contest between Ahmadinejad and Mir Hussein Mousavi transformed the social and political face of the nation. Enthusiasts of "reform," from the well-off to the middle classes and working people—many of whom had refused to vote in the previous poll in 2005—utilized the electoral schedule and a rift within the power elites to turn their years of quiet discontent into a spectacular open mobilization. Women and young people in particular turned energetically to grassroots activism, organizing mass street marches with a quasi-carnivalesque atmosphere. But the outcome of the elections—victory for Ahmadinejad, amid plentiful evidence of fraud—dashed the hopes of many, inspiring a profound moral outrage that in turn fed into a broad-based protest movement of a kind unseen in the history of the republic. It was called the Green Movement.[110]

This movement, neither a middle-class struggle against a pro-poor government nor a secularist war against religious rule, embodied a post-Islamist democracy movement to reclaim citizenship within an ethical order. It articulated the long-standing yearnings for a dignified life free from fear, moral surveillance, corruption, and arbitrary rule. Emphatically indigenous and principally nonviolent, it represented a green wave for life and liberty.[iii]

The movement started strongly but soon faced a violent crackdown by the Islamic regime. The thinking class (strategists, campaigners, writers) was immediately incarcerated; the reformist media was almost completely shut down; and free communications among citizens were suspended. The state intimidation and violence (at least seventy were killed and four thousand were arrested), a neurotic propaganda campaign in the state-controlled media, a Stalinist-type mass trial of opposition figures broadcast on television, and psychological warfare weakened the street showdowns. Amid the continuing collective dissent and fear of an impending uprising reminiscent of the "Arab Spring," the government in 2011 put the two key leaders of the opposition, Mir Hussein Mousavi and Mehdi Karroubi, under house arrest. Even though the Islamist regime, faced with numerous internal feuds, has thus far survived, many things have changed. The ruling circle has faced an unprecedented legitimacy crisis and a profound divide, while the supreme leader has become a central target of popular contention. The issue has gone beyond electoral fraud toward challenging the very ability of Islamist rule to accommodate the desires of its rights-conscious citizens. The Green Movement, notwithstanding its own drawbacks and differentiation, signaled the profound crisis of Islamism both in ideas and in governance and heralded the ascendancy of a post-Islamist polity for the future of Iran.

Notes

1. This chapter is based almost entirely on chapters 3 and 4 of my book *Making Islam Democratic: Social Movements and the Post-Islamist Turn* (Stanford: Stanford University Press, 2007). All quotes from Persian are my own translations.
2. Seyed Hossein Serajzadeh, "Non-attending Believers: Religiosity of Iranian Youth and Its Implications for Secularization Theory" (paper presented at the World Congress of Sociology, Montreal, 1999); *Aftab*, 8 Ordibehesht 1380 (2001); A. Kazemipur and A. Rezaei, "Religious Life under Theocracy: The Case of Iran," *Journal for the Scientific Study of Religion* 42, no. 3 (September 2003): 347–361.

3. See Morteza Nabawi, in *Resalat*, October 27, 2001, 2.

4. See Jean-Michel Cadiot, AP report, IranMania.com, August 20, 2001.

5. Charles Recknaged and Azam Gorgin, "Iran: New 'Morality Police' Units Generate Controversy," Radio Free Europe, July, 25, 2002, www.rferl.org/content/article/1100367.html.

6. See Ali Akbar Mahdi, "The Student Movement in the Islamic Republic of Iran," *Journal of Iranian Research and Analysis* 15, no. 2 (November 1999): 10.

7. Mohammad Jawad Larijani, in *Resalat*, 9-10-1373 (December 30, 1994).

8. Farzad Taheripour and Masoud Anjam-Sho'a, "Gostaresh-e Amoozesh-e Aali va Touse'e-ye Jam'iyyat-e Daaneshjoui" [The expansion of higher education and the growth of student body], *Barnaameh va Touse'e* 2, no. 5 (Spring 1372 [1993]).

9. For a perceptive analysis, see Majid Mohammadi, *Daramadi bar Raftaar-Shenasi-ye Siyasi* (Tehran: Intisharat-e Kavir, 1998).

10. See Jawad Rahimpour, "Maziyyat-e Jonbesh-e Daneshjooi: Pratic ya Estrategic," *Iran-e Farda* 49 (Aban–Azar 1377 [1998]).

11. According to student leader Heshmat Tabarzadi, interview in *Hoviyat-e Khish*, May 1, 1999, 8.

12. See Daftar-e Tahkim va Vahdat-e Anjoman-haaye Eslami, "The Manifesto of the DTV," DTV Web site, 16 Azar 1376 (1997).

13. *Nourooz*, 11 Tir 1380 (2001), 10.

14. See Parvin Paydar, *Women and Political Process in Iran* (Cambridge: Cambridge University Press, 1995).

15. See Zahara Karimi, "Sahm-e Zanan dar Bazaar-e Kaar-e Iran," *Ettelaat-e Siyassi-Eqtisadi* 179–180 (Mordad–Shahrivar 1381 [2002]): 208–219.

16. Azar Tabari and Nahid Yeganeh, eds., *Under the Shadow of Islam* (London: Zed Books, 1982), 17.

17. See *Payam Hajar* 1 (19 Shahrivar 1359 [1980]): 2.

18. *Zanan* 42 (Farvardin–Ordibehesht 1377 [1998]): 3.

19. Cited in *Zanan* 26 (1995): 3.

20. Maryam Behroozi, cited in *Ettelaat*, 3 Esfand 1361 (1982), 6.

21. Shahin Tabatabaii, "Understanding Islam in Its Totality Is the Only Way to Understand Women's Role," in *Under the Shadow of Islam*, ed. Azar Tabari and Nahid Yeganeh (London: Zed Books, 1982), 174.

22. *Zanan* 27 (1995): 42.

23. Masserat Amir Ebrahimi, interview in "Tehran: Fragmented and Feminized," *Bad-Jens*, 6th ed. (December 2002), www.badjens.com/sixthedition/i2.htm.

24. Abbas Abdi and Mohsen Goudarzi, *Tahavvolat-e Farhangui dar Iran* [Cultural developments in Iran] (Tehran: Entesharat-e Ravesh, 1999), 148.

25. *Zanan* 30 (1996); see also *Zanan* 9 (Bahman 1371 [1991]).

26. Post-Islamist women activists were especially encouraged by the collaborative approach of some secular feminists. For a discussion and attempts to build an

alliance of post-Islamist and secular feminists, see Nayereh Tohidi, *Feminism, Islamgarayi va Demokrasy* (Los Angeles: Ketabsara, 1996); also Nayereh Tohidi, "Islamic Feminism: Women Negotiating Modernity and Patriarchy in Iran," in *The Blackwell Companion to Contemporary Islamic Thought*, ed. Ibrahim Abu-Rabi (Oxford: Blackwell, 2006), 624–643.

27. Afsaneh Najababdi, "Feminism in an Islamic Republic: Years of Hardship, Years of Growth," in *Islam, Gender and Social Change*, ed. Yvonne Haddad and John Esposito (Oxford: Oxford University Press, 1998), 59–84.

28. Gerda Lerner, *The Creation of Feminist Consciousness* (Oxford: Oxford University Press, 1993), 138–166; Jane Bayes and Nayereh Tohidi, eds., *Globalization, Gender and Religion: The Politics of Women's Rights in Catholic and Muslim Contexts* (London: Palgrave Macmillan, 2001), chap. 2.

29. Attention to children is emphasized in such verses as "al-maal wa bonoun" (Kahf: 46), and the *ahadith* "Children are the *parvanehaye* [butterflies] of heaven" and "No sin is bigger than ignoring children" exemplify the centrality of care for children. See *Zanan* 38 (Aban 1376 [1997]): 2–5.

30. *Zanan* 23 (Farvardin–Ordibehesht 1374 [1995]): 46–57.

31. See, for instance, Mehranguiz Kar, "Mosharekat-e Siyassi-e Zanan: Vaqeiyyat ya Khial," *Zanan* 47 (1998): 12–13.

32. Clerics such as Ayatollah Bojnordi of Qom Seminary; see *Farzaneh* 8.

33. *Jomhuri-ye Eslami*, 12 Mehr 1376 (1997).

34. *Sobh Weekly* 32 (Aban 1375 [1995]); and *Sobh Weekly*, 28 Farvardin 1375 (1996).

35. For the list, see *Zanan* 28 (Farvardin 1375 [1996]): 3.

36. *Zanan* 38 (Aban 1376 [1997]): 38.

37. But women's share in the parliament, 6 percent, was still far short of the world average, 11.6 percent, though greater than the Arab countries' average, 4.3 percent; see *Zanan* 33 (1997): 76.

38. Cited in *Zanan* 34 (Ordibehesht 1376 [1997]): 4; *Zanan* 37 (Shahrivar–Mehr 1376 [1997]): 8; http://womeniniran.com, May 21, 2003.

39. For a good study of the Reformation, see Euan Cameron, *The European Reformation* (Oxford: Clarendon Press, 1991).

40. Mohammad Khatami, *Beem-e Mowj* (Tehran: Sima-ye Javan, 1993), 139.

41. Ibid., 198–205.

42. A. Soroush, "Religion and the Contemporary World" (lecture in Los Angeles, 1997), cited in *Kiyan* 36 (April–May 1997): 56.

43. Sadeq Zibakalam, *Maa Chegooneh Maa Shodim?* [How we became us?] (Tehran: Intisharat-e Rowzaneh, 1994).

44. See Hamidreza Jalaiipour, *Pas az Dovvom-e Khordad* (Tehran: Intisharat-e Kavir, 1999), 76–78.

45. See Akbar Ganji, *Tarik-khane-ye Ashbaah* (Tehran: Tarh-e Nou, 1999), 106–107; also A. Soroush, "Eideology va Din-e Donyavi," *Kiyan* 31 (Tir/Mordad 1375 [1996]): 2–11.

46. *Kiyan* 26 (1995): 9.

47. Mohsen Kadivar, *Baha-ye Azadi* [The price of freedom] (Tehran: Nashr-e Ney, 1999), 153–154.

48. Abdullah Nouri, *Shukaran-e Eslah* (Tehran: Tarh-e Nou, 1999), 256.

49. According to A. Soroush, interview by Roger Hardy, BBC World Service program on Islam and democracy.

50. Mohsen Kadivar, "Freedom of Thought and Religion in Islam" (paper presented at the International Congress on Human Rights and the Dialogue of Civilizations, Tehran, May 2001). See also his statement in *Hambastegi*, January 4, 2001, 3.

51. A. Soroush, "Horriyat va Rouhaniyat," *Kiyan* 24 (Farvardin–Ordibehesht 1374 [1995]): 2–11.

52. For instance, ibid.; Hashem Aghajari, "Islamic Protestantism," at http:// groups.yahoo.com/group/MewNews/message/8635; and Hashem Aghajari, *Hokumat-e Dini va Hokumat-e Demokratik* (Tehran: Moassesse-yeNashr va Tahghighat-e Zikr, 2002).

53. Nouri, *Shukaran-e Eslah*, 242.

54. Ibid., 243.

55. A. Soroush, "Khadamat va Hasanat-e Din," *Kiyan* 27 (Mehr–Aban 1374 [1995]): 12–13; A. Soroush, "Tahlil-e Mafhum-e Hokumat-e Dini," *Kiyan* 32 (Shahrivar– Mehr 1375 [1996]): 2–13.

56. Soroush, "Khatamat va Hasanat-e Din."

57. Mojtahed Shabastari, interview by the author, Berlin, October 7, 2003.

58. Mustafa Malekian, a teacher in the Qom Seminary, interview in *Rah-e Nou* 13 (Tir 1377 [1998]): 18–26.

59. See, for instance, Richard Plantinga, ed., *Christianity and Plurality* (Oxford: Blackwell, 1999); Richard Wentz, *The Culture of Religious Pluralism* (Boulder: Westview Press, 1998).

60. See *Kiyan* 5, no. 26 (August–September 1995): 46–49.

61. According to Masha'allah Shmasulwa'ezin, editor of *Kiyan*, interview by the author, Tehran, January 4, 2004.

62. Mustafa Tajzadeh, interview in *Payam-e Emrooz* 41 (Mehr 1379 [2000]): 42–43. See also Saiid Hajjarian, interview in *Waghaye-e Ettefaghieh*, 27 Tir 1383 (2004).

63. As discussed in Adam Przeworski, "The Role of Theory in Comparative Politics: A Symposium," *World Politics* 48, no. 1 (1996): 1049.

64. Saiid Hajjarian, interview in E. Baqi, *Baraye Tarikh* (Tehran: Nashr-e Ney, 2000), 45–46.

65. Nouri, *Shukaran-e Eslah*, 262.

66. Ibid., 226. See also Hamidreza Jalaiipour, interview in David Hirst, "Modernists Take on Iran's Mullas," December 4, 1998, at www.walfie.guardian.co.uk.

67. See Jalaiipour, *Pas az Dovvom-e Khordad*, 191; Akbar Ganji, in *Rah-e Nou* 20 (14 Shahrivar 1377 [1998]).

68. See, for instance, Youssefi Ashkevari, interview in *Shahrvand* 491 (June 20, 2000).

69. Hashem Aghajari, a leader of the Organization of the Mojahedin of the Islamic Revolution and an MP, in *Iran*, 5 Ordibehesht 1379 (2000).

70. See Hamidreza Jalaiipour, untitled article on Rooydad, 15 Mehr 1381 (2002), http://rooydadnews.blogspot.com/.

71. Such as Ayatollah Abdulqasim Mousavi Khoii, Ayatollah Kazem Shariatmadari, Ayatollah Muhammad Reza Golpaygani, Ayatollah Araki, and Ayatollah Montazari (who saw only a supervisory role for wilayat al-faqih). Also Ayatollah Shirazi, leader of Bahraini Shi'is, and Sheikh Muhamad Fadlullah (Lebanese Shi'i leader) did not support Khomeini's wilayat al-faqih (interviews by the author, Beirut, December 2005).

72. Sohrab Behdad, "A Disputed Utopia: Islamic Economics in Revolutionary Iran," *Comparative Studies in Society and History* 36, no. 4 (October 1994): 775–813.

73. This figure is cited by Mohsen Rezaii, the former commander of the Revolutionary Guards, in *Iran-e Farda* 44 (Tir 1377 [1998]): 16.

74. For the urban riots of the 1990s, see Asef Bayat, *Street Politics: Poor People's Movements in Iran* (New York: Columbia University Press, 1997), 106–108.

75. Mohammad Maleki, "The Students and the Cultural Revolution," *Andishe-ye Jamehe* 25/26.27 (Shahrivar/Mehr/Aban 1381 [2002]): 18.

76. Akbar Torbat, "Farar-e Maghzha az Iran beh Amrika" [Brain drain from Iran to the United States], *Aftab* 32 (Dey–Bahman 1382 [2003]): 70–79.

77. *Ettela'at*, 15 Farvardin 1377 (1998), cited in *Iran-e Farda* 42 (Ordibehesht 1377 [1998]): 34.

78. Report given by Hojjat al-Eslam Muhammad Ali Zamm, head of the Cultural and Artistic Department of Tehran Municipality, cited in *Bahaar*, 15 Tir 1379 (2000), 13.

79. See Kambiz Nowrouzi, "A Look at Judicial Figure," *Rah-e Nou* 1 (5 Ordibehesht 1377 [1998]): 15.

80. Editorial, *Kiyan* 12, no. 3 (Khordad 1372 [1993]): 2.

81. Kadivar, *Baha-ye Azadi*, 156.

82. See, for instance, Abdullah Nouri's defense of such concepts during his trial, in *Shukaran-e Eslah*, 265–268.

83. Homa Hoodfar, "Devices and Desires: Population Policy and Gender Roles in the Islamic Republic," *Middle East Report* 24, no. 190 (1994): 11–17.

84. Reported in Mohammadi, *Daramadi bar Raftar-Shenasi*, 102 n. 21.

85. Abdolali Rezaie, "Nime-ye Por-e Livan," in *Entikhab-e Nou* [New choice], ed. A. Rezaie and A. Abdi (Tehran: Tarh-e Nou, 1376 [1997]), 118.

86. Only half of Iranian youths considered a main goal to be to "make their parents happy," compared with 80 percent of the young in Egypt and 86 percent in Jordan. Mansour Mo'addel, "Religion, Gender, and Politics in Egypt, Jordan, and Iran: Findings of Comparative National Surveys" (unpublished report, 2002), 9.

87. Sohrab Behdad and Farhad Nomani, "Workers, Peasants, and Peddlers: A Study of Labor Stratification in the Post-revolutionary Iran," *International Journal of Middle East Studies* 34, no. 4 (November 2002): 667–690.

88. Alireza Rejaii, "Poverty and Political Developments in Iran," in *Poverty in Iran*, ed. F. Raiis-dana, Z. Shadi-tala, and P. Piran (Tehran: School of Behzisti va Tavanbakhshi, 1379 [2000]).

89. According to Minister of Science and Technology Mustafa Moin, in *Nourooz*, 11 Tir 1380 (2001), 10.

90. For a theoretical discussion regarding "social movement animation," see my "Islamism and Social Movement Theory," *Third World Quarterly* 26, no. 6 (July 2005): 891–908.

91. Reported in the daily *Iran*, April 27, 2002. On women's NGOs, see Hamidreza Jalaiipour, *Jame'e Shinasi-ye Jonbeshha-ye Ejtimaii* (Tehran: Tarh-e Nou, 2003), table 4. Also see the Web site of Mohammad Ali Abtahi, 24 Esfand 1382 (2003), www.webneveshteha.com/.

92. Reported in *Aftab-e Yazd*, December 14, 2000, 5.

93. *Hayat-e Nou*, August 29, 2000.

94. *Hambastegi*, June 23, 2001, 5.

95. Issa Saharkhiz, lecture, Amsterdam, June 24, 2004.

96. Reported in *Kiyan*, November–January 1999, 57.

97. Reported in *Al-Hayat*, February 19 and March 2, 1999.

98. Kian Tajbakhsh, "Political Decentralization and the Creation of Local Government in Iran," *Social Research* 67, no. 2 (September 2000): 377–404.

99. For a discussion of the influence of Iran in the Middle East, see Asef Bayat and Bahman Baktiari, "Revolutionary Iran and Egypt: Exporting Inspirations and Anxieties," in *Iran and the Surrounding World*, ed. Nikki Keddie and Rudi Matthee (Seattle: University of Washington Press, 2002), 305–326.

100. Cited in *Khordad*, 7 Aban 1378 (1999).

101. Reported in *Kiyan* 30 (June 1996): 43.

102. Reported in *Azad*, 11 Mehr 1378 (1999).

103. Cited in *Hayat-e Nou*, September 30, 2000, 3.

104. Cited in *Khordad*, 5 Mehr 1378 (1999).

105. Cited in *Khordad*, 27 Shahrivar 1378 (1999).

106. Cited in *Hambastegui*, March 12, 2001, 2.

107. In *Litharat*, cited in *Iran-e Farda* 41 (Farvardin 1377 [1998]): 37.

108. According to Intelligence Minister Ali Yunesi, in *Ettelaat*, 6 Shahrivar 1378 (1999).

109. These discussions draw on Asef Bayat, "Green Wave for Life and Liberty," *Open Democracy*, July 7, 2009, at www.opendemocracy.net/article/iran-a-green-wave-for-life-and-liberty.

110. Ibid.

111. For a detailed analysis of the Green Movement, see Asef Bayat, *Life as Politics: How Ordinary People Change the Middle East*, 2nd ed. (Stanford: Stanford University Press, 2013), chapter 14, "The Green Revolt."

3

Post-Islamism à la Turca

Ihsan Dagi

> Before anything else, I'm a Muslim. As a Muslim, I try
> to comply with the requirements of my religion. I have a
> responsibility to God, who created me, and I try to fulfill
> that responsibility. But I try now very much to keep this
> away from my political life, to keep it private. A politi-
> cal party cannot have a religion. Only individuals can.
> Otherwise, you'd be exploiting religion, and religion is so
> supreme that it cannot be exploited or taken advantage of.
> RECEP TAYYIP ERDOGAN, leader of the Adalet ve Kalkınma
> Partisi and the prime minster of Turkey

Islamism is not dead; some within it are transforming in a self-critical and creative manner to face an ideological and political impasse. Post-Islamism, as a new set of language and the grounds of the justification to continue engaging in politics, is the response. When Islamists turn to *democracy* as an effective political strategy to deal with their authoritarian opponents by appealing to the masses through legitimate means and to *pluralism* as the grounds to reach out and work with diverse social segments without targeting their differences, thereby they arrive at post-Islamism. As such post-Islamism is neither an "antithesis" to Islamism nor "Islamism under disguise" but, rather, Islamism fused with democracy and pluralism.[1] It represents Islamism's potency to develop a new political language and strategy and generate new actors.

The responsiveness that marks the emergence of post-Islamism out of Islamist movements demonstrates the "learning capacity" of the Islamists and their ability to transform themselves to answer the challenges that they have faced. Building on the accomplishments of the Islamists but determined to overcome their theoretical and political impasses, the post-Islamists have gone through a process of "rethinking" the old Islamist vocabulary and utopia.[2]

Conceiving Islam as a comprehensive social, political, and economic order to be constructed through the apparatus of the state made Islamism into a modern political project. The distance between modern times and the original Islam was bridged with a textual reading of the Quran. Envisaging the revival of a "total" Islamic community was not nostalgia for the past but a deliberated political choice to build a "new" society via the state power under a monopolized understanding of Islamic interpretations. As such Islamism was very close to the totalitarian ideologies and political strategies of the twentieth century.

Claiming to be loyal to the "original" message of the Quran, the Islamists sought to resurrect an Islamic society by fighting against the un-Islamic rulers at home and the Western powers abroad that corrupted these rulers and poisoned Muslims' minds. For the Islamists reinstalling the reign of Islam was a matter of survival that necessitated and prioritized a political struggle using any available means.

Over the years Muslims' relations to politics have changed under the impact of globalization, market forces, and the spread of new media and expansion of educated elites as well as the apparent failure of the Islamist political agenda. It has become increasingly difficult to depict a "single" mode of the relationship between Muslims and politics. The regime changes in the Arab world starting with Tunisia and followed up by Egypt, and the role performed by the Islamists in these countries, have now added new urgency to developing fresh approaches to the Muslim view on politics.

One element of the new Muslim view on politics can be described as "post-Islamism," as an *attitude* and as a *political strategy*. It is a new attitude that takes Islam as a source of reference yet recognizes a plurality of interpretations, strategies, and models generating from Islam. Such a post-Islamist attitude therefore does not envisage the monopoly of a single understanding of Islam and its imposition by the coercive apparatus of the state, leaving wide space for freedom and choice.[3]

Post-Islamism also includes a political strategy that utilizes democracy within a new language that enables building coalitions with different political and social groups. This new strategy takes the society as it is, with its diverse identities, lifestyles, and ideologies, thereby accepting its inherent plurality, and rejects the old Islamist project to transform it in a revolutionary manner. Post-Islamism, in this way, instead of proposing the idea of constructing a "new society" that ends up with a totalitarian political model, points to a "new thinking" that is inclusive, plural, and participatory in the social realm. It does not, though, abandon altogether preaching the virtues of a moral society based on Islam.

The critical question is whether the Post-Islamists in government would refrain from using coercive state power to materialize such a society. Post-Islamism is a movement that is not preoccupied with the state, capturing it and using it as a transformative agency. Instead it reflects the belief that what is solid and durable is entrenched in existing social and economic institutions. As such post-Islamism represents the supremacy of the social over the political. Instead of looking to the state as the agent of change, post-Islamism turns to society and its capabilities to settle political disputes.

Post-Islamism is not only about changing strategies for political struggle. It is deeper and more fundamental: abandoning the idea and ideal that an Islamic state is both *theoretically and politically* possible. This has a very significant implication for Muslims' relations to politics. If the idea of an Islamic state is a fallacy, then Muslims face a question of defining and deciding about a proper political model. Out of this search emerges *post-Islamism as an attempt to conceptualize a polity for Muslims in a world in which there is no preset divine order called the Islamic state.* Post-Islamists thus have come to embrace participation, inclusion, tolerance, emancipation, and human rights and liberties blended with Islamic morality, brotherhood, and solidarity in order to compensate for the loss of the divine in shaping the model of governance.

Why, then, if not to build an "Islamic state and society," do post-Islamists engage in politics? In answering this question the Turkish post-Islamists have replaced *Hak* (God) with *halk* (people). They engage in politics not in the name of Islam any longer but in the name of the people, whom they have to count on to come to power in order to serve them in return. Such a raison d'être requires adopting democracy and pluralism as the political and social constituting principles of the polity. In this vein the Turkish post-Islamists have justified their engagement in politics with the idea of emancipating the people through democratization and providing them with services. A Turkish motto, "Halka hizmet hakka hizmettir" [Service to people is equal to service to God], has given the ex-Islamists a reason for their continued engagement in politics.

Gathered around the Adalet ve Kalkinma Partisi (AKP, Justice and Development Party), the post-Islamists of Turkey have demonstrated the effectiveness of this new thinking in a competitive political environment. The AKP stands out among the most important successes of the post-Islamist movement. Having won three consecutive elections, it has been in power since 2002, a performance that would have been impossible for an Islamist party. It proved that post-Islamists acting within the rules of democracy could come to power through the ballot box and that democracy would accommodate a transformed Islamist movement. The Turkish case has thus settled the question of whether democracy will be able to accommodate the post-Islamists and whether the post-Islamists could accept the norms of democracy and work within its premises.

Turkish post-Islamism has developed out of a "particular context" in which Islamists were treated as "anomalies" by secularist state institutions and their social-economic allies. Though it may sound strange, Turkish post-Islamism is also about changing attitudes toward secularism as a pillar of the democratic state. Though it may be argued that post-Islamism cannot be "secular," within the particularities of Turkish politics, the post-Islamists have had to act within a strict secular constitutional order and have come to settle on an Anglo-Saxon version of secularism that separates the state from religious norms but in return grants religion full liberty in the social realm.[4] Engaging in a long battle with the radical secularists led the post-Islamists to "rethink" secularism along with democracy, pluralism, and human rights. Among others, it is the secularist constitutional order and institutional powers such as the judiciary and the military that have compelled the Islamists to rethink their political attitudes, strategies, and objectives.

Turkish post-Islamism therefore owes its emergence to the political impasse brought about by secularist suppression employing constitutional and social leverage against the Islamists and the Islamists' resourcefulness in responding to the crisis encountered. Thus, both a challenging social/political environment and a resourceful Islamist movement had existed in Turkey, which gave way to post-Islamism. Asef Bayat asserts that "Turkey has barely experienced typical Islamist politics: instead, its major religious parties (... particularly the Justice and Development Party) have espoused a largely post-Islamist disposition." A central attribute of this "disposition" is cited as advocating a "pious society in a secular democratic state."[5]

However untypical, there were Islamist intellectual and political currents in Turkey before the rise of the AKP as a post-Islamist experiment. The idea that Islam is not only a religion but also an ideology that regulates social, political, cultural, and economic domains is not unknown in

Turkey. Turkish Islamists too conceive of Islam as a comprehensive ideology and a utopia that envisages a "new society" to be constructed through the apparatus of the state. This would be possible only if what is "Islamic" is kept away from the poisonous impact of "Western modernity" and its concepts and values, such as democracy, secularism, nationalism, progress, and liberties, all of which are alien to Islam and the Islamic polity.[6]

Such views gained ground particularly in the 1980s when Islamism in the Middle East was in its heyday, while at the same time secular intellectual and political movements were severely suppressed in Turkey following the 1980 military coup. Islamists, then overconfident, believed in an "Islamic alternative" and the possibility of forming an Islamic state and society.[7]

Due to the reasons explained in this chapter, Islamists lost their self-confidence and hope for the possibility of the Islamization of the state and society in the late 1990s. Mainstream Islamists by then abandoned the idea of constructing an alternative social and political order. Displaying features of a post-Islamist turn, they searched for alternatives not in Islam but in modern political institutions, which are expected to secure within their democratic and pluralistic principles a place for Islamists. That is to say, the post-Islamists have abandoned the early 1980s sharp views of Islam, which was conceived of as an ideology capable of forming a new society and building a new state, and have made a shift not only in their views but also in their political strategy to prioritize the deepening of democracy, political pluralism, and even secularism to ensure their existence vis-à-vis an authoritarian Kemalist state. Mehmet Metiner, an ex-Islamist and now a member of parliament from the post-Islamist AKP, reflects the change in his simple but sharp statement: "Islam is not an ideology, and the Quran is not a constitution."[8] The ex-Islamists, while keeping their Islamic identity, started to ground their demands not in Islam but on the universality of political modernity, that is, human rights, democracy, the rule of law, and respect for differences.

Thus the intellectual and political fantasies of the 1980s to Islamize the state and society have largely come to an end, as abstract theories about an Islamic society, state, and economy had no relevance to the problems the Islamists encountered in the late 1990s. This is so because a continued usage of Islamist language with references to the model of governance and society could only have justified and intensified the repressive policies on all sorts of Islamic groups, as their main opponents were constantly pointing to the danger of the "Islamization" of the state and society. So the search for security and survival in the face of an oppressive state resulted in a process of ideological transformation of the Islamists starting from the late 1990s, giving way to a new thinking that could be described as "post-Islamism."

Therefore analyzing the dynamics, process, and outcomes of Turkish Islamists' transformation would shed light on the roots and content of "post-Islamism, a la Turca." The Turkish case proves that the transformation of Islamism into post-Islamism brings about empowerment for Islam's social and political representatives. Post-Islamism therefore does not indicate the failure of political Islam but, rather, shows the ability of the Islamists' to transform themselves in response to challenges and crises.[9]

This chapter explains the emergence of "post-Islamist politics" out of the transformation of Turkish Islamism by exploring its main political agent, the ruling Adalet ve Kalkinma Partisi (AKP). It examines the processes and dynamics that have led the Islamists in Turkey to discover democracy, secularism, pluralism, globalization, and Europeanization and the way in which this "discovery" has empowered Islamic activities in the social realm and ex-Islamist politicians. The chapter will start with an explanation of the rise of Islamist political movement and then explore the crises encountered in the late 1990s. After an assessment of the need and push for transformation, the chapter will focus on the AKP as a post-Islamist response.

Islamism in a Secularist Political Environment

The establishment of an outright Islamist political party is constitutionally not possible in Turkey. The Turkish constitution and the Law on Political Parties have never allowed political parties with a religious disposition, either ideologically or programmatically. This ban is based on the principle of secularism, which has been a constitutional principle since 1937, although a contested one. For those who put this principle into the constitution and have implemented it for decades, secularism means more than a separation of religion from the state and the freedom of conscience; it is a "way of life."[10] Such a notion of secularism denies Islam a place not only in the political but also in the social space, as it is kept solely in an individual's conscience and is thus socially invisible. While secularism is employed to deny the Islamists a share in power, the Islamists have contested the model of secularism as implemented by the Turkish state.

As a matter of fact, the secularism of the republic has been problematical. If secularism presumes the separation of the state and religion, it does not hold in a Turkey where religion is not separated from the state but, rather, taken under its control. The Directorate General of Religious Affairs (the Diyanet) is part of the state, with thousands of staff and hundreds of local branches, and enjoys a monopoly on religious services. Religious groups, circles, and dervish orders do not officially exist, let alone enjoy autonomy from the state. The government interferes in religion and religious activities while it expects religion to be subservient to the state.

If secularism requires the neutrality of the state toward all religions, sects, and creeds, the Turkish practice again presents an awkward model, in which the state's directorate for religious affairs provides services to Muslims only. It does not serve or represent the non-Islamic religions that are observed by some Turkish citizens. Moreover the directorate teaches, preaches, and practices not just Islam but a particular form of Islam—the Sunni-Hanefi version—which leaves the Alevis, a sect within Islam, without recognition or services. Finally, teaching a compulsory course on religion, which is Islam with a Hanefi interpretation, is a constitutional principle of this strange model of secularism.

However "unusual" it may be, secularism in the formative years of the republic served to break with a past that had been shaped by Islam and its influence over society. Through secularizing policies the new elite tried to empty the social realm of its Islamic content and insert their own authority and codes of legitimacy. Thus the process and eventual success of secularism became part and parcel of the political struggle to form a hegemony over the Islamic social space.[11] The Islamists in return rejected the Kemalist notion of secularism as being antireligion and designed to eliminate Islam in the public and political spheres.[12] These debates have turned modern Turkish history into a history of secularist/Islamist struggle.

Even the liberal opposition was silenced under the pretext of defending secularism. The first such case happened in 1925, when the first liberal party of the new republic, the Progressive Republican Party, was closed based on an article in its program that said that the "party is respectful to religious beliefs." The fact that this was viewed as sufficient to label the party "reactionary" indicates how secularism narrows down the political space, denying existence to any kind of Islamist political organization even at a time when secularism was not yet a defining characteristic of the state.

During multiparty politics in the 1950s, the religious groups that survived the single-party years sided with the Democrat Party, a party that seemed to have abandoned the radical and exclusionary secularism of the early republican period. The religious periphery found in the Democrat Party a political outlet where it could be represented. Relieved from radical secularist pressure, religious groups went through a process of revival in the 1950s and 1960s under center-right governments. However, in the process of restructuring Turkish politics following the 1960 military intervention, Islam became increasingly popular, and its political appeal grew. Its first outright political expression emerged with the establishment of the Milli Nizam Partisi (the National Order Party) under the leadership of Necmettin Erbakan. Over the years the names of the parties changed, but the movement has always been known as "Milli Gorus" (the "National View").[13]

In the formation process of the party Erbakan had the blessing of Zahid Kotku, an influential Nakshibendi sheikh. In its founding declaration Islamic references were explicitly made, such as "God's path," the Islamic notion of "commanding right, forbidding wrong" (*emr bi'l-maruf ve'n-nehy ani'l-munker*), and "being loyal to God." The party set out its objective in its program as establishing a "new and superior civilization," a civilization inspired by Islam. It also opposed the interest in banking and membership in the European Economic Community. The emblem of the party was a hand showing its index finger—Shahadah finger—which is a symbolic description of the testimony to be a Muslim.

Such a degree of Islamic symbolism was too much to tolerate. Following the March 12, 1971, military memorandum, when politics was under the surveillance of the military, the Constitutional Court closed down the Milli Nizam Partisi on the grounds that the party exploited religion for political purposes and thus engaged in antisecularist activities.

From this time onward, Islamist political parties have disguised their ideological stand behind symbolic language and conduct in order to avoid persecution and closure. Thus they have had to operate in a restricted political environment, hiding their true identity and twisting their discourse, which has made it difficult to trace Islamist parties, as it was constitutionally impossible to be one. Since they could not confess to being Islamist and explain their inspiration from the Quran for their program and vision, they had to engage in acts of symbolism. Their "ideology," for instance, was referred to as the "National View," and the social and political order to be established was described as the "just order." In fact the

Islamists were forced to make use of *takiyye*, hiding one's true belief when in danger, a practice that is allowed under Islamic jurisprudence.

In 1972 the "National View" movement established its second political party, the Milli Selamet Partisi (MSP, the National Salvation Party). Neither the leadership nor the ideology changed, just the name. The new party continued to use the symbolism of the first, especially in its emblem, which was an old key on the tooth of which a hidden word, *Allah*, was written in Arabic in the Qufi style. Because of the warnings of the public prosecutor, the party removed the word, but its emblem, the key, for some the "key to heaven," remained. The most popular slogan of the party in this period was a verse from the Quran: "Hak geldi, batıl yok oldu" [Truth has (now) arrived, and Falsehood perished] (Isra, 81).

The "National View" claimed to embody the "essence" of the nation and its "values." The nation was presumed to have a civilization of its own, derived from its history and culture, which were shaped by Islam. The movement was thus there to resurrect this authentic civilization. Ambiguous references to history and criticism directed against "cosmopolitanism" as opposed to the "national" constituted what the "National View" was all about.[14] However ambiguous it may be, under the disguise of a historical and cultural discourse, the "National View" referred to Islam as a political idea.

The MSP differentiated itself from other political parties with its critical stand toward the West and the history of Turkish Westernization. For the party Turkey, historically, culturally, and geographically, did not belong to the West; instead, it shared its past, values, and institutions with the Islamic world. A lack of spiritual values and social decadence were among the features of Western civilization that were to poison Islamic civilization.[15]

Besides the West there was another question: Westernization, presuming the possibility of a civilizational shift that was, for the Islamists, a rejection of Islam and the uniqueness of Islamic civilization. Westernization was understood as a denial of traditional Islamic values, attitudes, and institutions. Moreover, Westernization has also meant a secularization that has swept Islam out of social and political visibility. The party also used strong anticapitalist language, with reference to the traditional notion of social justice. The anti-Western and anticapitalist ideological stand of the MSP was appealing especially for the "men of the bazaar" in provincial towns who were responding to their growing weakness in the face of the capitalist big businesses spreading into Anatolia. Though it engaged in democratic processes by taking part in elections, the movement down-graded democracy to a "Western invention."

The Rise and Fall of Islamism

Receiving 12 percent and 9 percent of the total votes in the 1973 and 1977 elections, respectively, the MSP joined in all the coalition governments between 1973 and 1980 and became a "key" political actor in Turkish politics.[16] When the military took over the government with yet another coup in September 1980, Erbakan and other party officials were arrested and put on trial for attempting to change the constitutional order by force. Erbakan remained under detention for around a year before he was released.

When the military regime allowed the establishment of political parties in 1983, the "National View" formed its third political party, the Refah Partisi (RP, Welfare Party). The new party's worldview had not changed, nor had the leadership. Although Erbakan was banned from politics by the generals in power with a provisional article of the new constitution, he remained the behind-the-scenes leader of the RP. The old ideological posture of the party remained intact. It continued to claim itself as the only hak (truth and virtues) party and that all the others were batil (corrupt) parties.

Its opposition to the West and Westernization visibly increased. The identities of the RP and of the other political parties, institutions, or individuals in Turkey were to be determined by their stand on the West, described either as advocating the "National View" or as an imitation of the West. As Turkey was debating EU membership Erbakan proclaimed that once they came to power they would put an end to the process of Westernization and stop the EU integration process, including the customs union.[17]

In the local elections of March 1984 the party received 4.8 percent of the total votes. Under the leadership of Erbakan, following the lifting of the ban on former political leaders imposed by the military regime in 1987, the party increased its share of the total vote to 7 percent in the general election in November 1987, yet this put it below the 10 percent country-wide election threshold, and it was therefore not represented in the parliament. To pass the national threshold the RP made an electoral alliance with two other right-wing nationalist political parties before the 1991 general elections. The result was a success, with nearly 17 percent of the total votes and sixty-five seats in the parliament, where the biggest party received only 28 percent of the vote.

This election was the beginning of change for the RP. After struggling to pass the 10 percent national threshold the party realized that it needed to reach out to new voters with no Islamic orientation. For the first time in its election campaign the party stressed social problems and not religious themes, using modern propaganda methods. While maintaining its ideological coherence and loyal members, it aimed at reaching out to the society beyond its core supporters. It particularly tried to mobilize the urban poor by capitalizing on the people who suffered from the liberalization policies of the 1980s. The party's call for production, investment, employment, and redistribution, in addition to its Islamic references, touched upon the sensitivities of the masses, particularly in urban areas. The RP turned out to be capable of mobilizing popular support with messages that combined the language of the sacred with that of the "social" (poverty).[18] The changing political vocabulary was accompanied by an inclusionary political strategy, as reflected in the new and moderate personalities joining the party. It should be noted that this "new approach" to politics was mainly designed and carried out in Istanbul, the biggest city in Turkey, where Recep Tayyip Erdogan was the chairman of the party branch.

While trying to transform itself from an ideological party into a mass political movement the RP was careful not to lose its traditional Islamic character and discourse altogether. It effectively used its slogan "Just order" to appeal to the poor of the urban periphery and the middle classes that were disturbed by the corruption of the "centrist" parties. "Just order" had, indeed, a double reference, to a "divine" order but also to a just distribution of wealth. As such it was a perfectly designed political discourse for cutting across various social and economic segments.

This new strategy continued right up to the March 1994 local elections, in which the RP proved its growing political power by getting 19 percent of the total votes and winning the mayoral elections in twenty-eight cities including Ankara and Istanbul, a shocking result for the centrist and secularist political parties. The results showed that the RP's moderate, inclusive, nonideological political strategy paid off. The personalities of the mayors elected in these two biggest cities were indicative of the change the party was going through. In Istanbul it was Tayyip Erdogan, who was the architect of the RP's new strategy of reaching out to all segments of society in big cities with a language of services, not Islamism. In Ankara the RP's elected mayor was Melih Gokcek, who was a former politician from the center-right Motherland Party.

The growth of the RP continued. In the general elections in 1995 it came first, with 21 percent of total votes. After a short-lived coalition government of center-right political parties, Erbakan, still the leader of the RP, formed a coalition government with the center-right Dogru Yol Partisi (True Path Party). For the first time in republican history an Islamist political party came to power in a coalition government holding the prime ministerial position.[19]

Before long the Kemalist/secularist circles led by the military launched a campaign against the RP government, justified by their concerns about the future of secularism. Within the General Staff of the Armed Forces a special unit, the "West Working Group," was formed to investigate Islamist activities in every part of society and the state. Soon the National Security Council (NSC), meeting on February 28, 1997, took a number of decisions to "reinforce the secular character of the Turkish state" and to eliminate the Islamist threat. The council, dominated by the military, advised the RP-led government to take measures to protect secularism against the pressures of the Islamists who were in fact sitting in the government. It was a military ultimatum later known as a postmodern coup. The council asked the government to maintain the official dress code in government offices and universities, to introduce compulsory eight-year elementary school education, to practically close down the middle school sections of the country-wide Imam-Hatip schools (prayer leaders and preachers), to impose strict control over Quranic courses and student dormitories run by religious groups and foundations, to reduce the number of Imam-Hatip schools, to establish a section within the prime minister's office to investigate reactionary/Islamic activities in the bureaucracy, and to pass a law enabling civil servants to be fired if they were found to be engaged in Islamist activities.[20] These were all designed to eliminate not only the political but also the social, economic, and cultural influence of Islamist circles throughout the country. In a "National Policy Paper" prepared by the National Security Council, the Islamist challenge was cited as the source of a threat more dangerous and immediate than secessionist Kurdish nationalism.[21]

In the ensuing clampdown some private companies described as representing "Islamic capital" were publicly identified, and investigations were conducted on their networks, source of capital, and activities. Quranic courses run by various religious foundations were closed down; and the remaining courses were strictly regulated, and the participation of students in these courses was made possible only after a certain age.[22]

The imprisonment of Tayyip Erdogan, then the popular mayor of Istanbul, was another case by which pressure on the political representatives of Islamism was demonstrated. Erdogan was sentenced to ten mounts for inciting hatred among people on religious grounds in a speech he made in Siirt in 1998.

As part of the campaign against the Islamists the public prosecutor lodged a file in the Constitutional Court in May 1997 for the closure of the ruling RP. Eventually the Erbakan-led government was forced by military-led secularist opposition to resign in July 1997, and not long after the Constitutional Court dissolved the RP on the grounds that it had become a center of antisecularist activities. This was the third party of the "National View" led by Erbakan to be closed down; Erbakan himself was banned from politics for five years.

Torn between Islamism and Post-Islamism

The episode of the rise and fall of the RP demonstrates that religious, social, and economic networks were hit the hardest when Islamism as a political force was at its peak. This was a dramatic learning experience for the Islamists, who realized the fragility of the political power they seemed to be enjoying. In the early 1990s, at the initial stage of their transformation, the Islamists had embraced a new political language based on social themes that went beyond religious symbols in order to reach out to wider social groups with no Islamist leanings. By the end of the 1990s, with the ex-Islamists having succeeded in obtaining the support of diverse social groups, the political Islam represented by the RP turned into a mass political movement. Their success turned out to be their curse, because the rising power of Islamism alarmed the Kemalist/secularist establishment. The response was a series of oppressive measures imposed by the military, judiciary, and media and supported by the secularist middle classes and business elite. As a result the Islamists became cautious and even defensive in order to preserve the power that they had generated through their new strategy. They were victimized when they reached the peak of their power, a truly traumatic experience that prompted a process of transition from Islamism to post-Islamism.

In this transition the Fazilet Partisi (FP, Virtue Party), which replaced the RP, was the first post-Islamist experiment in Turkey. The piecemeal changes of Islamism gave way to wholesale transformation. The new party was indeed a new one, except its leadership, nominally headed by

Recai Kutan but effectively ruled by Erbakan, who was banned from politics after the close of the RP. The FP was different from its predecessor in many respects, including its approach to the questions of secularism, democracy, and the West. It was no longer antagonistic to the West and adopted a moderate, pragmatic, and cooperative position unheard of in any Islamist movement. Moreover, the party adopted "modern" political values such as democracy, human rights, pluralism, and the rule of law as part of its new political lexicon.[23]

The new party even claimed that it was abandoning its fundamental concepts such as "Just order" and the "National View" on the grounds that these were "misunderstood, misrepresented and misinterpreted" by some people.[24] Instead the party seemed to be more interested in democratization and the EU accession. Its chairman declared: "Political power should not be attained by non-democratic means," the "National Security Council [the military-dominated security council that included some members of government and the top military commanders] should be rearranged according to the principles of a western model democracy," and "secularism should not be a means to limit freedom of religion and belief." The party was also in favor of a free market economy and asked for speedy and comprehensive privatization.[25] The FP changed its stand on the EU too and advocated Turkey's integration into it, in contrast to its former views of the EU as a Christian club. The party leaders pushed the government and other political parties to comply with the Copenhagen political criteria and bring Turkey into the accession process.[26]

The fast break with the tradition of the Islamist "National View," which used to be skeptical of secularism, democracy, and the West, however, gave rise to justified questions about the sincerity of the FP leaders. Neither the "cause" (da'wa) nor the language of the movement had ever involved democracy, human rights, pluralism, or the rule of law. The old Islamists were distant from liberal democracy, had fundamental questions about the origins of democracy, and had claimed that it was the offspring of Western civilization, values, and institutions that were alien to Turkey and Islamic civilization.

However, the public positioning in favor of democracy, human rights, and the rule of law seemed to have gradually infected the leaders and the grassroots, which resulted in questioning about the leadership, ideology, and direction of the party. The process initiated by external pressures penetrated into the movement and forced its evolution into a post-Islamist position. This became evident in the May party congress of 2000, where

Kutan, the chairman of the party under Erbakan's tutelage, was challenged by post-Islamist Abdullah Gul, a moderate MP close to the former mayor of Istanbul, Tayyip Erdogan, for the leadership. This was an unprecedented event in the history of the movement, which had been a close-knit community in which obedience to the leader (enhanced by a reference to the Islamic concept of *biat*) was regarded as a central political virtue. It may be due to the challenge put up against this tradition that Gul referred to the congress as "the day the movement met politics for the first time in its history."[27] The post-Islamists were trying to emancipate themselves from the chains of the leadership, tradition, and old discourse and strategies.

Though the FP looked more post-Islamist in its discourse and program, the old guard at the top of the party administration did not want to hand the party over to the new post-Islamist cadets. Political figures close to Erbakan accused the opposition, the post-Islamists, of plotting to split the party by inserting functionalism (*nifak*).[28] It was obvious that Gul stood for the party leadership against the wishes of the leader of the movement, Erbakan, who called on the delegates not to break with tradition.[29] The contest was close, and Gul received support from almost half of the delegates despite Erbakan's direct and open lobbying against him. Based on the support Gul received one could infer that the discourse of change and democracy recently adopted by the leadership was taken seriously by the grassroots of the party as well.

Gul described the congress as the first occasion when the movement engaged in self-criticism before the public. He said, "By this congress the party got out of the aquarium and started to swim in the open sea."[30] This meant that the young and ambitious generation, the post-Islamist reformers, wanted to bring politics back to the movement and expand the limits imposed on them by tradition.

The fourth political party of the Islamist "National View" movement, the FP, was closed down by the Constitutional Court in June 2001 on the grounds that the party had been the center of antisecular Islamist activities like the preceding RP. After the decision the movement split in two. While the traditionalists established the Saadet Partisi (SP, Felicity Party), the post-Islamist reformers formed the Adalet ve Kalkinma Partisi (Justice and Development Party), with the participation of some influential figures from the center right under the leadership of Tayyip Erdogan.

While the SP rolled back to its origin by reembracing the old "National View," the AKP, abandoning Islamism altogether in its political vocabulary, has opened up as a mass political movement with a conservative

center-right outlook. In three general elections since the parties' formation, the Islamist old guard, the SP, received 2 percent, 4 percent, and 2
percent of the votes, respectively, whereas the AKP, with its post-Islamist
features, claimed 34 percent, 47 percent, and 50 percent. The transformation from Islamism to post-Islamism not only secured the survival of
ex-Islamist political cadets but has brought them into power.

Explaining What Was Changed and Why

The transformation of the Islamists has often been explained by references to the oppression they were subjected to during the February 28
process in the late 1990s. Although change had started earlier in order
to broaden the electoral base of the Islamists in the early 1990s, with the
February 28 process the Islamists became aware of the "limits of Islamist
politics" as they faced the power and determination of the secularist forces
in the state apparatus, civil society, and media.

It is not only the February 28 process that taught such a great lesson to
the Islamist circles that they started to "behave themselves." The transformation of the Islamists also owes a great deal to the economic and social
opening to the world during the 1980s and 1990s, which resulted in the
emergence of an Islamic middle class with entrepreneurs and intellectuals who demanded their share of power and benefits from the system and
who did not want to challenge but, rather, accommodate the Kemalist/
secularist establishment.[31]

Broader Islamic elements such as religious orders, groups, and rising
businessmen as well as intellectuals began rethinking the prudence and
wisdom of Islamism and questioning both the feasibility of Islam as a
political project and the conformity of the idea of an Islamic state to Islam
itself. One influential Islamist intellectual, Ali Bulac, who had been jubilant about the possibility of an Islamic state, now declared that "the project
of an Islamic state has collapsed."[32] Religious groups took note that the
social and economic networks of Islam had been damaged most when
"Islamism" was at its peak (1995–1999). Consequently Islamic institutions,
orders, and groups, including the religious business class that had started
to flourish, withdrew their support from the Islamist political movement.
They did not want to risk losing all their accumulated power and wealth by
contributing to the provoking success of the Islamists. Instead of "political
representation" by the Islamists, strong religious circles in all walks of life
sought a conservative-centrist political representation that was expected to

secure the survival of the social and economic networks of Islam. It was such thinking that paved the way for the transformation of Islamists and the emergence of the AKP from its ruins as a post-Islamist formation.

Democracy had turned into a matter of survival. The problem was that Islamists had never taken democracy seriously until the February 28 decisions of the NSC, through which they were ousted from power. After that they understood that despite their popular support they were and would always be seen as an "illegitimate" political force, an anomaly in Turkish politics in the Kemalist/secularist establishment.

It was not only the pressure of sympathetic circles but also the pressure of the military and judiciary, coupled with the secularist media, that compelled the Islamists to search for legitimacy and the virtue of "people power."[33] The popularity of Islamist politics displayed through elections was considered a valuable "asset" in their quest for "protection" and "recognition" from the secularist forces. As a result a call for democracy has become the main political discourse of the Islamists in political and intellectual debates, pushing them gradually to a post-Islamist position.

The new language of democracy and human rights was meant to build a protective shield and help the party acquire legitimacy. Democracy was to display the "popular legitimacy" of the Islamists, which in turn was expected to build security vis-à-vis the secularist forces of the establishment. Moreover, speaking the language of the "modern," that is, democracy and human rights, provided the Islamists with "discursive legitimacy" and supremacy over their opponents, who could not categorically reject these calls. Thus, the Islamists' love for democracy, at least at the start, was based on pragmatic calculations that it would contribute to their protection in the face of Kemalist/secularist assaults. But in the end the Islamists-turned-post-Islamists have moved from denying or devaluing democracy to investing in its rules, processes, and outcomes in search of protection and legitimization.

The Islamists went through similar experiences concerning their defense of human rights and the rule of law as they saw their political parties closed down, leaders banned from political activities, and associations and foundations intimidated. As a result they, in their post-Islamist stage, embraced the language of civil and political rights that was to provide effective leverage and protection against the pressures of the secularist state.

The Islamists have also dropped their historic opposition to the West in general and EU membership in particular. This was a clear break from their very tradition, as represented by Erbakan and the "National View," which was based on an open "crusade" against the West, a deep suspicion about modern political values, and an objection to the Turkish history of Westernization. A symbolic sign of change in this direction was Erbakan's decision to take the case of the party closure before the European Court of Human Rights in 1998, which demonstrates that under political and legal pressure exerted by Kemalist/secularist forces, Turkey's Islamists sought protection from Western institutions like the European Court of Human Rights.[34] "Rethinking" the West at this juncture was another moment that transformed the Islamists, for whom it was previously unthinkable to look for allies and protectors in the West. One of the emerging features of Turkish post-Islamism has been the abandonment of historical animosity toward the West.

They needed new allies outside Islamist circles at home and abroad. Supporting EU membership was an attempt to forge new alliances. Besides, the Islamists by then had realized that European demands for democratization and human rights overlapped with their search for protection against the Kemalist/secularist state apparatus, the military, and the judiciary. The expectation was that the military's interventions in politics would be significantly lessened as a result of the further democratization that had already been raised as a precondition for Turkey's entry into the EU. Thus the West and the EU emerged as allies to reduce the influence of the military and to establish democratic governance within which the Islamists would be regarded as a legitimate player. In this context they came to see that a Kemalist state ideology guarded by the military would not be sustainable in a Turkey that was an EU member.

This was a revolutionary "new repositioning" in Turkish history in which the demands and priorities of the post-Islamists and the West overlapped in outmaneuvering the Kemalist establishment, which had been disillusioned by democracy because it was democracy that brought the Islamists to power, by human rights because it was human rights mechanisms that protected the Islamists, and by the West because it was the West that was pressing for democracy and human rights and thereby providing shelter for the Islamists. The post-Islamists understood well that their opponents, the Kemalists, were vulnerable to an offensive in the name of democracy, human rights, and EU membership. As the old Westernizers became Western skeptics, the ex-Islamists gained confidence and went even further with their rapprochement with the West and modern political values, thus adding to the anxiety of the Kemalists/secularists.

An example of the changing discourse and strategy of the Islamists may be discerned in the head scarf debate. In the 1980s, when the head scarf was banned at universities, Islamists confidently defended wearing the head scarf as an "Islamic obligation" without giving any thought to defending it on other grounds. But in the late 1990s, they came to defend the wearing of the head scarf, still banned at universities, via references to the idea of human rights, equality, the right to choose, the right to education, and the principle of nondiscrimination. By then they knew that Islamic self-references did not explain much, did not justify any demand, and moreover did not bring about any change in the circumstances in Turkey. With their shaking self-confidence, the Islamists in their march toward post-Islamism discovered "universal" norms and values to protect Islamic symbols and identity. That is to say that in order to preserve the "particularities" of Islam, the post-Islamists embraced the "universal," defending their particularities with the secular language of modernity.[35]

Apart from such changes in political strategy and discourse, one person and his political vision shaped the process of the Islamists' transformation. This was Recep Tayyip Erdogan, who had moved into Islamist politics in the 1970s and became mayor of Istanbul with the RP in 1994. While in the ranks of the RP he uttered strong Islamist statements like "My reference is Islam," "Sovereignty in material and immaterial levels belongs to Allah," "You should be either Muslim or secular[;] you cannot be both," and "Democracy is not an objective but an instrument," which were frequently quoted by his opponents to invoke his Islamist past.[36] But he changed, distanced himself from his Islamist past. After establishing the AKP Erdogan was hailed for "taking off the shirt of 'national view,'" a phrase used to describe the change he had gone through. Though he underlined that his political ideas had not changed but "evolved," Erdogan as the leader of the AKP significantly differed from his own past self, let alone his former party. He disassociated himself from the Islamist "National View" movement. Did his imprisonment have an impact on him? To such a question he responded with, "Prison matures you."[37] He was certainly a different person politically when he got out of prison and intended to lead a new political movement.

To explain his post-Islamist transformation one should note the experience of the Islamists in the municipalities that they won in 1994. Erdogan was the mayor of Istanbul, a local politician. His experience in Istanbul certainly influenced him a great deal to turn into a pragmatic, service-oriented politician abandoning "lofty ideas" to build a new (Islamic) society and state. As a mayor he viewed politics as non-ideological but instrumental for solving the daily problems of people: politics as problem solving, not as a means to build an ideologically oriented Islamic community. Local politics, which is about "services" and not about great ideas, social transformation, bringing up a new generation through education, and so on, seemed a teaching experience for the Islamists.[38] Seeing, acknowledging, and recognizing the differences in a cosmopolitan city like Istanbul is likely to have had an impact on Erdogan with regard to the inherent pluralism in society. In his election campaign in 1994 Erdogan did not restrain from visiting nightclubs and bars in Beyoglu, the entertainment center of Istanbul.[39] Recognizing the differences in the social space that encircles cities, mayors have to be cooperative and pragmatic, able to form alliances with others in order to get various services delivered.

In this context, the Islamic motto often repeated by Erdogan that "service to people is service to Allah" has been effective in justifying and also secularizing the AKP's new policy line. If there is no ideological (Islamist) base left that justifies Islamists' involvement in politics, that is to say, if politics is not all about establishing an Islamic state, then the notion of "Service to people is service to Allah" (halka hizmet Hakka hizmettir) would justify their continuing presence in the realm of politics.[40] Such thinking has provided the ex-Islamists with an ideological justification for engaging in secular political processes with "material" objectives to achieve. As they have abandoned the idea of Islamizing the state and society, the reason that they should continue to engage in politics is formulated as service to people. The strictly secular activity of politics is then justifiable by a reference to "service to God" that goes through "service to people."

For the AKP leaders it was clear that the rise of Islamism in the political arena was detrimental to Islam's social and economic influence in Turkey. The new cadres, therefore, defined the new party as "conservative-democratic" in an attempt to escape from the self-defeating success that Islamism had experienced in the late 1990s. They saw how not only Islamists but also Islam's social base, with its educational, commercial, and solidarity networks, were crushed as a result of the "success" of Islamism in politics. They became more interested in keeping Islam's social and economic base intact as the ground of "political conservatism" and declared the end of ideologies, including Islamism, in the age of globalization.

The Rise of the AKP: Beyond Post-Islamism

The AKP is both the mirror that reflects the "new thinking" on Islamist politics and its principle agent and embodiment. The founders of the party, from the beginning, wanted to reach out to people outside the Islamist "National View" tradition and build a wider political ground. To appeal to those people they made it clear that the party would not be religious based but, rather, conservative and democratic.[41]

The party program was about "development and democracy," bringing together two fundamental themes of center-right politics in Turkey since the 1950s, a sign that the new party placed itself in the center-right tradition. Furthermore, the party declared its commitment to basic rights and freedoms; not only legal guarantees but also the proper implementation of human rights provisions were promised. The "individual" was referred to as the constituting unit of society, whose happiness was stated as the ultimate objective of the party.

Among the issues that took a central place in the party program and election campaigns were basic rights and freedoms, democracy and civil society, the rule of law, and the restructuring of the state. Different social, ethnic, political, and religious identities were declared a source of richness, not of a threat. On the political front the AKP of the ex-Islamists committed to democracy while upholding pluralism in its view of differences in the social realm. A limited state that would respect the expanding role of the private sector and NGOs was promised. The party also claimed that it would broaden the realm of politics vis-à-vis the historical domination of the civilian and military bureaucracy. In short, the statements of its leaders, program, and election declarations posited the new party to be a democratic, liberal, and pluralistic political movement, much akin to the post-Islamism that was emerging.[42]

From the moment it was established questions have been asked about whether the AKP is an Islamist party. The leadership, including Erdogan and his top aides, were coming from Turkey's Islamist political movement, the "National View." No doubt Erdogan, who grew up politically at a time when the ideas of Sayyid Qutb of the Muslim Brotherhood and Mawdudi of Cemaat'al Islami got into Islamic circles in Turkey through a translation boom in the 1970s, had a doctrinaire Islamist background. Yet as the leader of the new movement he has continually disassociated himself and his party from the "National View" movement and Islamist politics.

Erdogan claimed that his views have "evolved," rejecting the idea that he has changed but noting instead that he has developed his political views.[43] But he seems to acknowledge his transformation by saying that "the world is a different place and I am a different person."[44] At any rate, Islam has remained a very important part of his personality:

> Before anything else, I'm a Muslim. As a Muslim, I try to comply with the requirements of my religion. I have a responsibility to God, who created me, and I try to fulfill that responsibility. But I try now very much to keep this away from my political life, to keep it private. A political party cannot have a religion. Only individuals can. Otherwise, you'd be exploiting religion, and religion is so supreme that it cannot be exploited or taken advantage of.[45]

From this it appears that Erdogan has deliberately separated his religious beliefs and political activities.

Erdogan from the beginning underlined that his party had three "red lines": refraining from religion-based, ethnicity-based, and region-based politics. Yet the Constitutional Court was not of this opinion when in 2008 it decided over the application of the chief public prosecutor that the AKP was an Islamist political movement and constituted a center of antisecularist activities.[46]

Notwithstanding the decision of the Constitutional Court, the AKP emerged with a new program and political language, both exemplifying and building upon the transformation of Islamic political identity in response to domestic political developments and debates internal to the Islamist movement in the late 1990s. The AKP seemed to have departed not only from the old leadership of Islamism but also from the ideology of the "National View." Under the "experienced" leadership of Erdogan the new party claimed to stand for "democratic conservatism," which essentially combines democracy with religiosity.

Conservative democracy is a mixture of morality, family values, and historical pride with democracy, the market economy, globalization, and EU accession.[47] The "conservatism" of the AKP refers to the cultural and social outlook of the party, while "democracy" underlines the preferred political model within which competition for power is conducted. For Hale and Ozbudun, the AKP's "religiously inspired conservatism is more cultural and social than political or ideological."[48]

However, this does not comfort some people who fear that their "secular lifestyle" is under threat of Islamization under the influence of the AKP and its social extensions, such as Islamic dervish orders and religious circles. Restrictions on the places where alcoholic drinks can be consumed, high taxation on alcoholic drinks, and social pressure on nonfasting individuals particularly in small towns are often raised as proofs of their concern. Prominent Turkish sociologist Serif Mardin has come up with a notion of *mahalle baskisi* (neighborhood pressure) to describe the social control and restraints on those who live a secular lifestyle during AKP rule.[49] While the majority is comfortable with the AKP's "conservatism," a small group with strong Kemalist/secularist views remains unpersuaded about its commitment to pluralism and respect for the different. Since the opposition to the AKP is largely centered around this issue, it seems that the party has failed to ease the concerns of secularists about their lifestyle, which is the main shortcoming of its post-Islamist social posture.

Islam is certainly an important source of identity for the party leader, Erdogan, who once said, "My reference is Islam."[50] Though the party leadership has Islamist roots, the party does not have an Islamist agenda. Its grassroots is very diverse and includes almost all segments of the population. It gets votes from all parts of Turkey and from all ethnic and religious groups.[51] To keep such diverse social ground the AKP could not afford to remain "Islamist" and had to develop a more inclusive political vocabulary and organizational network.

The leaders of the AKP remain individually committed to Islam as a religion but refrain from developing an Islamic political agenda. This is not just a personal choice of the AKP leadership but also a realistic political strategy, given the social, political, and institutional limits of an Islamist political endeavor. Islam as a political project does not enjoy widespread support in Turkey. Less than 10 percent of the Turkish people would approve of a shari'a-based state.[52] Therefore it would be a self-defeating move on the part of the AKP to confine itself within such a limited space for politics, given the fact that it is a party that reached 50 percent support in the 2011 elections. It can be argued that the AKP has been imprisoned by its own success and is thus bound to move ever away from Islamism toward post-Islamism. As Olivier Roy notes, "Political logic won over the religious."[53]

The AKP is also restrained by the changing voting behavior of the electorate in Turkey, as evidenced by the general elections held over the last twenty years. In the five general parliamentary elections from 1987 to 2002, five different political parties came first. Fluctuations in voting behavior place a serious constraint on any political party, including the AKP. Therefore, to survive politically the AKP does not have the luxury of engaging in ideological politicking at the expense of a service-oriented approach to politics.[54]

Understanding this well, Erdogan has repeatedly said that the AKP is not religiously oriented but a conservative party of "average" Turkish citizens. Hale and Ozbudun argue that the AKP displays the typical characteristics of a center-right party in Turkey.[55] Likewise Erdogan refers to the Democratic Party of the 1950s, the Justice Party of the 1960s, and the Motherland Party of the 1980s, all mass center-right political parties, as its political predecessors.[56] In line with these, the AKP has emphasized the themes of democracy, national will, people power, and economic development as well as membership in the EU.

Striving for EU Membership and Democratization

One of the features of the AKP's post-Islamist credentials is its pro-EU integration stand. Such a stand marks a fundamental departure from Islamism, which takes anti-Westernism and the struggle against the West as inherent elements of Islamic identity. As soon as the AKP won the 2002 election, its leader, Erdogan, declared that their priority was to speed up the process of joining the EU, once called a Christian club by the Islamist "National View" movement from which the AKP and its leadership came.[57] Full membership in the EU has been the AKP's persistent policy in government. To demonstrate his commitment to EU membership, Erdogan asked, on a visit to Italy in late 2002, for a "Catholic marriage between Turkey and the EU," a statement that demonstrates a dramatic change in the mentality of a politician who once served in the ranks of Islamist politics.[58]

Certainly the needs of the AKP overlapped with the demands of the EU and the requirements for membership. The party wanted to limit the power of the military over domestic politics, enhance civilian control over the military, strengthen civil society including Islamic associations and endowments, expand freedom of expression, and make party closures more difficult. These were also the demands of the EU. Thus the AKP instrumentalized the EU accession process and reform agenda in order to carve out a secure place for itself in Turkish politics.[59]

As such EU membership was taken as an opportunity to broaden the scope of legitimacy for the AKP and build new coalitions with modern/secular social segments in Turkey and abroad. The post-Islamists obviously wished to expand the scope of their dialogue to reach out to their natural supporters. Eventually it paid off; the EU objective brought the support not only of big business but also of big media and social democratic and liberal circles, including intellectuals and NGOs, all significant actors in shaping public opinion.

What is important in the sense of the change the Islamists went through is that integration with the West and the maintenance of an Islamic identity at a social level are no longer seen as mutually exclusive choices, a realization that marks a radical shift from the traditional Islamist stand. Moreover, the AKP's pro-EU policy is not confined to its leadership but, rather, has also spread to its grassroots, as reflected in public opinion surveys in which pro-EU views are highest among AKP voters. For instance, an opinion poll conducted by MetroPOLL in December 2010 found that 69 percent of AKP voters favor EU membership, 15 percent above the national average of 54 percent, indicating that the AKP has transformed its traditionally EU-skeptic grassroots.[60]

EU membership would not only anchor Turkey in the West via treaty; it would also require the meeting of certain political preconditions concerning democracy, human rights, the rule of law, and respect for minorities. In regard to this, the AKP did its homework well. In this vein the government has introduced reforms on the Kurdish issue, and human rights in general, and civil–military relations, with the "harmonization packages" passed by the parliament, and even seemed ready to compromise on the long-standing Cyprus dispute.[61]

With the harmonization packages, freedom of association, deterrents against torture and mistreatment, and safeguards for the rights of prisoners were enhanced. The closure of political parties was made more difficult and now requires a three-fifths majority in the Constitutional Court. Article 8 of the anti-terror law was abolished in July 2003, along with the provisions that allowed political propaganda in local languages such as Kurdish. The reforms also ended the lessening of sentences for so-called honor killings and removed the NSC representatives on the censor board and the Radio and Television Supervision Board.[62] With another law, the auditing of military expenditures and property was made possible by the Court of Auditors, and the executive powers of the NSC's general secretary were repealed.[63] The State Security Courts were abolished, the death penalty was removed from the penal code, international treaties concerning human rights were accorded precedence over Turkish law, the military representative on the higher education board was removed,[64] and at the same time the state-owned TRT started to broadcast in Kurdish.[65]

Furthermore, a number of international conventions were signed and ratified by the AKP government. Among them are the International Covenant on Civil and Political Rights; the International Covenant on Economic, Social and Cultural Rights; Protocol No. 6 of the European Convention on Human Rights; the Optional Protocol of the Convention on the Rights of the Child; and Protocol No. 13 of the European Convention on Human Rights.

All these reforms were finally recognized as meeting the Copenhagen political criteria by the European Council, and accession negotiations started in October 2005. It was an irony of history that a political party with Islamist roots brought Turkey ever closer to EU membership, an objective it used to oppose strongly. The EU's decision to negotiate full membership with Turkey under the AKP on the grounds that the democracy criteria had been sufficiently met is a vindication that under the post-Islamists Turkey has not been Islamized but, rather, Europeanized.

Engaging with Globalization

Another issue that reflects the new post-Islamist "identity" of the AKP is its stand on globalization and engagement with global actors. The AKP's program, election declarations, and performance in government concerning globalization and international economic interactions have been strikingly in contrast to an Islamist stand. This has been a party friendly toward foreign capital, multinational corporations, and international financial institutions.

During the AKP years Turkey has integrated ever more into the global capitalist economy. Turkey's foreign trade tripled during the AKP years. In 2002 Turkey's total foreign trade stood at $87 billion; in 2008 this peaked at $334 billion, an almost fourfold increase. This figure dropped to $243 billion in 2009 due to the global economic crisis and slightly recovered in 2010 at $299 billion. In 2011, though, it jumped to a record $375 billion.[66]

When the AKP came to power in 2002 the number of foreign companies active in Turkey stood at 498. The number of companies registered as foreign reached 22,250 in 2009 and 25,927 by 2011. This certainly reflected Turkey's economic performance and prospects but also resulted from the welcoming attitude of the government and its policies of easing the activities of foreign companies. Such a policy could hardly be possible within the paradigm of Islamism.

Likewise during the AKP years the amount of foreign capital inflow significantly increased compared with earlier periods, as the party promised in its election manifestos to encourage the entry of foreign capital into the Turkish economy.[67] The record inflow of foreign capital was in 2007, with $22 billion. In 2002, when the AKP came to power, this was merely $1.5 billion. The post-Islamist AKP of foreign capital–friendly messages has not scared off foreign investors who view Turkey as a developing market, which is likely to continue to strengthen democracy and open Turkish society under the rule of the AKP. The AKP, whose leadership has an Islamist past, has apparently placed Turkey on an irreversible path toward globalization.

Turkey's increasing integration with the world was also manifested in the numbers of tourists visiting Turkey every year. During the AKP years the number of tourists visiting Turkey tripled from twelve million annually to twenty-nine million, mostly from European countries. This indicates not only a commercial but also a social interaction with the world under the government of the former Islamists.

During the AKP government, the market economy was underlined as the principle economic model. An aggressive privatization scheme was devised and implemented despite stubborn resistance from the Kemalist judiciary, which repealed some sales. During the AKP years privatization revenue reached $30.6 billion.[68] Some big privatization projects such as Turktelekom went to foreign capital amid criticism that the AKP was selling out Turkey's assets to foreigners.

While Erdogan talked of "marketing Turkey abroad," his opponents accused him of selling out the country to foreigners. In return he claimed that his opponents were "capital racist" and challenged his critics who said that they were not engaging in capital racism (indicating that they would not be interested in looking into the national origins of capital invested in Turkey). He called on international financial circles to come and invest in Turkey, promising that they would eliminate all barriers for foreign investment in Turkey.[69]

A similar cooperative attitude could be seen concerning the AKP's relations with the IMF, the World Bank, and other international financial institutions. A standby agreement reached with the IMF in early 2002 continued to be implemented by the AKP government. After its successful completion, another standby agreement was signed in 2005. The AKP thus worked together with the IMF in its implementation of economic policies.

In short, the AKP did not sink into an anti-globalist position, as would be expected due to its Islamist roots. But for the AKP, the performance of the government in providing services to the people mattered, and services could not be provided without Turkey being involved in global economic interactions. Thus it played within the rules of global capitalism by abandoning the Islamist rejection of globalization.

Redefining Secularism

Secularism was one of the toughest questions the Turkish post-Islamists had to tackle. It has been a constitutional principle since 1937 and was accepted by many in Turkey as a corollary to democracy. Yet it was also in its name that the suppression of Islamist movements was carried out, their political parties were closed, and their foundations were shut down. Islamists thus viewed secularism as practiced in Turkey primarily as an instrument of the Kemalist establishment to suppress what was Islamic. In the words of Ali Bulac, an influential Islamist, "Religion was suppressed and tradition was disrupted under interventions by the enlightening state....Islam turned into a protest movement against the interventions by the center."[70]

This was correct to some extent because the Kemalist establishment defined secularism as irreligiosity, which was later formulated as "a way of life" that excludes religion from social life. For instance, the secularist president Ahmet Necdet Sezer, speaking at a meeting organized by the Diyanet, asserted that "secularism is a way of life.... [A] secular individual would certainly not allow his religious beliefs to affect worldly matters."[71] Similarly the National Security Council's declaration of February 28, 1997, claimed that "secularism in Turkey is not only the assurance of political regime but also...a way of life."[72] The Constitutional Court in its decision to close down the RP referred to secularism as the "separation of social life, education, family, economics, law, manners, dress codes, etc. from religion." For the court, secularism was both "a civilized way of life"[73] and "Turkey's philosophy of life."[74] In short, secularism as understood by the Kemalists meant a nonreligious social space in which Islam was barred from being visible and was kept in the individual's conscience. Militant secularism of this kind has been a device to exclude, suppress, or at least control non-Kemalist social, political, and economic groups.[75]

This understanding, practice, and function of secularism was opposed by the post-Islamists not in the name of Islam but on behalf of a "moderate" Anglo-Saxon version of it. Such a model of secularism was acceptable to the Turkish post-Islamists because it does not interfere in social life to erase the influence of religion and, on the contrary, leaves the social realm open to the influence of religion. So, the post-Islamists were ready to settle with a "redefinition."

Along this line the AKP attempted to redefine secularism in a more "liberal, democratic, and Anglo-Saxon" way. Ahmet Kuru argues that this was a quest to transform an assertive-interventionist notion of secularism into a "passive secularism."[76] The speaker of the parliament and the chairman of the Constitutional Commission openly put this forward in the Turkish parliament. Both called for the need for a "reinterpretation" of secularism.[77]

Part of this effort of reinterpretation was to link up secularism with social peace and coexistence. Bulent Arinc, the former speaker of the parliament and one of the three leaders who founded the AKP, asserts that

> to build social peace a reinterpretation of secularism is required. We do not have any objection to the principle of secularism but we must define what we make of secularism. Rigid secularist policies should not turn social life into a prison. The understanding of secularism as a matter of peace and liberties and recognize it as the freedom of religion and conscience while not interfering in their beliefs will serve to build social peace.[78]

The party, in its program, considers "religion as one of the most important institutions of humanity" and secularism "as a prerequisite of democracy, and an assurance of the freedom of religion and conscience."[79] Erdogan asserts that secularism "needs to be crowned with democracy."[80] The attempt to link secularism with democracy as well as social peace is important since this is expected to cleanse the built-in authoritarian political content of radical secularism as implemented in Turkey that has been used against religious groups.

The AKP also emphasizes two important aspects of secularism: impartiality and the equal treatment of all religions by the state. Erdogan defines secularism "as an institutional attitude and method that ensures the state to remain impartial and equidistant to all religions and thoughts."[81]

Thereby secularism is essentially regarded as freedom of religion and conscience. Erdogan argues that "for women who use the Islamic head scarf secularism is an assurance."[82] In parallel to this point the party program reiterates that "secularism is a principle that allows people of all religions, and beliefs to comfortably practice their religions, to be able to express their religious convictions and live accordingly."[83] It is added that this is also the right of nonbelievers. The AKP presents its notion of secularism as a model of coexistence for all religions and belief systems. On the anniversary of the adoption of secularism Erdogan issued a statement emphasizing the centrality of secularism as an emancipatory guarantee for different beliefs and lifestyles.[84]

The AKP, by rejecting the "interpretation and distortion of secularism as enmity against religion," criticizes prevailing radical understandings of secularism in Turkey.[85] The presence of an Islamic social space is ensured by redirecting the state from its mission to secularize society. This implies that the state should not compete with religion in the social realm and in return religion withdraws from its claim to have a say on the state. That is to say that the post-Islamists try to secure the social space from the secularizing interventions of the state by calling for a passive model of secularism along Anglo-Saxon lines.

In return the AKP opposes the use of religious values in politics. Erdogan claims that they

> do not think it right to conduct politics through religion, to attempt to transform government ideologically by using religion.... To make religion an instrument of politics...harms not only political pluralism but also religion itself.[86]

Discrimination against religious people for their choices is regarded as antidemocratic: "It is also unacceptable to put pressure on people who think and live differently by using religion."[87]

What is also criticized is the view that takes secularism as an attribute of the individual rather than that of the state.[88] For Erdogan, "secularism is not a religion but Islam is. Thus we cannot treat them as same.... It is not an individual but the state that is secular."[89] This means that the AKP leader expects the state to be secular but not individuals. With such an approach the AKP challenges an understanding of secularism as a way of life. While welcoming the "secular state" as a framework guaranteeing freedom of religion, they oppose the secularization of the social space by public authority. For the post-Islamists, therefore, secularism is not an anathema; it can be properly defined and as such accepted.

Ali Bulac, the post-Islamist who declared in the late 1990s the failure of Islamism, formulates the basic elements of the post-Islamist reinterpretation of secularism as follows:

> There is no contradiction between Islam and secularism if the latter is defined as "the protection of religious freedom and freedom of consciousness; prevention of domination by a certain religious group over the others; ensuring that people from every religion and faith freely express themselves; absence of domination by a religious elite in the governance; recognition of the right to be present in the public domain to the individuals; and ensuring that state is equally distant to all religious, philosophical and ideological groups." This sort of definition provided for the concept of secularism is consistent with Islamic precepts and the historical experience by the Muslims.[90]

Such an accommodationist approach to secularism may go beyond the position of post-Islamist movements in other Muslim countries; as Bayat states, "Post-Islamism is neither anti-Islamic, un-Islamic, *nor is it secular.*"[91] But the place of secularism in the constitutional order and in the founding ethos of the republic has compelled the post-Islamists to seek an accommodation with secularism not as a way of life and the supremacy of the state over religion but, rather, as the separation of the state and religion as well as freedom of conscience.

Conclusion

The search for survival in an environment of secularist extremism and political authoritarianism has led mainstream Turkish Islamists to settle for democracy, globalization, EU membership, and an Anglo-Saxon form of moderate secularism. The emergence of Turkish post-Islamism was thus triggered, as in the other cases of post-Islamism, by the crisis of Islamism, a crisis that occurred at the time when Islamism was at its strongest stage, in the late 1990s. This may have added to the trauma experienced by the Islamists but may have also facilitated the transformation and the birth of post-Islamism.

The Adalet ve Kalkinma Partisi has been both an agent of this transformation and its embodiment. What made the party unique was its
experimentation in merging an Islamist past with a democratic and liberal
political agenda. It gathered people with diverse ideological backgrounds
and lifestyles around a democratic ideal and developed a globalist,
market-oriented, and pro-EU political discourse without ideological rigidity. As such the AKP exemplifies the capability of Islamist political cadres
to regenerate themselves by embracing attributes of post-Islamism such
as democracy, pluralism, and moderate secularism in a politically competitive environment and in connection with European political networks
and global economic institutions.

Recognizing the secular characteristics of politics, the Turkish
post-Islamists, including their political representative, the AKP, have
abandoned their "claims" for an Islamic government. The withdrawal of
their Islamic identity from the political arena where secular programs
compete with one another has given strength to the post-Islamists for
their activities in the social realm, while their political representatives
did very well in competing with the other political actors in the political
realm. As the political space is occupied by the conservative-cum-secular
AKP, then the social/individual space is left for Islam's influence. Thus,
departing from the political has in fact accelerated post-Islamists'
engagement in the social arena, where they could expand "Islamic
values" under the protection of the redefined principle of secularism.
Democracy is valued at this juncture as the institutional and principle
framework to enable the post-Islamists' participation in the power game
and to keep secularism as a legal/institutional guarantee of immunity
from state interference in Islam's individual and societal power. The
result is the emergence of a post-Islamist politics that is prepared to
embrace values and instruments of political modernity but is also capable of expanding its social and individual reach within the boundaries of
this political modernity.

It must be reiterated, however, that in rethinking their past identity, political strategy, discourse, and objectives, the post-Islamists have
abandoned the notion of an Islamic state—not only out of political prudence. They have questioned the feasibility and wisdom of constructing
an Islamic state. Its feasibility is questioned because, first, oppression
has worked: the Islamists were rolled back when they were at the top
of their power. Second, post-Islamists have increasingly recognized the

social and ideological plurality even within Islam itself as it has withdrawn into the social realm under the pressure of the political scene. Third, the experiences in the Middle East have taught them the difficulties of defending an Islamic government in the age of globalization, where all forms of ideological state formations are very hard to maintain.

Post-Islamists who withdrew from the political claims of Islamism seem to have understood that democracy, pluralism, and human rights would present a powerful, legitimate, and widely supported alternative to the Kemalist/secularist establishment.[92] Therefore, instead of presenting an Islamic alternative to the secular/Kemalist regime, the post-Islamists have proposed a secular/modern alternative out of the conviction that the Kemalist order can hardly be approved of by modern political values, principles, and institutions.

In conclusion, the AKP certainly reflects features of a post-Islamist movement, keeping its ties with Islam in the social realm while abandoning it as a political program.[93] At any rate it envisages a "pious society," even though in a "secular democratic state."[94] But it also goes beyond the post-Islamism "project" in the sense that the AKP *as a political agent* acting in a secular constitutional order does not "fuse religiosity and rights, faith and freedom, Islam and liberty" in its *political agenda*, notwithstanding the private choices of its members. It does emphasize "rights instead of duties, plurality in place of singular authoritative voice, historicity rather than fixed scripture, and the future instead of the past."[95] But still Islam is an unspoken ideal for the AKP, which deliberately refrains from being labeled a "Muslim democrat" party in parallel to the "Christian democrat" parties of Europe. Instead the party defines itself as "conservative democratic." The AKP's conservatism is blended with democracy to express the party's "ideological" position, which is a soft reference to religious values. What emerges from this is a political identity that takes Islam in the name of conservatism as an implicit reference point for valuing family, social solidarity, and the past. As noted, what Hale and Ozbudun make of the AKP's "religiously inspired conservatism" implies that the party's relationship with Islam is "more cultural and social than political or ideological."[96] "Conservatism" defines the AKP in relation to society, whereas "democratic" reflects its political identity. The resultant post-Islamism of the AKP is thus socially conservative in appeal and politically democratic in discourse.

Notes

1. A. Bayat, *Making Islam Democratic: Social Movements and the Post-Islamist Turn* (Stanford: Stanford University Press, 2007), 11.

2. I. Dagi, "Rethinking Human Rights, Democracy and the West: Post-Islamist Intellectuals in Turkey," *Critique: Critical Middle Eastern Studies* 13, no. 2 (2004): 135–151.

3. A. Bayat, *Islam and Democracy: What Is the Real Question?* ISIM Paper, 8 (Leiden: Amsterdam University Press, 2007), 17–20.

4. A. Kuru, "Reinterpretation of Secularism in Turkey: The Case of the Justice and Development Party," in *The Emergence of a New Turkey: Democracy and the AK Parti*, ed. H. Yavuz (Salt Lake City: University of Utah Press, 2006), 136–159.

5. Bayat, *Making Islam Democratic*, 189.

6. Ismail Kara, ed., *Turkiye'de Islamcilik Dusuncesi*, vol. 1 (Istanbul: Risale Yayinlari, 1986); Ismail Kara, ed., *Turkiye'de Islamcilik Dusuncesi*, vol. 2 (Istanbul: Kitabevi Yayinlari, 1997); Ismail Kara, ed., *Turkiye'de Islamcilik Dusuncesi*, vol. 3 (Istanbul: Kitabevi Yayinlari, 1998). For Ali Bulac, a contemporary intellectual with a strong Islamist standing who was influential in the making of an Islamist generation in Turkey, Islam is "an alternative way of thought, system of belief and the way of life" (*Cagdas Kavramlar ve Duzenler* [Istanbul: Pinar Yayinlari, 1987], 199).

7. Kenan Cayir, "The Emergence of Turkey's Contemporary 'Muslim Democrats,'" in U. Cizre, *Secular and Islamic Politics in Turkey: The Making of the Justice and Development Party* (London: Routledge, 2008), 64–66; A. Gunes-Ayata, "Islamism versus Authoritarianism: Political Ideas in Two Islamic Publications," in *Islam in Modern Turkey: Religion, Politics and Literature in a Secular State*, ed. R. Tapper (London: I. B. Tauris, 1994), 254–279.

8. M. Metiner, *Yemyesil Seriat, Bembeyaz Demokrasi* (Istanbul: Dogan Kitaplari, 2004), 216.

9. For the "failure" argument, see O. Roy, *Failure of Political Islam* (Cambridge: Harvard University Press, 1994); G. Kepel, *Jihad: The Trail of Political Islam* (Cambridge: Harvard University Press, 2002).

10. When annulling a law permitting the use of head scarves on university campuses, the Constitutional Court ruled that "secularism is a civilised way of life" (E. 1989/1, K. 1989/12 no, dated 7.3.1989, at www.anayasa.gov.tr/files/pdf/kararlar_dergisi/kd_25.pdf.

11. N. Gole, "Secularism and Islamism in Turkey: The Making of Elites and Counter-Elites," *Middle East Journal* 51, no. 1 (1997): 46–58.

12. S. Mardin, "Ideology and Religion in the Turkish Revolution," *International Journal of Middle East Studies* 2, no. 2 (1971): 197–211.

13. Ahmet Yildiz, "Politico-religious Discourse of Political Islam in Turkey: The Parties of National Outlook," *Muslim World* 93, no. 2 (2003): 187–209.

14. N. Erbakan, *Milli Gorus* (Istanbul: Dergah Yayinlari, 1975); N. Erbakan, *Turkiye'nin Temel Meseleleri* (Ankara: Rehber Yayinlari, 1991); H. H. Ceylan, ed., *Erbakan ve Turkiye'nin Temel Meseleleri* (Ankara: Rehber Yayinlari, 1996).

15. Erbakan, *Turkiye'nin Temel Meseleleri*, 99–100; *Milli Gazete*, September 21, 1995.

16. B. Toprak, "Politicization of Islam in a Secular State: The National Salvation Party in Turkey," in *From Nationalism to Revolutionary Islam: Essays on Social Movements in the Contemporary Near and Middle East*, ed. S. A. Arjomand (Albany: State University of New York Press, 1984), 119–132.

17. *Milli Gazete*, December 4, 1995.

18. Z. Onis, "The Political Economy of Islamic Resurgence in Turkey: The Rise of the Welfare Party in Perspective," *Third World Quarterly* 18, no. 4 (1997): 743–766.

19. M. H. Yavuz, "Political Islam and the Welfare (Refah) Party in Turkey," *Comparative Politics* 30, no. 1 (1997): 63–82.

20. The historical irony is that those demands were signed by pro-Islamic prime minister Erbakan along with the generals; see "Recommendations of the State Council Meeting and Comment," *Briefing*, March 10, 1997, 4.

21. *Hurriyet*, November 4, 1997.

22. For the February 28 decisions of NSC, see "Recommendations of the State Council Meeting and Comment," 4.

23. *Yenibinyil*, May 21, 2000.

24. *Radikal*, December 18, 1998.

25. Ibid.

26. W. Hale and E. Ozbudun, *Islamism, Democracy and Liberalism in Turkey: The Case of the AKP* (London: Routledge, 2010), 10–11; *Hurriyet*, May 4, 2000.

27. *Milliyet*, May 20, 2000; *Radikal*, May 20, 2000.

28. *Yenibinyil*, May 6, 2000; *Milliyet*, April 15, 2000.

29. *Milliyet*, April 29, 2000; *Hurriyet*, May 10, 2000.

30. *Milliyet*, May 20, 2000; *Radikal*, May 20, 2000.

31. H. Yavuz, "Introduction: The Role of the New Bourgeoisie in the Transformation of the Turkish Islamic Movement," in Yavuz, *Emergence of a New Turkey*, 1–19.

32. Ali Bulac, "Islam devleti projesi coktu," interview by Nese Duzel, *Radikal*, December 21, 1999.

33. I. Dagi, "The Justice and Development Party: Identity, Politics, and Human Rights Discourse in the Search for Security and Legitimacy," in Yavuz, *Emergence of a New Turkey*, 88–106.

34. The court's verdict came in 2001, ruling that the Constitutional Court of Turkey did not breach Article 11 of the European Convention of Human Rights and that the closure of the Welfare Party was justified because it aimed at destroying democracy and democratic liberties. That was a shock that brought back some degree of traditional animosity toward the West, which was described as having double standards, prejudices, and a historical dislike toward the "crescent." See *Refah (The Welfare Party) and Others v. Turkey* (41340/98 41342/98 41343/98 41344/98), February 13, 2003, 39–49.

35. K. Canatan, "Cagdas Siyasal Islam Dusuncesinin Gelisim Seyri," *Bilgi ve Dusunce* 1, no. 3 (December 2002): 31–38; Y. Akdogan, "Siyasal Islam'dan Muhafazakar Demokratliga...," *Bilgi ve Dusunce* 1, no. 3 (December 2002): 17–23; A. Bulac, "AB Disi Secenegin Kritigi," *Zaman*, March 13, 2002.

36. "Erdogan: Referansim Islam," *Hurriyet*, August 28, 2001.

37. D. Sontag, "The Erdogan Experiment," *New York Times*, May 11, 2003. Over the court's verdict he called for a country that abided by the rule of law. He said that his struggle for the supremacy of law and democracy would continue; see *Sabah*, April 22, 1998.

38. In a personal conversation, a minister in the AKP government who had been elected a mayor in 1994 told me that when he was elected he knew much about the problems of the umma, such as the Palestinian question, the situation in Kashmir, and Muslims' problems here and there, but nothing about the problems of his own city. But he realized that in order to be reelected, what mattered was to solve the local problems.

39. H. Besni and M. Ozbay, *Bir Liderin Dogusu: R. Tayyip Erdogan* (Istanbul: Meydan Yayinlari, 2010), 154.

40. H. Yavuz, "The Transformation of a Turkish Islamic Movement: From Identity Politics to Policy," *American Journal of Islamic Social Sciences* 22, no. 3 (2005): 105–111.

41. *Hurriyet*, July 7, 2001; also see the Adalet ve Kalkinma Partisi program, "AK Parti Kalkinma ve Demokratiklesme Programi," at www.akparti.org.tr/site/akparti/parti-programi.

42. Adalet ve Kalkinma Partisi, *Hersey Turkiye Icin: AK Parti Secim Beyannamesi* (Ankara: AK Parti Yayinlari, 2002); Adalet ve Kalkinma Partisi, *Nice AK Yillara: Guven ve Istikrar Icinde Durmak Yok Yola Devam* (Ankara: AK Parti Yayinlari, 2007); AKP, "AK Parti Kalkinma ve Demokratiklesme Programi."

43. For an early description of Erdogan as a moderate politician, see M. Heper, "Islam and Democracy: Toward a Reconciliation?" *Middle East Journal* 51, no. 1 (1997): 37.

44. D. Frantz, "Turkey, Well Along Road to Secularism, Fear Detour to Islamism," *New York Times*, January 8, 2002, www.nytimes.com/2002/01/08/world/turkey-well-along-road-to-secularism-fears-detour-to-islamism.html.

45. Sontag, "Erdogan Experiment."

46. I. Dagi, "AK Party Survives the Closure Case: What Is Next?" *Policy Brief*, SETA, no. 19, Ankara, August 1, 2008.

47. For the theoretical background for the idea of conservative democracy, see Y. Akdogan, *Muhafazakar Demokrasi* (Ankara: AK Parti Yayinlari, 2003). Akdogan has been a political adviser to Prime Minister Erdogan since the establishment of the AKP and was elected as a member of parliament in the 2011 elections. For a short English version, see Y. Akdogan, "The Meaning of Conservative Democratic Political Identity," in Yavuz, *Emergence of a New Turkey*, 49–65.

48. Hale and Ozbudun, *Islamism, Democracy and Liberalism in Turkey*, 29.

49. R. Cakir, *Mahalle Baskisi* (Istanbul: Dogan Kitapcilik, 2008).

50. "Erdogan yargilandi," *Milliyet*, April 1, 1998, www.milliyet.com.tr/1998/04/01/haber/haboo.html.

51. For instance, Armenian Orthodox Patriarch Mesrob II announced before the July 2007 elections that his community would vote for the AKP; see "Ermeni cemaati secimlerde AK Partiyi destekleyecek," *Yeni Safak*, April 6, 2007, http://yenisafak.com.tr/politika/?q=1&c=2&i=48782&Ermeni/Cemaati/se%C3%A7imlerde/Ak/Partiyi/destekleyecek. Also see Vahram Ter-Matevosyan, "The Armenian Community and the AK Party: Finding Trust under the Crescent," *Insight Turkey* 12, no. 4 (2010): 93–111.

52. A. Carkoglu and B. Toprak, *Religion, Society and Politics in a Changing Turkey* (Istanbul: TESEV Publications, 2007), 81.

53. O. Roy, *Globalised Islam: The Search for a New Ummah* (New York: Columbia University Press, 2004), 61.

54. I. Dagi, "Turkey's AKP in Power," *Journal of Democracy* 19, no. 3 (2008): 25–30; I. Yilmaz, "Muslim Democrats in Egypt and Turkey: Participatory Politics as a Catalyst," *Insight Turkey* 11, no. 2 (2009): 93–112.

55. Hale and Ozbudun, *Islamism, Democracy and Liberalism in Turkey.*

56. *Milliyet*, July 15, 2001.

57. "Avrupa'ya net mesajlar," *Radikal*, November 7, 2002, www.radikal.com.tr/haber.php?haberno=55890; Philip Robins, "Confusion at Home, Confusion Abroad: Turkey between Copenhagen and Iraq," *International Affairs* 79 (2003): 547–566.

58. "Erdogan, AB ile 'Katolik Nikahi' kiymak istiyor," *Zaman*, November 14, 2002, http://arsiv.zaman.com.tr/2002/11/14/pdetay.htm.

59. B. Duran, "JDP and Foreign Policy as an Agent of Transformation," in Yavuz, *Emergence of a New Turkey*, 281–305.

60. MetroPOLL, *Turkiye Siyasal Durum Arastirmasi* (Ankara, December 2010), 64.

61. For political reforms under the AKP government, see Hale and Ozbudun, *Islamism, Democracy and Liberalism in Turkey*, 55–67.

62. *Briefing*, May 5, 2003, 6.

63. *Briefing*, July 28, 2003, 9.

64. *Briefing*, April 26, 2004, 8–9.

65. *Briefing*, June 14, 2004, 14.

66. Official figures of the Turkish Statistics Institution, at www.tuik.gov.tr/Gosterge.do?id=3488&metod=IlgiliGosterge.

67. I. Grigoriadis and A. Kamaras, "Foreign Direct Investment in Turkey: Historical Constraints and the AKP Success Story," *Middle Eastern Studies* 44, no. 1 (2008): 53–68.

68. Figures between November 2002–May 2010 as declared by Minister of Finance Mehmet Simsek, at www.hurriyet.com.tr/ekonomi/15086024.asp.

69. "Racism over Capital Drives Foreign Investment Away," October 15, 2005, at www.turks.us/article.php?story=20051015103640151&mode=print.

70. Ali Bulac, "Islam and Politics," *Today's Zaman*, July 13, 2007, www.todayszaman.com/columnist-116522-islam-and-politics.html.

71. "Zirvede Laiklik Atismasi," *Radikal*, September 21, 2004, www.radikal.com.tr/haber.php?haberno=128665.

72. Cited in A. Kuru, *Secularism and State Policies towards Religion: The United States, France, and Turkey* (Cambridge: Cambridge University Press, 2009), 161.

73. Constitutional Court decision E. 1989/1, K. 1989/12 no, dated 7.3.1989.

74. Cited in Hale and Ozbudun, *Islamism, Democracy and Liberalism in Turkey*, 22.

75. D. Jung, "Secularism: A Key to Turkish Politics," *Intellectual Discourse* 19, no. 3 (2006): 129–154.

76. Kuru, *Secularism and State Policies towards Religion*, 161–201; Kuru, "Reinterpretation of Secularism in Turkey."

77. "'We respect Turkey's principles of secularism, but these need to be re-interpreted,' said Burhan Kuzu, chairman of the constitutional commission in parliament" (Ibon Villelabeitia, "Turkey Needs to Re-interpret Secularism—Senior MP," *Reuters*, October 13, 2010, www.reuters.com/article/idINIndia-52167920101013).

78. "Arinc: Sosyal hayati cezaevine cevirmeyelim," *Hurriyet*, April 25, 2006, http://hurarsiv.hurriyet.com.tr/goster/haber.aspx?id=4312365&tarih=2006-04-25.

79. AKP, "AK Parti Kalkinma ve Demokratiklesme Programi."

80. R. T. Erdogan, "Conservative Democracy and the Globalization of Freedom," in Yavuz, *Emergence of a New Turkey*, 336.

81. Ibid.

82. R. T. Erdogan, "Basini ortenlerin guvencesi laiklik," *Radikal*, October 17, 2010, www.radikal.com.tr/Radikal.aspx?aType=RadikalDetayV3&Date=&ArticleID=1024098&CategoryID=78.

83. AKP, "AK Parti Kalkinma ve Demokratiklesme Programi."

84. "Erdogan: Laiklik hayati bir oneme sahip," February 2, 2010, at www.ntvmsnbc.com/id/25053875/.

85. For Erdogan's view that "secularism is not antireligion," see "Erdogan: Laiklik ve demokrasi aractir," *Sabah*, May 16, 2007, http://arsiv.sabah.com.tr/2007/05/16/haber,1DE0E4E466C84DA58BFBB5D18F0D42D9.html.

86. Erdogan, "Conservative Democracy and the Globalization of Freedom," 336.

87. AKP, "AK Parti Kalkinma ve Demokratiklesme Programi."

88. See the interview with the speaker of Parliament, one of the three senior politicians who established the AKP, Bulent Arinc, May 5, 2006, at www.tbmm.gov.tr/develop/owa/tbmm_basin_aciklamalari_sd.aciklama?p1=34166.

89. "Erdogan: Laiklik ve demokrasi aractir."

90. Bulac, "Islam and Politics."

91. A. Bayat, "What Is Post-Islamism?" *ISIM Review* 16 (2005): 5; emphasis mine.

92. Dagi, "Rethinking Human Rights, Democracy and the West."

93. I. Dagi, "Transformation of Islamic Political Identity in Turkey: Rethinking the West and Westernization," *Turkish Studies* 6, no. 1 (2005): 30.

94. Bayat, *Making Islam Democratic*, 189.

95. Ibid., 11.

96. Hale and Ozbudun, *Islamism, Democracy and Liberalism in Turkey*, 29.

4

Islam and the Retrenchment of Turkish Conservatism

Cihan Tuğal

In the last four decades, a multistranded Islamic mobilization has shaken the secular Turkish republic. Religious intellectuals and communities, formerly props of secular center-right politics, slowly gained a voice of their own and challenged basic tenets of the system. Within the previous decade, however, they "returned" to their original hearth—the Turkish center right—while also considerably transforming it. Below, I will argue that the religious field tilted toward an "Islamism" at odds with the Turkish state from the 1970s to the 1990s but many Islamists converted to "conservatism" beginning in the late 1990s. Since much of the argument here will refer to Turkish conservatism (center-right politics), a definition is in order. Turkish conservatism is based on an acceptance of modernization (and indeed partial Westernization), but it reacts against the top-down modernization of the secular elite. Turkish conservatives propound democracy as the voice of the "real nation" against the allegedly Westernized and "alienated" elite. In this imaginary, the nation is constructed quite monolithically, as the holder of the true Turkish and Islamic values. Minorities (such as the Shia-influenced heterodox Alevis) are suspect, and they are believed to be in cahoots with the alienated elite. The piety of the citizens and (initially, less so) the rulers is at the core, but making the institutions (procedures, rules of the game, laws, etc.) more Islamic is not a priority. Individual piety is also seen as the key to success against competing nations and internal enemies. Like its Western counterparts, Turkish conservatism is in favor of private property and staunchly antisocialist. In sum, Turkish conservatism is strongly pro-development, but it sees the muting of internal differences and social opposition as a precondition of healthy change and growth.

The project dates back to the Ottoman Empire (e.g., Prince Sabahaddin's resistance to the Young Turks). Its most influential actors in recent decades were the Democrat Party (1950s), the Justice Party (1960s–1970s), and the Motherland Party (1980s). All were supported by certain religious communities. Most of these communities were of Nakshibandi (Sufi) origin, though some of them (such as the İskenderpaşa community and some of the Nurcus) had less traditional platforms than the others (such as the Menzil and İsmailağa communities). While many aspects of Turkish conservatism resonate with classical Western conservatism, there are slight differences such as the heavy role of organized and multiple religious communities (instead of a hierarchical church) in Turkish conservatism.

The "Islamist" agenda, from the 1970s onward, centered on increasing the role of religion in education, foreign policy, economic decision making, political discourse, and everyday life. Due to heavy secular laws against religious propaganda, Islamist parties (the Milli Salvation Party in the 1970s, the Welfare Party in the 1980s and 1990s) could not always voice these demands openly in their programs but propagated them through action and insinuation. For example, demanding the application of shari'a as a legal system is forbidden, but through their jurisprudence columns, Islamic newspapers (e.g., *Milli Gazete*) and magazines push people to shape their own lives according to shari'a principles (in matters ranging from divorce to inheritance). In other words, Islamism sought to reorganize the whole society and state based on religious principles, whereas in Islamic conservatism, the emphasis was on the preservation of national culture through mobilizing Islam, rather than an Islamic purification of that culture. Islamists differentiated themselves from Islamic conservatives by arguing that existing national culture had been corrupted by non-Islamic elements throughout the centuries—elements that had to be removed. Moreover, in line with Islamist departures from conservative Islam elsewhere (Ayubi 1991), Islamists organized resistance against the allegedly impious state, whereas in medieval (and later conservative) Islam, even impious rulers and state cadres were deemed legitimate to the degree that they protected unity and order within the Islamic *ummah*. Various wings of the Islamist movement were in line with Asef Bayat's (2007, 11) characterization of Islamism before the post-Islamist turn: the Islamic mobilization in Turkey emphasized duties, sought to speak with a single authoritative voice,[1] and based itself on fixed scripture (though each wing differed with respect to the true meaning of the scriptures).

Yet it is crucial that not all the Islamic communities joined the band-wagon of Islamism. *Community*, or *cemaat*, is a word used in Turkish to refer (in most cases) to Sufi groups and their offshoots. We should note that, while in some Western scholarship Sufism is counterposed against textual Islam as a representative of heterodoxy against orthodoxy (Gellner 1991), most of Ottoman and Turkish Sufism has combined elements of what has been called heterodoxy (tomb visits, reliance on intuition rather than clas-sical Islamic texts, mystic interpretations of those texts, leader cults) with orthodoxy (impersonal and strict adherence to medieval interpretations of the texts). Nakshibandis are the prime example of this, while Kadiris have also moved less consistently in this direction (and there are remarkable exceptions such as the Shia-influenced and heterodox Alevis).

Due to their large following in modern Turkey, the political positions of *cemaats* have been crucial. Among the larger, the İsmailağa commu-nity sided with the Islamists beginning from the 1970s, while the Erenköy community was on the center right. The İskenderpaşa community had a fluctuating relation with the Islamists but eventually made a decisive shift to the center right in the 1990s. Hence, sizable Sufi groups remained loyal to the secular state and the center right.

Among religious communities, some started to differentiate their posi-tions from that of the traditional Sufis, roughly from the 1950s onward. They combined tenets of mystic Islam with a systematic embrace of the natural sciences and also a somewhat rationalistic understanding of scripture. I will call these communities "post-Sufi." Post-Sufi groups (most significantly the Nurcus and Süleymancıs in Turkey) also tend to be more nationalistic and more formally organized when compared with the Sufi groups. Both the Nurcus and the Süleymancıs share roots with Sufi groups such as the Menzil, İsmailağa, Erenköy, and İskenderpaşa communities: they all trace their genealogies to the Nakshibandi tradi-tion, which differentiates itself from other Sufi traditions by its marriage of Sufi Islam and scriptualist Islam. The Nurcus and Süleymancıs have added a strong dose of modernism (especially an emphasis on science, modern education, and an embrace of the nation-state) to this synthe-sis. İsmailağa and İskenderpaşa communities are still more concerned with preserving traditional morality and relatively more scripture-focused (though unlike the Islamists they also give a lot of weight to Hadith and medieval jurisprudence).

Even the non-Islamist Sufi and post-Sufi communities wanted a more pious state and citizen, but unlike the Islamists, they did not think that this required a rupture with the mainstream of Turkish politics and society. The application of Islamic law was not one of their central concerns.

Some of these post-Sufi groups' turn to Western values predates post-Islamism. These groups have never been either Islamist or post-Islamist. If we define post-Islamism along the lines suggested by Bayat (2005)—as a project and a condition where liberty, rights, and freedom are fused with Islam, religiosity, and faith—we can see the differences more clearly. For these groups, the main goal was combining Islam not with the free spirit but with the science and power of the West. They also desired to link Islam with the power of the Turkish state and Turkish nationalism. As much as these groups were interested in making the state and its citizens more pious, they were also invested in strengthening the nation and the state against its neighbors and its internal enemies (leftists and ethnic separatists). These groups were also characterized by a cult of the leader (e.g., more puritan Islamists claim that Nurcu groups deify Said-i Nursi).

What has characterized Turkey during the previous decade (more specifically, following the anti-Islamist coup in 1997) is the ultimate religious, intellectual, and political victory of these post-Sufi communities, especially the (Nurcu) Gülen community among them, over Islamism. The changing balances within Islamic parties are a major sign of this. While the Islamist parties of the 1980s and 1990s excluded the post-Sufis and incorporated but subordinated some Sufi communities, the largest Islamic party of the 2000s (the Adalet ve Kalkınma Partisi [AKP]) comprises both the more modernist Sufi communities (e.g., Erenköy and İskenderpaşa) and the post-Sufis. As will be seen below, the ideological outlook of the AKP has merged with that of the post-Sufis, and there are speculations that especially the post-Sufi Gülen community (an offshoot of the Nurcu line) wields more power within the party than its publicly more visible ex-Islamist leaders. This signals not a gradual shift to post-Islamism but, rather, a retrenchment of Turkish conservatism.

Turkish Secularism: Nationalist, State-Controlled, and Contested

In order to have a thorough understanding of the conservative reaction to the elite and the later Islamist challenges, it is also necessary to consider the peculiar meaning that "secularism" (laiklik) has had for the Kemalist state. Between 1919 and 1923, with the defeated Ottoman Empire effectively partitioned by the entente powers, the founding wars for the Turkish republic waged by Mustafa Kemal's troops had appealed not only to the national liberation "dream" of fatherland and freedom but to the Muslim duty to resist the infidel occupation. Religious homogenization was an important constituent element of national unity, with the birth of the republic attended by the expulsion of Orthodox Greeks, as pendant to the 1915 massacres of Armenians. In short, *Turk* came to mean also "Muslim": the implicit definition of the nation was from the beginning quasi-religious. Mustafa Kemal held the Muslim title of *gazi*, warrior for the faith. The question, rather, was of the relation between religion and the state.

Secularization—as expanding state control over religion, rather than the simple removal of religion from the center of public life—had become an official project starting with the nineteenth-century Tanzimat reforms. However, there were serious conservative revisions of this tendency, most notably under Sultan Hamid (the Second). With the twentieth century, secularism became an explicitly stated and basic element of official ideology. In 1924, the founding constitution of the republic retained Islam as the state religion, even as the caliphate, fez, religious courts and schools, and so on were swept away and the Latin alphabet and Western legal code were introduced; the clause was removed in 1928. Secularization was formally enunciated as one of the six principles of the Kemalist Republican People's Party's program in 1931 and was finally incorporated into the constitution in 1937.

In the official view, rehearsed by many Western scholars, the 1924–1925 modernizations constitute categorical proof of the disestablishment of religion in Turkey.[2] With Islam removed from every official public site, this argument runs, religious sectors of the population would eventually adapt to the ruling reality and become thoroughly secularized. Others have argued, however, that the Turkish state has controlled and institutionalized Islam, rather than disestablishing it (Bromley 1994; Heper 1985; Keddie 1997; Mardin 1983). Thus the (nonelected) Directorate General of Religious Affairs exercises a monopoly power over the appointment of preachers and imams throughout the country and controls the distribution of sermons. In this view there are clear continuities between the Turkish republic and the Ottoman system, in which state and religion were deeply imbricated.

Arguably, however, Turkish secularization may best be seen as an ongoing struggle over the nature and development of an "official Islam," characterized by the public use of religion for national cohesion. Rather than reproducing some universalist (or Ottoman) logic,[3] the secularization project was continually remade, its (partially unintended) outcomes the result of a series of interventions by different social forces. This process has involved conflicts both within the ruling power bloc constituted by the reforms of the late Ottoman period and the early years of the republic and with social layers excluded from it. Since the 1930s, the dominant sectors within this bloc—the military leadership, the modernizing layers of the civil bureaucracy, an officially protected industrial bourgeoisie, and a West-oriented intelligentsia—have favored a more or less authoritarian exclusion of religion from the public sphere. The bloc's subordinate sector—conservative elements of the bureaucracy and professional middle class, an export-oriented bourgeoisie, merchants, and provincial notables—tended to advocate a larger space for Islam, albeit still under "secular" control. This could also mobilize broader popular layers—workers, peasants, artisans, the unemployed, small provincial entrepreneurs, clerics—against the dominant sector and often succeeded in extracting concessions from it. The Kemalist Republican People's Party has long been the political vehicle of the dominant, statist sector of this bloc, while the more traditionalist-religious layers have been represented by a variety of different parties since the end of single-party rule in 1950: Adnan Menderes's Democrat Party in the 1950s, Süleyman Demirel's Justice Party in the 1960s and the 1970s.

The Contested Islamist Departure from Conservatism

The rise of Islamism challenged both Kemalism and conservatism. During the early 1970s, Islamist politics had mainly been the resort of small provincial entrepreneurs, on the defensive against state-industrial policies, rising labor militancy, and rapid Westernization. It was the lack of response from the established business organizations and parties to the needs of small enterprises, facing extinction in an import-substitution economy, that led the ex-president of the Union of Chambers of Turkey, Necmettin Erbakan, to found the Milli Order Party (MNP), in 1970. As well as defending the economic interests of provincial businessmen and traders, the MNP also appealed to their religious feelings and their distaste for Western consumer culture. This stance won support from the more pious of peasant farmers and artisans, who were also attracted by Erbakan's rather sketchy program of economic development based on communally owned private enterprise, shielded and regulated by the state: Erbakan's promise of a "third/communal sector" seemed to be a barrier against the growing power of big business. Some of the religious intellectuals and communities shifted their support from the center right to this party in the course of the 1970s. There were two dynamics behind this shift: Some of the more staunchly pious communities found the center right too secular and modern; and at the other end of the spectrum, many intellectuals, publishers, and scholars (along with their students) wanted an Islamic line independent from the state. Against the communities and the state allied with the West, their motto was "Neither the East nor the West."

Closed down by the military in 1971, the MNP was refounded in 1972 as the Milli Salvation Party (MSP), with virtually no change in its program. The MSP's most significant gain during the 1970s was increased freedom of operation for the country's Imam-Hatip schools, whose graduates would provide the main activists and leaders of the Islamist movement in the coming decades. These were officially intended to educate prospective preachers (*hatips*) and prayer leaders (imams). But since it was not possible for students to observe the precepts of Islam in regular public schools, they also attracted enrollment from religious families who did not necessarily want their children to become preachers or prayer leaders. In time, this generation of Imam-Hatip graduates came to occupy important public positions, constituting a religious middle class capable of competing with the secularist intelligentsia in economic, cultural, and political realms. In a country where intellectuals had previously been equated with the Left, the emergence of this new avowedly Muslim intelligentsia would be a significant element in the construction of Islamism as a hegemonic alternative.

The 1979 Iranian Revolution came as a watershed for the Islamist movement. In the minds of many Muslims this mass upheaval, overthrowing one of the most oppressive Western-backed regimes in the region, shook the accustomed identification between Islam and obedience and redefined Islamist politics as the revolutionary struggle of the *mustazafin*—the oppressed. This was an electrifying message for the impoverished young workers streaming toward the cities in hope of jobs. Under conditions of increasing inequality, the Left was politically and ideologically absent after the 1980 military crackdown. The squatters of the neoliberal period, who encountered the consumerist wealth of the city without being able to partake of it, could look neither to the social-revolutionary option that had mobilized earlier generations nor to the hope of joining an expanding industrial working class. In this environment, a militant, socially radical Islamism had much to offer. Religious responses multiplied to fill the political vacuum, while faith-based welfare substituted for the formal social security system gutted by expenditure cuts. The MSP had been closed down by the military in 1980. When parties were once again allowed to organize in 1983, Erbakan's Welfare Party (RP) embodied this transformed Islamism.

The 1980 coup was a turning point in the state's relation to Islam. Crushing the challenge from the left, the ruling bloc also initiated a highly controlled opening to religious groups. Islamic studies were introduced as part of the national school curriculum, while the emphasis on scientific theories such as evolutionism was reduced. Certain hitherto semiclandestine religious communities were now afforded increased public visibility, under the protection of the state. In this environment, especially the (post-Sufi) Gülen and Süleymancı communities expanded and were perceived by official circles as antidotes against both the Left and the Islamists (Çakır 1990).

In the 1982 constitution drafted for the junta, the definition of "Turkishness" included unprecedented references to Islam (Parla 1995). These concessions can be seen as an attempt to contain and defuse the appeal of the Iranian Revolution and of socially radical Islamism through a "passive revolution" at home, in the classic Gramscian sense—the absorption of (possible or actual) popular demands by counterrevolutionary regimes, as a typical response to revolutions abroad. The other side of this process was the demobilization of potential revolutionary forces. Such "revolution-restoration," as Gramsci (1971, 114–120) put it in the context of post-1815 European responses to the French Revolution, kept ruling-class regimes intact while partially satisfying the popular sectors. During the 1980–1983 military dictatorship, the Turkish regime likewise took some steps toward implementing Islamist demands while defusing their insurgent potential.

Yet, while these changes were intended to consolidate rather than undermine secularization, they nevertheless opened the way to further conflict, as they increased the weight of religious sectors in a nation that defined itself as secular. If the center-right parties and pro-state religious communities were the intended beneficiaries of these reforms, Islamist circles and parties were the unintended victors. The Islamist vote rose from 8 percent in 1987 to 16 percent in 1991 and then passed 20 percent (whereas all other parties gradually came to be stuck below 20 percent).

Despite their internal tensions, the Islamists emerged as the leading party in the 1994 municipal elections, taking over the administration of most key cities. Islamist municipalities channeled more services to poorer districts and distributed free coal, food, and clothes. In contrast to the majority of Turkish politicians, united across party lines by their pursuit of the spoils of privatization, the ideological impetus of the Welfare Party had enabled it to stay clean in the post-1980 environment; simply by curtailing municipal corruption, the Islamists achieved a notable improvement in the quality of urban services.

This mounting urban challenge also had an architectural dimension. In Turkey, as throughout the Middle East, Islamist intellectuals in the 1980s were developing notions of the ideal Muslim city—centered around a mosque, further surrounded by markets, schools, and cultural centers: Architectural modesty and harmony with nature would be its defining features; urban development would respect the historical texture of the city. Buildings should reflect humility before God: high-rise developments, the very symbol of an aggressive, atheistic modernity, were to be banned. Moral propriety and a rather underspecified sociopolitical egalitarianism would flourish.[4]

The victory of Erdoğan and the RP in the 1994 metropolitan municipal elections created both panic and euphoria in the city, at the prospect that this Islamist urban imaginaire would be applied wholesale. Passionate controversy raged around a "second conquest" of Istanbul, with the Ottoman seizure of the city in 1453 as the first. Both Islamists and their opponents compared the secular inhabitants of the city center with the Christians of Byzantine times. Celebrations on the anniversaries of events in 1453, traditionally a focus for mobilizations of the political Right, became a symbol of growing Islamist strength (Bora 1999).

In fact, the Islamist intellectuals were divided over their plans for urban development, and not least in their attitudes toward the squatters. Some glorified the pious squatters as agents of retribution against the godless urban elite.[5] Others were more ambivalent, at times applauding their creative contribution to the cityscape, at others scolding them for pillaging history and nature. But an influential section of the RP leadership saw the "conquest," and prospective sidelining, of the secularist establishment as a way to integrate Istanbul more successfully with the world economy and exploit its rich Ottoman history to attract more tourists. These strategists were also less forgiving toward the squatters, whom they perceived as nomads, at odds with the urban spirit of Islam, and a potential problem for the reconquered Istanbul of the future. The egalitarianism and pro-squatter populism of earlier Islamist thinking were stripped away in this current's approach.[6]

The RP, as a pragmatic party, gave voice to all these concerns. Under Mayor Erdoğan, the Istanbul metropolitan authority tightened control on alcohol consumption, recentered Islamic symbols in public places, and introduced prayer rooms in municipal buildings (Çınar 2005). It sought, without success, to reconvert Hagia Sophia into a mosque and to build another mosque in the center of Taksim Square, Istanbul's main public space.

Islamism roused more hope and fear as it built up from urban to national victories. The Welfare Party emerged as the largest force in the general election of 1995 largely on the basis of its achievements in local government. After several months of resistance by the secularist establishment, Erbakan managed to form a coalition government with the True Path Party. Among its first acts, the Islamist-led coalition implemented the highest wage increases since 1980 and moved to limit profits on interest. In the municipalities, the RP started to organize well-publicized events to advertise its sympathy for the Palestinian struggle and for Islamic causes. Initially Erbakan signaled an intention of working toward a "global democracy" based on the cooperation of Muslim nations under Turkish leadership (Özdalga 2002). However, he soon caved in to pressure from the Turkish military elite, even signing a historic military cooperation agreement with Israel.

Other religious trends of the 1980s and 1990s were as follows: an expanding place for ritual in everyday life, especially in poorer neighborhoods; a flourishing of Islamic publishers, radio and television channels, and press; further growth of pious schools and dormitories; increasing numbers of mosques and Quranic schools; and an increasingly public struggle among Islamic groups regarding the correct definition and practice of Islam. Along with an Islamic attack on secularism, the Turkish republic thus witnessed Islamist attacks on many beliefs and practices hitherto believed to be Islamic (tomb visits, the Sufi *dhikr*, and even the Friday prayer in a secular republic!). While the post-Sufi groups participated in some of these trends, they did not join the struggle against traditional Sufi practices (though they had themselves dropped most of these practices, most notably the *dhikr*).

Erbakan also talked frequently about the need to open more Imam-Hatip schools, a particular bugbear of secularist military leaders, and hosted a prime ministerial dinner to which prominent Sufi *şeyhs* were invited. Such a gathering was a first in the history of the republic, and hard-liners interpreted it as a formal recognition of religious orders that had been banned since the early Kemalist reforms. Such were the grounds on which, in February 1997, the military once more intervened in Turkish political life, demanding that the Erbakan government restrict Imam-Hatip schools, increase obligatory secular education from five to eight years, and control religious orders. The Welfare Party proved too divided to mount an effective resistance, and the government resigned. The generals proceeded to shut down the party, banned Erbakan from political activity, and initiated another round of torture and repression, though not on the scale of the 1980s. At this stage, too, the military undertook a thorough purging of Islamists from its ranks.

After the crisis of 1997–1998, the Islamists initially regrouped as the Virtue Party, which was likewise kept under close scrutiny by the authorities. But they could now hope to gain some external backing from the European Union, which by this stage was funding extensive networks of human rights and civil society NGOs in Turkey; the country would be granted candidate status for accession in December 1999.[7] The Islamists toned down their criticism of the establishment, but they also ventured to put up a head-scarfed woman as a parliamentary candidate. The ban on the head scarf in government buildings was a linchpin of Turkish secularization, and though the Welfare Party had frequently hinted that it should be rescinded, it had never dared to take such a major step while in office. Now its ideologues started to reframe the veil as a matter of human rights, rather than of religious obligation, in the expectation that the EU would intervene on their behalf. In the short term, their tactics backfired. Merve Kavakçı, the head-scarfed deputy, had to leave the Meclis before she could be sworn in, as the secular-establishment parties forgot their old quarrels to unite in violent condemnation of the "intruder."

The Long Way Home: Return to the Conservative Nation

This changing balance of forces was a crucial determinant in the Islamists' shift toward a thoroughgoing Americanization. The term is used here to mean not only political support for Washington and the global capitalist order but a much broader allegiance to American economic, social, and religious models. If the first two of these have always been dear to the establishment elite in Turkey, the Islamists' breakthrough would lie in naturalizing a new version of all three of them among much broader layers.

After the crisis of 1997, when it became clear that larger concessions were necessary to win the toleration of the ruling elite, a new generation of Islamists began to challenge Erbakan's leadership. In the late 1980s and early 1990s, this generational conflict had been expressed as a clash between ardent young radicals and a more conservative mainstream. The youth had become avid readers of (the Egyptian thinker) Sayyid Qutb and (the Iranian thinker) Ali Shariati, shifting the discourse in a more revolutionary direction and partially reducing the influence of the relatively more party-sanctioned (Pakistani thinker) Mawlana Mawdudi. Though intellectually not as deep and sustained, similar radical ideas were voiced by Turkish figures such as İsmet Özel. All of the authors above envisioned an Islamic society and state entirely different from secular, democratic capitalism, though there were also differences among them (with Shariati propounding a more egalitarian order and Mawdudi remaining loyal to free private property; Qutb was in between the two).

After 1997, the former radicals were quick to adopt a free market, "moderate Muslim" position. Prominent among them were R. Tayyip Erdoğan, Abdullah Gül, and Bülent Arınç, all of them differentiated from the old guard by their professionalism, media savvy, and attentiveness to the pro-business agenda. Erdoğan, though his family was from the city of Rize in the Black Sea region, was born in Istanbul in 1957 and raised in the rundown neighborhood of Kasımpaşa, where he attended an Imam-Hatip school. A university graduate and soccer player, he honed his charisma during years of grassroots work as an activist and organizer. Gül is from Kayseri, a Central Anatolian city closely integrated with global markets. Born in 1950, he received a Ph.D. from an Istanbul university in 1983 and studied in England. He was an economist at the Islamic Development Bank until 1991, when he became a full-time politician. Arınç, a lawyer, was born in 1948 in Bursa, a conservative city in the industrial Marmara region, and has been politically active since his youth. Arınç retained links with his old Islamist party, while Gül served as a bridge between the Islamists and international business, Turkey's ruling elite, and the liberal intelligentsia. This new generation of political entrepreneurs was far more receptive to cooperation with the West.

These top political leaders, operating still in a secular legal framework with restrictions on the explicit politicization of religion, did not explicate the theological basis for their change of heart. However, among the former radical intellectuals, attention was shifting from Qutb, Mawdudi, and Shariati to Abdulkarim Soroush and Muhammad al-Jabiri. Their more liberal Islamic theologies, which reject not only the viability but even the idea of an "Islamic state," started to dominate public debate. At the same time, journalists (such as Abdurrahman Dilipak) and religious scholars (such as Hayrettin Karaman), known for their arguments about the distinctiveness and superiority of Islamic political structures and states, started to say that democracy was the closest political structure to Islamic ideals under the existing conditions. Even though most theological debates centered around the legitimation of democracy, secondary debates about the desirability of coexistence with other religions (rather than struggle or war with them), the need to promote the Turkish state's strength (indeed an old conservative theme), and the necessity of working with Western states (while at the same time opening up to the Islamic world) were also commonplaces in this decade. These theological shifts were not articulated by the party leaders but, rather, by journalists in the AKP-connected newspapers *Yeni Şafak* and *Vakit* (later *Akit*) and partially in the party booklet *Conservative Democracy*.

While some hard-liners interpreted these changes as selling out (as voiced by the newspaper *Milli Gazete*), most interpreted them in two different (sometimes overlapping) ways. The publicly available line was that the old goal of a completely different Islamic order was unrealistic and the pious had to adjust to the realities of Turkey and the world. Another line, mostly circulated among activists rather than announced to the larger public, was that the goal was intact but the leaders had discovered longer-term and more roundabout ways of realizing it, adjusting their strategies to the realities of Turkey and the modern world. In my extended ethnography of a formerly radical Islamic region within Istanbul (Tuğal 2009), I found that people could shift quite often between these positions, or sometimes even combine them, in a far-from-consistent fashion. The straight and uncompromising rejection of these shifts remained restricted to a minority.

Thus a new alignment emerged from the seeming impasse of 1997. It had become clear that the ideological differences among the Islamists were too sharp to be contained within a single party. There were insoluble tensions between the liberalizing business wing and those who wanted to stick to old-style Islamism. The authoritarian structure of the party did not allow aspiring young activists to have a say in decision making. In 2001 the rebels established their own organization, the Justice and Development Party (or AKP), having failed to take over the existing structures at a major party congress. Erdoğan and the other AKP leaders moved quickly to reassure the military and media establishments that religion would not be used for political purposes and that the AKP would not challenge the head scarf ban. They were also vociferously pro-European. They made frequent trips to the United States, holding meetings whose agendas have remained private. Gül helpfully explained to an American audience that the members of the AKP were "the WASPs of Turkey." It was clear that the new leadership was trying to reclaim the territory of the center right in Turkish politics—in effect, to reconstitute an updated version of that alliance of provincial businessmen, religious intellectuals, and the state elite at which the subordinate fraction of the ruling power bloc had traditionally aimed but which had become impossible with the rise of radical Islamism. Now, this alliance could also offer to strengthen the hand of the neoliberal and export-oriented sectors of Turkish capital. Large numbers of center-right politicians, intellectuals, and supporters soon swelled its ranks.

The AKP named its new platform "conservative democracy," and *Islamism* became an unwanted word. The word was already anathema to Islamic conservatives in the 1990s and before, whom secular discourse lumped with Islamists under categories such as "religionist," "Islamist," and "reactionary"; Islamists did not like being grouped with conservatives either.

The appeal of the AKP to liberals and intellectuals in 2002 rested primarily on its pro-democratic, pro-European stance. Yet, on democratization, the party has never demonstrated more than a pro forma commitment. Erdoğan is well known for his authoritarian tendencies, and as the can-do mayor of Istanbul between 1994 and 1998 he ruled with an iron fist.[8] At the AKP founding congress, its leadership had pledged itself to a regime of internal party democracy, but initial moves in this direction were soon overturned. In 2003, the AKP's Board of Founders annulled internal elections to the Central Committee and invested the party president, Erdoğan, with sole authority to appoint or dismiss members of the Central Committee. These authoritarian moves had their counterparts in the relation of the party to the people. While Erdoğan's government legislated a series of democratic reforms at the instigation of the EU, it also disregarded the most basic norms of representativity and accountability with regard to its electorate. Rather than taking popular grievances seriously, Erdoğan publicly scolded anybody who talked to him about hunger, unemployment, or housing problems. At party rallies he has told the poor to pull themselves together and do something for themselves, instead of expecting the government to do it for them. Recently, in May 2010, he told the families of the victims of a mining accident that the suffering of miners is an inseparable part of their job, indeed their "fate"!

Erdoğan has likewise blamed flood and earthquake victims in a couple of poverty-stricken areas of being responsible for their plight (as they had picked dangerous locations for and used low-quality construction material in their buildings) and denied official responsibility in the face of social protest (which followed these events). When his proclamations about "fate" (regarding the mining accident in 2010) roused criticism in the press, the prime minister questioned the faith of his critics (as they had objected to his argument that this accident was a part of fate). He told them to discuss the matter with the Directorate General of Religious Affairs. In other words, Erdoğan manipulated religious discourse to shut off public debate about the mining industry.

In short, Erdoğan resorts to three weapons in fighting social protest: the theme of individual responsibility, an authoritarian personalistic style, and the instrumentalization of religion. This combination of authoritarianism, individualism, and traditional religion is a far cry from the post-Islamist reinterpretation of religion along the lines of individual freedom rather than individual duty. The new Turkish conservatism, in other words, exemplifies not a shift from duty to rights (the post-Islamist transformation) but a shift from the communalistic understanding of responsibility (characteristic of Islamism) to individual responsibility.

A further test of democratization—and another stumbling block for EU entry—is the official approach to the Armenian massacres of 1915. The military elite has always denied any responsibility for these killings, and it is a criminal offense to say that they constituted genocide. In 2005, with expectations of democratization rising, an international group of scholars attempted to organize a conference at which the genocide thesis could be openly debated. AKP Interior Minister Cemil Çiçek reacted by saying that the conference organizers were "stabbing the nation in the back." The scholars first called the meeting off and then moved it to a different university. While holding such a gathering would probably have been harder, if not impossible, under any previous government, the incident was a stark reminder of the nationalist-authoritarian tendency within the AKP, of which Çiçek is a leading figure.

Some analysts perceive demilitarization and the government's position on the Kurds as proofs of its allegiance to democracy. But even here the blessings have been mixed. During the course of the famous Ergenekon case, the pro-government prosecutors and journalists have courageously attacked some murderous groups within the state. However, a lot of opposition figures (at best) loosely or ideologically connected to these murderous groups have also been imprisoned. Moreover, any opposition to the government has been labeled publicly as "pro-Ergenekon" without any proof (such as a major strike in 2010 by Tekel workers who lost their rights as a result of privatization). On the one hand, ethnically oppressive laws were rescinded. On the other hand, the courts and security forces have ratcheted up the pressure against legal Kurdish parties and associations, alleging that they have ties to the illegal guerilla. Even children are put on trial for participating in demonstrations organized by legal Kurdish parties. While secular and religious liberals have celebrated the Ergenekon and Kurdish processes, critics (Kemalists, secular-nationalist Kurds, and socialists, now all losing their ranks to an expanding pro-AKP liberal intelligentsia) have raised the suspicion that the AKP is democratic only to the extent that it benefits the party. One can probably take a more cool-headed stance than both camps and argue that the AKP has strengthened democracy within the framework of Turkish conservatism: a democracy that is designed to reflect the "true" culture and morality of the nation and thus marginalize (if not purge) the (perceived) enemies of the nation.[9]

Just like the Islamist challenge had a spatial dimension in its heyday, so does the absorption of Islamism into Turkish conservatism. Even before 1997, Mayor Erdoğan had been using Istanbul's religious heritage as a means of attracting global capital and tourism, rather than as the basis for an Islamic republic. The process accelerated after 2002, when the former Islamists began championing the construction of skyscrapers in the city's new financial center. More importantly, in contrast to the protests that greeted Dalan's pro-corporate mayoralty, the Islamic free market conservatives succeeded in further integrating Istanbul into the circuits of global capital without mobilizing opposition in the sprawling squatter neighborhoods that ringed the city. This was the urban-spatial dimension of Turkey's passive revolution: absorbing the challenge of Islamism into free market Atlanticism. The pious Muslims of the AKP—who now held that they were no longer Islamists but, rather, conservatives—would henceforth mobilize religion to reconstruct the city in ways that contradicted their earlier radical aspirations.

The market-oriented turn in the Islamization of the city has many expressions. During the 1990s, fast-breaking tents for the poor during the month of Ramadan were a symbol of Islamism's rising political challenge.

They signaled both the impoverishment of the masses under the rule of the "secular" elite and the existence of a god-fearing material alternative. Increasingly, however, fast-breaking tents have become sites of collective consumption. The AKP-controlled municipalities began to organize nightly Ramadan festivities that went on till daybreak, where people of all classes would go to enjoy Sufi music (along with pop and rock), narghile, stand-up shows, and a wide variety of food. While some of this was free, merchants and shopkeepers also participated on a cash basis. Muslim tourists came from all over the region, especially to the historic mosques in Sultanahmet and Eyüp, boosting the "world city" image. There is a certain irony here: in the 1990s, Islamist newspapers used to contrast their puritanical Ramadan to the consumer-oriented fast-breaking of wealthy secularized Muslims, with their expensive feasts. Now the sectors have merged, thanks to the passive revolution, which has assimilated the month of fasting into the sphere of public entertainment.

"Ottomanization" has been another theme. Superficially, this celebration of the age of the caliphate may seem in line with the Islamist urban imaginaire; yet, rather than preserve the historical fabric of the city, the current AKP metropolitan municipality seems set on pulling down the original Ottoman buildings and reconstructing ersatz versions. It is secularists, rather than Islamists, who are now resisting such redevelopments, accusing the municipality of wanting to re-create the historic center of Istanbul in glossy tourist fashion. Similarly, in commemoration of the Ottoman "Tulip era" of the 1720s, the AKP has taken to decorating the city with the flowers. This was an act of defiance against the anti-Ottoman puritanism of Kemalist ideology, which has traditionally attacked the import of expensive tulip bulbs as a sign of the sultanate's degeneracy. The period involved a precocious experiment with petty industrialization, the printing press, and the aestheticization of art and architecture. It was brought to an incendiary end in 1730 by a popular rebellion against aristocratic ostentation, led by the ex-janissary, secondhand clothes dealer Patrona Halil: The palaces were pillaged, and leading modernizers were killed.[10] The AKP's current tulip mania not only celebrates the Ottoman reformers—and their luxurious excesses—but also signifies, through the overflow of tulips from the upper-class neighborhoods to the squatter districts, that conspicuous consumption is now for the enjoyment of all. The garish illumination of the Bosphorus Bridge, attacked by angry Kemalists as "nightclub"—*pavyon*—lighting, also signals the political will to make ostentation available to all, breaking the bourgeoisie's monopoly. Such a strategy is intended to ensure that there will be no Patrona Halils in the republic's "Tulip era."

A more transnational arena where consumerism and Islam (rather than freedom and Islam, as in post-Islamism) are fused is the latest Umrah "fashion." In the Turkish elite secular perception, Hajj and Umrah have been coded as signs of backwardness, the reproduction of unnecessary relations with the Arab world, and so on. This perception is now being turned on its head, as members of the elite (including businesspeople, popular singers, and top secularist journalists) go on the Umrah. One journalist (Ertuğrul Özkök) wrote extensively about his experiences, normalizing this trip and introducing it to the elite mainstream. In public discourse, this tendency is explicitly dubbed as "Umrah fashion," indicating the element of elite distinction that has accompanied the normalization of this Islamic ritual.

Post-Sufis: From Foe to Friend

One of the most significant religious changes in Turkey is the shifting status of a post-Sufi community. The Gülen community (arguably the largest Islamic community in Turkey) was a frequent target of attack before the coup in 1997. Islamists perceived the community as an ally of the Turkish and American states. In the 2000s, the community became not only a necessary ally against an oppressive secularism but also a quite respected member of the now expanded Turkish/Islamic/conservative camp.

The Gülen community is based on some of the central themes of the Said-i Nursi line, including a scientific (some would say positivistic)[11] understanding of Islam, a silent (rather than armed and public) struggle against the Left, support for the center right (rather than an independent Islamic political party), a synthesis of the Sufi and textualistic elements of Islam, and an overall strategy that focuses (at least publicly) on Islamicizing the individual rather than the state. However, this community has significantly shifted more toward the center when compared with other Nurcu groups, especially by supporting cooperation between Turkey and the West and dialogue among religions. The community is Turkish nationalist. The schools they build all over the world emphasize Turkification more than Islamization. Central Asia is one of the central loci of activity, and some speculate that the community has the West's blessing (since Russia, China, and Iran, along with Sunni Islamic radicals, are the other major players in this region). Covering is not one of the priorities of the community, but some have commented that in all other issues pertaining to gender, its internal relations are quite patriarchal (Turam 2007). The public discourse of the community (as voiced by quite powerful media channels such as the newspaper *Zaman* and the television channel Samanyolu) is not based heavily on Islamic references but, rather, seeks to instill national pride, a mainstream and pragmatic foreign policy vision, and a stance against authoritarian secularism. However, the internal structure is quite complex, and as one moves toward the inner circles (which are less and less public), the importance of Islamic culture increases. Finally, the key word in the Gülen community is not *freedom* but *responsibility*—resonating with Islamist duty but also contrasting with it, as its understanding of responsibility is more individualist and market-oriented. In all these senses, the community is Islamically conservative and nationalist, rather than Islamist or post-Islamist.

Despite its centrist and nationalist tendencies, the Kemalists see the Gülen community as one of the major threats against secularism: they argue that they have a stealth agenda of building a caliphate-like and extremely conservative state in Turkey. These fears are supported by the growing numbers of Gülen supporters in some key state institutions (e.g., the police and the judiciary) and the community's opaque internal structure and apparently unquestioning allegiance to its leader (Fethullah Gülen).

Before 1997, relations between Islamists in Turkey and the community were not only conflict- but also sometimes violence-ridden, as Islamists struggled to save the youth from Gülen's pro-Western understanding of Islam. In other words, Islamists' perception used to be the opposite of the Kemalists' (Gülen as a barrier to Islamization). In the 1980s and 1990s, conservative sectors of the state marketed the Gülen community (along with another post-Sufi community, the Süleymancıs) as antidotes to Islamism, both in Turkey and in other parts of the world. Up until the 1999 elections, the Gülen community publicly supported center-right (and once, center-left-nationalist) parties and openly attacked Islamists (e.g., Gülen verbally attacked the Islamist mobilization for the legalization of the veil on university campuses). As a parallel to these tendencies, the community was on good terms with the military. It welcomed the military coup in 1980 and (in oblique fashion) the 1997 military intervention against Islamic groups and parties (though it eventually fell victim to the latter intervention).

After 1997, not all Islamists became members of this community, but they started to declare that it has a more realistic Islamic agenda than old-style Islamism. Key to this turn was the purge of Gülen followers from the army in the aftermath of the 1997 secularist coup. Gülen emigrated to the United States after the coup, reinforcing his image as a victim of rigid secularism. Today he lives in Pennsylvania and aims to build a bridge between the Islamic world and Washington, based on dozens of quite influential NGOs inspired by his reinterpretation of Islam. In Turkey too, the community's influence was restored after the AKP came to power in 2002. In this process, the tone of the Islamist press gradually switched from critique to praise and admiration. The Gülen community is now perceived as an unquestionable member of the Islamic camp against the Kemalists. It should also be noted that the relation between the AKP and the community goes beyond a simple alliance and (despite many lingering tensions) at times resembles a merger, as many Gülen followers are now AKP members and leaders.

Post-Islamism or Absorption of Islamism?

How should we interpret these changes? I will here advance the thesis that we are witnessing the absorption of Islamism into a conservative project, rather than the flowering of a full-fledged post-Islamism. I base this claim on the AKP's relations to secularism, liberty, ambiguity, and plurality. However, as will be seen below, one could still argue that there are elements of post-Islamism within the AKP's line, due to Islamism's thorough transformation of Turkish conservatism.

While post-Islamism implies the secularization of the state paralleled by the maintenance of religious ethics, a further Islamicized conservatism implies the instrumentalization of religion and possibly even a partial decline in religious ethics. There are quite contradictory trends in Turkey regarding individual piety and ethics. One encounters less ethics and piety among former activists. This actually gives rise to many internal criticisms, with some pious journalists criticizing their comrades and lamenting how unethical they have become. One common trope used in religious publications to characterize this trend is *dünyevileşme* (this-worldization), which refers to the turn of former militants from an obsession with religion to a growing obsession with money, luxurious consumption, upward mobility, and career. At the same time, however, pious lifestyles have started to spread among some formerly secularized sectors. While formerly marginal and radical activists are becoming more secular, elite and visible individuals are becoming more religious.

Moreover, in a post-Islamist condition, public debates revolve around how to reconcile Islam with liberty. In present-day Turkey, debates and political struggles, rather, revolve around how to reconcile Turkish/ Islamic culture with certain Western values, where the main model is an American-type conservatism rather than the more freedom-oriented values of the West. The outstanding overlap with American conservatism is the emphasis on individual responsibility in a market society. In a related fashion, whereas ambiguity is a basic tenet of post-Islamism, there is only *some* ambiguity in current Turkish Islamo-conservatism. The project is, rather, marked by certain characteristics imagined to be fixed. More specifically, what is less ambiguous in American conservatism and the Turkish/ Islamic synthesis is also less ambiguous in Turkish Islamo-conservatism. Examples include obedience to the leader, the value of national unity, and the centrality of Turkish/Islamic values to a united society and state.

Finally, whereas post-Islamism comes with plurality, there are serious limits to the pluralism of the new Turkish conservative project. Certainly, Turkish Islamo-conservatism is more pluralistic than the Islamism of the 1970s. However, certain sectors are firmly excluded from its seemingly all-accepting embrace. These sectors partially overlap with the sectors excluded from the American conservative project (e.g., organized labor), but there are also Turkish specificities (e.g., the exclusion of Alevis, despite apparent calls of inclusion, which Alevis of different stripes find insincere).

However, despite these tendencies of assimilation into conservatism, Islamism has also influenced the Turkish conservative project. First and most important, piety is now defined more rigorously. While older conservatives were content with rulers who performed their Friday prayers and some of their other daily prayers, now there is more public scrutiny regarding regular prayer. Some provincial center-right leaders used to consume a small amount of alcohol, though they also performed their religious duties. Now, it is out of the question for most provincial leaders to consume alcohol. However, it is dubious whether the making of this new political elite is an Islamicization of modernity or the pacification of potential threats to secularism.

Two other spheres—international relations and new business sectors— provide further potential basis for thinking that Turkey might be shifting to a post-Islamist atmosphere. In the sphere of international relations, it is questionable whether Turkish foreign policy has taken an Islamic turn. But certainly, it is understood and legitimized in Islamic terms among

some sectors. Under Ahmet Davutoğlu's intellectual and political leadership, and with considerable probing from Washington and the EU in
search of a "moderate Islamic" alternative to Tehran, Ankara has opened
up to its neighbors. These neighbors were seen by earlier administrations
as backward and useless, if not hostile to Turkish interests. Some argue
that this is a realistic shift in foreign policy rather than an Islamic one. But
inside and outside Turkey, the governing party's Islamic roots, as well as
Davutoğlu's reputation as an Islamic thinker, are taken as proof of Islamic
motivation. In the coming years, the AKP's ongoing revision of Turkey's
relations with Israel will provide further material to test this claim.

The growing power of the pious business class is also in the same
gray area. There is real, public excitement regarding the new businesspeople of Anatolia, who look different and presumably act different from
the established businessmen and -women of the big cities. Yet it is still
open to question whether this class constitutes an enactor of an authentic
and/or alternative modernity or a local parallel of the global pious rebellion against the secular and regulated bourgeoisie (and bureaucracy), the
prime example of which rebellion is the conservative American business
class. Of course, this comparison by no means renders the Turkish pious
business class "less real," but only casts a shadow on its originality or
distinctive Islamicness.

What are the causes of Turkey's differences from Iran, where there is
a more distinctly post-Islamist current? Answering this question would
require a long discussion. The present chapter will conclude only with
a suggestion based on Bayat's work. Bayat has pointed out that the reason post-Islamism has gained a lot of ground in Iran while remaining
restricted in Egypt is the difference between the political trajectories of
these two countries. Iran went through a revolution, despite the lack of a
sustained and organized Islamic movement for decades. Egypt, by contrast, had witnessed a sustained and organized Islamic movement but
no Islamic revolution, at least at the time of Bayat's initial statement of
the post-Islamism thesis. The revolution in Iran caused disenchantment,
which was one of the reasons for shifts to post-Islamism (Bayat 2007,
191). Turkey, however, has neither gone through a revolution nor experienced a sustained revolutionary uprising. The revolutionary Islamists
either made their presence felt by putting pressure on the mainstream
Islamist party or remained outside the major political conflicts. Islamism
did constitute a challenge to the state and market in the 1980s and 1990s,
but this never turned into a well-coordinated and full-scale Islamization

of the state and society. For a full understanding of the weakness of post-Islamism in Turkey, it seems, one would have to turn to political processes.

References Cited

Armağan, Mustafa. 1997. *Şehir, ey Şehir*. Istanbul: İz Yayıncılık.

Ayubi, Nazih. 1991. *Political Islam: Religion and Politics in the Arab World*. New York: Routledge.

Bayat, Asef. 2005. "What Is Post-Islamism?" *ISIM Review* 16, no. 5.

Bayat, Asef. 2007. *Making Islam Democratic: Social Movements and the Post-Islamist Turn*. Stanford: Stanford University Press.

Bora, Tanıl. 1999. "Istanbul of the Conqueror: The 'Alternative Global City' Dreams of Political Islam." In *Istanbul between the Global and the Local*, ed. Çağlar Keyder, 47–58. Lanham, Md.: Rowman and Littlefield.

Bromley, Simon. 1994. *Rethinking Middle East Politics: State Formation and Development*. Cambridge: Polity.

Çakır, Ruşen. 1990. *Ayet ve Slogan: Türkiye'de İslami Oluşumlar*. Istanbul: Metis.

Cansever, Turgut. 1997. *Kubbeyi Yeri Koymamak*. Istanbul: İz Yayıncılık.

Çınar, Alev. 2005. *Modernity, Islam, and Secularism in Turkey: Bodies, Places, and Time*. Minneapolis: University of Minnesota Press.

Davison, Andrew. 1998. *Secularism and Revivalism in Turkey: A Hermeneutic Reconsideration*. New Haven: Yale University Press.

Freely, John. 1998. *Istanbul: The Imperial City*. London: Penguin.

Gellner, Ernest. 1991. "Civil Society in Historical Context." *International Social Science Journal* 43:495–510.

Göçek, F. Müge. 1987. *East Encounters West: France and the Ottoman Empire in the Eighteenth Century*. New York: Oxford University Press.

Gramsci, Antonio. 1971. *Selections from the Prison Notebooks of Antonio Gramsci*. London: Lawrence and Wishart.

Heper, Metin. 1985. *The State Tradition in Turkey*. Huntingdon: Eothen Press.

Keddie, Nikki R. 1997. "Secularism and the State: Towards Clarity and Global Comparison." *New Left Review* 1, no. 226: 30–32.

Keyder, Çağlar. 2004. "The Turkish Bell-Jar." *New Left Review* 28:65–84.

Kutlu, Mustafa. 1995. *Şehir Mektupları*. Istanbul: Dergah.

Lerner, Daniel. 1967. *The Passing of Traditional Society: Modernizing the Middle East*. New York: Free Press.

Lewis, Bernard. 1961. *The Emergence of Modern Turkey*. New York: Oxford University Press.

Mardin, Şerif. 1983. "Religion and Politics in Modern Turkey." In *Islam and the Political Process*, ed. James Piscatori, 138–159. Cambridge: Royal Institute of International Affairs.

Mardin, Şerif. 1989. *Religion and Social Change in Modern Turkey: The Case of Bediüzzaman Said Nursi.* Albany: State University of New York Press.

Özdalga, Elizabeth. 2002. "Necmettin Erbakan: Democracy for the Sake of Power." In *Political Leaders and Democracy in Turkey,* ed. Metin Heper and Sabri Sayarı, 127–146. New York: Lexington Books.

Özdenören, Rasim. 1998. *Kent İlişkileri.* Istanbul: İz Yayıncılık.

Özyol, İdris. 1999. *Lanetli Sınıf.* Istanbul: Birey Yayıncılık.

Parla, Taha. 1995. *Türkiye'nin Siyasal Rejimi.* Istanbul: İletişim.

Sezal, İhsan. 1992. *Şehirleşme.* Istanbul: Ağaç Yayıncılık.

Tuğal, Cihan. 2006. "The Appeal of Islamic Politics: Ritual and Dialogue in a Poor District of Turkey." *Sociological Quarterly* 47, no. 2: 245–273.

Tuğal, Cihan. 2009. *Passive Revolution: Absorbing the Islamic Challenge to Capitalism.* Stanford: Stanford University Press.

Turam, Berna. 2007. *Between Islam and the State: The Politics of Engagement.* Stanford: Stanford University Press.

Notes

Parts of this chapter were published in the *New Left Review* 44 (2007): 5–34 and 51 (2008): 65–80.

1. However, there was always competition among Islamic groups about who should ultimately be the single voice, and therefore there was a field of Islamic voices rather than one single Islamic authority (Tuğal 2006).

2. The Western versions include Lerner 1967 and Lewis 1961.

3. Andrew Davison (1998) has argued against both accounts (the "establishment" perspective and the "control" perspective) by stating that separation and control were not two conflicting goals in the minds of the Turkish modernizers. Assuming that secularist policies constituted a coherent world of meaning, he has carried out a hermeneutic reading of them. More particularly, he contends that Kemalists enacted separation between religion and education, and religion and legal codes, in a way that would expand their control over society. The separation of religion and politics and the privatization of religion allowed them to eliminate opposition at home and legitimate the new republic as a Westernizing country abroad. While Davison presents a rather complex account, his resolution in framing the balance between separation and control as internally coherent poses some problems. I contend here that we would have a better grasp of the complexity and dynamism of Turkish secularization if we approach it via dialogical, rather than hermeneutic, tools, to decipher the multiplicity of voices and conflicts, which with hindsight sometimes seem to blend into a logical whole, a total "culture."

4. For the best exemplars, see Armağan 1997; Cansever 1997; Özdenören 1998.

5. For this populist line, see Özyol 1999.

6. These views are voiced in Kutlu 1995; Sezal 1992.

7. For more details of EU involvement in Turkey, see Keyder 2004, 78.

8. Mehmet Metiner, "Dünden Bugüne Tayyip Erdoğan," *Radikal İki*, July 6, 2003.

9. This chapter was finalized in December 2010. Ever since, the AKP became (or appears to have become) much more Islamist within the boundaries of its conservative framework (e.g., it has expanded religious education and intensified the regulation of alcohol). Also, the tensions between its leaders and Gülen (alluded to at the end of this chapter) have become more public. Such developments have led to a decline in liberal and intellectual support for the party, as these sectors were more comfortable with a more Gülen-type conservatism (though the liberals' own public rationalization of muted support is framed in terms of the party's weakened commitment to democracy and the EU process, rather than a change in its religio-political position).

10. Halil controlled the city for a while, after which the sultan massacred seven thousand janissaries along with him (Freely 1998, 252–253). On Western impact during the Tulip era, see Göçek 1987.

11. For the argument that Said interpreted Islam in a positivist way, see Mardin 1989.

5

Moroccan Post-Islamism:

EMERGING TREND OR CHIMERA?

Sami Zemni

Since 9/11, the debate on the nature of Islamist movements and on the presumed essence of Islam has loomed large in academic as well as public contexts. It has become obvious that "the nature of the relationship between the West and political Islam" is not solely restricted to questions of political and sociocultural change in the Arab and/or Islamic world; it has also "become a defining issue for foreign policy."[1] There is indeed an emerging "Islamist question" arising within Western public debate, in which both public intellectuals and scholars intervene, referring to whether Islamic politics and Islamist parties are ready to play a democratic role in the political arena. This question is the topic of frequent, passionate debates between believers and nonbelievers, between those who see Islamist movements as a potent force for the modernization and democratization of the Arab world[2] and those who see in them an Islamic brand of fascism that will capture power democratically, only to cancel democracy afterward.[3]

There are two main problems with these debates. First, they tend to be very ideological and normative, as they are abstracted from actually existing Islamic movements and focused on unearthing essences. As Asef Bayat has rightly pointed out,[4] asking the question of whether Islam and democracy are actually compatible is less interesting than asking the question about under which conditions Muslims can make them compatible. Second, the Islamist question in European and U.S. debates is more reflective of our own obsession with all things Islamic, rather than a conscious and honest analysis of what happens on the ground. The debates on Islamism (and more and more on Islam in general) are flawed in the sense that they start from essentialist positions and have much more to do with Western material interests, changing ideological and political fault lines within Western polities, and difficulties in dealing with issues of migration and integration.

This chapter will take a much more pragmatic and academic stance toward the issue. Instead of positing any a priori assumption of what Islamist parties are or are not, what they can or cannot become, I will focus on what these movements have done in the past and do today, that is, how these movements evolved and changed over time. As Islamist ideology, abstracted from its concrete practicalities, has always been a poor predictor of political behavior, I will analyze the changing Moroccan Islamist political landscape, capturing its dynamic and depicting its evolutions. To understand the ideological changes as well as the strategic options of the different movements, it is necessary to take into account the contextual limits of mobilization and participation, as well as the regional and global environment in which the movements operate. Looking into the internal ideological debates of the movements should also be reflective of the wider sociological evolutions (generational divide, urbanization, communication, etc.) of society as well as take into account the relationships among the different Islamic movements. Morocco, with its "Commander of the Faithful," has a rich political scene and a diverse landscape of parties, movements, and trends. The Islamist trend is fragmented over various parties and movements, reflecting different conceptions of the relationship between politics and religion, divergent strategic and tactical options, and dissimilar goals and aims. Furthermore, Moroccan Islamist movements have—like their counterparts elsewhere—evolved and changed, influenced as they were by internal changes (ideological shifts) and shifting local sociological realities (generational impact of membership changes, urbanization, modernization), as well as external influences. In other words; Islamist movements interact with the environment in which they thrive.

The aim of this contribution is not to rewrite the history of Moroccan Islamism, as others have done so in a much more detailed and nuanced fashion,[5] but, rather, to think about the modalities of change affecting Moroccan Islamism. I will try to conceptualize this change against the backdrop of larger debates on the relation between Islam and politics. More specifically, I will interrogate the notion of post-Islamism as a possible conceptual tool to broaden our understanding of political movements referring to Islam.

From Islamism to Post-Islamism?

Ever since the 1979 Iranian Revolution, an abundant literature on Islamism has emerged that has produced as many valuable insights as contradictory

analyses. As the amount of factual knowledge and data on Islamic movements and organizations grew, more systematic analyses ensued, and
attempts at theory-building emerged. Social theories try to condense and
organize knowledge about the world in a system of interconnected abstrac-
tions; it became clear that the elementary building blocks of the theories,
that is, the concepts used to define and describe the phenomena under
scrutiny, were ambiguous. What in fact is Islamism? Or should we talk
about political Islam? Or what about Islamic fundamentalism, Islamic
resurgence, or Islamic revival?[6]

Raising the question of concepts and their definition is not just a matter of theoretical debates in the "ivory tower" of academia. On the contrary,
I see it as a necessary venture both for understanding scientifically the
phenomena under scrutiny and for the dissemination of more coherent
knowledge to a larger public. There is still a need to drain the swamp
of analytical confusion, as Guilain Denoeux suggested ten years ago.[7]
This undertaking has become all the more important (and interesting,
one could add) because of the growing reflexivity of the movements and
persons under scrutiny. Different Islamic parties, movements, and per-
sons have regularly rejected the label—constructed and defined mainly
by outsiders—they have been given. On numerous occasions, Saad Eddin
al-Othmani, former secretary-general of the Moroccan Parti de la Justice et
du Développement, has refused the appellation of "Islamist party," favoring instead the more vague "party with an Islamic reference."[8]

In order to be able to speak about what *post-Islamism* can come to designate, it is necessary to flesh out what exactly I mean by *Islamism*. I define
Islamism as an ideology that strives to appropriate the political space through
the mobilization of religious (Islamic) resources and modes of social action
ranging from the *da'wa* (predication) to the jihad (violence, terrorism) through
which certain social groups manifest their desire to control the state or to
overthrow or oppose the state and to install an order that is called "Islamic."[9]
Central to the practice of Islamist ideology—and its distinguishing feature
from the religion of Islam—is the question of politics. Islamism conflates
the question of the political order (its legitimacy and organization) with a
(partially reinvented) theological interpretation of Islam. Whether coined in
terms of the caliphate, the imamate, or the Islamic state, the question of a
polity ordered by and based on Islamic Law (shari'a) runs central to the ideology. The advantage of this definition is that it can easily accommodate the
notion of transformation and change in Islamist movements, as groups can
(and have) changed their ideology, program, strategy, and tactics.

Post-Islamism, then, comes to refer to something that is different from and beyond Islamism; it has come to denote several different things. While the term was first used by Asef Bayat in his 1996 seminal essay "The Coming of a Post-Islamist Society,"[10] the term grew to prominence especially in French academic debates after the publication of a special issue of the *Revue des Mondes Musulmans et de la Méditerranée* in 1999 under the title "Le Post-Islamisme."[11] While for Bayat *post-Islamism* seemed to capture the dynamics of societal secularization at work in Iranian society during the 1990s, the French academic debate reframed the concept "primarily as an historical rather than an analytical category, representing a particular era or an historical end."[12] Post-Islamism was therefore quickly encapsulated in the specific debates on "the failure of political Islam" (or Islamism), as the catchy title of Olivier Roy's 1992 book states.[13]

The question then was mainly geared toward the chronology of Islamism, hypothesizing about the rise of Islamism and its failure. According to this narrative, Islamist movements failed to reach their goals (whether they took over power, as in Iran, or tried to capture it, as in Egypt), prompting the movements to reconsider their ideological, political, and strategic aspirations. Within this narrowed-down framework, it is obvious that the concept of post-Islamism attracted negative comments and critique from different angles.

While post-Islamism tried to "systematize empirical data from the past thirty-five years into a coherent historical pattern,"[14] it failed, according to many, to account for the particularities of different contexts. Lauzière has analyzed the shortcomings for the Moroccan context,[15] while Yilmaz shows the limits of the concept within the Turkish context.[16] A second line of critique argued that only the revolutionary form of Islam, with its top-down strategy of taking power, had become outmoded. Therefore post-Islamism does not so much describe a shift in the nature of Islamism as it represents a specific brand of it.[17] Finally, a third critique focused on the problematic definition of Islamism that lays at the basis of the post-Islamism thesis. François Burgat, for example, raises the following important question: "Should we—and this is the crux of the matter—tar all Islamists with the literalists brush and deny thereby the existence of everything that does not fit in with this pattern?"[18]

In 2007, Asef Bayat further elaborated post-Islamism as an analytical category as he saw additional evidence of a major shift and transformation in the ideas and practices of (ex-)revolutionary Islamists in Iran. Post-Islamism thus became defined as both a condition and a project. As a condition it refers to the fact that "Islamism becomes compelled, both by its own internal contradictions and by societal pressure, to reinvent itself";[19] while as a project it encompasses the "attempt to conceptualize and strategize the rationale and modalities of transcending Islamism in social, political, and intellectual domains."[20] Post-Islamism signals a qualitative shift,

> an endeavor to fuse religiosity and rights, faith and freedom, Islam and liberty. It is an attempt to turn the underlying principles of Islamism on its head by emphasizing rights instead of duties, plurality in place of singular authoritative voice, historicity rather than fixed scriptures, and the future instead of the past. It wants to marry Islam with individual choice and freedom, with democracy and modernity.[21]

While Bayat coined the term in reference to the Iranian experience, it is not always clear if the term is applicable in other settings and if so, under what conditions. For example, does post-Islamism as a condition apply only to settings where Islamists have come to power and realized, after ruling for some years, that there is a big discrepancy between their ideological and programmatic ideals and the necessary pragmatism of rule? How can we then apprehend the Moroccan case, where there have been no Islamists in power but where the ruling monarchy has grounded its legitimacy for a very long time in Islam? Could the manner in which the Moroccan monarchy has defined Islam over the last decades be depicted as post-Islamist even when it is not Islamists but, rather, a long-standing ruling monarchy attempting to rethink Islam in relation to politics and society?

While it is not necessarily so, Bayat states that post-Islamism may be "embodied in a master (or multi-dimensional) movement."[22] Therefore, rightfully in my opinion, post-Islamism seems to refer more to a societal trend than to the categorization of specific political movements. The difference is noteworthy, as the former embeds the concept of post-Islamism into the field of the sociology of religion (focusing on issues such as the individualization of faith, the secularization of practices, etc.),[23] while the latter sees the term more as a yardstick, as a norm, to differentiate among different types of movements that refer in one way or another to Islam.

I will operationalize the inquiry into the possible existence of Moroccan post-Islamism by revisiting the modern history of Moroccan Islamist movements from the angle of the *problématique* of post-Islamism. In order to get a better grasp of the dynamic of change I prefer a thematic periodized approach instead of describing each movement or trend separately. Therefore I will describe first the gradual autonomization of Islamist movements in relation to the "official" Islam in the 1970s. Second, I will describe the changing patterns of Moroccan Islamism in the political transition period known as *alternance*. Third, I will focus on the consequences of 9/11, the Casablanca attacks, and the question of violence. Finally, I will look into the impact of the Arab revolutions of 2011 on Moroccan Islam in general and Islamism in particular. In each of these sections I will focus on the internal dynamics of change (the impact of failing strategies and of repression, changing socioreligious environment, generational impact, etc.) as well as external forces (e.g., al-Qaeda's type of violence, 9/11, the process of democratization, etc.).

Islam in Postcolonial Morocco

Although complete control has never been fully obtained, the Moroccan monarchy has always tried to organize and manage the religious field. Since independence, the monarchy, the conservative wing of the Istiqlal Party, and the leading *'ulama* (Muslim scholars) have shared the same political and religious culture, in which Moroccan Salafi Islam and the Maliki rite played a crucial defining role.[24] In 1962, for example, three followers of the Baha'i faith were found guilty of holding beliefs that were considered heretical and in flagrant contradiction to Moroccan's Islam and its Maliki rite. In this affair Allal al-Fassi, leader of the Istiqlal Party, played a leading role, trying even to outdo the king in showing his commitment to the Islamic cause.

The monarchy developed its own interpretations of Islam as the foundation of its power and legitimacy through the promotion of the Arab/Islamic identity of Morocco. The institution of the monarchy has become the object of a process of sacredness, its veneration kept alive until today through the amalgamation of the triad state-nation-Islam, thus putting the form of the regime in the register of sacredness.[25] With the promulgation of the first constitution in 1962 the king became the constitutional head of state and "Commander of the Faithful," and his person was invested with complete inviolability.[26] The king as the Commander of the Faithful constitutes the summit of religious authority in the country, and the constitution refers several times to Islam. The monarchy has always encouraged the development of religious associations that were based on its interpretation of Islam (a conservative but tolerant Islam as a pillar of its legitimacy) while, at the same time, trying to neutralize politically more popular religious figures. King Mohammed V and his heir, Hassan II, certainly succeeded in giving high-profile positions to leading religious figures within the monarchical organization. Thus, the king tried to "tame" the 'ulamas and de-solidarize them from the political parties.[27]

The religious centrality of the monarchical institution has always constituted a bone of contention between the king and some Islamic clerics either belonging to the official clergy or belonging to important families in the country. Even if the 'ulama were mostly confined to the cultural sphere, from the 1970s onward the late king Hassan II "used" their services to counter the growing power of leftist movements, on the one hand, and the discourse of the first Islamist movements in the country, on the other. During the same decade, a newer, self-proclaimed autodidact 'ulama stood up to challenge the monarchy.

Two major brands of Islamism emerged in the 1970s. The first one, the Chebiba Islamiyya (Islamic youth) of Abdelkrim Mouti'i, was very much influenced by Sayyid Qutb's writings and embraced revolutionary action. The Chebiba was bolstered and supported by the authorities to counterbalance the growing influence of leftist movements and their secular ideologies on the university campuses throughout the country. Just like in other countries, however, the alliance between authorities and Islamists turned sour when the Chebiba took its actions outside the confines of the university. After the Chebiba was accused of the murder of Workers' Union leader Omar Benjelloun in 1975, a vast repression against the movement was launched. While the leadership fled the country and tried (in vain) to ignite the fire of revolt from abroad, a larger group of sympathizers quickly entered into a long phase of discussion and self-reflection. This reevaluation of the movement's violent strategy led to the fragmentation and splintering of the group into numerous different organizations.[28] It is from this nebula of groups that emerged, eventually, a participationist current wanting to enter the legal political field, as I will discuss further.

The second type of Islamism that emerged in the 1970s was formed around the charismatic figure of Sheikh Abdessalam Yacine. Born in the 1920s and of Berber descent, Yacine received a traditional Islamic education but became an inspector of French-speaking education at the Ministry of Education. He was the first public figure to officially reprove the king for his policies. In 1974, he wrote his first open letter to Hassan II, his first major political act. In this letter, "Islam or the Downfall," a typical form of *nasiha* (warning) written in his characteristic acerbic but eloquent manner, he disputes the legitimacy of the Moroccan monarchy and positions himself and his movement as an alternative. In the letter Yacine promotes Islam as the solution to all the political problems the country was facing and urges the king to follow this route. He begs the king to forsake un-Islamic ideas, such as the cult of monarchy, and return to the pure teachings of Islam. In particular, Yacine's disputation of one of the central elements of the monarchy's legitimacy—the king's authority as the Commander of the Faithful—put him at odds with the monarchy. Initially, the king did not know what to do with a man who unashamedly criticized the royalty but who stayed clear of the political stage. Therefore, Yacine was incarcerated in a psychiatric institution and afterward placed under house arrest for ten years, being freed only in 2000.

Placing himself firmly in an Islamic tradition, Yacine quickly became the charismatic leader of a movement called al-Adl wa al-Ihsan, Justice and Beneficence (officially created in the period between 1981 and 1983). Led by the sheikh, the movement has always rejected the monarchy's legitimacy but has simultaneously also always refused to participate in the framework of legal politics. Some observers have therefore stated that the movement is functioning more as a millenarian sect than as a political or social movement,[29] in the sense that it is involved in nonstop criticism of the king, the monarchy, and Moroccan politicians but refuses to enter any legal and/or institutional framework, waiting for the time when the Islamic order will automatically come to the fore.

This reading, however, underestimates the originality of Yacine's movement. Al-Adl wa al-Ihsan is in the first place a spiritual movement, in the sense that its identity is to call people to God "through education,...kind preaching, teaching, persuasion and exhortation."[30] The movement is convinced that the "illness" of the country, that is, *fitna*, can only be cured with the medicine of religion. Only "real spiritual education and any genuine repentance" can form the basis of work interested in the "commonwealth of the umma."[31] From this follows the idea that political action and social action are integral parts of the spiritual revival. As such, Lauzière rightfully and astutely points out that Yacine and his movement transcend the Salafist epistemology of monarchical Islam,[32] as well as that of other Islamist movements including the violent Salafi groups of the 2000s, as I will discuss further. Al-Adl wa al-Ihsan, while not fully dismissing scripturalist Islam, stresses inner faith through the rehabilitation of mystical and spiritual concepts—something that puts the movement in a particular position in relation to the question of Islamism.

Islamism and the Question of Political Alternance

Beginning at the end of the 1980s but mostly during the 1990s Islamist movements reacted to the new institutional environment that the king was trying to establish. From the beginning of the 1990s, Hassan II promoted and tested the idea of a "homegrown" process of democratization, locally referred to as *alternance*. With the disappearance of the Soviet Union, the continuous diplomatic problems surrounding the question of the Western Sahara, an economic and social crisis, growing political oppositions and urban revolts, his deteriorating health, and the pressure of the EU and other international institutions, Hassan II wished to bring the so-called historical opposition of the nationalist movement—unified in the Koutla al-demouqratiyya, or Democratic Bloc—into government. This was to be complemented with the installation of a political and economic order based on the rule of law and the inclusion of some form of legal Islamist politics. The reforms were further carried out by Hassan's son and heir, Mohammed VI.

The Islamists did not play a direct role in the debates around the question of *alternance* but had, obviously, to "respond" to this new situation. A group of ex-militants of the Chebiba, mainly organized around Abdellilah Benkirane, had been in favor of political participation since the second half of the 1980s. As early as 1976 Benkirane had made his criticism of the Islamic trend and concluded not only that the violent option was leading nowhere but that it was essentially counterproductive. He contended that only action within society could bring about a more Islamic system. Mohammed Yatim, an Islamist MP, summarizes:

> We went from a project of change to establish an Islamic state from the top, with all that comes with it in practice (living and working in hiding, denial of participation,...) influenced by "the literature of the trial" of the East; to the establishment of a new mentality that has a more positive relationship with reality. We realized that the problem in Morocco is not to build an Islamic state. The state is constitutionally established and there is no discussion on the legitimacy of the presence of religion in society and the constitu-

tion.... Since 1985, the movement has been freed from the legacy of the Chabiba, we favor dialogue within the movement.[33]

In 1982–1983 Benkirane created the Jamiyya al-islamiyya, a charitable organization that wanted to work within the legal confines of the law as it did not question the Islamicness of the monarchy and the state. Opening the way to some sort of collaboration with the authorities, he tried to integrate with the political arena. However, in both 1989 and 1992 Benkirane saw his official requests for the formation of an Islamist party turned down. After the government refused to recognize the movement as a political party, Benkirane changed the name of the organization a first time into al-Islah wa al-Tajdid (Reform and Renewal) and a second time in 1996 to Harakat al-Tawhid wa al-Islah (Movement for Unity and Reform, MUR). The name changes were brought about by internal discussions on the movement's new political strategies and ideology and by the incorporation of independent Islamic think tanks and Islamic cultural organizations into the movement.[34]

Knowing full well that this was still a movement and not an official political party, Benkirane looked for a way to enter the political realm. An adept political strategist, he understood that integration into the newly emerging political field depended on the existence of a political party and contesting the elections. He chose a political party that had been more or less inert since 1965, the Mouvement Populaire Constitutionnel et Démocratique (Popular Constitutional and Democratic Movement) of Dr. Khatib, ex-leader of the Moroccan Army of Liberation. The merger of the MUR and the Mouvement Populaire Constitutionnel et Démocratique would lead a couple of years later to the official name change into the Parti de la Justice et du Développement (PJD). The fusion of the two movements was made possible because they agreed on the following points: recognition of the Commander of the Faithful, the complete renouncement of violence, recognition of the Maliki rite as the constituting rite of the country, and respect for the constitution.[35]

The Islamists won nine seats in the 1997 elections, but through partial elections and defections in other parties they ended the legislature with fourteen MPs. They entered parliament and followed a course of critical parliamentary majority, meaning that they voted with the governmental majority while remaining outside the government itself. In the 2002 elections, the PJD was able to gain forty-two seats, becoming the third-biggest party in parliament. The entrance of the Islamists into electoral competition was a success for the monarchy's inclusive and consensual approach to the new political game. Not only did it bring a part of the oppositional voice into the realm of legitimate politics, but it also used the party as a stabilizing force during a period of economic turmoil and social change.

Thus, the PJD fulfilled a stabilizing role within the process of *alternance*. One of the ideas behind the integration of the PJD into the legal political field, although it was not openly or officially endorsed, was to make sure that a movement close to large parts of the population would be able to speak openly and thus bar the way for more radical movements.[36] As stated above, in the 2002 legislative elections, the PJD became the third-biggest party in the country. But as Michael Willis states, the role of the PJD in those elections was a "strange case of a party that did not want to win,"[37] as it was content to downplay its own success by running in a limited number of electoral districts. Through this strategy, the PJD wanted to show its commitment to the democratic game, lessen the fear of an Islamist party coming to power, and demonstrate that its commitment to work for the benefit of all Moroccans was more important than its own possible electoral gain. This trajectory at least shows the pragmatism and reformism of the movement. In the 2003 municipal elections many PJD members were elected onto local councils or into the position of mayor. This triggered an important learning phase for the PJD. The party stresses that its municipal work has been a tremendous success based on efficient urban management, tight budgetary controls, and anticorruption measures as well as a very pragmatic use of its moralizing agenda.[38]

The reformism of the PJD is based on a reevaluation of *ijtihad*. Abdellilah Benkirane repeated several times that the PJD is a political party attached to the Islamic current and not a religious party. It departs from the *marjaiyya islamiyya* and through *ijtihad* comes to a political platform. Within this approach the concept of *maslaha* (public interest, general welfare) plays a crucial role in expanding classic notions of *shura* so that it can possibly encompass democratic ideas. Not only does this lead to the acceptance of electoral politics as a legitimate means to organize the body politic, it also opens the possibility to resort to reason as a way to think politics and to put moral and ethical principles before specific injunctions of dogma, orthodoxy, or tradition.

The ideological changes are mostly elaborated within the confines of the MUR. Officially an educational and cultural association, the pietistic movement is based on the principle of the invocation of God, and its actions are geared toward the elaboration of an Islam that is adapted to Moroccan sensibilities. In contradistinction to the PJD, the MUR strives for the application of the shari'a but remains vague as to what this actually means. The relationship between the party and the MUR is a complex and difficult one. Even though the organization tries to keep its autonomy from the party, it functions nevertheless as the de facto think tank of the party and as a major recruiter of militants. The president of the association, Ahmed Raisouni, has become an influential public *'alim*, having even been asked to deliver speeches at the royal palace during Ramadan. The MUR denounces violence, supports the monarchy and the principle of *bey'a* (allegiance), and respects the rules of democracy. However, the movement also speaks about the necessity of establishing a *khilafa intikhabiyya*, an elected caliphate, based on electoral choice and consultation.[39] Asked what this exactly means, Raisouni has stressed that the prophetic model is not closed or final. More than any specific political model or regime (presidential or monarchical), the prophetic model is, rather, an inspirational source. He prefers, in the end, to look for new modalities of Islamic governance adapted to the times in the spirit of the teachings of Islam than to promote a finalized template of a model.

Yacine's Adl movement, on the other hand, held onto its position of rejecting participation in what was deemed an illegitimate political order. After the passing of Hassan II, Sheikh Yacine actually wrote a new open letter, this time to the new king. In it Yacine criticizes the monarchy for not being able to tackle the issues of poverty, exploitation, and corruption, but he goes even a step further. Yacine says to Mohammed VI that his father, Hassan II, was a sinner but that he offered him the possibility to repent by paying back the millions of dirhams that the monarchy had "stolen" from the people (an amount Yacine estimates at $30 million) so that it could be used to pay off the huge Moroccan financial debt.

While still immersed in the classic Islamic idea of "nasiha," the leadership of the movement understood that in the changing political environment (but also with the growing success of the social services of the movement demanding more efficiency), it became necessary to provide the movement with more structure. At the national level a political circle was formed that "deals with all affairs pertaining to the commonwealth. Its mission is to communicate and propagate the opinions and positions of the movement regarding political, economic, and social issues."[40] The political circle, led by Fathallah Arsalane, has five missions: that is, to train potential political activists; to conduct research and prepare

programs that propose viable alternatives; to work for wider communication with the various actors of society, namely, those having moral,
economic, or political influence; to lay out a framework that unites all
those who serve the cause of Islam in the country; and to prepare the
Islamic Covenant.

Stressing very clearly that the establishment of the political circle is
not a separation from its earlier strategy and underscoring that it is "not
a novelty in the thinking of the movement or its tendencies," the movement—evidently positing politics as a derivative of spiritual renewal—
has noted that the circle should "combine the affairs of the State with the
objectives of the Call rather than separate them. The separation of the two
fields is purely functional."[41] It is clear that since its inception the political
circle has become a de facto political body, dealing with issues discussed
throughout the country. Regardless of ideology, it is obvious that the circle
has gained prominence in the movement and has proved that al-Adl did
not want to remain isolated in the *alternance* dynamic. Even though the
movement did not want to formally enter the political realm, it is clearly a
political actor, thus showing its interaction with and response to a changing environment.

Throughout the 1980s it became apparent that the state had lost its
religious monopoly on producing Islamic norms. While still the central
and most important institution, the monarchy had to compete with different types of Islam looking for public recognition. While the monarchy decided to integrate the PJD into the formal political game and to
ban Yacine's al-Adl wa al-Ihsan, it also "imported" traditionalist forms of
Islam affiliated to Saudi Salafi milieus as a way to further fragment the
Islamic offer. Indeed, since the 1990s the monarchy promoted or at least
accepted the spread of more conservative and literalist trends of Islam
within the Kingdom through the dissemination of religious discourses
coming from the Middle East and the Gulf countries. With the different
types of Islamism being politically institutionalized in various ways, the
state created for itself different spaces where it could better intervene and
control these Islamic trends. This institutional fix seemed, at least for a
while, to account for what numerous observers have called the "Moroccan
exception," that is, a politically moderate Arab country with "controlled
Islamists" and an absence of political violence engaged in democratic
reform or *alternance*. This image, however, was shattered on May 16,
2003, when suicide attacks in Casablanca killed more than forty Moroccan
citizens.

The Casablanca Attacks: Political Violence and the Islamist Question

Even though the mainstream Islamist movements were not connected to the violent groups and have on several fronts denounced the use of violence, the question nevertheless remains of how these parties align themselves in relation to the issue of violence carried out under the banner of Islam. The question is politically important. With the attacks in Casablanca on May 16, 2003, the king and some of the (secular) political parties overtly and directly assessed the question of Islamism and its presence in the Moroccan polity.

The state's inadvertent support for the importation of Wahabism in the 1980s—first seen as a status quo ideology intent on maintaining the power and privileges of the Makhzen[42]—to counter the growing power of Islamist movements has given way to radical and violent groups denouncing Islamism as a perversion of Islam.[43] This *salafiyya jihadiyya* authorizes violence against any person involved in "immoral behavior" that departs from its static definition of shari'a. At first apolitical and puritan, this type of fundamentalism found resonance with some uncompromising traditionalist scholars (such as the influential *'alim* al-Zemzemi) as well as with the most marginalized groups of the country. When some militants in the most destitute suburbs of the cities and their shantytowns married this puritanical form of Islam with a more violence-prone reading of Qutb and the likes of bin Laden and al-Qaeda, a new politicized form of jihad emerged in the country.[44]

This prompted Mohammed VI to reclaim, more than before, his central role in the religious architecture of the country and to reorganize the religious field.[45] The king asserted that he, and only he, is the sole representative of Islam. Besides stressing his central role in religious matters, the announced reforms were carried out to ensure the tolerance of Moroccan Islam "so as to uphold the values and tenets of the generous, tolerant Islamic faith and preserve the unity of the Maliki rite." This is done, according to the king, "by adopting an open-minded form of Ijtihad, which is consistent with modern times, in order to protect our youth against foreign, destructive trends."[46] The king has reiterated on numerous occasions that the threat is not inherently Moroccan but, rather, that it is imported! Therefore, he argues, Islam cannot be used for projects of hatred and war, as the Moroccan identity is distinctively tolerant. Throughout his speeches since 2003, Mohammed VI has stressed the fact that Moroccan Islam is by definition tolerant and nonviolent: "Being the religion of the just middle, it reposes on tolerance, honors human dignity, advocates (peaceful) coexistence and rejects aggression, extremism and the quest for power in the name of the religion."[47]

The new agenda for Islam, the violence of jihadist movements in the country, and the involvement of Moroccans in attacks throughout the world have, of course, resonated with the place, role, and ideas of the Islamist formations. The PJD had always found an equilibrium between the demands of its base and the demands of the monarchy, channeled through the office of the Ministry of the Interior. The leadership of the party, which at the time of the attacks was organized around Saad Eddin al-Othmani, Abdellilah Benkirane, and Lahcen Daoudi, clearly opted for a nonconfrontational strategy toward the regime, while other members— supporters of the president of the parliamentary group, Mustapha Ramid— chose to denounce the interference of the Ministry of the Interior. The Casablanca attacks gave certain elements in the security apparatus and political field the opportunity to attack the party. Many Moroccan newspapers and journals thought that some "pact" had been formed between the PJD leadership and the Ministry of the Interior in the weeks prior to the local elections of September 2003. The PJD renounced any ideas of making massive strides in the local elections, while the ministry decided not to dismantle or ban the party. The PJD's decision to go along with the regime's dictates has put much pressure on the party and its ability to control its constituency.

While the relationship with the Makhzen—the political and administrative apparatus surrounding the monarchy and governing the country— seemed to have stabilized after 2005, several national and international observers thought that the 2007 legislative elections would bring about an Islamist electoral landslide victory. These fears or hopes (depending on the stance of the observer) were disappointed as the PJD came in as the third-biggest party. Even though the 2007 election did not meet the party's expectations, it is now obvious that the PJD is one of the major political actors in the country, firmly embedded in Moroccan political life. The 2007 elections signaled a new phase in the growth of the movement, in that it has now come to terms with the difficulties and dilemmas associated with participating in a semi-authoritarian political environment.[48] Indeed, since 2007 the PJD has been constantly engaged in securing its position on the political field vis-à-vis the other political parties but most of all vis-à-vis the government and monarchy, as the latter have tried to curb the success of the party on numerous fronts.[49] Political life in the Kingdom seemed, until recently, centered around the question of how to contain the PJD's influence and power. Fouad Ali Himma, a personal friend of and adviser to the king, created, ex nihilo, the Authenticity and Modernity Party (Parti Authenticité et Modernité), which observers saw as the main challenger for the Islamists. This plan, however, had to be pushed aside as the unfurling logic of the Arab Spring of 2011 quickly changed the political rules of the game.

Islamists Facing the Arab Revolutions

The Arab Spring has also taken root in Morocco. The February 20 movement symbolizes Morocco's own take on the Arab aspirations toward more freedom and justice. Moroccans, on February 20, 2011, in over fifty cities across the country, took their grievances to the streets and pressed for meaningful political and economic change. While the number of protesters was not as massive as in Egypt or Tunisia, February 20 signaled the start of a new social movement that has changed the rules of the Moroccan political game. Morocco's controlled policy of gradual reform was challenged by the February 20 movement, as the main question for the monarchy and the ruling elites was how to define a strategy toward the popular movement while not losing control over its own policy options regarding the question of reform. The royal speech of March 9, in which the king called for the writing of a new constitution, was historical less for its content than for the fact that it was the first time in Moroccan postcolonial history that a royal initiative directly answered a popular demand.

It is interesting to analyze how the main Islamist movements have approached the February 20 movement as the king has regained control over the reform agenda. The movement has different bases of support. Besides the so-called Facebook youths, the movement is actively supported by the Amazigh (Berber) movement, a large group of progressive journalists from Rabat and Casablanca, the movement of the *diplômes chômeurs*, and the radical parties of the Left, with a prominent role for the human rights organization Association Marocaine des Droits Humains, the Marxist-Leninist party Annahj Addemokrati (Democratic way), and al-Adl wa al-Ihsan of Sheikh Yacine. Yacine's movement has been one of the major supporters of February 20, while the PJD has been opposed to it, opting instead for the royal initiative. Especially PJD Secretary-General Abdellilah Benkirane has voiced his opposition to the protest movement, which has led to the first cracks in the tight organization of the party. Benkirane prohibited the youth organization of the party to join the protests and has, on several occasions, put pressure on any party member who seemed to sympathize with the protesters. Several top politicians of the party threatened to resign from the party, but as the parliamentary elections of November 25 came closer, the party closed ranks, hoping to become the winner of the elections. According to the new constitution, approved in July, this would mean that the leader of the winning party would automatically be asked by the king to become the prime minister and form a new government. In the run-up to the elections, Benkirane stated that the party did not support the February 20 movement "because we felt that the monarchy was in danger.... [W]ith the monarchy we are the Morocco that we know today but without the monarchy I do not know what we would become."[50]

Al-Adl wa al-Ihsan has looked to make alliances with other political movements and civil actors such as the far Left and the Berber movement. This shows that the movement is able to build political bridges with different political and ideological currents.[51] Of course, as an oppositional force, al-Adl was more or less obliged to look for alliances if it did not want to end up as an isolated political faction. Al-Adl has reiterated its commitment to democratic institutions but has never had any chance (or opportunity) to take practical responsibilities in this matter. The rhetoric of democracy has proved an interesting tactical device to forge alliances with other oppositional movements, but the question remains as to how al-Adl can find a synthesis between certain aspects of democracy and its religious agenda.

The PJD, on the other hand, is committed to democratic procedures in the Moroccan polity (and within the party), but again, it is difficult to apprehend how the movement resolves possible contradictions between liberties and Islamic values, between the demands of citizens and the proclaimed goal of creating a moral polity. As the PJD plays the "sidekick" of the monarchy, it can always deny any responsibility in the debates over the question of freedoms, for it is the king who sets the agenda and judges accordingly. The PJD is in a way constrained by the institutional and political role it plays and its aspiration to construct an ideal Islamic society. The party gets its legitimacy not from religion but from the monarchy itself. The moralization of politics constitutes a specific terrain of action that the PJD can use to "make a political difference." As a parliamentary force, it has not been able to really tackle difficult problems such as poverty and illiteracy; but it has invested a lot of energy in moralizing campaigns.

While there is no doubt that these campaigns are part of electoral strate-gies, the theme of the moralization of public life is a crucial area of politi-cal interest for the party. While the PJD has always been careful to couch its moralizing campaigns in the form of *da'wa* and nasiha (admonition), thus not directly requesting the prohibition of something, one has to ask the question of whether a constant reminder that specific habits are bad or un-Islamic does not produce such pressure as to empty some personal freedoms of their content. In the end, the party, not being able to make deep changes to legislation, is concerned more with reducing the space of secular politics through the promotion of Islamic morals than with the introduction of specific Islamic rules and/or laws. In this way the PJD is trying to present Islam not as an alternative to secularism, democracy, or modernity but as a way of dealing with the de facto secularization of behaviors and norms in Morocco. The PJD is post-Islamist in the sense that it is not so much striving to reestablish the "original Islamic city" as it is trying to create a social order where justice is guaranteed through a respect for Islamic values that have their genealogy in the sacred texts.

In the end, the PJD is synchronously emphasizing the rights and duties of the individual. While classic forms of Islamism were mostly concerned with the duties of individuals as part of the Islamic community in regard to their righteous state, today's forms of Islamic politics seem to stress more the rights of the individual citizen. However, it is clear that this does not automatically or necessarily lead to a post-Islamist stance where inalien-able rights are granted to citizens but, rather, a situation in which Islamist parties are constantly rethinking their political projects in relation to the changing sociocultural and political environment in which they thrive.

With its electoral victory, the PJD now has to live up to the expectations of the voters. Benkirane, officially nominated by Mohammed VI as prime minister, is now confronted with the difficult task of finding a balance between living up to electoral promises and the necessary pragmatism of public affairs. It is too early to judge the ability of the party to make the conversion from an oppositional to a ruling party, but it is clear that the interplay between the palace and the Islamist prime minister will become an important post of observation to analyze the PJD's political behavior.

Toward Some Tentative Conclusions

Post-Islamism seems to become more and more a social reality in Morocco, as Islam, while still prominent in public and private matters, has become much more individualized, more a matter of personal choice than of coercion or tradition. However, just as post-Islamism is a poor indicator for political behavior, it is perhaps, for the Moroccan case, not the best concept to describe the dynamics of Islamist movements. It is, in other words, not always clear what "happens" when we describe the PJD as a "post-Islamist" movement. The concept does not explain the movement; nor does it necessarily help in predicting political behavior. The value added of the concept lies more in its general outlook on the nature of religiosity, public displays of religion, and the transformation of Islamist movements (as Asef Bayat meant) than in its description of a clear category grasping the behavior of Islamist movements. In fact, if we hold onto the term and want to make it "useful" (from an academic point of view), then we must take care not to make something that we need to understand change and transformation into something that essentializes these movements.

Nevertheless, *post-Islamism* seems indeed to cover a vast terrain of change in Islamist ideology. It points to certain interesting features of change that encompass post-Islamism as a concept and as a project. While Islamist political formations have been quite astute in embracing the democratic ideals of procedural techniques, that is, the ways in which power is exercised (elections, parties, accountable governance, transparency, the rule of law, etc.), they have had more trouble in situating themselves in discussions concerning the ways of constituting the body politic, that is, the ways in which power is legitimated. While the PJD states clearly that the sovereignty and legitimacy of power belong to the people, there are still questions remaining as to how this inclusionary rhetoric translates into political reality. While it is obvious that the PJD is not striving to establish a religious state or theocracy, and while it stresses rights instead of duties, it is perhaps not always clear how the ideal of societal harmony and unity—as expressed by the movement—translates when it is faced with the de facto plurality of interests in society: a very daunting task for any political party, let alone a party that is asked to rule for the first time.

Notes

All translations from French and Arabic into English are mine.

1. Michael Emerson and Richard Youngs, eds., *Political Islam and European Foreign Policy. Perspectives from Muslim Democrats of the Mediterranean* (Brussels: Center for European Policy Studies, 2007), 1.

2. For example, see François Burgat, *L'islamisme en face* (Paris: La Découverte, 2005); François Burgat, *Face to Face with Political Islam* (London: I. B. Tauris, 2003); Asef Bayat, *Making Islam Democratic: Social Movements and the Post-Islamist Turn* (Stanford: Stanford University Press, 2007); John L. Esposito and John O. Voll, *Islam and Democracy* (New York: Oxford University Press, 1996).

3. Sheri Berman, "Islamism, Revolution and Civil Society," *Perspectives on Politics* 1, no. 2 (2003): 257–272; Magdi Khalil, "Egypt's Muslim Brotherhood and Political Power: Would Democracy Survive?" *Middle East Review of International Affairs* 10, no. 1 (2006): 44–52.

4. Asef Bayat, *Islam and Democracy: What Is the Real Question?* ISIM Papers no. 8 (Amsterdam: Amsterdam University Press, 2007).

5. Malika Zghal, *Les islamistes Marocains. Le défi à la monarchie* (Casablanca: Ed. Le Fennec, 2005); Mohsen Elahmadi, *Le mouvement Yasiniste* (Mohammadia, Algeria: Imprimerie de Fédala, 2006).

6. And what about terms in other languages, such as the concept of *intégrisme* in French scholarship?

7. Guilain Denoeux, "The Forgotten Swamp: Navigating Political Islam," *Middle East Policy* 9, no. 2 (2002): 56–81.

8. See, for example, Saad Eddin al-Othmani, interview by Narjiss Rerhaye, *Le Matin*, April 21, 2003.

9. My definition bares the traces and influences of numerous other definitions and analyses of Islamism, such as François Burgat, *L'islamisme au Maghreb. La voix du Sud* (Paris: Karthala, 1988); Burgat, *L'islamisme en face*; Olivier Roy, *L'islam mondialisé* (Paris: Le Seuil, 2002); and Bobby Sayyid, *A Fundamental Fear. Eurocentrism and the Emergence of Islamism* (London: Zed Books, 1997).

10. Asef Bayat, "The Coming of a Post-Islamist Society," *Critique. Critical Middle East Studies* 9 (1996): 43–52.

11. Olivier Roy and Patrick Haenni, eds., "Le post-islamisme," theme issue, *Revue des mondes musulmans et de la Méditerranée* 85–86 (1999).

12. Bayat, *Making Islam Democratic*, 17–18.

13. The French version of Olivier Roy's *The Failure of Political Islam* was published under the title *'L'échec de l'islam politique* (Paris: Le Seuil) in 1992.

14. Henri Lauzière, "Post-Islamism and the Religious Discourse of 'Abd al-Salam Yasin," *International Journal of Middle East Studies* 37, no. 2 (2005): 241–261, at 257.

15. Ibid., passim.

16. Ihsan Yilmaz, "Beyond Post-Islamism. A Critical Analysis of the Turkish Islamism's Transformation toward Fethullah Gülen's Stateless Cosmopolitan Islam" (2008), at www.gulenconference.net/files/Georgetown/2008_IhsanYilmaz.pdf (accessed December 14, 2010).

17. Salwa Ismail, "The Paradox of Islamist Politics," *Middle East Report* 221 (2001): 34–39.

18. Burgat, *Face to Face with Political Islam*, 160.

19. Bayat, *Islam and Democracy*, 19.

20. Ibid.

21. Ibid.

22. Ibid., 18.

23. LeVine, for example, talks about a post-Islamist public sphere. See Mark LeVine, "Heavy Metal Muslims: The Rise of a Post-Islamist Public Sphere," *Contemporary Islam* 2 (2008): 229–249.

24. For a historical account on Salafism in Morocco, see Abdeljalil Badou, *Al-athr al-Shatibi fi-l-fiqr al-salafi bi-l-Maghrib* [The influence of al-Shatibi on Salafi thought in Morocco] (Mohammadia, Algeria: Seliki Ikhwan, 1996). For a more political analysis of modern Salafi movements, see Abdelhakim Aboullouz, *Al-Harakat al-salafiyya fi-l-Maghrib (1971–2003). Bahth enthroupoulougi soucioulougy* [Salafi movements in Morocco (1971–2003). A socioanthropological study] (Beirut: Markaz dirasat al-whada al-arabiyya, 2009).

25. A Moroccan schoolboy was jailed in 2008 for assumedly insulting the king after he had altered the phrase "God, the Nation, the King" on the school blackboard to read "God, the Nation, Barcelona."

26. Mohsen Elahmadi, *La Monarchie et l'islam* (Casablanca: Najah al-Jadid, 2006).

27. Exceptions of religious leaders within the parties were Allal al-Fassi and Abou Bakr Kadiri in the Istiqlal and Larbi al-Alaoui in the Union Nationale des Forces Populaires/Union Socialiste des Force Populaire. Others were "bureaucratized" through their integration into a public function (education, administration, and so forth).

28. Different revolutionary groups tried to keep the idea of jihad in Morocco alive. A Moroccan jihad organization that was mainly implanted in France and Belgium published a pamphlet entitled "The Islamic Revolution: Morocco's Fate" in 1984 that would become a source of inspiration for *jihadi* fighters in the late 1990s.

29. Mohammed Chekroun, *Jeux et enjeux culturels au Maroc* (Rabat: Editions Okad, 1990).

30. Al-Adl wa al-Ihsan, "Our identity," at www.yassine.net/en/Default.aspx?article=jsm_EN&m=1&sm=16 (accessed October 31, 2011).

31. Ibid.

32. Lauzière, "Post-Islamism and the Religious Discourse of 'Abd al-Salam Yasin."

33. Mohammed Yatim, interview, *al-Raya*, March 23, 1992, cited in Mohammed Tozy, *Monarchie et islam politique au Maroc* (Paris: Presses de Sciences Po, 1999), 245.

34. 'Abd al-Illah Benkirane, *Al-haraka al-islamiyya wa ishkaliyat al-minhaj* [The Islamic movement and the problematics of the current] (Casablanca: Mashourat al-Forqan, 1999).

35. Both Dr. Khatib and Benkirane recognize that it was Benkirane who initiated the project. Khatib posited two conditions for the Islamists to join his party: that they recognize the legitimacy of the monarchy and respect the constitution.

Khatib presented these conditions as his own. However, Mohammed Tozy, a leading Moroccan political scientist, has a more nuanced view on the deal, as he explained to me: "I don't think it was all that clear. Khatib has a close history to religion....I think it happened in stages. There was a demand from Benkirane, the most pragmatic of the Islamists: He would ally himself with the devil; he has no complexes. I think, that given his [Dr. Khatib's] inroads in the palace, indirectly, passing through different counselors and saloons....They have never told him to integrate Islamists in his party, but they have suggested it allusively....[I] t's typical of the Moroccan political system. There was never a letter saying 'Dear Khatib, please...'" (interview by the author, March 10, 2000).

36. Graham Fuller, *The Future of Political Islam* (Houndmills, England: Palgrave Macmillan, 2003).

37. Michael Willis, "Morocco's Islamists and the Legislative Elections of 2002: The Strange Case of the Party that Did Not Want to Win," *Mediterranean Politics* 9, no. 1 (2004): 53–81.

38. Miriam Catusse and Lamia Zaki, "Gestion communale et clientélisme moral au Maroc: Les politiques du Parti de la justice et du développement," *Critique Internationale* 42 (2009): 73–91.

39. Zghal, *Les islamistes Marocains.*

40. Al-Adl wa al-Ihsan, "Our identity."

41. Ibid.

42. *Makhzen* is a term to describe the central authority in Morocco. It dates back several centuries and was embodied in the sultanate and the local power centers. Today it is more a pejorative term to describe the central power structures and elites that gather around the monarchy.

43. Anouar Boukhars, "The Origins of Militancy and Salafism in Morocco," *Terrorism Monitor* 3, no. 12 (2005), www.jamestown.org/programs/gta/single/?tx_ttnews%5Btt_news%5D=157&tx_ttnews%5BbackPid%5D=180&no_cache=1 (accessed December 15, 2011).

44. Sami Zemni, "Moroccan Islamism. Between Local Participation and International Islamist Networks of Influence?" in *Interregional Challenges of Islamic Extremist Movements in North Africa*, ed. Muna Abdalla (Pretoria: ISS, 2010), 77–98.

45. For a more elaborated analysis of the reorganization of the religious field after 2003, see Sami Zemni, "Islam between Jihadi-Threats and Islamist Insecurities? Evidence from Belgium and Morocco," *Mediterranean Politics* 11, no. 2 (2006): 231–253.

46. Ministry of Communication, "Discours de SM le Roi a' l'occasion de la Fête du Trône," subheading "French" and "discours du roi" (July 30, 2004), at www.maroc.ma.

47. Ministry of Communication, "Discours de S.M le Roi Mohammed VI suite aux attentats de Casablanca du 16 mai 2003," subheading "French" and "discours du roi" (May 29, 2003), at www.maroc.ma/.

48. Amr Hamzawi, *Party for Justice and Development in Morocco: Participation and Its Discontents*, Carnegie Papers, no. 93 (Washington, D.C.: Carnegie Endowment, 2008).

49. In 2009, for example, several PJD mayors were deposed after allegations of corruption. The very popular mayor of Meknes, Ahmed Belkora, was one of the targeted mayors, although the case against him appeared to be very thin. It is more likely that this was a clear message to the PJD not to change its electoral base and constituency by using the services of local notables outside the large urban centers. Curbing the ambitions of the PJD is a concern for the monarchy as it wants to keep a certain control of the movement at a distance (without resorting to direct repression).

50. Abdellilah Benkirane, interview, *Tel Quel* 493 (October 22–28, 2011).

51. Franscesco Cavatorta, "Civil Society, Islamism and Democratisation: The Case of Morocco," *Journal of Modern African Studies* 44, no. 2 (2006): 203–222.

6

Post-Islamist Politics in Indonesia

Noorhaidi Hasan

Has the threat of Islamism, largely defined as political discourse and activism that aim to change the secular system of society and the state to create an Islamic country by exploiting religious symbols and identities, come to an end in Indonesia?[1] This question should be posed given the demonstrations by radical Islamists who have actively pushed for the implementation of the shari'a (Islamic law) and even jihad in several areas of communal conflict in Indonesia since the fall of Suharto in May 1998. These events are very much alive in our collective memory. As a consequence of the rising tide of Islamist radicalism, many observers during the first decade of post-Suharto Indonesia imagined a bleak future for the most populous Muslim country in the world, one that may today be no different from Pakistan or even Iraq, countries that are gradually being sucked into a maelstrom of political and religious violence. However, after less than fifteen years it has become apparent that these observers need to adjust their pessimistic accounts, in line with Indonesia's growing democracy, which is now characterized by flourishing political activities based on electoral politics within the framework of a democratic system.

Some skeptics still judge Indonesia's emergent democracy as superficial, based on their assumption that it remains procedural rather than functional and is driven by political money and manipulation. Nonetheless, one cannot deny the reality of an electoral democratic system that guarantees much broader public participation in politics, although this participation may lack depth. Moreover, since democracy allows multiple opinions to emerge and claim space on the surface, it guarantees that radical Islamists' attempt to take control of the Indonesian public sphere will end in failure. Indeed, the ongoing consolidation of democracy has contributed to the weakening influence of radical Islamist movements that reject multiculturalism and citizenship, the foundations of democratic life. There is reason to believe that the era of high-profile politics staged by the militant

Islamist groups has shifted toward a strategy of implementing the shari'a from below. Attempts to give the shari'a constitutional status and thereby enforce it at the state level ended in failure, attracting insufficient support in the People's Consultative Assembly. This failure ultimately serves to highlight the marginal position of militant Muslims and their unsuccessful efforts to popularize their discourse glorifying militancy and violence.

This chapter aims to understand the shifting patterns of Islamic political activism in post-Suharto Indonesia and how this phenomenon is related to the nation's ongoing democratic consolidation and the moderate Muslims' campaign for democratic Islam. The central question to be tackled here is whether Indonesia is in the throes of forging a post-Islamist path. After a brief theoretical discussion on the concept of post-Islamism, this chapter looks at the historical context of the rise of Islamist radicalism that has threatened the burgeoning of democratic Islam in Indonesia and how it has been changing toward the call for implementation of the shari'a at the personal level through *da'wa* (Islamic proselytizing). Next, it discusses the relentless effort by moderate Muslims to call for democratic Islam that has contributed to the weakening of the influence of radical Islamism. Finally, it examines the way the Prosperous Justice Party has negotiated its Islamist identity and ideology with the pragmatic politics of power sharing in the realities of the democratic electoral process.

Post-Islamism

Recent academic debates on the Muslim world have seen a major shift in the pattern of Islamic activism, from collective activism that is revolutionary in character toward an individual activism that accepts the imperatives of modern life. If the first is shaped by ideologies, what Asef Bayat defines as "post-Islamism" distances itself from political nuances and collective militancy while still ensuring harmonization and parallelism between Islam and modernity.[2] Post-Islamism is conceptualized by Bayat as a "conscious attempt to strategize the rationale and modalities of transcending Islamism in social, political, and intellectual domains." Representing "an endeavour to fuse religiosity and rights, faith and freedom, Islam and liberty," it renders religion into a plural reality with multiple meanings and accommodates aspects of democratization, pluralism, multiculturalism, and human rights. Bayat further argues that

> post-Islamism serves primarily as theoretical construct to signify change, difference, and the root of change.... The advent of

post-Islamism does not necessarily mean the historical end of Islamism. What it means is the birth, out of the Islamist experience, of a qualitatively different discourse and practice.[3]

Post-Islamism is embedded in the process of cultural transaction that reflects how global cultures are assimilated in a locality. In today's society it seems difficult to separate the process of social, cultural, and political change from the development of global dynamics. Undeniably, the advancement of information and communication technology has significantly affected everyday lives in almost all parts of the world, with several significant repercussions. Globalization has not only changed the way people relate to space but also contributed to the creation of a homogenized culture, toward a synchronization of taste, consumption, and lifestyle.[4] On a more positive note, globalization has also deepened the penetrative forces of modern values such as democracy, tolerance, and human rights.

In parallel with the rapid process of globalization, the Muslim world has in fact seen major transformations. These include a greater sense of autonomy for both men and women and the emergence of a public sphere in which politics and religion are subtly intertwined. Mass education and mass communications have facilitated an awareness in Muslims of the need to reconfigure the nature of religious thought and action, create new forms of public space, and encourage debate over meaning. Within this context Islam has become the subject of dialogue and civil debate. Open contests over the use of the symbolic language of Islam and its meanings have increasingly shaped this new sense of public space that is discursive, performative, and participative. In such engagements, publicly shared ideas of community, identity, and leadership take new shapes.[5]

One noticeable effect of these developments is the proliferation of forms of piety that appear as congruent with the principles of individual freedom and democracy and are removed from their traditional religious moorings. Islam is presented in a way that is sophisticated, fresh, and hybrid, in order to make it an appealing alternative to urban, capitalist cultures. This has given rise to a sense of personalized Muslimhood, which conceals a clear shift from the earlier emphasis of Islamism on the Islamist polity to one on personal piety.[6] The model of Muslimhood presents both a challenge and an opportunity to rethink the established boundaries between the private and the public. Now individuals can choose from an expanded range of options among a wider assortment of religious representations, both traditional and secular, manufactured, packaged, and retailed by specialized service agencies. This free choice in turn offers individuals the opportunity to patch religious fragments together into a subjectively meaningful whole and transform them into powerful symbols able to be enacted in public.[7]

In the same vein Göle has argued that post-Islamist identities have enabled Muslims to experience the "banalization process." Actors from diverse backgrounds are involved in shaping the face of Islam in the public space and may enter into the modern urban context with little hesitance. By using global communication networks they participate in public debates, track patterns of consumption, and study the rules of the market while at the same time embracing individualistic, professional, and consumerist values.[8] This statement does not mean that Islam no longer functions as a source of guidance in Muslim life. Although its traditional function of stirring collective actions in society has faded, it serves as an inspiration imbued in the social and cultural imagination of the community, whereby society has transformed itself to accommodate modernization and globalization. It is as if we are seeing a synthesis between the wave of Islamism, on one hand, and, on the other, the growth of modern and secular education, and of free market values and democratic idioms, in the Muslim world.

Post-Islamism can be seen as an alternative that gains ground amid the failure of the project that attempts to position Islam as a political ideology and is thereby changing the political landscape of Muslim states. The experiences of many Muslim states confirm that the Islamist project has instead stigmatized Islam and transformed it into an enemy of modern civilization. As an alternative to religious radicalism, post-Islamism offers Muslims a way to actualize religious beliefs and values while still following the path of modernity and globalization, without plunging into violence and joining a cycle of militancy. Democratic values, which form the foundations of practical Islam and the politics of contemporary Muslim society, suggest that being a democratic Muslim is no longer an oxymoron.[9]

In the context of Indonesia the roots of post-Islamism began to gain ground in tandem with the rise of the new Muslim middle class, which has gotten involved in the debates about objectifying Islam. Their rising demands for a more nuanced lifestyle—as the Islamic revival has swept across Indonesia since the 1980s—urged them to adopt Islamic symbols as a mode of modern cultural expression in public spaces.[10] Islamic symbols appear in middle-class attempts to construct new narratives of themselves and their place in the world from creative blends of their own cultural inheritance and global influences.[11] In response to the growing demand for the availability of religious space within the urban landscape of metropolitan and big cities, luxury Islamic centers, with a large mosque as the main building surrounded by training and educational buildings, shops, and a hotel, have been constructed on large tracts of land in major cities such as Jakarta, Surabaya, and Makassar. The new Muslim middle class comes to these places to engage in reciting the Quran, chanting *dhikr* (the profession of the faith), and the like while discussing various aspects of Islam. In this way Indonesian Islam has experienced a process of commodification, favoring global high technology and catering to consumerist Islamic appetites.[12] Styled in accordance with the (upper) middle class and new wealth's appetite and symbolized by religious insignia of all kinds, the post-Islamist identity has fostered a pluralist vision of Islam that contributes to the burgeoning of democracy.

Shades of Militant Islamism

The proliferation of the seeds of democratic Islam faced a serious challenge when the wave of Islamist radicalism erupted in the aftermath of the collapse of Suharto's New Order regime in May 1998. By that time, a number of militant Islamist groups had come to the fore and achieved notoriety by taking to the streets to demand the comprehensive implementation of the shari'a (Islamic law), raiding cafés, discotheques, casinos, brothels, and other reputed dens of iniquity and, most importantly, calling for jihad in the Moluccas and other Indonesian trouble spots. They had (and have) names such as the Front Pembela Islam (Defenders of Islam Front), the Laskar Jihad (Holy War Force), the Majelis Mujahidin Indonesia (Indonesian Holy Warriors Council), the Jemaah Islamiyah (JI, Islamic Community), and the Hizbut Tahrir Indonesia (HTI, Indonesian Islamic Party of Liberation), to mention but a few. They sought to impose a totalitarian world order by disseminating religious doctrines and via activism that espoused norms, symbols, and rhetoric imbued with animosity. The challenge posed by these groups intensified when bombs exploded in a nightclub at Legian, Bali, in October 2002. This bombing was followed by explosions at the Marriot Hotel in Jakarta in 2003, outside the Australian Embassy in Jakarta in 2004, again in Bali in late 2005, and more recently at Jakarta's Marriot and Ritz-Carlton hotels. While a moderate understanding of Islamic doctrines apparently remains the foundation of mainstream Indonesian Islam, the series of bombing attacks has served as a reminder that anti-civilian violence is a recurrent phenomenon in Indonesia today.

The expansion of militant Islamist groups was clearly emblematic of the expansion of Islamist ideology and violent activism in the political arena of post-Suharto Indonesia. This ideology asserts the shari'a as the highest law and the single source of all legislation. Militant Islamists define the shari'a as containing all of God's rules derived from the Quran and Sunna, which provide a comprehensive and universal guide and solution for every problem facing humankind. Their sense of urgency is perhaps heightened by the recent and protracted economic, political, and social crises that have afflicted Indonesian Muslim society. True and faithful Muslims therefore have no choice but to abide by the shari'a. Abu Bakar Ba'asyir, the commander (*amir*) of Indonesian *mujahidin* (holy warriors) and leader of the *ahl al-hall wa'l aqd* (advisory council) of Majelis Mujahidin Indonesia, gave a speech to the first national congress of *mujahidin* in August 2000. He proclaimed that application of the shari'a is a nonnegotiable imperative and argued that its rejection must be countered by jihad.[13] He stated his belief that application of the shari'a would lead Indonesia to solve its various crises. In his eyes the shari'a proved itself by being the leading political system for about fourteen centuries. It expanded throughout the world, bringing peace, justice, and prosperity. It was not until 1924, when worldly temptations (*penyakit kemewahan*) began to overwhelm the Muslim *ummah* (community), that its superiority was undermined by secular ideologies.[14] In an interview, he insisted that the shari'a is final (*harga mati*). It is not to be negotiated or debated. Rejecting the shari'a might even lead a Muslim ruler to apostasy.[15]

HTI's leader, Muhammad al-Khaththath, saw the importance of the shari'a as an alternative to secular ideologies, including nationalism, socialism, and capitalism, which are claimed to have exerted domination over the world but to have failed to bring humankind to a full realization of both its material and its spiritual dimensions. The shari'a is asserted as a means of establishing the *khilafa* system, which is the main goal of the organization. In al-Khaththath's opinion, the failure to enforce the shari'a will steer Indonesian Muslims clear of the only Islamic system that will bring them out of their crises and allow them to achieve prosperity, wealth, and justice.[16] Considering the necessity to establish the *khilafa* system, the chairman of HTI's Central Leadership Board, Hafidz Abdurrahman, has highlighted that every Muslim is obliged to participate in any attempts toward the implementation of the shari'a.[17] HTI's spokesperson, Muhammad Ismail Yusanto, has emphasized that the existing secular system has been flawed since the beginning. It simply marginalizes the role of religion in the Indonesian public sphere, as the system treats religion as merely a personal or private matter.[18] Members of the organization took to the streets to champion the slogan "Save Indonesia with the shari'a." HTI's belief is that Indonesia's dependence on Western countries, which has brought nothing but severe economic and political crises, can only be eliminated through the shari'a. Yusanto maintains that the shari'a is a mercy for all humankind. It is relevant to all problems faced by all people, regardless of ethnicity or religion. Its universality is predicated on the universality of Islam as a religion revealed by God.[19]

Toward the Shari'a from Below

The militant Islamists' discourse emphasizing the need for a change in the political structure as a means to implement the shari'a in a comprehensive manner has gradually shifted toward the application of the shari'a from below, in tandem with the efflorescence of Islamic popular culture. Trendy, colorful *jilbab*s (head scarves) for women and *baju koko* (Muslim shirts) for men have achieved prominence as symbols facilitating the interest of the Muslim middle class in demonstrating their religious identity as well as social status. They are involved in Islamic teaching sessions at five-star hotels and mass ritual programs such as *dhikr akbar* (remembrance of God) organized at grand mosques in metropolitan cities such as Jakarta and Surabaya. Coupled with the expansion of new da'wa genres, such as cyber da'wa and cellular da'wa, the growth of Islamic popular culture has offered Muslims alternatives in actualizing their religious beliefs and practices. Hence the irrelevance of militant Islamists' repudiation of the state democratic system claimed to have blocked the Islamist dream of making Islam visible and victorious.

Many militant Islamist leaders who had been at the front line to call for jihad in the conflict areas in the Moluccas and Poso, Central Sulawesi, now put new emphasis on the need to apply the shari'a at the personal level. This is considered a prerequisite for the establishment of a Muslim society. The attempt to raise individual awareness of the importance of the shari'a as guidance for Muslims in their everyday life is believed to be more crucial than its application by the state. After his release from prison in mid-2006, even Ba'asyir stated his opinion that the attempt to impose the application of the shari'a at the state level could disturb the main purpose of Muslim struggle, that is, upholding the principle of *tawhid* (obedience to God) as a foundation of Muslim belief. Individual consciousness of consistently applying the shari'a at the personal level—being a manifestation of one's total obedience to God—would automatically change the nation's political landscape as a whole. In Ba'asyir's opinion, his call on Muslims to participate in armed jihad against Christian enemies in early 2000 was linked up with the escalated conflicts between Muslims and Christians in the Moluccas and Poso. He was convinced that the conflicts that had killed thousands of Muslims and displaced other thousands was a result of the state leadership's idle disregard for the fate of Muslims and also their neglect of their main task to make Islam's victory into a reality. Instead, he argued, they served as a *taghut*, evil power, that collaborated with the Zionists and the West to undermine Islam and the ummah. As a result, Indonesia had become a *dar al-harb* (realm of war) where jihad was necessitated. The fact that the conflicts have come to an end in parallel with the opening of more opportunities for Muslims to express their religious beliefs and identities, according to Ba'asyir, has rendered the status of Indonesia as the *dar al-harb* no longer relevant. In his eyes, Indonesia is now a *dar al-aman* (realm of Islam) that enables da'wa to flourish.[20]

While supporting the idea of implementing the shari'a from below, other militant Islamist leaders, such as former JI commander Nasir Abbas, stridently criticized Osama bin Laden's *fatwa* on the compulsion for every Muslim to participate in jihad, meaning killing Americans and their Zionist allies wherever they are.[21] In Abbas's point of view, bin Laden's jihad ideology and his pseudo fatwa on the compulsion to fight jihad against Americans and their allies were based on a false understanding about the essence of jihad.[22] His criticism of bin Laden's fatwa marked the shift in the ideological position of the JI leadership concerning jihad, resulting in conflict among them. In the same vein, Laskar Jihad former commander Ja'far Umar Thalib insisted that bin Laden was not qualified as a *mufti*, so his fatwa should be abandoned. Reiterating his persistent criticism of jihadist proponents, he highlighted what he understood as a danger of jihad when interpreted and applied wrongly by the followers of *bid'a* (reprehensible innovation). In his opinion, jihad is only legitimate under some conditions, among them that permission had to be obtained from the authorities and that it would only be for defense purposes.[23] Both

Abbas and Thalib were of the opinion that bin Laden's call for jihad has instead brought disunity among Muslims and put the Muslim world into a war with the West.

Aware of the political change occurring in Indonesia that facilitated the peace process in various conflict areas such as the Moluccas and Poso, as indicated above, the militant Islamist leaders did not simply criticize bin Laden's interpretation of jihad; they no longer saw any relevance for jihad as a means of realizing the application of the shari'a. Instead, they argued that da'wa (Islamic proselytizing) is more appropriate to make Indonesian Muslims aware of their duty to uphold the supremacy of the shari'a. On many occasions Ba'asyir himself promoted nonviolent endeavors to defend Muslim solidarity and struggle for the application of the shari'a. He now claimed that violence gives Islam itself a bad image. In response to demonstrations against the Israeli war in Lebanon and George W. Bush's visit to Indonesia in late 2006, Ba'asyir warned that demonstrators should hold peaceful protests and avoid any violent act. It was not the first time that Ba'asyir had called for peaceful demonstration. He even showed his disagreement with the path taken by Azahari and Noordin M. Top, two Malaysians believed to be behind terrorist bombings in Indonesia. In Ba'asyir's opinion, violence associated with armed jihad is only legitimate when enemies are attacking Muslims, who are thus in a defensive position to protect their dignity as part of the Muslim ummah.

As Ba'asyir has pointed out, the most suitable strategy for implementing the shari'a in Indonesia today is not jihad but, rather, informing Indonesian Muslims of the magnificence of the shari'a. In his eyes, this is consistent with the Prophetic strategy of da'wa to give hope (*tabshir*) and threat (*indhar*): the hope of heaven and the threat of hell. Following the Prophet, Ba'asyir related the implementation of the shari'a to the relationship between a person's life in this world and that in the hereafter. Every individual is a leader: a leader for oneself, one's family, one's village, and above all for one's country. Individuals are responsible in the hereafter for whatever they have done in this world. Political leaders who do not create laws to prevent their people from being condemned to hell will face retribution in the hereafter; they will be responsible for all people's sins.[24] However, this does not mean that Ba'asyir totally neglects the importance of jihad; he just sees da'wa as more appropriate to Indonesia's current situation. He sees da'wa and jihad as twin concepts, as alternate ways to establish God's laws on earth. In his eyes, the West has demonized and criminalized jihad because they are afraid of Muslims' return to the past glorious victory of Islam. Ba'asyir argued that Islam becomes weak if it is separated from jihad. Only with jihad will Islam gain honorable victory. However, he maintained that jihad should not be understood simply as holy war. It connotes any efforts to establish God's laws, and da'wa in this context is considered the most suitable way to realize the spirit of jihad.[25]

Commenting on the need to conduct da'wa in order to bring about the application of the shari'a, Yusanto emphasized the basic nature of Islam as a peaceful religion. In his opinion, jihad should be interpreted in its broadest sense, as any struggle for doing good deeds. This includes the commitment to perform daily prayers, fasting, the pilgrimage to Mecca, serving other people, and assisting the poor. In other words, jihad is no different from da'wa itself, meaning *amr ma'ruf*, "enjoining good," and *nahy munkar*, "opposing vice."[26] On a similar note, M. Rahmat Kurnia, another HTI activist, said that HTI promoted "nonviolent da'wa" (*dakwah tanpa kekerasan*). In his opinion, "violent da'wa simply engenders negative impacts on Muslims and jeopardizes their struggle as a whole."[27]

Moderate Muslim Response to Radical Islamism

The change in the militant Islamists' discourse toward calling for the implementation of the shari'a from below is indubitably associated with the ongoing democratic consolidation occurring in Indonesia, which has witnessed a transition away from authoritarianism over the last decade or so. This dynamic began with the downfall of Suharto in May 1998, which brought his New Order authoritarian regime that had been in power for more than thirty-two years to an end. The collapse of the New Order regime heralded the Reformasi, which has had a tremendous impact on the current dynamics of Indonesian politics. Coupled with the weakening of state power, the far-reaching process of liberalization and democratization that followed Suharto's demise opened a space in which large numbers of Indonesian people could discuss and develop opinions on the issues that affected their lives. A variety of groups, identities, and interests thus emerged, competing for the newly liberated public sphere. At the dawn of the Reformasi era, B. J. Habibie came to power as Suharto's replacement and embarked on a course of political reform. He promised to reschedule elections, release political prisoners, decentralize political power, allow political parties to operate freely, and liberalize the press. His initiatives to meet the demands for reform brought the first free and fair parliamentary elections since 1955, which were held in 1999 and led to the election of the late Abdurrahman Wahid as president.[28] More importantly, Reformasi paved the way for Indonesia to embark on a democratization process that extended people's rule to an increasing number of institutions and issues and thus guaranteed popular control and political equity.[29] Within this context Law No. 22/1999 was ratified on regional autonomy, devolving much of the administration's authority to local governments. This law promoted democratization, thereby allowing Indonesian people to get involved in political life and the decision-making process.[30] The last two successful general elections, held in 2004 and 2009, brought victory to the Democratic Party and brought its founder, Susilo Bambang Yudhoyono, to power as the first president directly elected by the people. Under the leadership of Yudhoyono the effort to strengthen democracy, good governance, and justice has continued.

No doubt, the ongoing democratic consolidation occurring in post-Suharto Indonesia has reduced the room to maneuver that had been available to militant Islamist groups. Broader spaces available for Muslims to express their interests and participate in politics have not only delegitimized the Islamist campaign for the establishment of an Islamic state but also moderated their vision about the ideal position of the ummah vis-à-vis the state. Moussalli has argued that there is a correlation between democracy and moderation in radical Islamist discourse, the development of which originated in a reaction to the political, economic, and international conditions of the Muslim world. He has further argued that radical violent Islamist discourse is only relevant when it is faced with isolation from society under conditions of social disunity, corruption, exploitation, and undemocratic regimes. The discourse automatically moderates when the state provides sufficient spaces and freedom for Islamists to participate in dealing with public issues and concerns.[31]

The narrowing of spaces for maneuver available to militant Islamist groups as a result of democratization has cohered with Indonesia's increasing awareness of the danger of Islamist radicalism and terrorism. Following the 9/11 terrorist attacks in 2001, Jakarta came under constant international pressure to act swiftly against the alleged terrorist networks operating in the country. In the context of the global campaign against terror, the Indonesian government eventually had no choice but to join the international coalition to fight against terrorism. After the first Bali bombing in 2002, the Indonesian government took more serious initiatives to tackle radical religious threats and allocate a bulk of its resources to act against terrorism. New regulations have been enacted to provide legal devices for combating terrorism. President Megawati Soekarnoputri issued, for example, the Government Regulation in Lieu of Statute No. 1/2002 on War against Terrorist Crimes and Presidential Instruction No. 4/2002, which instructs the coordinating state minister of politics and security affairs to take the necessary steps to implement the regulation. These regulations were strengthened by Law Nos. 15 and 16/2003 on anti-terrorism. President Yudhoyono has continued the campaign by strength-ening counterterrorist capabilities through networking and programs of training and education, seminars, conferences, and joint operations. As a result, many terrorist cells have been destroyed, and their operational spaces have been tightened. For instance, Dr. Azahari was shot by antiter-ror police in a raid operation in his hideout in Malang, East Java. His sup-porting cells in Semarang, Wonosobo, Surakarta, Sleman, and Surabaya were subsequently discovered.

In tandem with the ongoing democratic consolidation and the war on terror, nascent opposition across the spectrum of Muslim democrats against militant Islamists has begun to gain ground in Indonesia. The wave of Islamist militancy marked by the mounting call for the shari'a and jihad has increasingly been seen as threatening three principles of democratic life: (1) the raison d'être of the *rechtstaat* (law state) and the rule of law, (2) the sovereignty of the people, and (3) the unity and plurality of Indonesian society. These three principles demand that state legislatures should be built, enforced, and developed in accordance with democratic principles. In other words, the application of the shari'a and jihad con-tradicts the principles of human rights, as guaranteed by the Indonesian constitution.[32] More and more Muslim moderates show an increasing awareness of the danger of the militant Islamists' call for the shari'a and jihad to multiculturalism and democracy. Together with local activists and elites outside the power circle, they are involved in movements campaign-ing for civic freedom.[33]

Moderate Muslims concerned with this matter set up a variety of NGOs as loci for their activism. Examples of these kinds of organizations include Jaringan Islam Liberal (JIL, Liberal Islamic Network), the International Center for Islam and Pluralism (ICIP), the Wahid Institute (TWI), and the Ma'arif Institute for Culture and Harmony, to mention but a few. JIL was set up in Jakarta in 2002 by a group of Jakarta-based young intellectu-als, such as Ulil Abshar Abdalla, Luthfi Assyaukanie, Saeful Mujani, and Ahmad Sahal. They organized discussions, seminars, and workshops to disseminate liberal, progressive views on Islam. They also established an active Web site and a moderated chat group on the Internet as an interactive forum for critical debates on Islam—which frequently provoked heated reactions from their critics. The Web site quickly expanded with the establishment of media syndication. Columns and articles discussing progressively varied aspects of Islamic teaching spread widely beyond the network and appeared outside Muslim-related publications. Popular radio stations set up chat shows to discuss day-to-day needs and offer answers to the problems of Muslims from the progressive point of view on air.[34] Similar to JIL, ICIP has been concerned with the dissemination of progressive, tolerant, and open-minded ideas about Islam. Under the leadership of Muhammad Syafi'i Anwar and Syafiq Hasyim, it actively organized discussions, seminars, workshops, and conferences with the main aim of strengthening pluralism and multiculturalism in Indonesia.[35]

While JIL and ICIP incorporated progressive Muslim thinkers from any segment of the faithful, TWI was established by a group of young Muslim intellectuals affiliated to the largest mainstream Muslim organization, Nahdatul Ulama (NU). The founders include Ahmad Suaedy, Rumadi, and Abdul Moqsith Ghazali. A forum to disseminate progressive ideas by the most outstanding NU scholar and liberal thinker, Abdurrahman Wahid, TWI has been active in organizing campaigns for tolerant Islam, pluralism, and religious freedom. Various innovative programs have been introduced both to facilitate communication and cooperation between Muslim and non-Muslim progressive intellectuals and to enhance Muslim intellectuals' capacity to raise awareness among grassroots Muslims of the importance of pluralism and democracy.[36] Progressive Muhammadiyah intellectuals led by Ahmad Syafii Ma'arif followed in the footsteps of their NU counterparts by establishing the Ma'arif Institute in 2003. Its main mission is to disseminate Islamic reform through interreligious dialogues and cooperation.[37] Through various programs and initiatives, the institute serves as a forum for young progressive Muhammadiyah intellectuals to promote critical thinking on religious issues relevant to contemporary Muslim interests.[38]

Beyond the boundaries of these organizations, representatives of mainstream Indonesian Muslims in NU and Muhammadiyah have also expressed their specific concern about the threats of militancy and radicalism. In response to the threats posed by militant Islamist groups who campaign for the shari'a, seek to circumscribe the rights of minorities, marginalize pluralist sentiments, and even call for jihad, these moderates have worked closely together to promote discourses on interreligious harmony, democracy, egalitarianism, and gender equality. At the same time, they continue to exercise a profoundly moderating and democratic influence on Islam and Indonesian politics, through their campaigns asserting that Islam and democracy are compatible and via their condemnation of Islamic radicalism. They have not only rejected proposals to implement the shari'a but also organized meetings to condemn terrorist actions committed in the name of Islam. To them, terrorism cannot be tolerated, since it is in total opposition to Islam.[39]

A former NU leader and president, the late Abdurrahman Wahid argued that the mounting calls for the shari'a were clearly against Indonesian democratic ideals. His unqualified conviction was that democracy cannot accept the application of Islamic law. In a democratic nation-state, the implementation of an Islamic legal system would subordinate non-Muslims to Muslim citizens, in effect making them second-class citizens.[40] Wahid's counterpart, former Muhammadiyah leader Ahmad Syafii Ma'arif, insisted that Islam upholds the principle of unity for all mankind, whereby a culture of tolerance is encouraged. In his opinion, democracy has a strong foundation in Islam.[41]

Ma'ruf Amin, the head of the fatwa committee of the Indonesian Council of Ulema (Majelis Ulama Indonesia, MUI), strongly condemned terrorism perpetrated in the name of jihad. He insisted that whereas terrorism spreads violence and fear, jihad, when performed correctly in accordance with its proper conditions and rules, brings peace for the people. In his eyes, jihad is, in essence, Muslims' utmost struggle to realize the common good. It is not terrorism. Consequently, suicide bombing claimed for the sake of jihad is totally forbidden in Islam.[42] Amin's opinion on jihad and terrorism represents MUI's official position as a semigovernmental body directly involved in the campaign against terrorism. Along with the Department of Research and Development (Balitbang) of the Ministry of Religious Affairs, MUI established a Special Team for Fighting against Terrorism through an Islamic Religious Approach (Tim Penanggulangan Terorisme Melalui Pendekatan Ajaran Islam). Within this context it issued a fatwa clarifying the distinction between jihad and terrorism.[43] It also actively promoted the peaceful understanding of Islam through so-called antiviolent religious sermons (khutbah anti-kekerasan). In a praiseworthy endeavor, it published a compilation of sermons in 2006 entitled Taushiyah dari Mimbar yang Teduh: Kumpulan Khutbah Anti Kekerasan (Admonition from the peaceful pulpit: Anthology of antiviolent sermons), to be distributed to thousands of mosques across Indonesia.[44]

The Prosperous Justice Party

The effort made by moderate Muslims to campaign against Islamist radicalism by disseminating tolerant, peaceful Islam has not only reduced the space to maneuver available to radical Islamist groups. This campaign also brought a new hope for Islam's inclusion in the state democratic system. In line with the transformation of Indonesia's political system, new political parties have arisen to represent a wide range of ideologies and interests, and these include parties that explicitly espouse the application of the shari'a (Islamic law) and other conservative positions. One such example is the Justice Party (Partai Keadilan, PK), which represented the growing strength of political Islam in Indonesia. This party was fundamentally different from the other Islamic parties: the United Development Party (Partai Persatuan Pembangunan), the National Awakening Party (Partai Kebangkitan Bangsa), the National Mandate Party (Partai Amanat Nasional), and the Moon and Crescent Party (Partai Bulan Bintang). Its differences were in its historical roots, its ideology, its political goals, and the broader electorate it appealed to. It was derived from the da'wa (Islamic proselytizing), Muslim Brotherhood–inspired movement that preaches Islam as a total way of life and which began to gain ground on Indonesian university campuses in the 1970s.[45]

As a party that drew its inspiration from the Brotherhood, PK defined Islam primarily as a political ideology and endeavored to position it at the center of Indonesian politics. Its vision of Islam was of a classical, complete, and universal system that comprehensively governs all spheres of social, political, economic, and cultural life. It proclaimed the shari'a as the only system that could rid Muslims of the multitude of problems and catastrophes that afflict them, all of which result from the implementation of secular systems. PK believed that only through the shari'a would Muslims be able to challenge the domination of the Western powers, which are in league with the Zionists to undermine Islam and the Muslim ummah.[46] Implicit in this rhetoric was a rejection of the existing nation-state system, seen as a weapon of the imperialist West to divide Muslim nations and demolish the *khilafat* (caliphate). It is not surprising that PK was very much concerned with issues of Islamic solidarity and the reestablishment of the caliphate.[47] PK's political manifesto demonstrated a clear tension between the ideal of the ummah and the reality of the nation-state. It was known as an avant-garde party of *ikhwan* and *akhawat*, popular terms used by *tarbiyya* members to address their fellow

activists. Its electoral campaign pushed Islamist viewpoints and emphasized its exclusiveness as an Islamist party. Significantly, PK garnered only
1.4 percent of overall votes in the 1999 elections and thus failed to meet
the 2 percent electoral threshold.

The result of the 1999 elections forced PK to rebrand itself as the
Prosperous Justice Party (Partai Keadilan Sejahtera, PKS), whose vision
further developed the ideology, thought, and systems of its predecessor
and its desire to establish Islam and the shari'a as the social, political, and
legal system of Indonesia.[48] However, it now gave a different emphasis to
the party's goals concerned more with the real issues facing Indonesian
Muslims. It now presents itself as the party of moral reform, and rather
than seeking direct political power it aims to show the public, through
da'wa, what a government based on the moral principles of Islam would
look like. The party used the slogan "Clean and caring" to launch popular campaigns focusing on the national issues of a weak economy and
rampant corruption.[49] To cope with the reservations shown by its secular
nationalist rivals and Indonesian people in general, PKS sought to create a new image as a moderate Islamist party, adopting the national and
democratic rhetoric. The party acknowledged the principle of a secular
political state as a prerequisite of liberal democracy,[50] the secular format
of the Indonesian nation-state, the state ideology of Pancasila, and the
1945 Indonesian constitution. It made these the framework of its political
participation in the electoral democratic system.

Despite the principle of God's absolute sovereignty held by most
Brotherhood theoreticians, PKS saw no contradiction between Islam and
democracy. It argued that the community has the right to define political
institutions via democracy, which it accepted as an instrument to infuse
Islam into Indonesian politics.[51] Reference was made to Yusuf Qaradawi,
a moderate Brotherhood thinker, who acknowledges that the people have
the right to govern themselves and that this does not detract from God's
ultimate sovereignty. This is the progressive, inclusive political Muslim
position, which increasingly perceives democracy as incorporating the values that Islam advocates, including consultation, enjoining what is good
and prohibiting evil, and resisting unbelief.[52]

Borrowing from the framework developed by Baker to analyze the
dynamics of political Islam in Egypt, it is interesting to look at the extent to
which the PKS's rise represents the birth of a new Islamism with a much
longer-term vision of social and political reform. As Baker argues, the
new Islamists' adoption of participatory government and their pragmatic

approach distinguish them significantly from the first generation of Islamists, who sought political power in order to reform the social order in accordance with Islam. They are more content to contest elections and take up whatever seats or offices they may win. Instead of cultivating a defensive discourse of Islam as a religion under attack, and thus calling on its followers to defend it against its enemies, the new Islamists call Muslims to participate in the task of improving society.[53] Their thinking might be characterized as holistic, inclusive, and favoring dialogue. Religion is seen as just one part of the solution. It needs to be viewed in conjunction with national interests, economic realities, and cultural traditions. Given their emphasis on the national interest, they are open not only to collaboration with other political forces and non-Muslims as equal partners but also to dialogue and collective deliberation. The new Islamists represent, as Mandaville has noted, "a broader generational and strategic shift identifiable in Muslim movements across several settings today."[54] PKS's decision to put an emphasis on national interest and dialogue in its political vision indeed reflects significant elements in a post-Islamist trajectory.

The opportunity to get involved in democratic, electoral, power-sharing-based politics served as the catalyst for PKS to dramatically break with its rigid ideology of the totality of Islam (*Islam kaffah*), as developed by the tarbiyya movement. It believes that the Pancasila, as the philosophical foundation of the state, can function as the main inspiration for the whole process of statecraft and governance. Yet PKS does not see the ideology of Pancasila as a bastion of secularization, blocking all other political aspirations. It suggests instead that the Pancasila and democracy can work together with Islamic values and principles. In an elegant maneuver, PKS proposed the implementation of the Medina Charter (Piagam Madinah), the constitution of the Medina city-state under the leadership of the Prophet Muhammad.[55] By referring to the Medina Charter, PKS demonstrated the compatibility of Islam with democracy and, at the same time, its determination to abide by the civic principles of pluralism and peaceful coexistence among and within diverse religious groups. During the campaigns in the run-up to the April 2004 parliamentary elections, PKS reiterated its vision as a party of moral reform concerned with the fight against the nation's core problems, including corruption, collusion, and nepotism. The image it presented was of a disciplined organization, outwardly and inwardly unsoiled, free of corruption, and morally pure. This strategy worked well. The party won significant electoral support, as much as 7.34 percent.[56]

PKS appears to have become more pragmatic in its drive to meet its political targets, particularly those of winning regional-level direct elections (*pemilukada*). It has been quick to provide loans for sympathetic intending candidates and has collaborated with other parties, including the nationalist-secular Indonesian Democratic Party of Struggle (Partai Demokrasi Indonesia Perjuangan) and the religious Christian Prosperous Peaceful Party (Partai Damai Sejahtera). In this way it has been able to promote its members and sympathizers to the posts of governor and head of district across Indonesia. PKS scored a prestigious victory in Depok, West Java, where its leading cadre and former minister of forestry under Abdurrahman Wahid's presidency, Nur Mahmudi Ismail, was elected as the city's mayor. It also nominated a former high-ranking police officer, Adang Daradjatun, and his running mate, Dani Anwar, for election as Jakarta's governor and vice-governor. At that time the party was confident that it did not need to collaborate with other parties. The PKS team was defeated by Fauzi Bowo and his running mate, Prijanto. Despite this failure, PKS participated in the 2008 election race in West Java by nominating its own cadre, Ahmad Heryawan. It collaborated with the National Mandate Party, whose candidate Dedi Yusuf stood as Heryawan's running mate. PKS won this election. This success was followed by another PKS victory, when its candidates Syamsul Arifin and Gatot Pudjonugroho were elected to the posts of governor and vice-governor of North Sumatra in the direct elections in the same year.

PKS's campaign to strengthen its image as a moderate Islamist party open to all segments of Indonesian society (a catchall party) intensified in the run-up to the parliamentary elections in April 2009. Its pragmatic politics place less and less emphasis on ideology, and many voters questioned whether PKS had abandoned its Islamist agenda and reconciled itself to operating within the framework of Indonesian nationalism. They ask if the priority the party gives to electoral victory means that it has downgraded its religious agenda or if this merely represents a tactical shift in its political strategy. This sort of skepticism echoes the reservations held by established Muslim organizations, as noted above. To counter some of this criticism PKS aired a series of media advertisements. One of these used the slogan "The party for all of us" and featured a series of comments from different people of diverse backgrounds, from an old garbage collector to a beautiful girl wearing a T-shirt and jeans (without a head scarf). Through these campaigns, the party sought to demonstrate its alignment with a moderate version of Islam. Despite their ambivalent position on certain issues, the party's elite did not hesitate to call for civic freedom and democracy. Likewise, the chairman of the consultative body, Hilmy Aminuddin, repeatedly rejected any affinity with Wahabism and denied allegations of their animosity toward traditional religious practices, such as *tahlilan, yasinan*, and *mawludan*. The leaders also affirmed their theological affiliation with mainstream Indonesian Islam, the *ahl al-sunna wa'l jama'a*.[57]

It is worth noting that PKS's ideological position and political pragmatism have also provoked criticism from the party's members and sympathizers. The involvement of this so-called da'wa party in electoral politics has sparked debate in numerous blogs. Will its commitment to da'wa reshape politics, or will politics steer PKS away from da'wa?[58] People have openly queried whether the PKS legislators still retain their credibility as preachers (*du'at*) committed to Islamizing society through politics or whether they are simply politicians pretending to be preachers. Some bloggers are even questioning whether the Islamic struggle for the supremacy of God's teachings can be pursued through the un-Islamic democratic game. Concerns about PKS's collaboration with secular parties, and particularly with a Christian party like the Prosperous Peaceful Party, provoke the most heated debates. In fact, more and more PKS members and sympathizers are worried that this short-term power-oriented political maneuver will deflect the party from its main mission of improving Indonesia's political systems and practices. They believe that this kind of coalition simply demonstrates the hypocritical nature of politicians and their hunger for power. In response to discontent spreading among party members and sympathizers, PKS intensified the cultivation of da'wa as a complementary strategy to dominate the political landscape of Indonesia. It developed various da'wa activities, including *halqa, daura, pengajian* (religious lectures), *liqa* (meetings), *rihla* (tours), *mabit* (staying overnight), seminars, and workshops, which are deemed necessary as a manifestation of the tarbiyya vision to build an Islamic society based on the eight Brotherhood principles laid down by Hasan al-Banna.

The strategy to accept democracy and balance its political pragmatism with da'wa successfully led PKS to win 7.89 percent of the overall votes in the 2009 general elections. This result put the party in the top four after President Yudhoyono's Democratic Party and the other two secular nationalist parties, Golkar and the Indonesian Democratic Party of Struggle, winning 20.45, 14.85, and 14.65 percent, respectively. As the coalition partner of the Democratic Party, PKS has continued to strengthen its position as a moderate Islamic party that respects civic freedom and human rights.

Conclusion

This chapter has sought to demonstrate that the influence of the radical Islamist ideology and movement that attempt to transform Indonesia into an Islamic state by calling for the comprehensive implementation of the shari'a and jihad in various conflict areas in eastern parts of the country has significantly faded away. Attempts made by radical Islamists to impose a totalitarian world order by disseminating religious doctrines and activism that espoused norms, symbols, and rhetoric imbued with animosity ended in failure, and this ultimately serves to highlight the marginal position of radical Muslims and their unsuccessful efforts to popularize their discourse glorifying militancy and violence. In the face of this failure radical Islamists have shifted toward a strategy of implementing the shari'a from below (or adopting it at the personal level), promoting da'wa (Islamic proselytizing), and nonviolent endeavors with the aim of making Indonesian Muslims aware of their duty to uphold the supremacy of Islam. The new course they have taken is considered more appropriate to deal with the current situation and the future challenges facing the ummah. The circle of militancy and violence is believed to only jeopardize the struggle for the victory of Islam.

There are some factors contributing to the radical Islamists' failure to change the political landscape of Indonesia and conversely, their changing strategy of calling on Muslims for the implementation of the shari'a at the individual level. These include the democratic consolidation that facilitated the opening of political opportunity in the era of Reformasi and the burgeoning of modern democratic idioms as a result of moderate Muslims' campaign against Islamist radicalism. The opening of the post-Suharto Indonesian public sphere has allowed moderate Muslims from diverse backgrounds to get involved in the debates about objectifying Islam, and this prevents militant Islamist actors from dominating religious symbols and the interpretation of religious creeds through their militant campaigns and from imposing their agenda of an Islamic state. For the sake of democracy, more and more Muslim moderates are showing an increasing awareness of the danger of the militant Islamists' call for the shari'a, as well as the need to disseminate multiculturalism, gender equality, justice, and civic freedom, the universal values believed to be embedded in Islam as a mercy for all (rahmat li'l 'alamin). In the midst of the celebration of democracy in Indonesia, the logic behind the call for the implementation of the shari'a as an alternative to the formerly totalitarian political system has automatically lost ground.

The Indonesian government's success in bringing the bloody communal conflicts in various parts of the country to an end—which occurred in parallel with the ongoing democratization process—is another factor that has urged militant Islamists to change their course, for the conflicts had been taken as legitimation by the militants to call for the need to apply the shari'a at the state level and fight jihad as a solution to the government's perceived failure to protect Islam and the Muslim ummah. No less important were the initiatives taken by the government in collaboration with civil society organizations to tackle the threat of Islamist radicalism and terrorism. In response to mounting pressures from the international community, the government joined the international coalition against terror, under the framework of which various political, legal, and strategic measures have been deployed.

There is reason to believe that Indonesia today is in the throes of starting along a post-Islamist path. A sort of synthesis between the call for Islam's importance for public life and democracy, post-Islamism has emerged as an alternative to Islamist radicalism. Through its endeavor to fuse religiosity and rights, faith and freedom, as well as Islam and liberty, this post-Islamist alternative has enabled Muslims to express and actualize their religious beliefs and practices, without plunging into violence and joining the cycle of militancy. Discussion on post-Islamism is relevant to studies on the shift in the Islamic political discourse and activism occurring in a democratizing Indonesia, which, like other parts of the Muslim world, has seen huge social change as a result of globalization. The growth of Islam's public visibility, which has occurred in tandem with the celebration of democracy, has become irrefutable evidence of the transforming dynamics of Islam in this country.

The phenomenon of PKS sheds light on the relevance of the discussion on post-Islamism in relation to the recent dynamics of Islam in Indonesia. As an Islamist party that drew its inspiration from the Brotherhood-inspired tarbiyya movement, PKS has participated in electoral politics and launched popular campaigns in order to expand its electorate and base of support—thus winning significant votes in the elections. Conveying alternative political visions to a wider audience, it has been active in promoting clean governance, anticorruption, and professionalism, deemed to be the prerequisite to get rid of corruption, an incompetent bureaucracy, poverty, and other fundamental problems faced by Indonesia as a nation. Its ability to package these issues was the key to PKS's success in garnering significant votes in the 2004 and 2009 parliamentary elections, capturing, respectively, 7.34 and 7.89 percent of the overall votes. Despite its ambivalence toward democracy, PKS has also increasingly developed an inclusive political platform and altered its basic perception about what is permissible in a democratic environment. It has no doubt learned how to get involved in the electoral democratic games and become a proactive force contributing to the process of further democratic deepening in Indonesia.

Notes

1. Scholars of political Islam such as Gilles Kepel, Oliver Roy, and John L. Esposito, to mention but a few names, have debated the appropriateness and usefulness of the term *Islamism*. For a new debate on the term and contested perspectives on its meaning inspired by events after 9/11, refer, for instance, to Richard C. Martin and Abbas Barzegar, eds., *Islamism: Contested Perspectives on Political Islam* (Stanford: Stanford University Press, 2010).

2. Asef Bayat, "What Is Post-Islamism?" *ISIM Review* 16, no. 5 (2005): 5; see also Asef Bayat, *Making Islam Democratic. Social Movements and the Post-Islamist Turn* (Stanford: Stanford University Press, 2007), 10–11.

3. Bayat, "What Is Post-Islamism?" 5.

4. Arjun Appadurai, "The Production of Locality," in *Counterworks: Managing the Diversity of Knowledge*, ed. Richard Fardon (London: Routledge, 1995), 208–229; see also Manuel Castells, *The Information Age: Economy, Society, and Culture*, vol. II: *The Power of Identity* (Oxford: Blackwell, 2000).

5. See, for instance, Armando Salvatore, "The Genesis and Evolution of 'Islamic Publicness' under Global Constraints," *Journal of Arabic, Islamic and Middle Eastern Studies* 3, no. 1 (1996): 51–70; Dale Eickelman and James Piscatory, *Muslim Politics* (Princeton: Princeton University Press, 1996); Dale Eickelman "Islam and the Language of Modernity," *Daedalus* 129 (2000): 119–135.

6. Jenny B. White, "The End of Islamism? Turkey's Muslimhood Model," in *Remaking Muslim Politics*, ed. Robert W. Hefner (Princeton: Princeton University Press, 2005), 87–111.

7. Jose Casanova, *Public Religions in the Modern World* (Chicago: University of Chicago Press, 1994), 36–37.

8. Nilufer Göle, "Islamic Visibilities and Public Sphere," in *Islam in Public: Turkey, Iran, and Europe*, ed. Nilufer Göle and Ludwig Ammann (Istanbul: Istanbul Bilgi University Press, 2006), 3–43.

9. Vali Nasr, "The Rise of 'Muslim Democracy,'" *Journal of Democracy* 16, no. 2 (2005): 13–27.

10. Moeflich Hasbullah, "Cultural Presentation of the Muslim Middle Class in Contemporary Indonesia," *Studia Islamika* 7, no. 2 (2000): 1–58.

11. Ariel Heryanto, "The Years of Living Luxuriously. Identity Politics of Indonesia's New Rich," in *Culture and Privilege in Capitalist Asia,* ed. Michael Pinches (London: Routledge, 1999), 159–187.

12. Mona Abaza, "Markets of Faith: Jakartan *Da'wa* and Islamic Gentrification," *Archipel* 67 (2004): 173–202.

13. Abu Bakar Ba'asyir, "Sistem Kaderisasi Mujahidin dalam Mewujudkan Masyarakat Islam," in *Risalah Kongres Mujahidin I dan Penegakan Syari'ah Islam,* ed. Irfan S. Awwas (Yogyakarta: Wihdah Press, 2001), 79–90.

14. Abu Bakar Ba'asyir, "Pemikiran Politik dan Dakwah Islam," in *Dakwah dan Jihad Abu Bakar Ba'asyir,* ed. Irfan S. Awwas (Yogyakarta: Wihdah Press, 2003), 136–137.

15. Abu Bakar Ba'asyir, interview by the author, Surakarta, August 2006.

16. Muhammad al-Khaththath, "Khilafah, Wajib Ditegakkan dan Perlu," *Al-Wai'e* 55 (March 2005): 75–77.

17. Hafidz Abdurrahman, "Menegakkan Khilafah Kewajiban Paling Agung," *Al-Wai'e* 55 (March 2005): 12–18.

18. Muhammad Ismail Yusanto, "Hizbut Tahrir Menolak Kepemimpinan Sekuler," Pernyataan Hizbut Tahrir Indonesia, no. 060/PU/E/09/04, issued during the demonstration in Jakarta, on September 11, 2004.

19. Ibid.

20. Abu Bakar Ba'asyir, interview by the author, Surakarta, August 2006.

21. For more detail, see, among others, Peter Mandaville, *Global Political Islam* (London: Routledge, 2007), 248–256.

22. Nasir Abbas, *Membongkar Jamaah Islamiyah (Pengakuan Mantan Anggota JI)* (Jakarta: Grafindo, 2008).

23. Ja'far Umar Thalib, interview, at www.alghuroba.org, accessed March 19, 2009.

24. Abu Bakar Ba'asyir, interview by the author, Surakarta, August 2006.

25. Ibid.

26. M. Ismail Yusanto, interview by the author, Surakarta, July 2006.

27. M. Rahmat Kurnia, interview by the author, Jakarta, 2005.

28. See Marco Bünte and Andreas Ufen, "The New Order and Its Legacy: Reflections on Democratization in Indonesia," in *Democratization in Post-Suharto Indonesia,* ed. Marco Bünte and Andreas Ufen (London: Routledge, 2009), 3–28; see also Dewi Fortuna Anwar, "The Habibie Presidency," in *Post-Soeharto Indonesia: Renewal or Chaos?* ed. Geoff Forrester (Singapore: ISEAS, 1999), 33–47.

29. Anders Uhlin, *Indonesia and the "Third Wave of Democratization": The Indonesian Pro-Democracy Movement in a Changing World* (New York: St. Martin's Press, 1997).

30. P. Pratikno, "Exercising Freedom, Local Autonomy and Democracy in Indonesia, 1999–2001," in *Regionalism in Post-Suharto Indonesia,* ed. Maribeth Erb, Priyambudi Sulistiyanto, and Carole Faucher (London: RoutledgeCurzon, 2005),

21–35; see also Henk Schulte Nordholt and Gerry van Klinken, "Introduction," in *Renegotiating Boundaries. Local Politics in Post-Suharto Indonesia*, ed. Henk Schulte Nordholt and Gerry van Klinken (Leiden: KITLV Press, 2007), 1–29.

31. Ahmad S. Moussalli, *Moderate and Radical Islamic Fundamentalism: The Quest for Modernity, Legitimacy and the Islamic State* (Gainesville: University Press of Florida, 1999), 104–105.

32. Tim Imparsial, "Penyeragaman dan Totalisasi Dunia Kehidupan Sebagai Ancaman terhadap Hak Asasi Manusia, Sebuah Studi Kebijakan di Indonesia" (research report, Jakarta, 2006).

33. Ihsan Ali-Fauzi and Saiful Mujani, *Gerakan Kebebasan Sipil Studi dan Advokasi Kritis atas Perda Syariah* (Jakarta: Nalar, 2009), 91–112.

34. For a further account on JIL, see, for instance, Zuly Qodir, *Islam Liberal: Paradigma Baru Wacana dan Aksi Islam Indonesia* (Yogyakarta: Pustaka Pelajar, 2003); Angela M. Rabasa, Cheryl Benard, Lowell H. Schwartz, and Peter Sickle, *Building Moderate Muslim Networks* (Santa Monica: RAND, 2004); and Ahmad Ali Nurdin, "Islam and State: A Study of the Liberal Islamic Network in Indonesia, 1999–2004," *New Zealand Journal of Asian Studies* 7, no. 2 (2005): 20–39.

35. On the establishment of ICIP and its main mission, see, for instance, K. Khudori, "ICIP: Menapaki Jejak Transformasi Pluralisme ke Pluralitas," in PSIK, *Pluralisme dan Kebebasan Beragama: Laporan Penelitian Profil Lembaga* (Jakarta: PSIK Universitas Paramadina, 2008), 149–176; see also Budhy Munawar-Rachman, *Reorientasi Pembaruan Islam: Sekularisme, Liberalisme dan Pluralisme Paradigma Baru Islam Indonesia* (Jakarta: LSAF, 2010), 77–88.

36. Ahmad Suaedy, director of the Wahid Institute, interview by the author, Jakarta, July 19, 2010; Rumadi, a Nahdlatul Ulama young intellectual, interview by the author, Jakarta, July 9, 2010.

37. Fajar Reza Ul Haq, director of the Ma'arif Institute, interview by the author, Jakarta, July 20, 2010.

38. On the profile of TWI, see its Web site, www.wahidinstitute.org; see also Munawar-Rachman, *Reorientasi Pembaruan Islam*, 101–110. As for the Ma'arif Institute, see M. Hilaly Basya, "Religious Leaders and Democratic Transition in Post–New Order Indonesia: A Study on the Role of Muhammadiyah Scholars in Reducing Radical Islamic Movements" (unpublished M.A. thesis, Leiden University, Leiden, 2010).

39. Masdar Farid Mas'udi and Masykuri Abdillah, two leading Nahdlatul Ulama intellectuals, interviews by the author, Jakarta, August 7, 2007, and August 1, 2010, respectively. Also Tarmizi Thaher, former minister of religious affairs and also a Muhammadiyah intellectual, interview by the author, Jakarta, August 4, 2010.

40. Abdurrahman Wahid, "Islam in a Democratic State: A Lifelong Search," in *A Celebration of Democracy. A Journalistic Portrayal of Indonesia's 2004 Direct Elections amongst Moderate and Hardline Muslims*, ed. Asrori S. Karni (Jakarta: Era Media Informasi, 2006), ix–xx.

41. Ahmad Syafii Maarif, "Islam in Indonesia and Democracy," in *A Celebration of Democracy. A Journalistic Portrayal of Indonesia's 2004 Direct Elections amongst Moderate and Hardline Muslims*, ed. Asrori S. Karni (Jakarta: Era Media Informasi, 2006), xx–xxiii.

42. Ma'ruf Amin, the head of the fatwa committee of the Indonesian Council of Ulema, interview by the author, Jakarta, July 18, 2007.

43. Indonesian Council of Ulema, *Fatwa MUI tentang Terorisme No. 3/2004* (Jakarta: Indonesian Council of Ulema, 2005), i–17.

44. Department of Religious Affairs, *Meluruskan Makna Jihad, Mencegah Terorisme* (Jakarta: Department of Religious Affairs, 2006).

45. On the *tarbiyya* movement, see Rifki Rosyad, *A Quest for True Islam: A Study of the Islamic Resurgence Movement among Youth in Bandung, Indonesia* (Canberra: ANU E Press, 2006); S. Salman, "The Tarbiyah Movement: Why People Join This Indonesian Contemporary Islamic Movement," *Studia Islamika* 13, no. 2 (2006): 171–241. And on its transformation into the Prosperous Justice Party, see Ali Said Damanik, *Fenomena Partai Keadilan Transformasi 20 Tahun Gerakan Tarbiyah di Indonesia* (Jakarta: Teraju, 2002); Mathias Diederich, "A Closer Look at *Dakwah* and Politics in Indonesia: The Partai Keadilan," *Archipel* 64 (2002): 101–115; and Yon Machmudi, *Islamising Indonesia: The Rise of Jemaah Tarbiyah and the Prosperous Justice Party* (Canberra: ANU E Press, 2008).

46. Aay Muhammad Furkon, *Partai Kedilan Sejahtera: Ideologi dan Praksis Politik Kaum Muda Muslim Indonesia Kontemporer* (Jakarta: Teraju, 2004), 149–157; M. Imdadun Rahmat, *Ideologi Politik PKS, Dari Masjid Kampus ke Gedung Parlemen* (Yogyakarta: LKiS, 2008), 55–57.

47. Furkon, *Partai Keadilan Sejahtera*, 53; Rahmat, *Ideologi Politik PKS*, 58.

48. Rahmat, *Ideologi Politik PKS*, 114.

49. Elizabeth Fuller Collins, "'Islam Is the Solution': *Dakwah* and Democracy in Indonesia," *Kultur, the Indonesian Journal for Muslim Cultures* 3, no. 1 (2003): 148–182; Elizabeth Fuller Collins and Ihsan Ali Fauzi, "Islam and Democracy: The Successful New Party PKS Is a Moderate Alternative to Radical Islamism," *Inside Indonesia* (online), no. 81 (January 2005), http://insideindonesia.org/content/view/192/29, accessed December 3, 2009; and Ary Hermawan, "PKS dan Perubahan Paradigma Gerakan Islam," *Republika*, April 10, 2004, 4.

50. Ziya Öniş, "Globalisation and Party Transformation: Turkey's Justice and Development Party in Perspective," in *Globalising Democracy*, ed. Peter Burnell (London: Routledge, 2007), 122–140.

51. Cholid Mahmud, one of the PKS leading figures in Yogyakarta, interview by the author, Yogyakarta, March 2008.

52. James Piscatori, *Islam, Islamists and the Electoral Principle in the Middle East*, ISIM Paper, 1 (Leiden: ISIM, 2000).

53. R. Baker, *Islam without Fear: Egypt and the New Islamists* (Cambridge: Harvard University Press, 2003).

54. Mandaville, *Global Political Islam*, 114.

55. PKS's chairman, Tifatul Sembiring, reiterated his party's denial of the impor-
    tance of the Jakarta Charter in a seminar in London on Indonesian politics and
    economic progress. According to him, what PKS has endorsed is the application
    of the Medina Charter that in essence guarantees religious pluralism. See Partai
    Keadilan Sejahtera, "Mengkaji Indonesia dari Inggris" (June 20, 2008), at www.
    pk-sejahtera.org, accessed March 26, 2010.

56. Francois Raillon, "Islam and Democracy: Indonesia's 2004 Election and
    Beyond" (paper presented at the European Institute for Asian Studies Special
    Briefing, Brussels, 2004), 2.

57. See the statement made by Hilmy Muhammad at a seminar in London as
    reported in "Ketua Majelis Syuro: Saya Sering Memimpin Tahlil dan Yasin,"
    July 22, 2008, at www.pk-sejahtera.com, accessed April 5, 2010; see also "PKS
    Menjawab Fitnah," October 25, 2008, at, accessed April 7, 2010. See also a
    sort of self-critique article by PKS cadre Yon Machmudi, "PKS Mengancam
    Eksistensi Ormas Islam?" spread in various blog spots.

58. See, for instance, debates at www.pkswatch.blogspot.com.

PART THREE

Change in Ambivalence

7

Egypt and Its Unsettled Islamism

Asef Bayat

At its height in the late 1980s, Egyptian Islamism represented a complex web of dispersed and heterogeneous organizations, activities, and sympathies around a distinct core embodied in the reformist Muslim Brotherhood (MB), which aimed to Islamize society at the grassroots and ultimately establish an Islamic state. To achieve the same end, militant Islamists of al-Gamaʿa al-Islamiya, meanwhile, combined social agitation and armed struggle against the state and Western interests. Challenged by these lay Islamists, the institution of Azhar (the religious establishment sanctioned by the state) expanded its *daʿwa* (or call to the "true" Islam), institutional, and social activities, contributing to the general spread of religiosity. Then stood the vast sector of "civil Islam," containing large religious welfare and professional associations, Muslim youth and women's groups, and Islamic activism at universities, at schools, and in neighborhoods. Individual Muslim celebrities and media personalities, such as Mustafa Mahmoud, Selim el-Awa, Hasan Hanafi, and Muhammad Emara, carried out their own daʿwa.

This movement caused significant change in society and posed the most serious challenge to the Egyptian regime. The Muslim Brothers' commitment to socioreligious change through daʿwa and associational work wrested much of urban society from state control. Through independent mosques, schools, youth associations, women's groups, clinics, and publications, ordinary people negotiated alternative ways of being and doing that MB's parliamentary activities aimed to turn into public policy.

The challenge of al-Gamaʿa al-Islamiya militants seemed even more dramatic. During the 1980s, in addition to controlling university campuses, they moved into poor districts of Cairo and spread their influence in southern towns and villages. They agitated in the streets and mosques, resolved local disputes, and imposed moral discipline (*taghiir al-monkar*) by preventing "vices" such as drunkenness and mixing of the sexes. As the "organic intellectuals" of the humble Saiidi (South Egypt) social milieu, the militants also offered welfare services, literacy classes, clinics, transportation, income-generation projects, and food for the poor.[1] By the early 1990s, they virtually ruled many southern towns and had established their "Islamic Republic of Imbaba" in the heart of the capital city. At this juncture of intense societal vigor, religion dominated the nation's political and cultural idioms, and the "Islamic solution" assumed an unprecedented currency. Islamic ethics found expression in language, behavior, physical appearance, dress codes, mosque attendance, radio and television programs, publications, and public spaces. It was also reflected in the spread of Islamic commodities, fashion, and leisure, which penetrated civil society, the military, and some state institutions. By the early 1990s, Egypt seemed to be going through an Islamic "revolution by stealth."

Things, however, proved to be more complex. Toward the end of the 1990s, the cumulative reform project reached its limits at the state's doorstep. The dilemma, which had also haunted Iran's political reform project, was a familiar one: How far could a reform movement march forward under a "weak" or nonhegemonic state threatened by social and economic forces and constrained by its own paternalistic attitudes toward sociopolitical change? On the one hand, the relative success of the movement in changing Egyptian society and in challenging the state partly caused its own downturn. On the other, the crisis of Islamism in the region, notably Iran, together with the new global sentiments in the aftermath of the 9/11 attacks pushed some trends within Egyptian Islamism to rethink their religious politics. The "Islamic Republic of Egypt," as some had predicted, never came.[2] Instead, the Islamist movement experienced in the 2000s a process of fragmentation accompanied by rising conservative religiosity and individualized piety before merging into a revolution that heralded the coming of a post-Islamist Egypt. This chapter chronicles the tumultuous contours of Islamism since the 1980s through the revolution of January 2011; it suggests that while the pre-revolution Egypt and its "seculareligious" state nurtured the dominance of Islamist discourse, the postrevolution Egypt under the Islamist Muslim Brothers ironically signals the rise of post-Islamist sentiments.

Decline of the Core

The Gama'a al-Islamiya originated from the "religious family" of the Islamic student associations, which President Sadat encouraged to grow as part of his policy to undermine communists and Nasserists. Dominating Egyptian universities, these associations went beyond student welfare activities, engaging also in moral discipline, opposing music, theatergoing, dancing, and mixing between the sexes. With the advent of the Iranian Revolution and Camp David Accords in 1979, two trends emerged in these associations. Moderates, based largely in Cairo and delta universities, aligned with the Muslim Brothers; and the radical trend, dominant in Upper Egypt, evolved into the Islamist al-Gama'a al-Islamiya. Assassinating President Sadat in 1981 in the hope of launching an Islamic revolution in the image of Iran, the Gama'a developed to become by the mid-1990s one of the most important militant Islamist groups in the Muslim world.

Al-Gama'a militants' comparative advantage (in relation to other political groupings) grew out of their intimate connection to the territories they controlled. In a sense, they represented the "organic intellectuals," the disenfranchised but educated youth of the depressed towns and villages of South Egypt (Saiid), which, by virtue of northward migration, had been extended to such Cairo slums as Ain al-Shams and Imbaba. Isolated from the modern north by mountains and desert, by socioeconomic marginalization, and by tribal social organization, the Saiid had already been rendered as modern Egypt's internal other.[3] With the central state effectively absent, local tribal and kinship confederations governed people's daily lives. As Nasser's land reform program gradually undermined this traditional social structure, al-Gama'a moved in to fill the void. When the militants began to operate in such Cairo slum districts as Imbaba and Ain Shams, they found familiar communities marginal to the modern Egyptian state—with no municipality, no effective police, no house numbers, and no maps, where a stranger could get lost in the maze of endless alleyways. Whereas the militants succeeded in penetrating Ain Shams and Imbaba, they failed to make inroads into the more integrated districts of Gamaliya, Bab el-Shariyya, Sayyeda Zeinab, Dokki, Zamalek, and Maadi. Because the Gama'a was able to operate only where the state was effectively absent, the movement was bound to assume a territorial or regional, and therefore local/endemic, character.

This territoriality, however, was as much an advantage as a limitation. Once the state reclaimed the Gama'a's territories, the militants were rendered out of place and on the run. They could neither defeat the state nor work within it; they could neither lead a revolution nor cause notable reform. Despite Aboud el-Zomor's claim that the Gama'a aimed for a popular revolution in the image of Iran, the group's vision of revolutionary change did not go beyond a military coup in which the people had almost no role except to "defend the new regime" once it was established.[4]

At the same time, the militants did not know how (because they did not wish) to operate within the existing political arrangement. The Gama'a's da'wa remained remarkably narrow and notoriously male. Focusing primarily on political and religious agitation, the militants failed to leave behind any novel ideas or practices, any institutional or discursive legacy through which to induce social change. There was little attempt, for instance, to hold free elections, practice local governance, establish NGOs, or supervise projects of self-development. Al-Gama'a's welfare provisions assisted some of the poor but were essentially meant to make people dislike the regime and believe in Gama'a's "Islamic solution." Da'wa focused primarily on people's moral obligations, on "forbidding wrongdoings" (nahye an al-monkar), rather than on their rights and potential as agents of their own destiny. Thus the likes of Shaykh Jaber of Imbaba in Cairo prowled with gangs, setting fire to video shops, closing down beauty salons, threatening to throw acid on unveiled women, preventing the genders from mixing, and even condemning music at weddings,[5] the last utterly contrary to Egypt's festive culture. At the national level, militants attacked Coptic Christian churches, gatherings, individuals, and property.[6] Violence against the Copts increased from fifty-two incidents during the 1970s to 111 during the 1980s and early 1990s, including forty-six murders from 1992 to 1994.[7] For Islamists, the proselytizing practice of Christian churches hindered the establishment of an Islamic society and state. While their welfare provisions, dispute settlements, and fighting of local bullies gained popularity, their severe moral order antagonized others, including powerful families.

What the Gama'a ultimately left behind was no more than a conservative religiosity and piety, one that was to be appropriated later by establishment Islam. Consequently, when the Egyptian state reclaimed these territories by a twin strategy of promoting arrests and NGOs, the militants were rendered socially redundant and politically fugitives, seeking refuge in underground cells, sugarcane farms, Europe, or the safe haven of the Taliban's Afghanistan. Of course, exiled members continued their agitation from abroad. Al-Murabitoun was published in Denmark, and al-I'tisam in Britain, while Yasser al-Serri established his Islamic Research Centre in London. Those such as Refai Ahmad Taha and Mustafa Hamza escaped to Afghanistan to gain guerrilla training and then give it to new recruits before sending them back to Egypt via the Sudan and Libya to carry out military operations. The assassination of the speaker of parliament in 1990 was the first of such attacks by these "returnees from Afghanistan." With its key "historical leadership" in custody and the other leaders in exile,[8] the Gama'a became further removed from the pulse of Egyptian society.

With the killing in October 1990 of the activist Alaa Muhyeddin and the subsequent siege of Cairo's Imbaba in December 1992, the movement, which had focused on da'wa and education, virtually transformed into a guerrilla military organization. Now, military leaders would issue fatwas and execute them without consulting the da'wa wing. In Asyût, beginning in 1992, military leaders became emirs and took charge of educational policies.[9] Both the target and the scale of its violence shifted from scattered incidents against civilians (nonconformists, secularists, and Copts) to widespread military attacks against the state. A semi–civil war seemed to be under way. The insurgents targeted police officers, top officials, foreign tourists, and Copts, opening fire on trains, vehicles, hotels, and banks. The four years from 1990 through 1993 were Egypt's bloodiest of the twentieth century. The death toll increased from 139 in 1991, to 207 in 1993, to 225 in 1994. Altogether, nearly 1,200 insurgents, police officers, civilians, and Copts perished between 1992 and 1996.[10] Police and the military erected checkpoints at every corner in southern cities and villages, while nightly raids into militant hideouts continued ceaselessly. Thousands, including many innocents, were rounded up; many were tortured and detained without trial.[11]

Between 1992 and 2000, some 101 death sentences were handed down by security forces and military courts.[12] Mediation attempts by al-Gama'a's lawyer Montasir al-Zayyat, a former member, were rebuffed by the government, and Interior Minister Abdel Halim Mousa was dismissed in 1993 for considering negotiations with the militants. As the insurgents became more hunted and desperate, their violence became more indiscriminate. It reached its apex in the Luxor massacre of November 18, 1997, when insurgents brutally murdered and decapitated fifty-eight Western tourists and four Egyptians in the Temple of Hatshepsut.[13] The sheer savagery of the attack shocked the Egyptian public, disoriented the security apparatus, and crippled the country's most important foreign exchange earner, the tourist industry, for three years. In the hours after the attack, thousands of foreign tourists flocked to airports to exit the country en masse, leaving behind deserted luxury hotels, abandoned tourist sites, millions of redundant workers, and a nation caught between the brutality of the insurgents and the state.[14]

The massacre, meanwhile, heralded the impending demise of militant Islamism. For two days after the killings, the Gama'a did not utter a word. Then there emerged a series of confused and contradictory statements. "Political leaders" in Europe expressed regret, the imprisoned or "historic leaders" in Egypt condemned the operation, while the "military leaders" based in Afghanistan claimed responsibility.[15] Montasir al-Zayyat, the Gama'a's lawyer, realized that the organization and its "Islamic alternative" were in profound crisis and conveyed to the leadership the futility of a violent strategy that had deeply alienated the average Egyptian.[16] The crisis of "frontal attack" then pushed al-Gama'a to pursue a fundamental shift in its strategy.

By July 1997, imprisoned leaders were ready to enforce a unilateral halt to bloodshed and return to peaceful da'wa. Privately jubilant, the Interior Ministry, however, remained defiant, rejecting any hint of concession to or dialogue with the militants.[17] The exiled leadership's initial hostility to the cease-fire call subsided when Sheikh Omar Abdel-Rahman, Gama'a's spiritual leader (jailed in the United States for ordering the 1993 bombing of the World Trade Center), endorsed it.[18] Although internal disputes and sporadic attacks by splinter cells continued, Gama'a finally reaffirmed on March 25, 1999, its decision to renounce antigovernment violence once and for all. Dismayed by the new strategy, al-Jihad leader Ayman al-Zawahiri, who by now had virtually been absent from the Egyptian scene, joined Osama bin Laden to establish the International Islamic Front to Fight the Jews and Crusaders in 1998. In response, al-Zayyat proposed and Abdel-Rahman endorsed an International Islamic Front to Defend Islam by Peaceful Means.[19] Although the latter remained merely an idea, it was followed by a number of initiatives for nonviolent activities. (Ex-)Militants made formal requests to establish political parties within the existing system: Hizb al-Wasat, the Islamic Party of Reform (Hizb al-Islamiya al-Islah),[20] and Hizb al-Shari'a. "Time has shown that violence and armed struggle have been harmful to all parties, to the country and Islam itself," militants concluded.[21] But the government turned down all the applications on the grounds that "religious parties" were not allowed. This infuriated Abdel-Rahman and Ahmad Taha, who threatened to abandon peaceful means and mobilize "people led by the army, clerics and university professors for a revolution."[22] However, legal activism was too compelling to the imprisoned leaders to be thwarted by such threats.

Aggressive Israeli policy under Benjamin Netanyahu and Arial Sharon, the crisis of the Algerian Islamist experience, the dramatic transformation of Iranian Islamism, and the ascendancy of post-Islamism under Khatami (which Gamaʻa leader Ahmad Taha observed while residing in Iran) persuaded Gamaʻa's "historic leaders" to remain committed to their new nonviolent vision. Now, Gamaʻa's new primary target was not Egyptian *"jahili* rule" but, rather, the Jewish state, against which all groups in Egypt and in the Muslim world should unite.[23] The historic leaders realized not only that they were incapable of defeating the Egyptian state but also that their violent method had subverted their aim of "guiding people toward the path of God." They concluded that their violent strategy had in fact benefited the "enemies of Islam": Israel, the United States, the West, and secularists.[24] These political realities conditioned the historic leaders to revisit their doctrine. To match their new political perspective they were compelled to craft new doctrinal arguments by reinterpreting the Islamic texts. In the end, militant Islamists found virtue in what the MB had been practicing for over six decades. But was the MB's strategy of societal transformation free from constraints?

The Muslim Brothers in Abeyance

In the early 1990s, the MB, or Ekhwan al-Muslimoun, was acting as though it was a shadow government. The MB controlled thousands of mosques, dominated the major national professional syndicates and the student unions in the north, ran various NGOs, influenced numerous schools, and formed the most powerful opposition in parliament. The Muslim Brothers, in short, had captured a sizable space in civil society and were beginning to permeate state institutions including the judiciary, universities, and Al-Azhar. However, at its peak, the movement seemed to be looming at the state's back door, ready to pounce. Primed by its clampdown on the Gamaʻa, startled by the 1995 assassination attempt on President Mubarak in Addis Ababa—feeling, in a word, threatened—the government set out to cripple the MB. An emergency law had already been deployed to bar public assemblies, and an anti-terrorism law passed in 1992 had made preventive detention legal and restricted the press. Against opposition outcries, the government marched on, weakening the Ekhwan's hold on universities and manipulating the election procedures of professional syndicates to exclude Muslim Brothers. It shut down the Lawyers Syndicate from 1996 to 2001, ignored dozens of court rulings

against that action, and then did the same to Ekhwan-dominated professional associations for three years beginning in 1996.[25] The Brotherhood's
monthly *Liwa al-Islam*, published since 1945, was shut down, while the
ruling National Democratic Party (NDP) continued to publish its own
Islamic weekly with the almost identical title *al-Liwa al-Islami*.

Then, beginning in June 1995, the government began in earnest, with
a spate of arrests and military trials of leading Muslim Brothers. Such
detentions were typically carried out prior to national elections to prevent Brothers from participating.[26] Prominent Islamist syndicate leaders
such as Essam El-Erian and Mohamed Saad (of the Doctors Syndicate)
and Mokhtar Nouh and Khaled Badawi (of the Lawyers Syndicate) were
jailed, and over five thousand MB offices throughout the country were
shut down. The state took over some sixty thousand mosques and forbade
preachers from conducting sermons without clearance from the Ministry
of Awqaf, depriving Islamists of a vital channel of da'wa.[27] By April 1997,
sixty-one leading Muslim Brothers had been sentenced to up to five years
in prison with hard labor. Finally, the suspension of the Islamic-oriented
Labor Party, an MB ally, and its paper *al-Sha'b* was a further blow to the
Ekhwan.

The Labor Party's support for Sudan's "Islamic project," its public
protests against government corruption, and its pro-Iraq campaign had
already angered state security forces. The last straw was *al-Sha'b*'s fierce
attack on the minister of culture for allowing the "blasphemous" novel
Banquet for the Seaweed to be republished. For weeks, *al-Sha'b* urged
Muslims "to join hands and avenge the insults which the Ministry of
Culture directed against God and Islam."[28] As al-Azhar students poured
into the streets in protest, Egypt went through one of its deepest political
crises. When the government consequently disbanded the Labor Party
and *al-Sha'b*, the Ekhwan's only channels of communication and legal
means to act were those professional syndicates it still controlled. It
appeared as though the MB's role of diverting youth from joining violent
Islamist groups had come to an end. The state had no need to tolerate
the group.

With its offices closed down, publications disbanded, mosques controlled, leading activists jailed, and organization under surveillance, the
MB was pushed to the sidelines. "We don't do anything anymore," admitted the spokesman, Mamoun al-Hudaibi, as early as March 1997.[29] Later,
only the MB-dominated syndicates, notably the doctors' association, could
manage public activity, for instance, raising public awareness on atrocities

committed against Muslims in the Balkans and Chechnya. Even this did not remain unpunished. The MB was forced to limit its congregations to such occasions as Quran-reciting sessions, Ramadan *iftars*, and funerals, though organizers did not hesitate to turn these events into political rallies.[30]

Some members had already accepted that "we do not aim to rule or aspire to power. Simply let us continue making our da'wa toward God."[31] Younger leaders echoed this in their arguments for an Islamism without an Islamic state. In February 2000, Essam El-Erian concluded that the MB's call for an Islamic republic was "a slogan that has passed its time.... The constitution already says that Egypt is an Islamic state and that shari'a is the basis of legislation." Thus the language of agitation shifted to a large degree from state power to public morality, virtues, and international issues. It was around such sensitive matters as "blasphemy," "insults to Islam," moral laxity, and the oppression of Muslims in Palestine, Chechnya, and the Balkans that the group rallied to agitate the public. Islamism, it appeared, ceased to be primarily a political project and was simply an "Islamic phenomenon,"[32] a struggle against secular values in order to elevate personal piety, morality, Islamic identity, and ethos—a process I like to call *cheap Islamization*.

El-Erian's argument that the Egyptian state was already Islamic did hold some degree of truth. The constitution had clearly authorized shari'a as the main source of law, and the government often framed its policies in religious terms. As I will show later, the state began to selectively appropriate the religious space left by the decline of political Islam. This demonstrated the complex dynamics of Islamism in Egypt. At one level, it reflected the hegemony of Islamism, which had imposed aspects of its frame, language, and institutions on the state. At the same time, however, the success of Islamism in changing certain social and cultural codes, institutions, and ethical moral structures deprived the core of the movement (al-Gama'a and the MB) of popular support for mobilization. For the reforms had appeased large segments of the constituency by fulfilling some of their fundamental ethical and moral needs. Thus, when *al-Sha'b*'s Magdy Hussein and the Freedom Committee of the Journalists Syndicate held a conference in 2000 to protest the detention of the MB's prominent members, few turned up, until "loads of youth cadres from the Labor Party were bused in to fill the empty seats."[33] There was nothing like the public outcry of 1995, when many protested similar detentions of Brothers.

The Muslim Brothers did survive the political shockwave, as they had done often in their long history, thanks to their reliance on associational activism, kinship ties, and maneuvering between active presence and abeyance. However, the internal dynamics of Islamist movements, in addition to the dramatic domestic and international events at the turn of the century such as the September 11 attacks, only reinforced the gradual change in the nature of Islamism from a political project challenging the state to one concerned with personal piety and global malaise. Political Islam in Egypt began to lose its earlier appeal, while militant Islamism, despite its sensational media coverage, experienced a deep crisis. Perhaps nothing was more telling about the movement's destiny than the afflicted state of Omar Abdel-Rahman, serving a life sentence in a New Jersey prison. Forgotten and frail in a foreign jail, blind and lonely with no access to anyone who spoke his language, the sheikh had only a few tapes of the Quran—its recitation and exegesis—as his companions. Locked up in his prison cell, the spiritual leader almost faded away from public memory. Egyptians could only hear his murmurs uttered through the lips of his son: "Why have Muslims abandoned me?"[34]

Islamization without an Islamic State

The unsettling of the Islamist core did not mean a waning of religious commitment and activism. On the contrary, many indications pointed to a growing, albeit fragmented, trend of conservative religiosity and piety. Across sixty-five societies included in the World Values Survey, Egyptians were the most pious, with 98 percent declaring their religiosity, compared with 82 percent of Iranians and Americans and 24 percent of Japanese, the least religious.[35] Comparative surveys of religiosity (in Egypt, Pakistan, Indonesia, Kazakhstan, Jordan, and Iran) confirmed that Egyptian Muslims revered devotional institutions and trusted ulema and imams more than they did intellectuals, the army, the courts, and the universities.[36] Egyptian Muslims continued to flock to Friday prayer sermons, overflowing from mosques and into the streets. The middle class and professionals in particular showed a great commitment to Friday prayer rituals.[37]

As did women to the veil. By 2000, the number of women wearing the *hijab* (head scarf) experienced a new upsurge, and in 2002 veiled women constituted a staggering majority of over 80 percent. In my survey of 466 women appearing in public in Cairo (at the Book Fair), 80 percent were veiled; the remainder included non-Muslims. Of the 374 veiled, 284 wore hijab; seventy-five, *khimar*; and fifteen, *niqab*. A similar survey in a shopping mall in Zamalek, the most "Westernized" Cairo neighborhood, showed that over 67 percent appeared in a veil.[38] This certainly was not the Cairo of 1969, when Janet Abu-Lughod observed, "One rarely sees jallaabi-yah....Almost no women are veiled."[39] Even Egypt's most liberal institution, the American University in Cairo, saw a slow but steady growth of public piety among staff and students. While in the 1980s the head scarf was a rarity on campus, by early 2000, veiling had become common among students and staff, albeit with the fashion and sophistication of their higher class background. In 2003, ten students appeared with fully covered faces, causing considerable legal and security complications. The university's prayer halls, nonexistent in the 1980s, were now filled with religious students who wished to pray, discuss, and forge new identities. Student activists of the Help Club held ceremonies to celebrate the entry of newly veiled women, born-again Muslims, to their midst. The hijab assumed an inertia of its own. As more diverse women turned to veiling, they rendered the hijab a hegemonic public symbol, conditioning, even pressuring, others to follow suit. With more and more women from the literate, intellectual, and affluent classes, including chic movie stars, wear-ing the hijab, veiling ceased to be a sign of fanaticism or "baladiness."

In this process, as Muslims became "more Muslim," Copts turned "more Christian." The largely middle-class Copts cemented a new reli-gious awareness, manifested in rising church attendance, public display of Christian icons, and anxiety over political Islam. "Welfare pluralism" or "NGOization," by offering opportunity on a sectarian basis, only exac-erbated the communal divide.[40] Coptic Christians adhered to a religious conservatism (in terms of scripturism, public morality, sexual conduct, family values, and gender politics) that could only be matched by their Muslim counterparts. Indeed, judged against Muslim women's modesty, lack of veiling among Coptic women often veiled their conservatism.

Perhaps nothing was more telling about the neoconservative social trend than the public's reaction to the personal status law proposed in par-liament in 2000. The long-standing bill, which favored official recognition of *urfi* marriage (a written contract concluded in front of two witnesses but not registered formally) and women's (conditional) right to initiate divorce and to travel abroad without men's permission, caused profound public anxiety, notably among men. An opinion poll in Cairo showed that half of respondents (both men and women) were against women having the right to initiate divorce (*khul'*); 85 percent were against the inclusion of this right in a marriage contract (isma); and a staggering 90 percent opposed women traveling abroad without men's permission.[41] Parliamentarians, by using Islamic language, forced a substantial revision of the bill. Even the traditionally liberal dailies such as Al-Wafd did not spare commentaries and cartoons that reflected deep anxiety over the new law and the fear that it would subjugate men and disturb the harmony and stability of the family.[42] The daily attributed the rise of divorce to "misguided" claims for gender equality, which it argued went against the Quran and shari'a.[43]

Art and music did not remain immune to the rise of pious passion. Nationalism, religiosity, and art converged in the profound moral outrage Arabs felt toward Israel's siege of Palestinian territories in 2002. Egypt's leading pop stars, among them Amr Diab, Muhammad Munir, and Mustapha Qamar, produced best-selling albums with religious and nationalist lyrics, often performed in the style of melancholic religious recitation. Muhammad Munir's high-priced al-Ard wa-Salaam, ya Madad ya Rasoul Allah sold 100,000 copies. The most popular Egyptian singers, including Ali al-Hajjar, Muhammad Tharwat, and Hani Shaker, joined voices to produce the religio-nationalistic album al-Aqsa ya-Allah. Distinct from traditional religious songs, which are upbeat melodies praising the saints or the Prophet Muhammad, the new genre carried powerful elements of spirituality, sorrow, and even tragedy. In passionate and sad lyrics, the singers plead with the creator to secure the nation from blunders and suffering.[44]

The new ethos found institutional and discursive expression in the vast, though fragmented, "Islamic sector," composed of Islamic media, publications, education, associations, business, halaqat (religious gatherings), art, entertainment, tastes, and fashion. Business quickly capitalized on this growing market for Islamic commitment and commodities. The likes of Ragab al-Sueirki, a notorious polygamist who married nineteen times, ran his clothing store chain under the name Al-Tawheed Wal-Nour:[45] "Islamic names bring baraka, raise peoples' trust, and attract them to business."[46] Many private schools and clinics chose Islamic names even though they differed little from the same, non-Islamic institutions.[47]

This represented a new trend in religiosity. Thick on ritual and remarkably thin on dissent, it signified a shift from Islamism as a political project to a form concerned primarily with personal salvation, ethical enhancement, and self-actualization. Mosques continued to pack them in for Friday prayers and informal sermons, but they were devoid of oppositional da'wa. In my experience of attending Friday prayer sermons for some six months in 1996 in Cairo's various mosques, from the poor Bulaq abul-Alaa to the rich al-Muhandessin, from the traditionally militant Kubri-Al-Gama'a and Amr Ibn-Aas to the *zawaya* of Old Cairo, I encountered only slight references to domestic politics. As the Ministry of Awqaf controlled all mosques, only Azhari preachers were allowed to deliver sermons, and they focused overwhelmingly on conventional religious ethos and injunctions. The star preachers of the late 1990s and early 2000s were no longer the militant Omar Abdel-Rahman or Sheikh Kisk, or even the traditionalist Sheikh Sha'rawi. Rather, they were the likes of the necktied and cleanly shaven Omar Abdel Kafi, Khalid el-Guindy, and Amr Khalid, whose sermons attracted massive crowds of youth and women from elite families.

Clearly, adherence to religious ethics and the search for spirituality were not new among Egyptian Muslims, including the rich and the powerful. In the course of sixteen years of interaction with various strata of Egyptian society, particularly with the elite, I observed how they revered the Book, the tradition, and the religious authorities in a more profound and widespread manner than those in Iran did. But theirs was a *passive* religious attachment: as believers, they ordinarily and unquestioningly went along with carrying out their religious obligations. What appeared to be novel from the late 1990s on, however, was that many lay Muslims, notably the young and women from affluent families, exhibited an *active piety*: not only did they practice their faith, they also preached it, wanting others to believe and behave like them. The adverse effect of this extraordinary quest for religious truth and identity became apparent before long. Unlike the passively pious, who remained indifferent about other peoples' religiosity, the actively pious began to judge others for what and how they believed, privileging their own forms of devotion, thus generating new lines of division and demarcation.

This kind of piety was largely the stuff of the comfortable and privileged classes. Indeed, there was little sign of religious transformation among the rural and urban poor, except perhaps for migrant laborers in the Arab Gulf states, many of whom returned to Egypt as pious petite bourgeoisie. Otherwise, the poor continued to practice folk piety, based on their own perceptions and social conditions. Most of them remained illiterate and thus "ignorant" about sacred texts and religious injunctions, upholding general conservative social mores (as on gender, for instance). They felt blessed for living in an Islamic environment, but they constantly lamented how "only a very few real Muslims were around." The harshness of their distressed lives often expressed itself in deep cynicism about fellow Muslims whose greed and betrayal had corrupted an imaginary moral community. "Since we are Muslims, then our society is surely an Islamic society," said Ramadan Abdul-Fotouh, an illiterate manual worker.[48] Many poor and rural families remained involved in Sufi orders of various kinds that had spread throughout the country, a faith line that centers on individual spirituality and universal love.[49] Others continued to construct new "saints," as in the image of Shaykh Sha'rawi or hundreds of others from the *awliyâ* revered in the villages of Upper Egypt.[50] The *mulids* of the well-known saints, Sayyid Badawi, al-Hussein, Sayyida Zeinab, Ayshe, and Nafissa, continued to attract massive crowds from all over the country. Some estimated that as many as half of all Egyptians attended Mawlid festivals.[51] They came with food and family and passed days and nights in the streets and alleyways around the shrines of the saints. The participants blended the mundane pleasures of picnicking and socializing with conducting *dikr* and experiencing spiritual ecstasy. In the evenings, children were busy with the deafening noise of carnival games, while young adults marched up and down the streets, to see and be seen, attending to their faith and enjoying affordable fun. The profane and festive mood of these sacred congregations made middle-class Islamists shun them as occasions that "have nothing to do with religion; these people simply try to have fun."[52] More austere religious commentators charged them with playing with paganism.[53]

The middle layers and well-to-do classes, women in particular, and not the poor, experienced new religious activism. While the middle- and lower-middle-class high-achievers had already embraced political Islam during the 1980s, the elites and the new rich inclined toward a piety that could accommodate their privilege and power. Middle-class migrants to the Gulf (teachers, doctors, and professionals) often returned home more pious: The women now wore hijab or *khimar*, while the men had grown facial hair, with both groups feeling "closer to God." Saudi religious tradition socialized Muslim migrants to new religious experiences, such as strict prayer times in mosques, attending religious lessons, forced veiling, and abstaining from watching movies. Upon their return, many continued to practice such ethos. Alongside this ritualistic piety came strong materialistic values and hierarchical snobbery, expressed in the heavy-handed treatment of maids, drivers, or cooks.[54] The popularity of a new genre of lay preachers (sheikh and *sheikha*) reflected, and became a catalyst for, the growth of this new active religiosity.

The "Phenomenon of Amr Khalid"

In the late 1990s, Amr Khalid, an accountant turned preacher, had become a Cairo household name. Khalid followed the lead of Omar Abdel Kafi and Khalid el-Guindy but surpassed them in popularity among well-to-do youths and women. A gifted orator in the style of televangelists, he lectured in private homes and exclusive clubs but soon rose to stardom at the pulpit of El-Hossari Mosque in the trendy al-Muhandessin, before he was forced by the authorities to move to 6th October City, a new posh community on Cairo's outskirts. His weekly lessons became a spiritual staple for thousands of young people who flocked from throughout the city's affluent districts to hear him. The crowd rushed hours in advance to get an ideal spot, filling the lecture hall and the surrounding sidewalks, often causing heavy traffic congestion. In 1999, Amr Khalid would deliver up to twenty-one lessons a week in socially prominent households, peaking at ninety-nine during Ramadan.[55] Amr Khalid's recorded sermons became unparalleled best sellers at Cairo's massive Book Fair in 2002,[56] and they traveled as far as the markets of East Jerusalem, Beirut, Damascus, and the Arab Gulf states. Youth subculture, elitism, and a pietistic Islam converged to produce this genre of da'wa against a backdrop of political Islam in crisis and profound stagnation on Egypt's intellectual and political landscape.

The new preachers deliberately targeted the young and women of the elite classes, "the people with influence," because "they have the power to change things," according to Khalid el-Guindy.[57] Since elite families generally kept away from traditional mosques located in lower-class areas, young preachers brought their message to the comfort of private homes, clubs, and the stylish mosques of posh neighborhoods. More important, in addition to face-to-face sermons to disseminate his message, Amr Khalid utilized a full range of media, including satellite television channels such as Dream TV, Iqra'a, and Orbit; his state-of-the-art Web site; and audio- and videotapes—media that reached the upper-middle and more affluent classes in particular.[58] For some time, popular state-sponsored magazines *Al-Ahram al-Arabi* and *Al-Ahram al-Riyadi* distributed his tapes as gifts to their readers. Khalid el-Guindy established a paid "Islamic Hotline" (Hatif el-Islami) for the public to seek advice from the sheikh.[59] Within a year, daily calls increased from 250 to one thousand. For his part, Amr Khalid traveled with his message to the stylish Agami and other upper-middle-class north coast resorts and later went on speaking tours to Arab states where his fame had already spread. By the early 2000s, Khalid was being treated like a pop star, with dignitaries such as Queen Rania of Jordan attending his lectures. The colorful decor and the talk show–like aura of his lecture halls, in contrast to the austere Azharite pulpits, reflected the taste of his main audience: the twelve- to thirty-five-year-old elite males and females who had never before been exposed to religious ideas in such an intense and direct manner.

Khalid resembled his audience. Young, cleanly shaven, often wearing blue jeans and a polo shirt or a suit and tie, Amr Khalid embodied simultaneously the hipness (*rewish*) of Amr Diab (Egypt's most revered pop star), the persuasive power of evangelist Billy Graham, and the unrefined therapy of American talk show host Dr. Phil (McGraw). For the young, Khalid was "the only preacher that embraced and tackled our spiritual needs" and someone who "makes us psychologically comfortable," who "treats us like adults, not children."[60] Unlike more orthodox preachers known for their joyless moralizing and austere methods, Khalid articulated a marriage of faith and fun. Speaking in sympathetic, compassionate tones and in colloquial Arabic, Khalid and his colleagues conveyed simple ethical messages about the moralities of everyday life, discussing issues that ranged from relationships, appearance, and adultery to posh restaurants, drunk driving, hijab, and the sins of summer vacations in Marina.[61] In a sense, the new preachers functioned as "public therapists" in a troubled society that showed little appreciation for professional psychotherapy. Emotional intensity, peace, and release (crying) often imbued Khalid's sermons. "You should attend my lessons," Khalid alerted his audience, "not for raising your knowledge but for touching your heart."

From the likes of Khalid, young people heard the message that they could be religious and still lead a normal life—work, study, have fun, and look like anyone else in society. Khalid's words assured the audience that they could be pious while maintaining their power and prestige. His message operated within the consumer culture of Egypt's nouveaux riches, where piety and privilege cohabit as enduring partners. Analogous to the Methodist Church of the well-to-do in the American Bible Belt, where faith and fortune are happily conjoined, Khalid's style made rich Egyptians feel good about themselves.

Khalid was not a scholar or interpreter of the Quran and did not issue fatwas. Rather, he was devoted to correcting individuals' ethical values and everyday behavior, fostering such values as humility, generosity, trust, loyalty, and repentance. However, he was no liberal Muslim thinker. Some of his ideas remained highly conservative, and many of his methods were manipulative. On the hijab, for instance, Khalid based the "integrity of society...on the integrity of women," and based that of the latter on "her hijab," because "one woman can easily entice one hundred men, but one hundred men cannot entice a single woman." Since, according to this logic, unveiled women are promoters of sin, a "complete, head-to-toe hijab is an obligation in Islam." Muslim women unconvinced of this were not really Muslim, he claimed in his tapes, because Islam, in literal terms, simply means "submission" to the word of God: "Even if you do not understand, you must obey him."

Armed with such logic and speaking with tremendous force and conviction, the preachers were determined to make converts. They patiently lectured detailed and practical guidelines for women, say, to start wearing the hijab. Thus, before long, many of their listeners began to make visible changes in their lives: veiling, wearing the niqab (something Khalid did not insist on), praying regularly in the mosques, and acquiring a pious identity. Khalid advanced a religious discourse that contained passion, clarity, relevance, and humor but lacked novelty, nuance, and vigor. While his style was highly imaginative, his theology remained deeply scriptural and lacked the perspective necessary to incorporate critical reason in his interpretations. This was not because he had never studied at al-Azhar. In fact, his doctrinal views hardly differed from those of orthodox Azharite sheikhs who dismissed him despite, or perhaps because of, his immense popularity. Rather, at that juncture in Egypt, when religious authority was fragmented and Islam showed little sign of innovation, Khalid appeared to be an innovator, even though only in style. The mass appeal of the likes of Khalid was a by-product of the crisis of Egypt's mass education, one that valorized memorizing, fragmenting knowledge, revering printed words, and nurturing authoritarian mentors. Compared with the patronizing manner of a typical Azhari sheikh, the amiable and compassionate Khalid appeared to be a true democrat—one who guided scores of well-off women to the path of active piety. But the halaqat, the network of semi-private women's groups, played an equally central role in re-Islamizing Egyptian women.

Re-Islamizing Women

The halaqat became a phenomenon in Egypt's religious landscape from the mid-1990s onward. Small, fragmented groups of between ten and sixty women, they tapped into the vast urban female population to cultivate active piety.[62] Most were presided over by female preachers, or sheikhas, who gave religious lessons in local mosques or clubs and often in private homes. Some, like Sherine Fathy, an ex-physician and a renowned elite preacher at al-Hilal religious complex, attracted hundreds of women from affluent families.[63] Less well-known sheikhas employed the simple language of da'wa, often framing their discourse in terms of their audience's socioeconomic desires, including "unlimited shopping in the hereafter."[64]

Women's quest for personal virtue compelled them not only to listen to preachers but also to conduct holy deeds through voluntary social services and charity work. They held initiation ceremonies to celebrate the rites of religious passage of born-again Muslims. In *haflat hijab*, or "veiling parties," they blessed the donning of hijab by young and old females who were ironically treated in the image of beauty pageants. Most activists came from middle-class and well-to-do families. Some used their private chauffeurs to visit homes, hospitals, and orphanages and reported back to their halaqat.

Although the ethics espoused by female preachers largely converged with the conservative tenet of patriarchy, the ulema expressed strong opposition to female-led da'wa. Even though the sheikhas encouraged women to "act as care givers in their homes and attend to their husbands" or encouraged educated women to express ideas on women's matters, the ulema viewed female preaching as "degeneration."[65] The Azhar clerics flatly rejected a woman's authority to issue fatwas, with the concern that the plurality of religious authority would undermine its monopoly of moral (and male) prerogative and might engender chaos and confusion among believers.

In a sense, Muslim women's participation as religious authorities implied a redefinition of gender roles. But there was a paradox—it empowered women and yet also reproduced patriarchal constraints. As such their activities did not represent any kind of "Islamic feminism" or struggle for gender equality articulated within an Islamic paradigm. It is true that historically, female activists in the Middle East such as Aisha Taymuriya, Zeinab Fawwaz, Nazira Zein al-Din, Malak Nasef, and Qadriya Hussein have always had to reinterpret Islamic precepts in order to further women's interests.[66] But "Islamic feminists" were distinct in that they saw an inherent privilege in religious discourse for Muslim women. Nevertheless, they all took women's rights as their fundamental point of departure and used religious language and practice to extend those rights.

Women active in the halaqat, however, seemed to have different concerns. Theirs was primarily a preoccupation with self-perfection to attain
proximity to God and to seek Islamic ideals of piety, discipline, and
self-enhancement.[67] Mundane acts of empowering women or serving
others were simply steps along the path toward personal salvation. This
renewal (*ihya*) could be achieved no longer by mere praying or fasting
(*ibadat*); da'wa, making others equally pious, was now paramount. This
could cause division by breeding competition and differentiation instead
of solidarity. Women of identical religiosity would associate among themselves (*sohba*) and shun the "less pious," nonreligious, or non-Muslim.
While individual women benefited from this "turn-to-religion" in terms
of enhancing their autonomy, by reproducing patriarchal constraints
they in effect shut down possibilities for other women who did not share
their ideology. Clearly, Egypt's Muslim activists were not, in contrast to
their Iranian counterparts, involved in political contestation for wom-
en's rights; for them, rather, Islamic activism provided "harmony and
self-contentment through perfecting such qualities as patience (sabr),
piety and discipline."[68] Their notion of self-enhancement differed from
liberal feminists' embrace of autonomy, freedom, and equality. Instead of
targeting patriarchy, they opposed Western feminists' emphasis on liberalism, individualism (as opposed to family), and tolerance (for instance,
of homosexuality). Indeed, being "good women" and "doing housework"
were considered acts of worship and fulfillment. "Each laborious task she
undertakes," argued the preacher Sherine Fathy, "every stuffed vine leaf
she meticulously rolls is not wasted, because in the end, it is an act of
worship."[69] It was perhaps such patriarchal theology that informed the
intimate relationship between Mona, a high-powered businesswoman
who covered her face with the niqab, and her husband. "When it comes
to my husband," she proudly declared, "I have to please him as religion
says. I have to have sex with him whenever he wants and never refuse.
It is exactly like praying and fasting."[70] Even more well-known activists
such as Safinaz Qasem who did speak out about gender imbalance and
were therefore labeled by some as "Islamic feminists" refuted the broader
feminist paradigm. They were primarily female Islamists for whom the
liberation of women depended on establishing shari'a. "Women's commitment to shari'a," according to Qasem, "is the highest degree of liberation women can achieve."[71]

How can we account for this genre of religious attainment among
Egypt's well-to-do women? If indeed this trend was rooted merely in

an ethical desire for "self-enhancement," a longing for inner clam, or the need for community and solidarity,[72] then why did it spread mostly among the *well-to-do*, generally among *women*, and at a particular *historical juncture*? A prominent Egyptian observer finds it "striking how rare it is to find examples of religious fanaticism among the higher...social strata of the Egyptian population." This is so, he suggests, because "they are exempted from the feelings of inferiority experienced by the aspiring lower middle classes."[73] There is indeed a recurring tendency to associate active religiosity with the lower class, the powerless, and the plebeian. Marx was famously concerned with the *politics* of religion, with how religion acted as the sigh of the oppressed masses. Elites appeared on the analytical scene only as exploiters of mass religiosity. This perspective continued to inform the mainstream Marxist paradigm. Although such thinkers as Michael Lowy, observing the rise of religious activism, pointed accurately to religion's both conservative and radical potential, they rarely addressed the religious attachment of the elites.[74] For Weber, too, the elites in general stayed away from religion. Exploring the religious orientations of nonprivileged classes, Weber suggested that the nobility's particular status, honor, was not compatible with such notions as sin, salvation, and religious humility.[75] These were too plebeian to be internalized by the elites. Privileged classes, for Weber, were scarcely prone to the idea of salvation. They were concerned instead with the "psychological reassurance of legitimacy."[76] Many of these interpretations had roots in the secular orientation of early social theorists, with the implicit assumption that the wealthy were modern and the modern were rationalist and thus secular.[77] It is now clear that religion might serve also as the "opium of the rich," as a source of tranquility to ward off their moral and spiritual (as opposed to material) helplessness, to offer the elites a meaning for what they cannot control, say, the mysteries of pain and death. Even a "feeling of inferiority," so often cited as causing "religious fanaticism," can be found among the "upper strata" of society, namely, among its women.

Elite Muslim women in general might be more prone to piety than other social groups, because the space of sin for them is far broader than for others. Affluent Muslim women, compared with men, the poor, and non-Muslims, showed a greater inclination to piety because their class position and lifestyle were, more than any other groups', associated with "sin" and therefore caused guilt. As members of a privileged class, they were likely to attend nightclubs, bars, or dancing or drinking parties and to date or appear "half-naked" on beaches. If they are unable to justify and accommodate such conduct with their Muslimness, then they are likely to suffer from moral anxiety and regret. Although affluent men also practice similar lifestyles, they are not subject to the same standard of sin and guilt as women. The centrality of the woman's body in moral judgments articulated in the "gender division of sin" subjects her to potentially disproportionate "sinful" acts. So, while Muslim men and women might appear half-naked on beaches, the woman, not the man, would be considered immoral; or only a woman's uncovered hair, not a man's, will provoke moral pressure. In in-depth interviews, "born-again Muslim"[78] women invariably talked about the agony of feeling guilty. Somaya, a thirty-eight-year-old interior designer, wearing a face cover, related how in her early thirties she "stayed out late at night, drinking and dancing." At those parties, "a man can laugh with you, touch you, and you cannot stop any of these acts." And "these violations made me always feel guilty." Hana, in her twenties, went through profound "psychological instability," as she put it, following years of "leftist intellectualism," not praying but drinking, dating, and doubting. Even though she never doubted God, Hana asked for guidance from an old pious woman. Her advice was: "There is nothing to read. Just obey God, and the rest will follow." The "real breakthrough in my religious awakening was when I watched my grandmother die," after which Hana left her graduate studies, got married, and began to teach in an Islamic primary school.[79]

An intense state of uncertainly seemed to spark women's turn to active piety. Incidentally, this class of women happened to be particularly susceptible to more uncertainty because they were exposed to too many "truths" to handle; they could afford to access diverse, often extremely different lifestyles, ideas, and options, the truth of which they were unable to determine. For some, even the plurality of fatwas by different sheikhs became a source of confusion and concern. In such a state of "existential anxiety," to use Giddens's term, the available mediums of practicing piety—listening to lay preachers like Amr Khalid, attending the halaqat, watching religious satellite channels such as Iqra'a—played a decisive role in turning individuals' confusion into comfort, their anxiety into peace. They offered women an authoritative life in a world of multiple options.[80]

There was still a social factor. Gender bias had created a class of well-to-do women who dressed well, attended exclusive clubs, and shopped in Western boutiques, but unlike their male counterparts, they remained socially obsolete. In other words, the women's "symbolic capital" did not match their economic standing, and this in a society that was intensely obsessed with the merit of social status. While their male counterparts were publicly and successfully engaged in business or bureaucracy, women either reluctantly undertook low-status "women's jobs" or preferred the isolation of housework to the humiliation of such "lowly" public positions. These social-psychological gaps in women's lives were filled by the structure of piety with its attendant components—identity, institutions, and rituals, bestowing feelings of certainty and of doing something useful.

But why did religiosity, and not something else, fill that gap? The hegemony of conservative sensibilities had drastically marginalized, in fact, suppressed, alternative modes of reasoning. Women's informal networks of clubs, private parties, and associations had already been turned into sites where new preachers such as Amr Khalid and Khalid el-Guindy could spread their evangelical messages among women. Ordinary women were often exposed to them casually by tagging along with friends or as a way of passing time or satisfying simple curiosity. However, once in the sessions, most of them encountered powerful words and penetrating arguments that they had neither the intellectual wont nor the moral courage to ignore. As they stoked a tormenting sense of guilt and self-blame over their "immodest" past, they needed to immerse themselves in a community of piety, which conditioned members to a prepackaged set of ideas, behaviors, and moral fixity, separating members from their past activities and associations. Here they could express their selfhood in a collective way, fulfill their longing for change and individuality, and yet remain committed to social norms. "I have killed my femininity by wearing the niqab to go to paradise"[81] represents the kind of self-actualization that Muslim women could get away with without their disgruntled husbands, fathers, or mothers being able to do anything about it. The more normalized pious behavior became, the easier it was for newcomers to join in, radically detaching these women from their mothers' generation, who lived a life with less pious passions.

Unlike the women of the old rich, who found meaningful public roles in volunteerism (NGOs), the nouveaux riche of the 1980s and 1990s displayed little interest in volunteer work. They were imbued with the general ethics of their class—hoarding wealth, pretending interest in the games of high culture, disdaining civic responsibility, valuing education so far as it brought status, or going after Western passports. This class embodied Egypt's post-Infitah mentality, where "possessive individualism" stood at the heart of its free market ethics.[82] The nouveaux riches' "nationalism" was confined to cultural populism, a sort of narrow-minded nativism that, ironically, juxtaposed, on the one hand, the snobbery of the dispossessed and, on the other, cosmopolitan connection and consumerism. Helping the poor for the sake of the poor meant little. Their disdain for volunteerism derived not only from an absence of social responsibility but also from an unsubtle dislike of associating with the poor. Only when the women of this class turned actively pious did they show concern for charity work, donating, helping orphans, and visiting widows, not necessarily out of inherent concern but, rather, religious obligation, one that remained deeply orthodox.

The Young and Religiosity

What about the religiosity of youth? In the 1990s, the globalizing youth in Egypt espoused a flexible piety that could accommodate their youthful habitus and in so doing further pluralized their religion. However, failing to forge any political clout, the young and their eclectic and inclusive religiosity remained marginal to and defensive before the orthodoxy. A decade earlier, young Egyptians were seen as Islamists waging guerrilla war, militants penetrating college campuses, or devotees memorizing the Quran in the backstreet zawaya, small mosques, of sprawling slums. Mainstream youths were expected to be pious and strictly adherent to Islamic moral discipline. Yet in their daily lives they defied their constructed image. "The youth of this country are rebelling against the old traditions," a defiant twenty-year-old female student stated in Cairo: "We are breaking away from your chains; we are not willing to live the lives of the older generations. Women smoking *shisha* is the least shocking form of rebellion going on."[83]

The media explosion about "Satanic youth" in January 1997 demonstrated not only a prevailing moral panic about the vulnerability of the young to Western cultural flows but the emerging self-assertion of globalized Egyptian youths. Every Thursday night, hundreds of well-to-do youngsters gathered in a large abandoned building to socialize, have fun, and dance to heavy metal music. Although six weeks of sensational media coverage and the arrest of dozens accused of "Satanism" put an end to the gatherings, they proved the existence of underground subcultures that few adults had noticed. Music-based subculture, however, did not die out after the Satanist affair. It later reappeared in the form of raving, beginning with small gatherings that grew rapidly after 1998. The Egyptian rave was largely sex-free, but it did involve alcohol and (unofficially) drugs (ecstasy pills). Indeed, experimentation with alcohol was not confined to the children of the well-to-do; one out of every three students in the cities had drunk alcohol (mainly beer).[84] And law enforcement professionals warned about the rise in drug use, notably of ecstasy.[85]

While in general a "culture of silence" prevailed with regard to sexuality,[86] premarital sex seemed to be considerable among Muslim youths, and this despite normative and religious sanctions. Approximate but indicative surveys of high school and college girls in Cairo showed that 45 percent had had some kind of sexual experience. Over 70 percent of male students said that they would not mind having premarital sex as long as they did not marry their partners.[87] Most used pornography and masturbated regularly even though they considered doing so religiously and physically wrong.[88] A more comprehensive study found "substantial rates of premarital sex among university students."[89] The phenomenon was confirmed by medical and health professionals, who expressed surprise about youngsters' knowledge about specific sexual practices.[90] Aside from the influence of satellite television and illicit videos, the changing structure of Egyptian households also seemed to play a role. Divorce, desertion, and migration had made one out of three Egyptian families fatherless. When mothers went out, the young had a place for romance.[91] In general, while elite couples sought romantic solace in dim discos, at raves, or at holiday resorts, lower-class youths resorted to such affordable fun as strolling along the Nile or meeting on the benches of inconspicuous Metro stations, a discreet privacy ensured paradoxically by the safety of public areas. There, couples sat and talked or romanced while pretending to wait for trains.[92]

These young people who struggled to inscribe their youthfulness through such behavior were deeply religious. They often prayed, fasted, and expressed fear of God. Heavy metal "Satanists" whom I interviewed were devout Muslims, but they also enjoyed rock music, drinking, and romance. The mainstream young combined prayer, partying, pornography, faith, and fun even though it might make them feel remorse and regret. Here is how a lower-class young man working in Dahab, a tourist resort visited by many foreign women, attempted to reconcile God, sex, and power in pursuit of both mundane and spiritual needs:

> I used to pray before I came to Dahab. My relationship to God was very strong and very spiritual. Now, my relationship to God is very strange. I always ask him to provide me with a woman and when I have a partner, I ask him to protect me from the police.[93]

This might sound like a contradiction, but it actually represents a consolation and accommodation. The young enjoyed dancing, raving, and having illicit relationships and fun but found solace and comfort in their prayers and faith. "I do both good and bad things, not just bad things; the good things erase the bad things," according to a law student in Cairo.[94] A religious man who drank alcohol and "tried everything" also prayed regularly, hoping that God would forgive his ongoing misdeeds. Many young girls saw themselves as committed Muslims but still uncovered their hair or wore the veil only during Ramadan or only during fasting hours. Many of those who enjoyed showing their hair found consolation in deciding to cover it after marriage, when their youthful stage was over. As a student stated, "During adolescence, all the young do the same; there is no *haram* or *halal* at such age."[95]

In this state of liminality, through such creative in-betweenness, the young attempted to reimagine their religion in order to reconcile their youthful desire for individuality with the existing moral order. Their eclectic mannerisms exemplified what I like to call an "accommodating innovation," a process whereby the young utilized prevailing moral codes and institutions to assert their youthful claims; they did not radically depart from these codes and institutions but, rather, made them work in their interest. The growing practice of "urfi marriage" (an informal oral contract requiring two witnesses) among the young, which officials described as a "danger" to "national security,"[96] reflected young people's use of this traditional practice to get around moral constraints on dating and economic constraints on formal marriage.[97] Yet this and other accommodating innovations occurred not against or outside of but within the boundaries of the dominant moral order and religious thinking. The Egyptian young never articulated their innovations as legitimate alternative visions but, in fact, remained remorseful, apologetic, and subservient to orthodoxy. Unlike their Iranian counterparts, they were free to listen to their music, follow their fashion, pursue their dating games, and have affordable fun, so long as they recognized their limits.

Indeed the appeal of "Amr Khalid" among the young may be seen in the context of such "accommodating innovation," in the sense of a reinvented religious idiom entrenched in conservative discourse. Egyptian cosmopolitan youths fostered a new religious subculture expressed in a distinctly novel style, taste, and language. These globalizing youth displayed many seemingly "contradictory" behaviors; they were religious believers but distrusted political Islam, if they knew anything about it at all; they swung back and forth from Amr Diab to Amr Khalid, from partying to prayers, and yet they felt the burden of social control exerted by elders, teachers, and neighbors. As young Egyptians were socialized in a cultural condition and educational tradition that often restrained individuality and novelty, they were compelled to assert them in a "social way," through "fashion." Thus, the religious subculture galvanized around the "phenomenon of Amr Khalid" was partly an expression of fashion in the Simmelian sense, in the sense of an outlet that accommodates contradictory human tendencies: change and adaptation, difference and similarity, individuality and social norms. Resorting to this type of piety permitted the elite young to assert their individuality and undertake change and yet remain committed to collective norms and social equalization.

Sharing Islam and the Nation

The pious sentiments of the late 1990s represented only one, albeit a major, aspect of Egypt's socioreligious change over the past two decades. Concurrent with this was another set of societal trends: conspicuous consumption, flamboyant shopping malls and gated communities, Western-style vacations, cable television, X-rated movies, and alternative lifestyles. While lower-class youth sought pleasure in backstreet teahouses, *mulid* festivals, or *Shamme nasim* holidays, the affluent socialized in standard global discotheques, shopping malls, and the resort paradises of Marina or al-Gouna. Rich youngsters formed a subculture of dating, illicit sex, heavy metal music, and "Satanic" parties, while the lower class resorted to urfi marriage and underground campus romances. In this midst, elite parents stood caught in the ongoing tension between seeking gratification from the abundance of global cultural products and deep anxiety over their "corrupting" impacts on their vulnerable children.[98]

This social cleaving, unseen in Egypt's postcolonial history, expressed itself most glaringly in its spatial dimension. The poor and the struggling middle classes were pushed into the sprawling urban slums and *ashwaiyat*, overcrowded informal cities, while the rich began a historic exodus to opulent gated communities on the fringes of the capital whose mere names—Dream Land, Utopia, Beverly Hills—spoke of a new cultural anomaly. There in those "dream lands," away from the daily anguish of plebeian life—poverty, pollution, filth, and "street bums"—the super-rich lived a fantasy life. They lived, worked, played, studied, and clubbed in urban enclaves that allowed little contact with ordinary Egyptians. Even their native maids were replaced by imported houseworkers from the Philippines, Thailand, or Bangladesh.[99]

By the late 1990s, it was as if the vast discrepancy in consumption had fractured Egypt's social and urban fabric, splitting the nation into disparate cultural universes. Yet the diverse Muslim fragments—rich and poor, old and new, local and cosmopolitan—all astonishingly shared two crucial discursive components: religion and nativism. Religious loyalty did not replace nationalist sentiment, principally because Israeli and U.S. regional dominance had caused a passionate national uproar. Instead, Islamic sentiment eroded nationalism's secular expression. In short, the "Islamic phenomenon" and nativist sentiment seemed to engulf the entire Muslim population, including the globalized upper class. Thus it was not uncommon for elite families to mix their California holidays with Hajj Umra or to hire private sheikhs to tutor their children in the teachings of Islam in the security of their luxurious habitat.

Some might call this a "hybrid reality," a mixing of "modernity" and "tradition." There is, however, little novelty or merit in such a characterization. For hybridity is not limited to the sociocultural practices of Egypt's new elites. Indeed, all cultures are more or less "hybrid." The impoverished middle classes in Egypt were not excluded. E'tiad's family represented perhaps a typical middle-class hybrid. In March 2000, my family and I visited E'tiad for a late lunch on the occasion of Eid al-Adha. E'tiad was a low-income veil-wearing teacher in a private Islamic school (al-Fath). Assertive and active in two Islamic associations and charity work, she was married to an articulate and opinionated man. As a retired state employee, he earned extra cash through freelance acting. He read daily papers and followed the news. He praised Nasser as a leader for standing up to Israel and the United States and despised radical Islamists, whom, he believed, were "terrorists supported by foreign powers such as the U.S., Iran, or Afghanistan." Their son, a slick, well-groomed teenager, studied engineering in a provincial university. He proudly showed us his brand-new computer and Internet connection, which the family praised for its importance in this age of information. Their soft-spoken seventeen-year-old daughter greeted us in a modest dress and head scarf, though she removed the hijab once she felt comfortable with us. E'tiad's family lived in a poor neighborhood of Old Maadi, in an extremely small flat of three tiny rooms packed with furniture and a small kitchen, with walls adorned with Quranic calligraphy. Everyone in the family was, rather typically, both religious and nationalist. They all agreed that "America has neither politics nor religion" and that the Arabs' many problems were manufactured outside the region. "The solution to the problems is for the Arabs to get together and fight Israel," they concluded.[100]

This blend of religiosity and nationalism, one that most Egyptians remarkably shared, was precisely what the Egyptian state both cherished and championed. In some ways, this societal tendency was reflected in and contributed to an "Islamization" of the secular state. At its height, the Islamist movement had not only captured a large part of civil society but significantly influenced the state, conditioning it to share and further appropriate religious discourse. Not only did it *socialize the state* to society's prevailing sensibilities, but Islamism, by penetrating the state apparatus, helped create a kind of "secularreligious" state.

Religiosity of the Secular State

In 1992 Interior Minister Muhammad Ali Mahjoub publicly announced that all laws in Egypt were based on Islamic shari'a and that the "Egyptian government would never allow the establishment of a secular state."[101] Similarly, the mufti of al-Azhar, Sheikh Tantawi, said, "Egypt has an Islamic state," even though "we do not have a religious party or a political religion."[102] Even an Islamist opposition leader, Essam El-Erian, of the MB, could publicly acknowledge in 2000 that "Egypt was an Islamic state." This remarkable convergence indicated the state's ideological direction. The constitution had already stipulated, since the presidency of Anwar Sadat, that Islam was the religion of the state and shari'a was the principal source of legislation. This meant that the state, according to Sheikh Tantawi, "does not accept the separation of religion from politics."[103]

Since the late 1970s, Egyptian governments simultaneously campaigned against political Islam while taking every opportunity to publicly display themselves as the guardians of religious values and morality. The political elites' embrace of Islam did not simply aim to secure political legitimacy; it also reflected their genuine belief in the religious supervision of society. The official outcries in recent years about the "Shiite conspiracy," "Satanism," "antireligious" literature, and homosexuality exemplified not only a real anxiety over moral disintegration but also efforts to project the state in a religious frame. The October 1996 discovery of an underground "Shiite group" allegedly led by preacher Sheikh Hassan Mohamed Shahata triggered extensive official media coverage of a "danger" that was "dividing our Islamic nation."[104] The campaign projected an image of the state as guardian of the people's religion, Sunni Islam, against corrupting alien thought.[105] Parliament called for deploying "religious caravans" to combat Shi'i thought, and al-Azhar ordered the confiscation of Shi'i literature.[106]

The arrest in May 2001 of fifty-two Egyptians accused of practicing sodomy on the tourist ship the *Queen Boat* reaffirmed that "contempt of religion" was a matter of state security.[107] The extensive publicity given to the *Queen Boat* case evoked the 1997 national convulsion over the permeation of "Satanism" among the young. Hundreds of articles, books, and interviews lamented what was in fact no more than youngsters listening to heavy metal music. This "alien phenomenon" was seen as an outcome of unfettered globalization, which threatened "our religious values." Later, the Ministry of the Interior began to monitor moral crimes and Internet users twenty-four hours a day; by July 2003 some 150 arrests had been documented.[108] Extending the Islamic holidays of Eid al-Adha, the Islamic new year, and broadcasting prayer calls in Cairo's Metro in 2002 were manifestations of the state-sponsored religious response.

This Islamic association inevitably pushed the government closer to official religious establishments: al-Azhar, the Ministry of Awqaf, and the Supreme Council for Islamic Affairs. As early as 1981, following the assassination of Anwar Sadat by al-Gama'a, President Mubarak had recognized Azhar's principal "mission" to rid "Egypt of the extremist and deviationist minority" and "to educate youth and give them a correct religious upbringing."[109] The mission later proved to be paramount when opposition Islamists launched their political onslaught. In turn, Sheikh Tantawi praised Mubarak's twenty-year presidency, which he and "establishment Islam" had helped him to achieve, because the president "observed the commandments of Islam," and under him Azhar's institutions grew from three thousand to six thousand.[110] Between 1986 and 1996, the fundamentalist Abdul-Sabour Shahin was President Mubarak's key adviser on Islam and the chairman of the ruling NDP's Religious Committee.[111] The weekly *Sawta al-Azhar* (published in 1999) joined the NDP's Islamic publication *al-Liwa al-Islami* and *Aqidati* in offering an alternative vision of Islam, filling the void created by the decline of political Islam. This was to be an Islam that was "not only a religion, but also a way of life."[112] Leaders of the main official religious establishments were members of the ruling NDP, which continued to reaffirm its commitment to shari'a as the primary source of law, to emphasize religious education and upbringing, to call on Islamic media to fight against "immoral cultural imports," and to focus on the moral guidance of the young.[113]

The government's attempt to reclaim religious space and to share moral authority earned it some legitimacy, but it also gave free reign to state religious authorities to aggressively pursue their Islamization project from the top, to influence cultural politics and public morality. Al-Azhar scrutinized scores of books, films, plays, and people.[114] Dozens of books on state and religion were barred from discussion or altogether banned in Cairo's Book Fair. Prominent secular judge and commentator on Islam Saiid al-Ashmawi himself was banned,[115] while Maxime Rodinson's *Muhammad* and Muhammad Shukri's *Al-Khubz al-Hafi* were stricken from classrooms along with some 250 religious and literary works. Among these, the publication of the novel *A Banquet for the Seaweed* caused an unparalleled uproar. The Islamist Labor Party printed provocative extracts from the novel to incite the public to unite in order to save Islam. Ensuing confrontations in the streets and within government brought Egypt to the brink of an intense political crisis. Parallel to al-Azhar, the Ministry of Awqaf had begun in 1996 to monitor Islamic da'wa by taking control of all 71,000 governmental and nongovernmental mosques and zawayas.[116]

Such a political climate fanned the smoldering embers of the virtually dead Front of al-Azhar Ulema (Jebhat al-Ulema al-Azhar), reviving it to become the most outspoken conservative group of the religious establishment. Founded in 1946 as a professional association for al-Azhar employees, by the late 1990s the front had become the mouthpiece of conservative ulema wishing to eliminate any secular tendency within the state and society. As part of its crusade, it charged the liberal minister of culture as well as freethinking intellectuals with staging "a coup" against Egypt's Islamic constitution.[117] Like the Azhar, schools were another critical medium through which Islamists quietly encroached on the state domain. Since the 1980s, Islamist instructors had clearly dominated a large number of higher education faculties, including engineering, science, and, most critical, the Teacher Training College (Dar al-Uloum). All Arabic language professors were reportedly members of the MB.[118] They trained future schoolteachers, who then carried Islamization into classrooms through basic education. What partially contributed to this trend was the Ministry of Education under Ahmad Fathi Sorour (1987–1991), who promoted greater religiosity in schools as a way to bolster the state's religious legitimacy.

Thus, the 1990s witnessed significant cases of indoctrination by teachers who turned schools into what Kamal Bahaeddin, the new minister of education, frantically called "factories of terrorism."[119] A ministry report to parliament in 1993 revealed that at least ninety schools and three hundred teachers had links to Islamist groups.[120] Despite the arrests between 1993 and 1995 of over one thousand Islamist teachers, religious sentiments and ideas continued to dominate the schools. A 1997 study of 354 "basic education" teachers confirmed that 86 percent adhered to a fundamental Islamist dictum: "Religious legacy has answers to all problems that Egyptian society is facing."[121] Classes on religion and Arabic often turned into sessions of religious and moral indoctrination. "If you or your mother do not wear hijab, you might end up in hell," students were warned. By early 2000 the veil had overtaken schools to such an extent that one could hardly find anyone without a head scarf, while some even wore niqab. And when the government banned niqab in schools, many students successfully challenged the government's decision in court.

The courts' sympathy attested to a lurking but systematic Islamist encroachment, through judges, attorneys, and thought, in the judiciary. Farouq Abdel-Aleem, the fundamentalist judge who convicted Nasr Abu-Zeid, appeared in court not in judicial robes but in traditional galabia. He decried Egyptian law because it was not, in his view, in conformity with shari'a.[122] Such judges and attorneys used their position not only to alter the judiciary system but to spread Islamism to the rest of society and other official institutions. They invoked the legal principle of *hisba* to justify the fight against secular thought. Derived from the Islamic injunction "encourage good and discourage evil,"[123] hisba entitled any Muslim to take legal action against anything or anyone he or she considered harmful to Islam, contributing to what an Egyptian anthropologist described as the "privatization of repression,"[124] at times with tacit state backing. It allowed courts to put ideas and beliefs on trial. Fundamentalist lawyers such as Nabih al-Wahsh and Yousef El-Badri, known as "blasphemy sheikhs," filed lawsuits against writers, professors, artists, and journalists whom they saw as "insulting" Islam, creating havoc in intellectual circles. Between 1995 and 1998, 134 hisba cases were filed against leading cultural figures such as Naguib Mahfouz, actress Yusra, and poet Higazi.[125] Writers such as Salaheddin Mohsen were convicted for suggesting in books that progress would come from science and not religion.[126] Feminist Nawal el-Sa'dawi was put on trial for calling the veil "nonobligatory" and Muslim scholars "obsessed with sex." Even the fundamentalist Abdul-Sabour Shahin, who had incriminated Nasr Abu-Zeid with apostasy, came under the same charge by his ex-associate Yousef El-Badri for his new book *Abi-Adam* (*Adam, My Father*), in which he analyzed the story of man's creation described in the Quran. The government-sponsored media, like the Islamic weeklies *al-Liwa al-Islami* and *Aqidati*, as well as well as radio and television contributed much to the rise of conservative religiosity in society.

The religiosity of Egypt's secular state resulted as much from the authorities' deliberate policy as from the Islamist movement's *socialization of the state* toward religious sensibilities. The political elites were compelled to adopt religious discourse in order to regain moral mastery over society and secure political legitimacy, but in this process they were conditioned to think and act religiously. Consequently, the state assumed a schizophrenic "secularreligious" disposition: it adopted laws with roots in both religious and secular values, based its authority on both discourses, and committed itself to both local religious and global secular standards and expectations. The post–September 11 global climate intensified this dual character.

The advent of "globalization," in its technological wonders, marketization, and flow of tourism, fascinated the Egyptian state. But its social costs and widening of class divisions bred social unrest, and its cultural imports threatened the "moral character" of children, causing panic among elders. Egyptian dailies decried how Internet links (some 1,600,000 in 2003) could debase "our moral values" and corrupt the young.[127] The late 1990s saw an "alarming" rise in violence among the young in a culture that cherished nonviolence.

How could this social rift, alienation, and cultural anomie be mended? What sort of ideological frame existed or could be deployed? Secular alternatives—technological advancement, democracy, and pluralism—that some officials claimed to offer the young failed to materialize.[128] Income disparity and deteriorating public education directed technological competence largely toward the elite,[129] while the pluralist vision fell victim to a growing "political de-liberalization" and cultural repression.[130] Facing conditions of political turmoil from within and moral-cultural onslaught from without, under a regime determined to pursue costly economic restructuring, no other discourse was seen as being as effective in safeguarding social integration and moral regulation as a combination of religion and cultural nationalism.[131] It was as though morals were invoked to secure the market and religion was besought to ensure rule. Safeguarding morals and the market, this farcical return to the function of the traditional *muhtasib* might be ironic. But it did depict Egypt's religious "passive revolution," characterized by the fusion of piety and power, the statization of religion and the religiosity of the state, with far-reaching consequences for religious and intellectual thought, democratic practice, and political change.

Unsettled Political Islam

What did this change in religious politics (the fragmentation of political Islam, the growth of individualized piety, and the religiosity of the state) mean for religious thought and intellectual practice? What did it imply for political change and democratic challenges? For the most part it meant little, until the later years of the first decade of the twenty-first century.

The Islamist movement in Egypt did undergo some rethinking in strategy, theoretical vision, and pragmatic dimensions. Al-Gama‘a al-Islamiya's decision to renounce violence, opting instead to pursue its goals through peaceful, legal political action within civil society, was, as some described, a "monumental strategic change." In a multivolume reexamination of their project, imprisoned al-Gama‘a leaders based their strategic shift on doctrinal grounds.[132] Drawing on the Quran and Sunna, they argued that violent method, "jihad," should not be allowed when peaceful da‘wa is possible, when opponents change their adversarial position, and when there is a possibility of reconciliation.[133] They decided, in addition, that Islam prohibits fighting against the "people of the book," especially killing women, children, the elderly, and the innocent, which Islam considers immoral acts. Murdering innocent tourists is described as particularly evil since, as *musta'meneen* (those needing protection), they were assured of safety by the natives.[134] Violence also tarnishes the image of Islam and harms the nation, they conclude. But a fundamental reason for Gama‘a's revised strategy was the failure of armed struggle to achieve its objective. In effect, the Gama‘a came to the conclusion: when you see that you cannot win, then stop fighting.[135] Although the Egyptian government continued to deny ex-militants from establishing political parties (as in the cases of Hizb al-Wasat, Hizb al-Islah, and Hizb al-Shari‘a in 1999), they persisted in calling on their members to pursue only a peaceful da‘wa.[136] Gama‘a's altered outlook brought it closer to the Muslim Brothers, who were also undergoing some transformations.

For the first time, in 1997, Mustafa Mashur, the leader of the MB, spoke of "pluralism," emphasizing that his organization was not a Muslim party (*gama‘at al-Muslimin*) but, rather, a party with Muslim membership (*gama‘a min al-Muslimin*).[137] The "younger" leaders such as Essam El-Erian went so

far as to attribute the globalized idioms of democracy, civil society, transparency, and accountability to the thoughts of Hasan el-Banna.[138] El-Erian
appeared to favor Mohammad Khatami's concept of "Islamic democracy,"
describing it as "blending democracy with the spirit of Islam, with our culture and civilization."[139] Some even spoke of women's and minority rights,
which they thought could be accommodated within an Islamic polity.
Undoubtedly, these modern concepts were a step forward from the MB's
earlier adherence to *shura*, a vague notion postulating that an authoritarian just ruler (in whom both temporal and spiritual authority is invested)
should be subjected to the principle of consultation. These revisions were
to deepen on the morrow of the Kifaya movement after 2005.

The perspective that informed the young al-Wasat Party went beyond
the new discourse of the MB. Indeed, the formation of al-Wasat represented a significant shift in Egyptian Islamist politics, signaling a possible
path toward a "post-Islamist" polity. Established in 1996 by young defectors from the MB (such as Abul-Alaa Madi, a former student movement
and Engineering Syndicate leader), al-Wasat denounced the authoritarian disposition of the Muslim Brothers, their underground activities, and
Islamist politics in general. Al-Wasat privileged modern democracy over
Islamic "shura," embraced pluralism in religion, and welcomed gender
mixing and ideological tendencies. Not only were Copts admitted to the
party: the main ideologue of the group, Rafiq Habib, was a Christian. In
al-Wasat's views, women played a role equal to that of men, serving in the
army or acting as judges.[140] Al-Wasat, therefore, was "not a religious party
but a civil party with an Islamic background," according to its leader.[141] It saw
Egyptian Islam not simply as a religion but as a civilizational and Arab cultural frame encompassing both Muslims and Christians.[142] Shari'a, which
the constitution considered the main source of law, should be subject to
modern interpretations, or *ijtihad*, and should not apply to non-Muslims
if it conflicts with their beliefs.[143] Al-Wasat's activists succeeded in 2000 in
establishing the Egyptian Society for Culture and Dialogue, an NGO that
aimed to legally pursue some of the party's objectives.[144]

Surely, these changes represented a new turn in Egypt's Islamist
politics. However, they remained remarkably marginal to conservative
orthodoxy in religious thinking. While a certain pragmatism evolved in
political strategy, in general religious thought, and therefore political
vision, experienced little innovation. Stagnation (*jomoud*) in *fiqh* was confirmed by Islamic thinkers ranging from Yousef al-Qaradawi and Selim
el-Awa to activists like Essam El-Erian.[145] The theology expressed by the

Islamists remained profoundly scriptural, with too narrow a perspective to historicize or bring critical reason to interpretations. The likes of Khalid Abdel-Karim, Saiid al-Ashmawi, and Nasr Hamed Abu-Zeid who attempted innovation faced censorship, threats, and charges of apostasy. Even moderate Muslim writers like Gamal el-Banna (the brother of Hasan el-Banna), whose three-volume *Nahw Fiqh Jadid* suggests tossing aside much of pre-twentieth-century *ahadith* (because they were fabricated) and who argued that hijab is not a religious obligation, were not tolerated.[146]

While the Gama'a's renunciation of violence was a great stride strategically, it did not change the doctrinal foundation of its politics: strict adherence to shari'a. Every new step and political position the "prison leaders" took, they defensively referred to the Sunna and shari'a as if politics beyond the boundaries of scripture did not exist, as though religion still held solutions to all human problems.[147] Their retreat from Ibn Taymiya's notion of "rebellion against the infidel ruler" was justified not on a critique of such fatwas in essence but, rather, on the grounds that the Egyptian state had ceased to be "infidel" because it had indeed accepted shari'a.[148] Otherwise, for these Gama'a leaders, overthrowing a secular state was still permissible. They continued to revere the spirit of Ibn Taymiya—his absolute supremacy of the sacred text and the indissoluble link between religion and the state: the very injunctions that had already inflicted enduring scars on religious thought and politics in Egypt.[149]

Like the new peaceful al-Gama'a, the MB's use of modern political vocabularies had serious limitations. Democracy was all right "so far as it did not contradict the scriptures, the Quran and Sunna."[150] For the MB, the value of democracy's principles lay in its procedures, primarily in serving to implement shari'a rather than in expressing the will of the populace to govern them. "What if in a Muslim society citizens decide to follow secular laws?" I asked Essam El-Erian. "Good true Muslims cannot and will not ignore shari'a," he presumed. The MB assumed that religious authority would safeguard society over people's own judgment of themselves. In fact, none of the existing Islamic factions, including al-Wasat, could tolerate a Muslim exiting his or her religion, the penalty for which is death. All favored the state crackdown on what they described as "immoral" lifestyles and artistic expressions and were impatient with nonreligious behavior.[151]

The only modernist voice came from a handful of "Islamic liberals" such as Muhammad Emara, Tariq el-Bishri, and Ahmad Kamal Abul-Majd, all of whom appeared to speak the language of *tanwir*, integrating notions of democracy, civil society, and human rights in their doctrines.[152] Although some critiques argued that these intellectuals used such modern concepts to counter secularists by their own idioms and to secure "recognition for the Islamic camp,"[153] the social impact of these religious intellectuals remained negligible. Neither their small following nor their "modernist" project made significant inroads into society. Far from turning into an intellectual basis for a religious reformation movement, the idea of "tanwir" progressively retreated, giving way instead to the fundamentalist-scripturist onslaught. The dominant voice remained that of the Salafies, the *ahl al-hadith*, who projected the Islam of the early *sahaba* (Prophet's companions) as simultaneously the "religion, the state, the prayer, and *hukm*" to fight innovation (*bed'a*), historicism, and pluralism. Their core institution, the semiofficial Gama'iyya Ansar al-Sunna al-Muhammadiya, controlling five hundred mosques and scores of schools and welfare associations, carried the banner of preserving a puritan Islam that "applied to all times and places."[154] Thus, there was little in Egypt's religious thought to match the critical edge of Iran's post-Islamism or the innovation and vigor of its Turkish and Tunisian counterparts. In the Egypt of the late 1990s, the dominant religious thought had in effect receded a century to the time prior to Rifa' al-Tahtawi, Muhamed Abdu, and Rashid Reda, the modernist protagonists who had carried the banner of religious reformation. The *al-Manar al-Jadid* of the late 1990s, seemingly the most innovative publication of religious thought, barely matched its predecessor, *al-Manar* (1896–1936),[155] in scope and perspective and was much more limited in its circulation.[156] The tanwir of the 1930s had lost to the textualist dogma of a revived Ibn Taymiya.

The degeneration in religious thought resonated in what was a deep stagnation in Egypt's intellectual life. Scores of Arab critics, including Edward Said, Muhamed Sid-Ahmed, Sabry Hafez, Samia Mehrez, Nasr Hamed Abu-Zaid, and Hazem Saghiya, deplored with great anguish the degeneration of intellectual quality in scholarship, journalism, artistic expression, political writing, and social criticism. "Egypt was once the *qibla* of progress and enlightenment in the Arab World," "a safe haven for all kinds of Arab and Muslim intellectuals and political activists," one lamented:[157] "It has now become one of the reasons for its cultural deterioration."[158] The cosmopolitan communities and culture and the flourishing intellectual and artistic life of the 1930s had declined to narrow-minded outlooks coupled with consumer culture.[159] In 1997, only 375 books were published in Egypt, compared with thousands of books and some two hundred newspapers and journals at the beginning of the Liberal Age in the 1930s.[160] Ironically, in this age of high piety, best sellers consisted overwhelmingly of sleaze literature.[161] Egyptian journalism, the oldest among Middle Eastern countries, regressed to "the profession of those without a profession," according to Said Adel-Khaleq of *Al-Wafd*.[162] Its oldest daily, *Al-Ahram*, deteriorated to the extent that, according to Muhamed Sid-Ahmed, intellectuals read it "mainly to see who died."[163] Egypt had produced better and freer cinema in the 1930s than it did in the late 1990s.[164] The nation's cultural production was relegated to the inelegant singer Sha'ban Abdul-Rahim, "Sha'bula," whose immense popularity and vulgarity compelled the Majlis al-Shura to debate this "phenomenon."[165] No wonder the veteran journalist Gamal Badawi mourned the "death of Egypt's enlightenment" in this "age of Sha'bula."[166]

In what Sabry Hafez describes as "these bleak conditions,"[167] the average Egyptian intellectual was imbued with a deep-seated "nativism," an outlook that fostered insularity, a particularistic mind-set, and intolerance.[168] He established a binary opposition between an "authentic" national self and the alien cultural "West," with an epistemological implication summed up in the dictum "Ta'âruf al-ashyaa biazdâdiha" (Things are known by their opposites). Thus, ideas and individuals were valued not on their own merits but for their imagined geographical origins. The nativist intellectual remained oblivious to the fact that the "indigenous" and the "alien" were in constant interaction and modification and that so many of his own cultural traits (dress code, food, entertainment) had originally been alien before they became "indigenized."

Uncritical exaltation of an imagined "golden age" and "indigenous" culture often blinded the nativist intelligentsia to domestic failures and shortcomings, making them seek justification outside the national self. Consequently, conspiracy theory, this antipode of critical inquiry, virtually turned into a paradigm to explain misfortunes. "Whoever follows the position of most of Egypt's intellectuals, journalists, and politicians," an Arab columnist put it sarcastically, "begins to think that the world wakes up every morning, rub its eyes, and exclaims: 'Oh my goodness, it's seven. I am late, I have to start immediately to conspire against Egypt.'"[169] The domineering regional policies of Israel and the United States made them the prime target of conspiratorial imaginations. The brutality of Israeli occupation was found not only in subjugating the Palestinian people but also in entangling the mainstream Arab intelligentsia in an unrefined and black-and-white view of the world. Thus, a spate of elaborate stories emerged in the print media and in public discourse on how, according to *Al-Ahram al-Arabi* and *Rose al-Yousef*, for instance, the Israeli Mossad and the CIA were behind the Luxor massacre.[170] The humiliating surveillance of Israeli–U.S. allies in the region drove generations of Arab intellectuals into a narrow-minded nativism and cultural nationalism that largely benefited authoritarian Arab states. The struggle to work toward democracy at home lost out to the fervent desire to regain dignity abroad.[171]

There was still the problem of confidence. A critique of the self demands self-confidence. One needs to be intellectually secure enough to publicly utter, "I do not know," or to acknowledge one's own shortcomings and one's opponents' achievements. A poverty of perspective and a shortage of intellectual courage make the nativist intelligentsia further inward-looking, defensive, and demagogic, often reluctant to engage, exchange, and modify ideas. The more insular one becomes, the less one learns about the complexities of the "other" culture, so that imagination becomes a substitute for inquiry. As much as they ignored or attacked the "culture" of "the other," nativists cherished anything they considered "authentic," religion being the most important. As an element of *turath*, Islam became a fundamental ingredient in intellectuals' worldview, with serious implications for cultural production in Egypt. By sharing the languages of religiosity and cultural nationalism, nativist intellectuals, the religious establishment, and the state formed a tacit discursive bloc, to the detriment of genuine "tanwir," rational inquiry, and critical thought. Indeed, the institutional structure of this shared discourse had already been established since at least the time of Nasser, who incorporated both religious elites and the intelligentsia (editors of newspapers and magazines, writers, artists, managers of cultural institutions) into the state structure, making them state employees. In this tense cohabitation, the "cultural actor" maneuvered between the "religious" and the "political," cultivating support on one side when threatened from the other. Thus the mainstream intelligentsia often sought protection instead of independence: "Rather than spearhead criticism, they have demonstrated compliance."[172] The ultimate casualties of this state of affairs were critical voices, independent minds, and innovative thinking. The ill-fated blend of authoritarian polity, religious morality, and nativist sensibilities progressively constricted the room to entertain democratic ideals, alternative thought, and self-criticism. It was within this paltry intellectual atmosphere that the likes of Amr Khalid rose to stardom and moral authority unintentionally cemented Egypt's Islamic passive revolution.

Toward the Post-Islamist Revolution

The tidal wave of Islamism that seemed poised to wash away the Egyptian state actually left it intact and subsided by the late 1990s. In fact, the state skillfully surfed the wave, weathered its initial crash ashore, and rode its smooth sprawl into society. But along the way society, state, and movement all went through significant change. The Islamist movement rendered the state more religious (as it moved to rob Islamism of its moral authority), more nationalist and nativist (as the state moved to assert its cultural Arab/Islamic authenticity), and more repressive, since the liquidation of radical Islamists offered the state the opportunity to control other forms of dissent. The "seculareligious" state both controlled and shared increasingly with conservative social forces, hindering the rise of innovative intellectual and political initiatives. Egypt's religious thought remained stagnant not because Sunni Islam had an intrinsic limitation that stifled innovation; after all, Turkish and Indonesian post-Islamists also came from a Sunni tradition. Rather, the rigidity of religious thought in Egypt owed a great deal to the absence of effective societal pressure, pervasive social movements, to compel the religious authority to rethink its orthodoxy, transcend strict adherence to scripture, and open up to a republican theology. Even the intellectual leadership remained largely complicit. Neither the state nor societal forces questioned the prevailing "fundamentalist" reading of Islam. Those who did fell victim to Islamist fury, since no effective popular outcry came to their rescue. A civil society dominated by Islamist sensitivities served the nation's authoritarian ethos and the state's undemocratic character. Via its ability to maneuver among religion, nation, and repression, the ruling elite managed to dodge popular anger unleashed by the volatile early post–September 11 years. Israel's violence against the Palestinians and the U.S. "war on terror" fueled nationalist-religious sentiments, which the elite deftly redirected toward external adversaries. Entrenched in "old-fashioned pan-Arab nationalism" and lured by the language of religiosity and moral politics, the political class failed to forge a movement to rectify authoritarian rule at home.

Egypt needed broad societal pressure to compel both the traditional political forces (political parties and the Islamist movement) and the regime to push for intellectual change and democratic reform. Only as late as 2004 did signs of an embryonic and fragmented movement seem to surface. Described as the "new dawn" in the nation's political life, it was reflected in the simultaneous constellation of several social happenings.

A number of new independent dailies, notably *al-Misri al-Youm*, *Nahdit Misr*, *al-Dostour*, and an energized *al-Arabi*, brought a breath of fresh air into the morbid body of the Egyptian press, so that even government publications began to raise more critical voices. Within the ruling NDP emerged a new trend calling for the democratization of the party, while a newly established Ghad Party seriously contested the Mubarak regime. More important was the formation of a nascent Egyptian Movement for Change (Kifaya), which placed democratic transformation at the top of its agenda. What marked the novelty of this movement was that it chose to work with "popular forces" rather than traditional opposition parties, brought the campaign into the streets instead of broadcasting it from headquarters, and concentrated primarily on domestic concerns rather than nationalistic demands. Resting broadly on the campaigns of intellectuals, rights activists, NGOs, women's groups, Muslims, and Coptic Christians alike, the Kifaya embraced activists from multiple ideological orientations, including Nasserists (notably their new Karamah group), nationalists, communists, liberals, and those with an Islamist orientation. Significantly, these developments converged against the background of an escalating spirit of protest in Egyptian society. After years of political intimidation and fear, Egyptians began to express grievances in the streets more daringly and audibly. The Kifaya and then MB supporters broke the taboo of unlawful street marches by staging numerous demonstrations and rallies in urban squares. Protesters chanted political slogans calling for an end to emergency law and torture and the release of political prisoners and urging President Mubarak to step down. Judges, journalists, students, workers, and college professors formed new institutions (as in the Popular Campaign for Change, the National Coalition for Democratic Transformation, the National Alliance for Reform and Change, Youths for Change, College Faculty for Change, the Street Is Ours, and the like) and organized rallies around explicitly political demands. A new political climate, a "Cairo Spring," imbued with a sense of optimism and hope had been created, one that reminded one of the Iran of the late 1990s.

How and why did such a mood and movement come to life suddenly after years of stagnation and nativist politics? They had a precursor, largely rooted in the sentiments and activities that surrounded the Egyptian Popular Committee for Solidarity with the Palestinian Intifada (EPCSPI). Set up in October 2000 to protest the Israeli siege of Palestinian territories in 2000 and then the U.S.-led occupation of Iraq, the EPCSPI had brought together representatives from Egypt's various political trends including leftists, nationalists, Islamists, women activists, and rights groups. It spearheaded a new style in communication, organizational flexibility, and mobilization. It set up a Web site, developed a mailing list, initiated charity collections, organized boycotts of American and Israeli products, revived street actions, and collected 200,000 signatures on petitions to close down the Israeli embassy in Cairo. The Egyptian Anti-globalization Group, the National Campaign against the War on Iraq, the Committee for the Defense of Workers' Rights, and some human rights NGOs adopted similar styles of activism.[173] Collecting food and medicine for Palestinians involved thousands of young Egyptian volunteers and hundreds of companies and organizations, while boycotting American and Israeli products drew in yet many more. Alternative news Web sites acted as the most important sites through which networks of critical and informed constituencies were fashioned. Satellite TV rapidly spread in the Arab world and helped bring in unusual information to break the hold of the barren domestic news channels.

The Kifaya, whose leaders had already been active in EPCSPI, built on this experience to foreground Egypt's nascent "democracy movement"; it did so within a global and national setting that had been seriously transformed. Emerging out of the new international conditions in which the language of "democracy" had been central, and triggered by the prospect of President Mubarak seeking a fifth term in office, the Kifaya (meaning "Enough") placed electoral reform at the center of its campaign. On the other hand, glaring inequality and declining purchasing power had already rendered lower- and middle-class Egyptians weary of a regime that had extended its repressive measures beyond the Islamist insurgents to ordinary citizens.[174] Egyptians could see, for instance, that in the aftermath of the Taba bombing in 2005, security forces had rounded up and held without charge some 2,400 people.[175] At the same time, President Mubarak had begun to lose the raison d'être of anti-Israeli rhetoric, which for so long had galvanized nationalist sentiments. With the prospect of declining tension in Palestinian–Israeli conflicts following the death of Yasser Arafat, the presidency of Mahmoud Abbas, and the outlook for an Israeli withdrawal from Gaza, Mubarak became increasingly close to Sharon. His new trade deal with the United States, which required the inclusion of Israel as a third party, exploded in the Egyptian media as the "second Camp David." Consequently, with international pressure mounting on Egypt, the regime became increasingly vulnerable and defensive, so that political activists found a space to be extraordinarily daring in their protest and mobilization. In this midst, the language of "reform" uttered by the "modernizing" faction of the ruling elite, led by Gamal Mubarak, supplied a political opportunity for activists to raise their voices in the street and in print. In the conditions in which the Kifaya appeared as the new effective player on Egypt's political stage, the MB resurfaced once again in a state of nervousness and yet determination. Maneuvering between cooperating with the Kifaya in a united front and yet acting as the sole opposition to the regime, the Brothers began to mobilize in earnest—in the streets, in institutions, and on college campuses. As usual, they utilized the occasions of Ramadan *iftars* and funerals to assemble; while their student organizations came out from underground, attempting along with the Socialist and Nasserist student groups to form an alliance of college student activism.

It was the collective sentiments around such a rudimentary "democracy movement" that galvanized international support and compelled the Egyptian government in May 2005 to amend the constitution to allow for competitive presidential elections. Beyond influencing the behavior of the regime, the unfolding movement also enforced some shifts in religiopolitical language. Compelled by the rising popularity of democratic demands, mindful of not falling behind the new popular dissent, and attempting to be in tune with the international discourse on democracy, the MB's younger leadership conceded to some aspects of democratic discourse. The MB seemed to move from the idea of establishing an Islamic *khilafa* based upon Quranic shura toward acknowledging the rights of the Coptic minority, behaving like a political party, and uttering the language of citizenship and political equality. Even though the MB leadership never abandoned their Islamism, adopting such ideas and pragmatic positions accounted for an important development in Egyptian politics. It would take a revolution for the MB to experience a serious ideological shake-up and disarray.

The "Cairo Spring" failed to cause deep and direct political reform in Egypt—the rigid political structure continued to reign the nation, the fraudulent and manipulative NDP continued to control the parliament, and the Kifaya remained largely the preoccupation of limited activists, rather than involving a broader national constituency. But the "new dawn" of which the Kifaya was an expression unmistakably set a new stage in the Egyptian political scene; it broke from the tired Arab nationalist and Islamist politics of the 1990s, inaugurating the emergence of a new way of doing politics. The few independent print and electronic media went on raising controversial issues. The opposition sustained its attack on

Mubarak's rule and democratic demands. Mubarak and his family could now be attacked publicly in the media. A new strand of advocacy NGOs shifted the issues of human rights, women's rights, and personal rights from the civil domain to political struggles. Youths, who previously had largely remained passive and demoralized, began to be remarkably active in the civil and voluntary sector, moving then into contentious politics, democratic claim making, and human rights. The new media, especially Weblogs, offered the young an unprecedented venue to express and discuss crucial social and political matters and remain connected in the networks of real and virtual collectives. While youth groups were engaged in civil activism, industrial workers, pushed by the relentless neoliberal onslaught (privatization, downsizing, labor transfer, and diminishing traditional entitlements), exhibited a renewed militancy. Starting in 2006, the industrial cities of Mahalla and Suez saw escalating unofficial strikes that came to haunt the political authorities. Mahalla workers marched in the streets and put camps on the main boulevard of the city; protests resumed again in 2009, the very same year when cement factory workers in Suez staged their own mini "revolution" to protest the company's sale of cement to Israel.[176] Even the "football nationalism" of 2009 (resulting from the violent clashes between Egypt's soccer fans and those of Algeria), which the regime tried to promote, could not detract Egyptians from pushing for democratic demands.

The spread of new communication technology, in particular social media, offered extraordinary possibilities to forge a new political consciousness, cement new alliances, and connect the emerging arrays of identities and activisms. The April 6 Youth Movement succeeded in linking the activism of the young to the protests of workers of Mahalla with the aim of launching a general strike. Thus, in this volatile political climate, the new generation of Ekhwani youth (*shabab el-Ekhwan*) seemed to assume a post-Islamist disposition; they publicly expressed anger at their old guard leadership and cooperated closely with the secular liberals, nationalists, and leftist groups. It was these youths of Ekhwan who eventually compelled their reluctant leaders to join the revolution when it arrived.

Against the backdrop of the crisis of Islamism worldwide (notably that of the Iranian and al-Qaeda version) in the post-9/11 aftermath, the failure of Arab nationalist politics to tackle Palestinian self-determination, and then the rapid expansion of new communication technologies and social media, Egypt's public sphere seemed to espouse a new political vision—one that was already expressed in the independent press, in the social media, among the new political class, and in the streets. By the late 2000s, Egypt seemed to develop a new public with a postideological and post-Islamist orientation—one that came to initiate the January 25 revolution of 2011. This was a post-Islamist revolution in which the call for "freedom, justice, and dignity" assumed the central place.[77] Yet this revolution entailed an aftermath in which, instead of the revolutionaries, the free riding Islamists (the MB and Salafis) dominated the political society thanks to their organizational capacity.

It might be ironic but expectable that the drive for a post-Islamist outlook may indeed accelerate in a post-Mubarak Egypt where the Islamist MB has assumed governmental power. The Brothers' push to monopolize power, insist on organizational discipline and secrecy, deploy the language of shari'a, and instrumentalize religion in the service of politics has already garnered substantial dissent from both within and outside the organization. Dozens of prominent members such as Abdul-Mon'em Abul-Fotuh and Mokhtar al-Nouh have broken away; other defectors have thus far formed five new political parties, including the post-Islamist Tayar Islami (Egyptian Current). Large numbers of youths from the MB have embraced the post-Islamist position without leaving the organization.[78] Never have the Brothers experienced such a decline in their legitimacy in such a short time. If in Iran it took a decade (due to the war with Iraq) to publicly disavow Islamist rule, the MBs' regime in Egypt augmented its disavowal in just over a year. But disenchantment with Islamist rule is one thing; and articulating a post-Islamist alternative is quite another. In Egypt this may have just begun.

Notes

This chapter is a modified adaptation of my *Making Islam Democratic: Social Movements and the Post-Islamist Turn* (Stanford: Stanford University Press, 2007), chapter 5. All unreferenced quotes are my own translations.

1. Hisham Mubarak, *Al-Irhabiyoun Qadimoun* (Cairo: Kitab al-Mahrusa, 1995).
2. E. Sivan, "The Islamic Republic of Egypt," *Orbis* 31, no. 1 (Spring 1987): 43–54; Cassandra, "The Impending Crisis in Egypt," *Middle East Journal* 49, no. 1 (Winter 1995): 9–27.
3. Over 82 percent of people in villages in the south and 74 percent of the city of Asyût were poor.
4. Mubarak, *Al-Irhabiyoun Qadimoun*, 181–182.

5. Ibid., 264–265.
6. Hamdi al-Basir, "Al-Unf fil-Mahaliyyat" [Violence in localities: A study of village of Sanbu in Dayrut, (Asyût Governorate)] (in Arabic; paper presented at the Second Annual Conference of Political Studies, "Politics and Localities in Egypt," Cairo University, Cairo, December 3–5, 1994).
7. Mubarak, *Al-Irhabiyoun Qadimoun*, 378.
8. The main figures from the first generation of leaders included Aboud el-Zomor, Karam Zohdi, Najih Ibrahim, Tariq al-Zomor, Farid al-Dawalibi, and Hamdi Abdul-Rahman.
9. Abdul-Hasan Saleh, a local leader and head of the city council in Asyût, interview in *Al-Hayat*, January 13, 1999, 8.
10. Egyptian Organization for Human Rights, 1991, 1992, 1993, 1994, 1995, 1996, and 1997 annual reports, Cairo.
11. Gamal Essam el-Din, "Parliament Scrutinizes Policing Policies," *Al-Ahram Weekly*, December 11–17, 1997, 2; see *Al-Wafd*, December 11, 1997, 3.
12. Khaled Dawoud, "Gama'a Militant Sentenced to Death," *Al-Ahram Weekly*, April 20–26, 2000.
13. *Cairo Times*, December 27, 1997, 5.
14. Ahmad El-Sherbini, "Azmat al-Siyaha al-Masriya wa Imkaniyat al-Ta'wid," *Ahwal al-Masriya* 4, no. 15 (Winter 2002): 151.
15. For details, see *Al-Ahram Weekly*, December 4–10, 1997, 3; *Al-Ahram Weekly*, December 11–17, 1997, 2. While exiled leaders in Europe (Osama Rushdi and Yaser Serri) regretted the incident, Ayman al-Zawahiri's al-Jihad group based in Afghanistan welcomed the massacre but said that future attacks should be focused on the Americans and Israelis; see *Al-Ahram Weekly*, November 27–December 3, 1997, 3. The imprisoned leaders in Egypt said that the attack was carried out "by young members...acting on their own" (*Al-Ahram Weekly*, December 11–17, 1997, 2).
16. See a profile of Montasir al-Zayyat in *Cairo Times*, January 22–February 4, 1998, 10.
17. *Al-Ahram Weekly*, August 28–September 3, 1997, 3; *Al-Ahram Weekly*, September 11–17, 1997, 2.
18. *Al-Hayat*, August 31, 1997, 4.
19. *Al-Hayat*, October 22 and 24, 1998.
20. The initiators included Salah Hashim (a founder of al-Gama'a and member of the "historical leadership"), Gamal Sultan (a former member of al-Takfir wal-Hijrah and editor-in-chief of *al-Manar al-Gadid* who also contributed articles to *al-Sha'b*), and Kamal Habib (an ex-Jihadi and a journalist at *al-Sha'b*).
21. Cited in *Cairo Times*, January 21–February 3, 1999, 5.
22. Cited in *Al-Ahram Weekly*, June 22–28, 2000, 4.
23. See interviews with the historic leaders of al-Gama'a in Tora Prison by *Al-Mussawar*'s editor-in-chief in *Al-Mussawar* 4054 (June 21, 2002): 4–22; see also *Al-Hayat*, October 11, 2000.

24. Al-Gama'a explained its strategic political change in four volumes discussed and written in the prison but later published in Cairo in 2002. The most important volume is Osamah Ibrahim Hafez and Assem Abdul-Maged Muhamed, *Mubadirat Waqf al-'Unf: Ruya Waqieyya wa Nazarat Shar'iya* (Cairo: Maktabat al-Turath al-Islami, 2002).

25. See *Cairo Times*, February 3–9, 2000, 11. For instance, just weeks before the parliamentary elections of 2000, the government detained some one thousand MB activists including a number of candidates in the elections.

26. *Cairo Times*, April 3–16, 1997, 6; *Al-Hayat*, October 17, 1999. Desperate to indict MB members, state security forces resorted at times to dubious evidence, turning the courthouses into laughingstocks. On one such occasion the prosecutor presented evidence, a videotape, of an alleged "secret meeting" of MB leaders in a private Cairo house. However, the videotape showed only the backs of some people entering a house, some wearing T-shirts with Nike signs. It became clear that the secret police had videotaped the wrong building (*Cairo Times*, February 3–9, 2000, 11).

27. According to Law 238-1996, no preacher could deliver sermons without clearance from the Ministry of Awqaf. This, according to Minister Mahmoud Zaqzouq, was intended to cut off the access of unqualified and extremist preachers. Between 1996 and 2001, nevertheless, some thirty thousand permits were issued; see Mahmoud Zaqzouq, "Hawl Shorout Bina'a al-Masajid," *Al-Wafd*, December 10, 2001, 9.

28. Cited in Khaled Dawoud, "Closing the Circle," *Al-Ahram Weekly*, October 5–11, 2000.

29. Cited in Steve Negus, "Down but Not Out," *Cairo Times*, April 3–16, 1997, 7.

30. See *Al-Halata al-Diniya fi Misr*, vol. 2, a report on the status of religion in Egypt (Cairo: al-Ahram Center for Political and Strategic Studies, 1998), 210–211. As early as 1997, Mustafa Mashur admitted, "We can no longer celebrate Ramadan. If we meet, it must be in secret." "Only when one of us dies we all get together at funerals," said a member. See *Cairo Times*, April 3–16, 1997, 6.

31. *Al-Hayat*, January 12, 1998, 1.

32. Dr. Essam El-Erian, interview by the author, Cairo, November 17, 2001.

33. Reported in *Cairo Times*, February 3–9, 2000, 11.

34. Interview with Abdel-Rahman's son in *Cairo Times*, August 2–8, 2001.

35. Cited in Mansour Moaddel, "Religion, Gender, and Politics in Egypt, Jordan, and Iran: Findings of Comparative National Surveys" (unpublished report, 2002), 5.

36. The most trusted institutions after the ulema and imams of mosques were intellectuals, the army, the courts, universities, and schools. Other institutions included in the survey were elders, TV, major companies, the press, civil service, parliament, and finally political parties as the least trusted. The survey was conducted by Riaz Hassan, a professor of sociology at Flinders University,

Australia. The Egyptian sample of 788 was taken from various governorates. The preliminary results of the survey were reported in Riaz Hassan, "Faithlines: Social Structure and Religiosity in Muslim Societies: An Empirical Study" (unpublished paper, April 1998). See also Moaddel, "Religion, Gender, and Politics in Egypt, Jordan, and Iran."

37. Surveys of the professional middle class carried out by my students Caroline Wahba, Christine Emil Wahba, Sherine Greiss, and Dana Sajdi (unpublished papers, Department of Sociology and Anthropology, the American University in Cairo, 1980, 1990).

38. The Cairo Book Fair survey was based on a random sampling of women lining up to enter into the fair on January 26, 2002. The Zamalek survey was carried out in July 2003 in a shopping mall, where 157 women entering the mall were surveyed. Of the total, fifty-eight were unveiled. I have subtracted an estimate of 25 percent from the latter on the assumption of them being Egyptian Christians and foreign expatriate women. I am grateful to Wesam Younis for helping to carry out this later survey.

39. Janet Abu-Lughod, *Cairo: The City Victorious* (Princeton: Princeton University Press, 1971), 239.

40. See Mariz Tadros, "NGO–State Relations in Egypt: Welfare Assistance in a Poor Urban Community of Cairo" (D.Phil. diss., University of Oxford, June 2004).

41. Some 83 percent were against urfi marriage. The poll was conducted by *Al-Ahram Weekly*, among 1,500 citizens in February 2001. The results were reported in Fayza Hassan, "The Meaning of Emancipation," *Al-Ahram Weekly*, March 1–7, 2001.

42. *Al-Wafd*, January 27, 28, and 30, 2000.

43. *Al-Wafd*, March 13, 2003, 14.

44. The main albums include Muhammad Rahim: *Al-Rahman Singing without Music*; Mustapha Qamar: *al-Quds*; Amr Diab: *ya Rasoul allah ya Muhhamd* and *Aakhar kalaam andina...al-Haqq haqq-e rabbina*; Angham: three albums with a Gulf state company; Samira Saiid: *Khaliq al-Azeem* and *Allah Akbar*; Muhamad Fuad: *al-Haqq*, plus a nationalist album called *Jenin*; Iman al-Bahr Darwish: *Izn ya Bilaal*, with ten songs; and Muhamad al-Hellow: *al-Quds Tasrakh*, including religious and nationalist songs. See Khalid Fuad, "The Season of Religious Songs," *Al-Qahira* 10 (May 21, 2002): 11.

45. *Cairo Times*, August 30–September 5, 2001, 8.

46. Stated by the owner of a drug store, cited in *Sawt al-Azhar*, February 25, 2000, 2.

47. See a report by Abir Abdul-Azim in *Sawt al-Azhar*, February 25, 2000, 2.

48. These observations are based upon in-depth interviews with thirteen low-skill workers (working in a cast iron foundry, an auto mechanic workshop, a small factory, and a plumbing workshop) conducted by Basma al-Dajani, the American University in Cairo, fall 1990.

232 CHANGE IN AMBIVALENCE

49. For a fine discussion of Sufi orders in Egypt, see Michael Gilsenan, *Saint and Sufi in Modern Egypt: An Essay in the Sociology of Religion* (Oxford: Clarendon Press, 1973). For the Sufi basis of "popular religion" in Egypt, see Ali Fahmi, "Addin al-Sha'bawi fi Misr," *Al-Dimuqratiya* 12 (October 2003): 49–51.

50. See Samuli Schielke, "Habitus of the Authentic, Order of the Rational: Contesting Saints' Festivals in Contemporary Egypt," *Critique: Critical Middle Eastern Studies* 12, no. 2 (Fall 2003): 155–175.

51. See Muhamed Hafez Diab, "Addin al-Sha'bi, al-Zakira wa Mu'ash," *Sutuh* 30 (1998): 16–18.

52. Dr. Essam El-Erian, a prominent leader of the Muslim Brotherhood, interview by the author, Cairo, November 2001.

53. Samuli Schielke, "Pious Fun at Saints Festivals in Modern Egypt," *ISIM Newsletter* 7 (2001): 23; also Schielke, "Habitus of the Authentic, Order of the Rational."

54. Based on interviews with twelve middle-class migrant families who had returned to Egypt after spending years in Saudi Arabia, conducted by Menna Al-Sheiby and reported in "The Social Impact of Labor Migration: A Closer Look at Migration to the Gulf (Saudi Arabia)" (Third World Development course, the American University in Cairo, spring 2002).

55. Hadia Mostafa, "In Layman's Terms," *Egypt Today* 21, no. 9 (September 2000): 81–83.

56. Amina Elbendary, "Books? What Books...," *Al-Ahram Weekly*, January 31–February 6, 2002, 14.

57. Cited in Mostafa, "In Layman's Terms," 83.

58. For this information I am indebted to my student Dalia Ahmed Mustafa and her term paper "Modern *Da'wa* and E-Piety: An Investigation of Amr Khalid and His Populist Islamic Micromobilization" (the American University in Cairo, fall 2001).

59. Hatef el-Islami was advertised in the weekly *Aqidati*, March 5, 2002, 5. A caller was to leave a question and would receive an answer after twenty-four hours. The advice fee was £1 per minute.

60. These are based on my interviews with Amr Khalid's fans, Cairo, May 2002, and those conducted by Dalia Mustafa and presented in "Modern *Da'wa* and E-Piety."

61. Marina is a popular upper-middle-class resort on the Mediterranean coast.

62. There is no precise figure as to the number of women's halaqat, but anecdotal evidence points to their vast numbers, with most people saying that there were such groupings in their neighborhoods.

63. See Sherine Hafez, "The Terms of Empowerment: Islamic Women Activists in Egypt" (M.A. thesis, the American University in Cairo, 2001).

64. In one such sermon in Cairo, a sheikha informed her audience of how in the hereafter God would reward devout women with "unlimited access to

shopping." "You can shop for whatever you desire and in whatever quantity you wish," she promised. Although pious men in the sheikha's view were to be rewarded with access to virgin women, virtuous wives would stand in a more advantageous position of being the men's favored sexual partners. Reported by Hania Shokamy, Cairo, December 2001.

65. Hafez, "Terms of Empowerment," 85–86.

66. Leila Ahmad, *Women and Gender in Islam* (Cairo: the American University in Cairo Press, 1998); Margot Badran, *Feminism, Islam and Nation* (Princeton: Princeton University Press, 1995).

67. Hafez, "Terms of Empowerment."

68. Ibid., 59.

69. Preacher Sherine Fathy, cited in ibid., 92.

70. Mona, interview by Noha Abu-Ghazzia, Cairo, spring 2003.

71. Cited in Azza Karam, *Women, Islamists and the State* (London: Palgrave, 1997), 219. Amira Howeidy, "Born to Be Wild," *Al-Ahram Weekly*, December 23–29, 1999, 19.

72. S. Duval, "New Veils and New Voices: Islamist Women's Groups in Egypt," in *Women and Islamization*, ed. Karin Ask and M. Tjomsland (London: Bridles Ltd., 1998), 45–73.

73. Galal Amin, *Whatever Happened to the Egyptian: Changes in Egyptian Society from 1950 to the Present* (Cairo: the American University in Cairo Press, 2001), 37–38.

74. Michael Lowy, *The War of Gods* (London: Verso Press, 1996).

75. See Max Weber, *The Sociology of Religion* (Boston: Beacon Press, 1964), 85.

76. Ibid., 107.

77. See Alan Aldridge, *Religion in the Contemporary World: A Sociological Introduction* (Cambridge: Polity Press, 2000).

78. Interestingly, women expressed how their moment of *hedaya*, guidance, would begin by taking a shower to cleanse their sins—something quite similar to the ritual of born-again Christians.

79. Somaya, interviews by Noha Abu-Ghazzia, Cairo, spring 2003; Hana, interview by the author, Cairo, spring 1995.

80. Anthony Giddens, *Modernity and Self-Identity: Self and Society in the Late Modern Age* (Stanford: Stanford University Press, 1991).

81. Middle-aged elite women, interviews by Noha Abu-Ghazzia, Cairo, spring 2003.

82. For a critical analysis of post-Infitah ideals and ethics, see S. E. Ibrahim, *New Arab Social Order* (Boulder: Westview Press, 1985).

83. Hoda's statement in response to my question, "What is it like to be young in today's Egyptian society?" interview by the author, Cairo, spring 2003.

84. The figure for the country was 22 percent. M. I. Soueif, G. S. Youssuf, H. S. Taha, H. A. Moneim, O. A. Sree, K. A. Badr, M. Salakawi, and F. A. Yunis, "Use

of Psychoactive Substances among Male Secondary School Pupils in Egypt: A Study of a Nationwide Representative Sample," *Drug and Alcohol Dependence* 26 (1990): 63–79, at 71–72.

85. Reportedly the quantity seized by the police jumped from 2,276 units in 2000 to 7,008 units in 2001; reported in *Cairo Times*, March 14–20, 2002, 16.

86. See Population Council, *Transitions to Adulthood: A National Survey of Egyptian Adolescents* (Cairo: Population Council, March 1999).

87. See Ayman Khalifa, "The Withering Youth of Egypt," *Ru'ya* 7 (Spring 1995): 6–10.

88. Ibid. This was confirmed by interviews with youngsters conducted by Rime Naguib, sociology student, the American University in Cairo, spring 2002.

89. Fatma el-Zanaty, "Behavioral Research among Egyptian University Students" (MEDTIC/FHI, Behavioral Research Unit, Cairo, 1996), reported in Barbara Ibrahim and Hind Wassef, "Caught between Two Worlds: Youth in the Egyptian Hinterland," in *Alienation or Integration of Arab Youth*, ed. Roel Meijer (London: Curzon Press, 2000), 163.

90. *Cairo Times*, May 15–28, 1997, 12. The active sexuality of youth was also confirmed by Mona, my M.A. student, in her thesis, for which she interviewed a number of "deviant" adolescents in a hospital in Cairo in the late 1990s.

91. Shahida El-Baz, cited in *Cairo Times*, May 15–28, 1997, 12.

92. Ironically, the partially segregated trains made traditional young women more mobile. Parents would not mind if their daughters took trains (as opposed to taxis or buses) since segregated trains were thought to protect their daughters from male harassment. Seif Nasrawi, "An Ethnography of Cairo's Metro" (term paper, Urban Sociology class, the American University in Cairo, fall 2002).

93. Cited in Mustafa Abdul-Rahman, "Sex, *Urfi* Marriage as Survival Strategy in Dahab" (term paper, the American University in Cairo, fall 2001), 18.

94. Cited in Rime Naguib, "Egyptian Youth: A Tentative Study" (unpublished term paper, the American University in Cairo, spring 2002).

95. Ibid.

96. Cited in *Al-Wafd*, May 4, 2000; *Al-Ahram*, May 6, 2000, 13.

97. A Central Agency for Public Mobilization and Statistics report about over five million bachelor boys and 3.4 million girls caused an uproar about the moral implications of so many unmarried individuals. Indeed the age of marriage reached thirty–forty for men and twenty–thirty for women; see *Al-Wafd*, January 1, 2002, 3.

98. The public expression of such anxiety spread in the media and academic conferences on the "ethics of the era of globalization." In May 2002, a large national conference organized by the Center for Educational Studies discussed the deterioration of moralities in Egypt in the current global context. It recommended a national project for "moral development"; reported in *Al-Wafd*, May 23, 2002, 15.

99. Based on my own personal observations in the late 1990s. Much of the discussion draws on Asef Bayat and Eric Dennis, "Egypt: Twenty Years of Urban Transformation," Urban Change Working Paper, no. 5 (London: International Institute for Environment and Development, 2002). For a political economy analysis, see Timothy Mitchell, "Dreamland: New Liberalism of Your Desires," *Middle East Report* 210 (Spring 1999), www.merip.org/mer/mer210/dreamland-neoliberalism-your-desires.

100. Home visit by the author, Old Maadi, Cairo, March 18, 2000.

101. *Al-Ahram* (daily), September 1, 1992.

102. Cited in *Sawt al-Azhar*, December 7, 2001, 4.

103. Ibid.

104. Statements by the state, cited in Jailan Halawi, "Police Clampdown on Shi'i Group," *Al-Ahram Weekly*, October 24–30, 1996.

105. For some reports, see *Al-Hayat*, October 22, 1996; and *Al-Hayat*, October 27, 1996.

106. Reported in *Aqidati*, October 29, 1996, 1.

107. See Atef Shahat Said, "Homosexuality and Human Rights in Egypt," *ISIM Newsletter*, January 2002.

108. Reported by Hisham Bahjat, a human rights advocate, lecture, the American University in Cairo, July 14, 2003.

109. *Al-Ahram* (daily), October 22, 1981.

110. Reported in *Rose al-Yousef*, October 6, 2001. See also *Al-Hayat*, January 15, 1999.

111. See Mary Ann Weaver, "Revolution by Stealth," *New Yorker*, June 8, 1998, 46.

112. According to Gamal Badawi, the editor-in-chief, reported in *Al-Ahram Weekly*, October 14–20, 1999, 3. It is interesting to note that Gamal Badawi was previously the editor of "secular" opposition daily *Al-Wafd*.

113. For documentation of NDP's Islamic discourse, see Jihad Awda, "Al-Hizb al-Watani wa Tatwir al-Khitab al-Dini," *Al-Dimuqratiya* 9 (January 2003): 9–22.

114. See various reports by the Egyptian Organization for Human Rights. For instance, Hamid Abu-Ahmad's translation of *Who Killed Palomino Molero?* by Mario Vargas Llosa was found to offend public morality, and Alaa Hamed was sentenced to eight years and a fine in 1991 for his *Distance in a Man's Mind* because it was seen as subversive to Islam. The Azhar found Farag Fouda's book *To Be or Not to Be* anti-Islamic, and Fouda was murdered by the al-Gama'a al-Islamiya for his "blasphemy" in 1992; see James Napoli, "Egyptian Sleight of Hand," *Index on Censorship* 21, no. 2 (1992): 23–25. In 1997, Azhar's Islamic Research Academy found Sayed el-Qimni's book *Rabb al-Zaman* denigrating both to Joseph and the Bible and to the companions of the Prophet Muhammad. The court, however, revoked the book's confiscation; see *Al-Ahram Weekly*, September 18–24, 1997, 3.

115. Reported in Adel Sarwish, "The Hydra Grows Another Head: The Fundamentalist Arab Governments in the Gulf Are Buying Out Journalists and Writers in Egypt," *Index on Censorship* 12, no. 6 (June 1992): 27.

116. Reported in *Al-Liwa al-Islami*, January 10, 2002, 4–5. Of course, the nationalization of mosques goes back to the Nasser era. Indeed, before the ruling in 1996, Law 157/1960 granted the supervision of all mosques in the country to the Ministry of Awqaf. The 1996 ruling simply began to enforce that law.

117. *Al-Hayat*, June 3, 2000, 5.

118. Reported in Weaver, "Revolution by Stealth," 47.

119. See Linda Herrera, "The Islamization of Education in Egypt: Between Politics, Culture and the Market," in *Modernizing Islam*, ed. John Esposito and F. Burgat (New Brunswick, N.J.: Rutgers University Press, 2002), 168–189.

120. Reported in *Rose al-Yousef*, May 10, 1993, 26–28.

121. Only 4 percent rejected this idea, and 10 percent did not express opinions. See Abdul-Salam Nuwir, *Al-Mu'allimoun wa al-Siyassa fi Misr* (Cairo: al-Ahram Center for Strategic and Political Studies, 2001), 157–158.

122. Weaver, "Revolution by Stealth."

123. Hisba was originally the name of the office of *muhtasib* or "Inspector of the Markets." The institution had come into Islam from Byzantine times, being Islamized by the Abbasids. For a discussion of this concept and for the details of Abu-Zeid's case, see Fauzi Najjar, "Islamic Fundamentalism and the Intellectuals: The Case of Nasr Hamid Abu-Zeid," *British Journal of Middle East Studies* 27, no. 2 (November 2000): 177–200.

124. Reem Saad, seminar, 1997.

125. See Alan Cooperman, "First Bombs, Now Lawsuits," *U.S. News and World Report* 121, no. 25 (1996): 38–40.

126. Reported in Jailan Halawi, "Detained for Deriding Islam," *Al-Ahram Weekly*, April 13–19, 2000.

127. In early 2003 there were seventeen Internet cafés in Cairo that young people between twenty and twenty-eight were using; *Al-Wafd*, March 2, 2003, 3.

128. Expressed by Minister of Youth Ali Eddin Hilal Desouqui, interview by the author, Cairo, November 3, 2001.

129. For the contour of social policies in Egypt, see Asef Bayat, "The Political Economy of Social Policy in Egypt," in *Social Policy and Development in the Middle East and North Africa*, ed. Masoud Karshenas and Val Moghadam (London: Palgrave, 2006), 135–155.

130. For a fine analysis of economic reform and political constraints, see Eberhard Kienle, *A Grand Delusion: Democracy and Economic Reform in Egypt* (London: I. B. Tauris, 2001).

131. The role of religion, especially Islam, in national integration and moral supervision has been emphasized clearly in the rationale behind the introduction of "teaching religion" in Egyptian schools. See Mahmoud Daba'a, "Ta'lim el-Din al-Islami fi Misr" (presentation on curriculum building for Egyptian schools at a workshop for Religious Education and Education of Religion in Egypt and Sweden, Alexandria, Egypt, September 19–21, 2002).

132. The volumes prepared by the Gama'a "historic leaders" in prison published under the Selselat Tashih al-Mafâhim (Series on the Correction of Concepts) included Hafez and Muhamed, *Mubadirat Waqf al-'Unf;* Najeh Ibrahim Abdullah and Ali Muhamed Ali Sharif, *Hormat al-Gholow fi-Ddin wa Takfir al-Muslemin;* Hamdi Abdul-Rahman Abdul-Azim and Najeh Ibrahim Abdulah, *Taslit ul-Adwa alaa Ma Waqa'a fil-Jihad min Ikhta';* and Ali Muhamed Ali Sharif and Osamah Ibrahim Hafez, *An-Nass wal-Tabiin fi Tashih Mafahim al-Muhtasebin* (all Cairo: Maktabat al-Turath al-Islami, January 2002). Because the books do not refer to state violence, Montassir al-Zayat feels a "smell of state intervention" in producing these books; see Montassir al-Zayat, "Recognizing the Religious Flow Helps Loosen the Political and Public Stress in the Arab World," *Al-Hayat,* May 13, 2002, 15.
133. Hafez and Muhamed, *Mubadirat Waqf al-'Unf.*
134. Abdul-Azim and Abdulah, *Taslit al-Adwa alaa Ma Waqa'a fil-Jihad min Ikhta'.*
135. Hafez and Muhamed, *Mubadirat Waqf al-'Unf.*
136. See a very interesting interview with imprisoned leaders in jail, in *Al-Musawwar* 4054 (June 21, 2002): 4–22.
137. Cited in Negus, "Down but Not Out," 7.
138. Essam El-Erian, interview by the author, Cairo, November 17, 2001.
139. Ibid.
140. Abul-Alaa Maadi, interview by the author, Cairo, March 2001. See also an interview with Abu-Alaa Maadi, the leader of the al-Wasat Party, in *Cairo Times,* August 2–8, 2001, 19.
141. Abul-Alaa Maadi, an al-Wasat leader, interview by the author, Cairo, March 2001.
142. The history and philosophy behind al-Wasat are documented in *Awraq Hizb al-Wasat* [Al-Wasat Party's documents], with an intro. by Rafiq Habib (Cairo: Hizb al-Wasat, 1996).
143. See *Awraq Hizb al-Wasat al-Misry* (Cairo: Hizb al-Wasat, 1998), 19–20.
144. See *Al-Ahram Weekly,* April 20–26, 2000; *Cairo Times,* April 13–19, 2000.
145. Al-Qaradawi believed that *fiqh,* among other things, was suffering from *jomoud,* or stagnation; see *al-Mokhtar al-Islami* 226 (September 2001): 74.
146. See Sana Negus, "Brothers' Brother," on the profile of Gamal el-Banna, *Cairo Times,* September 30–October 13, 1999, 16; Gamal el-Banna, *Nahw Fiqh Jadid,* 3 vols. (Cairo: Dar al-Fikr al-Islami, 1995, 1997, 1999).
147. See, for instance, al-Gama'a leader Hamdi Abdul-Rahman (emir of Sohâg) in an interview in *Al-Musawwar* 4041 (March 22, 2002): 26–29.
148. Interviews with Gama'a's leaders in Tora Prison, *Al-Musawwar* 4054 (June 21, 2002): 4–22.
149. On Ibn Taymiya, see H. Laoust, "Ibn Taimiyya," in *The Encyclopedia of Islam,* ed. C. E. Bosworth, E. van Donzel, B. Lewis, and Ch. Pellat (Leiden: Brill, 1986).
150. According to Essam El-Erian, interview by the author, Cairo, October 2001.

151. According to Abul-Alaa Maadi, interview by the author, Cairo, March 2001.

152. Raymond Baker's *Islam without Fear: Egypt and the New Islamists* (Cambridge: Harvard University Press, 2003) focuses on a small number of such religious intellectuals who have little influence on Egyptian religious discourse. Baker's otherwise interesting book overestimates a more sophisticated but marginal trend in the Egyptian intellectual landscape.

153. See Mona Abaza, "*Tanwir* and Islamization: Rethinking the Struggle over Intellectual Inclusion in Egypt," *Cairo Papers in Social Science* 22, no. 4 (Winter 1999): 92.

154. For the Salafi influence on Egypt's religious thought, see Jihad Owda, "Al-Salafiun fi Misr," *Ahwal Misriya* 23 (Winter 2004): 8–24.

155. On Rashid Reda, the publisher of *al-Manar*, see Emad Eldin Shahin, *Through Muslim Eyes: A. Rashid Reda and the West* (Herndon, Va.: International Institute of Islamic Thought, 1993).

156. According to Essam El-Erian, interview by the author, Cairo, October 2001.

157. Bashir Nafi, a professor of modern Islamic history, interview in *Al-Ahram Weekly*, January 14–20, 1999, 4. See also Edward Said, "Enemies of the State," *Al-Ahram Weekly*, June 21–27, 2001.

158. Hazem Saghiya, "Problems of Egypt's Political Culture," *Al-Hayat*, July 29, 2001.

159. The cosmopolitanism of Cairo and Alexandria in prerevolution Egypt has been discussed in Sami Zubaida's unpublished paper, "Cosmopolitanism in the Arab World" (2004).

160. Weaver, "Revolution by Stealth," 42.

161. The 1996 best sellers were the following: *Secret Channels: The Inside Story of Arab–Israeli Peace Negotiations* by Mohammad Hasnein Heikal (200,000 copies sold), *The Age of Fifi Abdou* by Emad Nassef (150,000), *A Journey to Paradise and Hell* by Mustafa Mahmoud (100,000), *Women from Hell* by Emad Nassef (100,000), *Girls for Export* by Emad Nassef (90,000), *The Red File* by Emad Nassef (70,000), *The War of the Whores* by Emad Nassef (70,000), *A Scandal Called Saida Sultana* by Mohammad al-Ghity (60,000), and *How Egyptians Joke about Their Leaders* by Adel Hamouda (60,000); see *Cairo Times*, April 17–30, 1997, 18.

162. Cited in *Al-Ahram Weekly*, January 6–12, 2000, 3.

163. Cited in Weaver, "Revolution by Stealth," 41.

164. Ibid., 42.

165. *Al-Wafd*, December 31, 2001.

166. Gamal Badawi, "The Age of Sha'bula," *Al-Wafd*, October 2002.

167. Sabry Hafez, "The Novel, Politics and Islam," *New Left Review*, 2nd series, 5 (September–October 2000): 141.

168. For an interesting discussion of "nativism," see Mehrzad Boroujerdi, *Iranian Intellectuals and the West: The Tormented Triumph of Nativism* (Syracuse: Syracuse University Press, 1996).

169. Saghiya, "Problems of Egypt's Political Culture."

170. See report in *Cairo Times*, November 27–December 10, 1997, 5.

171. According to a poll conducted by the American Zogby Institute one year before Sharon came to power, 79 percent of Egyptians said that the Palestinian issue was for them personally the most important and pressing political issue; cited in *Rose al-Yousef*, July 28, 2001.

172. Samia Mehreaz, "Take Them Out of the Ball Game: Egypt's Cultural Players in Crisis," *Middle East Report* 219 (Summer 2001): 10–15.

173. These passages draw on Asef Bayat, "The 'Street' and the Politics of Dissent in the Arab World," *Middle East Report* 226 (March 2003): 10–17.

174. Mona El-Ghobashy, "Egypt Looks Ahead to Portentous Year," *Middle East Report Online*, February 2, 2005, www.merip.org/mero/mero020205.

175. Joel Beinin, "Popular Social Movements and the Future of Egyptian Politics," *Middle East Report Online*, March 10, 2005, www.merip.org/mero/mero031005.

176. *Independent*, August 7, 2011.

177. An opinion poll in November 2011 showed that 75 percent of Egyptian respondents favored a "civil state" as opposed to a "religious state"; only 1 percent wanted a "military regime." See *Al-Masry al-Youm*, November 12, 2011. For details on the Arab revolutions, see Asef Bayat, *Life as Politics: How Ordinary People Change the Middle East*, 2nd ed. (Stanford: Stanford University Press, 2013), chapter 13, "The Post-Islamist Refo-lutions."

178. Interestingly, the Rand Corporation, which advises the U.S. government, also identifies the Muslim Brotherhood's youths (the future leaders of the organization) as "post-Islamists," with whom the United States should engage; see Jeffery Martini, Dalia Dassa Kaye, and Erin York, *The Muslim Brotherhood, Its Youth, and Implications for U.S. Engagement* (Pittsburg: RAND, 2012).

8

Hizbullah's Infitah:

A POST-ISLAMIST TURN?

Joseph Alagha

In the "Arab Spring," the Lebanese Shiite resistance movement Hizbullah issued political declarations blessing the Tunisian and Egyptian people, in particular, and the Arab masses, in general, for their drive for "freedom and dignity."[1] Hizbullah's secretary-general, Sayyid Hasan Nasrallah, added, "This is the true path when people believe in their resolve.... [T] his is the new Middle East created by its own people." He concluded, "Your Spring has begun; no one can lead you to another winter. Your belief, vigilance, and resilience will overcome all difficulties and make you triumphant."[2] Within this regional context, Hizbullah managed to affect a tangible change in the political system by democratic means. It virtually succeeded in ruling Lebanon after it obtained a majority of sixty-eight MPs in the 128-seat legislature, a constitutional move that allowed it to name the prime minister and wield significant political power over the cabinet, the council of ministers. This is unprecedented in Lebanese politics, since instead of resorting to political violence, the militant-Islamist organization followed constitutional and institutional channels, engaging the other constituents of Lebanese society in diplomacy, negotiations, and bargaining, even though Hizbullah's military power is by far greater than that of the Lebanese Army.

A "terrorist organization" in the eyes of the United States, Israel, Canada, Australia, the Netherlands, and other Western countries, after almost thirty years since its founding, Hizbullah seems to care less about its regional ambitions such as the "destruction of the state of Israel and the liberation of Jerusalem,"[3] as its 1985 Open Letter or Manifesto affirmed. How did the rapid evolution of Hizbullah from a marginal splinter group to a dominant group in national and international politics come about? Why did Hizbullah content itself with a domestic agenda of having the upper hand in Lebanese politics? What happened to its regional aspirations and confrontation with the so-called two "Satans," the United States and Israel? Was that apparent policy change only in semantics, or is the organization capable of enforcing its regional agenda, as it managed to put its teeth firmly in Lebanese politics? What is the role of geopolitics in this respect?

In this chapter, I show how Hizbullah, through the years since its inception, has transformed its ideas, discourse, theory, practice, and strategies, highlighting the organizational changes that took place along the way. I discuss why such changes have happened: Were these due to internal causes, Hizbullah's inability to materialize its blueprint, or due to international pressure? What role did 9/11 and its aftermath play? In what way have the changes in Iran since Ayatollah Khomeini's death impacted Hizbullah? This chapter also presents a concerted effort to map the DNA of Hizbullah, not only by studying its discursive shifts but also by analyzing the organization's new policy orientations and identity construction and reconstruction in the past three decades.

Departure from Islamism?

Asef Bayat coined the term *post-Islamism* as early as 1996 and distinguished himself from other scholars who later on employed the concept, but apparently with different connotations.[4] According to Bayat, post-Islamism represents in the first place a *condition*, a social and political one, in which the appeal and the sources for legitimacy of Islamist politics are exhausted after a phase of experimentation. The adherents become aware of the anomalies and shortcomings of their system while attempting to moderate and institutionalize their movement.[5] Post-Islamism is also a *project* representing a conscious attempt to transcend Islamism in social, political, and intellectual domains. Thus, it is an endeavor to overturn the underlying singular authoritative voice of Islamism and replace it with a plurality of voices of authority, in other words, "emphasizing rights instead of duties; historicity rather than fixed Holy Scriptures; freedom instead of rigidity; and the future instead of the past." Yet it is neither anti-Islamic nor un-Islamic or secular; rather, it is an undertaking to fuse "religiosity and rights, Islam and liberty, faith and freedom." The Islamic social movement's ideology comes to be plural in this state, not basing itself solely on Islam but, rather, becoming capable of including other (secular) ideas and denominations.[6]

My interviewees from Hizbullah's rank and file defined Islamists as fervent Muslim believers or pious (religious) youth and Islamism as religiosity and strict adherence to the divine laws. They defined post-Islamism as a process of *infitah*, or opening up to global cultural trends while preserving indigenous values as an Islamic moral alternative.[7] How post-Islamist, then, has Hizbullah become, if at all? Is Hizbullah on a trajectory of post-Islamism, or is its infitah to be understood, as Mandaville characterized, as bottom-up Islamization in disguise?[8]

In truth, Hizbullah witnessed remarkable transformations in the past three-plus decades. From its founding as an Islamic movement of social and political protest during 1978–1985, it evolved into a full-fledged social movement between 1985 and 1991 and then into a parliamentary political party from 1992 to the present. Since its inception, Hizbullah has adopted Ayatollah Khomeini's theory of *wilayat al-faqih* (guardianship of the jurisprudent) as its ideology in the Lebanese social and political conditions. Khomeini's wilayat al-faqih was imported to Lebanon, serving as a blueprint for a progressive Islamic state to be emulated by Hizbullah in its constituencies. Illustrating the vital importance given to becoming a member of "Ummat Hizbullah," a Hizbullah cadre told me, on condition of anonymity, that a person who tried to join the party but failed the process of screening (*ta'tir*) that Hizbullah's prospective members undergo three times returned with an assault rifle and killed his recruiting officer. Another member told me that as a practice of indoctrination and as an initiation ceremony, new Hizbullah recruits had to repeatedly state: "If the jurisprudent told you to kill yourself, then you have to do it."[9] This illustrates not only indoctrination but also the total obedience to the *faqih*.

In the early 1980s, Khomeini instructed 'Ali Khamina'i, who was at the time deputy minister of defense, to take full responsibility of the Lebanese Hizbullah. Since then, Khamina'i has become Hizbullah's "godfather." That is why, since its inception, Hizbullah, based on a religious and ideological stance, fully abides by the ideas and opinions of Khomeini as communicated by Khamina'i. During that initial period, the religious/ideological bond between the Islamic Republic of Iran and Lebanon could be examined from the following declarations by Hizbullah and Iranian officials—Shaykh Hasan Trad: "Iran and Lebanon are one people in one country"; Sayyid Ibrahim Amin Al-Sayyid: "We do not say that we are part of Iran, we are Iran in Lebanon and Lebanon in Iran"; Ali Akbar Muhtashami: "We are going to support Lebanon politically and militarily like we buttress one of our own Iranian districts"; Shaykh Hasan Srur: "We declare to the whole world that the Islamic Republic of Iran is our mother, religion, *Ka'ba*, and our veins."[10]

In the 1980s, Hizbullah advocated the establishment of an Islamic state in Lebanon and maintained the *ahl al-dhimma* category with respect to non-Muslims.[11] In spite of its exhortation of Christians to convert to Islam, Hizbullah did not seek to impose this conversion by force. Rather, the party applied its theory of tolerance to those Christians living in its constituencies, as well as to other Christians, as long as they were not "treacherous or aggressive." In conformity with the Prophetic tradition and the Quran, Hizbullah stressed that there should be "no compulsion in religion" (Quran 2:256) and an "equitable world" (Quran 3:64) or common ground that should guide relationships between Muslims and Christians. As such, it emphasized that the common ground between ahl al-dhimma and Muslims involves the social values of mutual tolerance, respect, brotherhood, and solidarity. On this basis, Hizbullah recognized the human freedom, that is, social and religious freedom, of Christians but *not* their political autonomy, as was the case in the 1926 French Mandate Constitution and 1943 Independence Constitution. Thus, in the 1980s, contrary to the Prophetic tradition that granted non-Muslims partnership in political structures, Hizbullah's "tolerance" or "inclusiveness" excluded Christians from political life, which could be regarded as a discriminatory practice. Hizbullah's then policy seemed to imply that tolerance is the responsibility of the "majority" and integration is the responsibility of the "minority."

Since 1985, there developed a number of changes in Hizbullah's ideological identification with Iran's ruling elite. Hizbullah argued that during the early phase of its formation, it needed a unifying religious-political ideology, rather than an elaborate political program. Thus, it based itself on wilayat al-faqih and regarded Khomeini as the jurisconsult of *all* Muslims.[12] In the beginning, the organization was, ideologically, completely dependent on Khomeini. Later on this dependency witnessed some leeway, in the sense that Hizbullah did not blindly follow the Iranian regime; rather, it had some specificity (*khususiyya*), since in his capacity as the Supreme Leader (Rahbar), Khomeini was endowed with the sole right to determine the legitimacy (legitimate authority) of Hizbullah. Khomeini highlighted certain precepts within which Hizbullah could move freely; however, he left their implementation to the party's discretion. Thus, although Hizbullah was ideologically dependent on the Iranian regime, it had some room to maneuver in its decisions pertaining to some cases in Lebanese domestic affairs. Even though the fragmentation of religious authority, that is, the multiplicity of *marja*'s among the Shiites, continued after Khomeini's death, in Hizbullah's case the issue of *marja'iyya* was determined on the doctrinal-ideological basis of following the official *marja' al-taqlid*, who is recognized by the Islamic Republic of Iran. Thus, Hizbullah's religious authority was and still is the Iranian faqih. This made the transition after Khomeini's death smoother.

Up until 1991, Hizbullah considered the Quran as the constitution of the Islamic umma and Islam as both a religious and a governmental order (*din wa dawla*). The party enjoined Muslims to strive, using all legitimate means, in order to implement the Islamic order, wherever they might be.[13] In the period 1985–1991, Hizbullah regarded the Lebanese political system, which was dominated by the political Maronites (Catholic Christians), as a *jahiliyya* (pre-Islamic pagan) system. It applied this classification to every non-Islamic system: be it patriotic, democratic, or nationalistic, even if it were governed by Muslims.[14] In other words, Hizbullah pursued the establishment of an Islamic state from the perspective of religious and political ideology. The religious ideology, as Hizbullah's leading cadres argued, enjoined adherents to instate God's sovereignty and divine governance on earth through *hakimiyya* and to execute God's law by instituting an Islamic order as a *taklif shar'i* (religious and legal obligation). According to the political ideology, Hizbullah did not want to impose an Islamic order by force unless an overwhelming majority of the Lebanese voted in its favor through a referendum. This should be taken with apprehension since Hizbullah's rhetoric was different from what it was actually doing on the ground; it was actively engaged in preparing the way for establishing an Islamic order, through a bottom-up process, at least in its constituencies.

In its third stage of evolution, from 1992 on, Hizbullah has experienced a considerable ideological shift. Since the early 1990s, it regarded founding an Islamic state as a "legal abstraction" and dropped its demands for its implementation in Lebanon. This paved the way for the party to employ the concept of *muwatana* (citizenship) instead of ahl al-dhimma. Hizbullah's intellectuals based this current practice on a novel interpretation of the Prophetic tradition, as sanctioned by Shiite jurisprudence. Thus, since the 1990s and into the twenty-first century, Hizbullah has made great strides forward in acknowledging the human, civil, economic, social, cultural, and most importantly, political rights of the so-called ex-*dhimmis*, recognizing their right to full citizenship, as citizens of equal status and rights. This is not a rhetorical shift; rather, it is a major policy alteration, which is being implemented, and it is aimed at making the "other" secure in a shared Lebanese polity that might one day be dominated by the Shiite majority.

With this new policy of alliances, diplomacy, negotiations, and bargaining, Hizbullah has been able to spread its wings and flanks to a tangible part of the Christian constituents of the country.

As a prelude to contesting the 1992 legislative elections, Hizbullah gained more resources, moderated its discourse, initiated several policies to broaden its appeal to a larger constituency, and embarked on further institutionalization. Sayyid 'Abbas al-Musawi, Hizbullah's second secretary-general, initiated a policy of openness and dialogue toward the Lebanese myriad. After his death, his student and successor Sayyid Hasan Nasrallah, the third secretary-general, continued this process of mobilization and organization at the grassroots level to support advocacy in and outside of parliament.[15]

The year 1992 was a central year in shaping Hizbullah's evolving identity. The party faced a challenge in deciding whether to participate in the parliamentary elections or not. Hizbullah's twelve-member committee took a positive decision after much heated internal debate and discussions, followed by Iranian arbitration (*tahkim*). Since the faqih is the one who determines "legitimacy" (even in practical political matters), Khamina'i had to intercede and grant legitimacy for participation. This caused a considerable schism within Hizbullah, because Subhi al-Tufayli, Hizbullah's first secretary-general, contested the decision and pursued a confrontational stance with the party and the Lebanese state. Al-Tufayli held a high post in the leadership of Hizbullah in the early 1980s. Nevertheless, he later created minor dissent in the party for reasons that apparently were socioeconomic ("Revolution of the Hungry" in 1997) but, in fact, involved control of the B'albak region. Al-Tufayli today represents that category of Hizbullah member who still upholds the Iranian revolutionary ideology of the 1980s. He repeatedly accused Hizbullah of "protecting the borders of Israel" since it prevents *jihadis* from targeting it or crossing the border, and he criticized Iran for "serving the interests of the US." Al-Tufayli emphatically stated, "This is not the Hizbullah I founded, and this is not the Iran of Khomeini."[16]

Asef Bayat has noted that Islamic movements like Hizbullah are constituted of many layers and orientations that make up a collectivity, but one that is fluid and fragmented. This collectivity remains coherent when its leaders are successful in creating a hegemonic reading of events that gains consensus among its followers. This means that there is always a danger of losing adherents due to integration or moderation. This can lead the more radical elements of the social movement, such as al-Tufayli, to leave the movement because they disagree with the course it is taking.[17]

By giving an extended interpretation to the doctrine of wilayat al-faqih (i.e., applying it to the Lebanese multiconfessional, multireligious society, rather than to "monolithic" Iran, with its predominantly Shiite majority), the committee strongly recommended participation in the elections. This was in harmony with Hizbullah's holistic vision, which favored living up to the expectations of the people by serving their socioeconomic and political interests. The committee added that Hizbullah's greater jihad and dedication to addressing the plight of the people did not contradict its priority of a smaller military jihad for the sake of the liberation of occupied land. As such, participating in elections would lead to the achievement of good political results and could also be regarded as a leading step toward interaction with others. By this, Hizbullah presents a novel experience in the infitah of a young Islamic party. The committee stressed that this participation was in accordance with the Lebanese specificities (khususiyyat) as well as the nature of the proposed elections, which allowed for a considerable margin of freedom of choice. In short, the committee concluded that the sum total of the pros (masalih) outweighed the cons (mafasid) by far. That was why participation in the parliament would be worthwhile, since it was viewed as one of the ways of influencing change and making Hizbullah's voice heard, not only domestically but also regionally and internationally through the podiums made available to the members of parliament.[18] Thus, it seems that Hizbullah was forced by political circumstances, the Ta'if Agreement, Lebanon's new 1990 constitution, and the end of the civil war, to adjust to a new phase in its history by propagating a matter-of-fact political program and by merging into the Lebanese political system.

A further shift occurred in the interpretation of the authority of the faqih when Hizbullah argued that it did not consider the current regime in the Islamic Republic of Iran as the jurisconsult of all Muslims and, in consequence, not all Islamic movements had to abide by the orders and directives of the faqih or the regime.[19] In May 1995, Khamina'i appointed Nasrallah and Shaykh Muhammad Yazbik, head of the religio-judicial council, as his religious deputies (wakilayn shar'iyyan) in Lebanon. This move granted Hizbullah special prerogatives and delegated responsibilities (taklif shar'i) that reflect a great independence in practical performance. Thus, Hizbullah consolidated its financial resources, since the one-fifth religious tax (khums) imposed on those Lebanese Shiites who followed Khamina'i as their authority of emulation (marja'), as well as their alms (zakat) and religious (shar'i) monies, would pour directly into Hizbullah coffers, instead of being channeled through Iran, as had been the case.

The interpretation of authority took another dramatic shift after the Syrian withdrawal in April 2005. In conformity with its policy to change when circumstances change, Hizbullah switches from Iranian to local authority when it suits its purposes. Although the watershed decision to participate in the Lebanese cabinet ideologically required the *shar'i* judgment and legitimacy of the faqih, Hizbullah set a precedent by securing religious approval and legitimacy from Shaykh 'Afif al-Nabulsi[20]—at the time, the head of the Association of Shiite Religious Scholars of Jabal 'Amil in south Lebanon—and not Khamina'i, a move that indicates even more independence in decision making.

Thus, Hizbullah heeds Lebanese religious authority in addition to the Iranian one, and therefore, its participation in the Lebanese cabinet was relegated to an administrative matter, not a doctrinal one. Consequently, Hizbullah's leadership was capable of taking independent decisions. Instantly, Hizbullah joined the cabinet with two ministers and proliferated in Lebanese state institutions and the administrative structure just before the conservative Iranian president, Mahmoud Ahmadinejad, and his government were sworn to power in Iran. This led to increased Lebanonization that is more in line with the specificities (*khususiyyat*) of Lebanese society, rather than blind adherence to Iran.

Therefore, Hizbullah moved from complete ideological dependency on Khomeini to much less dependency after his death. The party gained more independence in decision making, not only in practical political issues but also in military and doctrinal issues, to the extent that it seems as if Hizbullah exercised almost independent decision making, at least in some cases. Even in military matters, Hizbullah does not always heed Iranian orders if they do not serve its overall interest (*maslaha*). Two cases in point that illustrate this trend are Sharon's "April 2002 West Bank counterterrorism offensive" and Barak's December 2008–January 2009 "Operation Cast Lead" in Gaza. Iran strongly urged Hizbullah to open the northern front across the Lebanese–Israeli border in order to release pressure on the Palestinians,[21] but Hizbullah adamantly refused because such a move was considered detrimental to its national interest (maslaha). This trend continued after Ahmadinejad won a second term in the controversial June 2009 presidential elections.

Although Hizbullah was inspired by the Islamic Revolution, it operates like any ordinary political party functioning within a non-Islamic state and a multireligious confessional and sectarian state. Hizbullah cannot go beyond being a political party operating within the Lebanese public sphere. That is why, for instance, in the parliamentary elections, it reached out and allied itself with secular parties and former enemies on the Lebanese scene, like any political party that accommodates protest via negotiations and bargaining, making compromises on some doctrinal aspects. In the process, Hizbullah moved from separation to integration into Lebanese society, eventually becoming part of the national state. Hizbullah's voting behavior in the legislature progressively shifted from (1) voting against granting confidence to the cabinet between 1992 and 1996 to (2) abstaining between 1998 and 2004 to (3) voting for confidence since 2005, the year the party joined the cabinet. Thus, Hizbullah granted its approval only after it participated.

These changed framing processes and new mobilization tactics are evidence of Hizbullah's attempts to transcend communal boundaries by creating imagined solidarities and having partially shared interests with other communities.[22] This is necessary since the existing Lebanese political system mandates intercommunity cooperation, which suggests that Hizbullah has learned to operate within the established political framework. Furthermore, the party needs to be careful not to revert to its extremist image because this could lead to a loss of the resources it gained due to its moderation. To conclude, Hizbullah as a social movement gained political power in this stage of its evolution. This empowerment reinforces its identification with its national context at the expense of transnational solidarities.

The tug-of-war between the Hizbullah-led opposition (March 8 Group), on the one hand, and the Lebanese cabinet and its supporters (March 14 Trend), on the other, led to bitter polarization, which plunged Lebanon into 537 days of stalemate and political deadlock, from December 1, 2006, to May 21, 2008. The "Doha Accord" of May 21, 2008, between March 14 and March 8, negotiated by the Arab League, granted Hizbullah veto power in the next national unity thirty-member cabinet by a margin of eleven ministers, while March 14 acquired sixteen ministers, and the president, three. Hizbullah ended its sit-in in downtown Beirut and dismantled its tent city. After six months of vacuum in the seat of the presidency, something unprecedented in Lebanese history, the consensus president, army commander general Michel Sulayman, was elected on May 25, 2008, by 118 votes out of 127 MPs.

A Post-Islamist Trajectory?

While pursuing policies so as to work within the electoral fabric of Lebanon, Hizbullah did not abandon its rhetoric vis the wilayat al-faqih. In fact it legitimized its political program of working within a multicultural, multireligious country with reference to wilayat al-faqih without encroaching upon its doctrinal-ideological, Islamic-religious convictions.[23] In May 2008, after March 8 gained veto power in the Lebanese cabinet, Nasrallah reiterated,

> I am honored to be a member of the party of wilayat al-faqih. The just, knowledgeable, wise, courageous, righteous, honest, and faithful faqih.... Wilayat al-faqih tells us [Hizbullah] that Lebanon is a multiconfessional, multireligious country that you have to preserve and uphold.[24]

With this unshakable commitment to wilayat al-faqih, Hizbullah reformulated what it meant by an Islamic state by making a categorical distinction between *al-fikr al-siyasi* (political ideology), which it maintained, and *al-barnamaj al-siyasi* (political program), which it promoted. From an ideological perspective, Hizbullah is committed to an Islamic state, and it will not be dropped as a legal abstraction. However, the party's political program has to take into account the political status quo and the overall functioning of the Lebanese political system. Hizbullah characterizes the Lebanese political situation as a complicated mold of sectarian-confessional specificities that prohibit the establishment of an Islamic state, not only from a practical perspective but also from a doctrinal one. Hizbullah's political ideology stipulates that an Islamic state should be established on solid foundations having full legitimacy and sovereignty from the people. Since the general will of the Lebanese people is against the establishment of an Islamic state, then it is not plausible to establish one.

On November 30, 2009, after revealing Hizbullah's Manifesto, or new political platform, which neither mentions the Islamic state nor refers to wilayat al-faqih, Nasrallah affirmed in answer to a question that there is no contradiction/opposition between Hizbullah's belief in wilayat al-faqih, on the one hand, and the erection of a strong institutionalized Lebanese state, on the other. On the contrary, wilayat al-faqih sanctions and allows Hizbullah's integration into the political system. Not only that, in line with the Vatican's position and papal guidance, Nasrallah added that Hizbullah believes that Lebanon is a blessing and has accomplished great historical achievements. He reiterated Imam Musa al-Sadr's stance that "Lebanon is the definitive nation to all its citizens," which is in conformity with the Lebanese constitution.[25]

Thus, Hizbullah shifted its position through its acceptance of and engagement in the democratic process under a sectarian-confessional political and administrative system. More dramatically, Hizbullah's political program modified its demand for the abolition of political sectarianism and adopted the political Maronite discourse, which stresses the abolition of political sectarianism in mentality before eradicating it in the texts. In line with the Ta'if Agreement and its earlier election programs, Hizbullah's 2009 Manifesto called for the establishment of a "National Body for the Abolition of Political Sectarianism," since sectarianism is perceived as a threat to consensual democracy and national coexistence.[26] Although Nasrallah deemed the sectarian system a tribal system, he clarified:

> Let us be realistic. The abolition of political sectarianism is one of the most difficult issues and cannot be accomplished overnight....[N]obody can dictate how to abolish it in a sentence or two. Rather, if after years of debate, ranging from five to thirty years, we find out that political sectarianism cannot be abolished, then let us be bold enough to say that what we agreed upon in the Ta'if Agreement cannot be realized. However, till then, the Lebanese need to found the "National Body for the Abolition of Political Sectarianism" in order to initiate the debate in a constructive manner.[27]

The 2009 Manifesto delineates an almost complete Lebanonization of Hizbullah, at least in discourse, since it no longer included transnational links such as wilayat al-faqih and the Islamic state in its primary frame of authority. Furthermore, it gives primacy to the national political arena for achieving national goals that would be beneficial to all Lebanese. Moreover, the manifesto represents Hizbullah's ideological shifts in assimilating into the political system to accomplish its goals through political initiatives and continued cooperation with other parties. In fact, this manifesto might signify Hizbullah's trajectory toward a post-Islamist trend in practice, thus transcending Islamism, its exclusivist platform, and evolving in the pluralistic political reality of Lebanon, even though certain Islamist rhetoric might still be voiced and even though Hizbullah's political interests, at least for the time being, may keep it an ally of the Islamist regime in Iran.

Hizbullah laid the groundwork for this precept of practice earlier. On May 26, 2008, the party celebrated the eighth anniversary of the nearly complete Israeli withdrawal from Lebanon through a fiery speech delivered by Nasrallah, who stressed that Hizbullah abides by the Ta'if Agreement, will honor the Doha Accord to the letter, and will continue to participate in the political system *as it is.* Nasrallah's stance remained the same after the fiasco of March 8 to acquire the majority of the seats in the June 2009 legislative elections. Hizbullah gave up its veto power and helped to broker a national unity cabinet on November 9, 2009, based on the previously agreed-on power-sharing formula: fifteen seats for March 14, five seats for the centralist coalition of the president, and ten seats for March 8. Thus, contrary to its military power and demographic strength, in an endeavor to uphold consensual democracy, Hizbullah contented itself with two ministers out of the ten allocated to March 8. Further measures of political compromise, such as conceding ministerial quotas to Sunni and Christian representatives in the cabinet, suggest that Hizbullah remains committed indeed to a mode of governance that is inherently communal, pluralist, and representative.

Conclusions

Through heavy reliance on a strict application of Khomeini's wilayat al-faqih in the 1980s, "Hizbullah—The Islamic Revolution in Lebanon" emerged as a strong internal organization with a limited following. Subhi al-Tufayli's firm, uncompromising political discourse, and his repeated references to the establishment of an Islamic state, which was unprecedented in Lebanese political discourse, backfired domestically, considerably alienating the party from other political and social movements and from the Lebanese public sphere. Thus, Hizbullah's policies were counterproductive, leading to a failure to integrate into Lebanese political life, especially after the party's initial vehement criticisms of the Ta'if Agreement.

Since the end of the civil war in 1990, Hizbullah has been confronting major developments in Lebanon: prominently, the emergence of a pluralistic public sphere and increasing openness toward other communities, political parties, and interest groups in the Lebanese myriad. Through a new interpretation of wilayat al-faqih, Hizbullah altered its discourse, priorities, and overall political outlook. The mixed confessional space in Lebanon led Hizbullah to move from marginalization to infitah, which allowed the party to become a major player in the Lebanese public sphere by participating in the parliamentary and municipal elections—and even obtaining a majority in the legislature in 2011. In short, in the early 1990s, Hizbullah started promoting its Islamic identity and agenda by following a pragmatic political program, mainly to allay the fears of Christians and other Muslims who were opposed to the Islamic state. In the meantime, Hizbullah remained faithful to its Shiite constituency by employing a bottom-up Islamization process and working within the Lebanese state's political and administrative structures while, at the same time, establishing Islamic institutions within civil society.

In the third stage, Hizbullah faced the problem of reconciling its political ideology with political reality. Thus, the party shifted from a *jihadi* outlook to a more flexible shari'a perspective. Hizbullah portrayed a distinguished expediency in its political program in an attempt to reconcile, as much as possible, its principles, aims, and political ideology, on the one hand, and its circumstances and objective capabilities, on the other hand, by relying heavily on the jurisprudential concepts of necessity, vices, and interests as a kind of Islamic prima facie duty. This is how Hizbullah's pragmatism was conducive to forging a marriage of convenience between political ideology and political reality, to the extent of pursuing a policy of infitah sanctioned by its political program. In this pluralistic Islamic cultural sphere, the concept of citizenship (*muwatana*) reigns, where all people have equal rights and duties and where coexistence and mutual respect are the main norms and assets among Lebanon's eighteen ethno-confessional communities.

Thus, the logic of operating within the bounds of the Lebanese state has prevailed over the logic of the revolution. The party justifies and legitimizes its political program by resorting to Quranic and jurisprudential bases. Significantly, the Shiite religio-political legacy conferred upon Hizbullah all the authenticity it needed in order to derive from it a political program based upon flexibility and pragmatism. Relying on the progressive nature of Shiite jurisprudence, Hizbullah remolded, constructed, and interpreted its authority in such a way as to bestow legitimacy on its participation in a pluralist polity based upon the quota system and patronage. And so, through this heavy reliance on Shiite jurisprudence, especially the concept of maslaha, Hizbullah was able to change parallel with the circumstances, through its pragmatic interpretation and metamorphosis of wilayat al-faqih. Hizbullah's metamorphosis could be attributed to changed historical and social circumstances and, more importantly, to the results of interactions with other political actors. Thus, the objective, sociological, and political reality of Lebanon compelled this originally Islamist movement onto the post-Islamist path, even though such post-Islamism remains inconsistent, selective, and pragmatic.

Notes

1. Quotations in English are my translations.
2. See Sayyid Hasan Nasrallah, speech delivered at the "Lebanese Political Parties' Festival in Support of Egypt's Arabism," February 7, 2011, at www.moqawama. org/essaydetails.php?eid=19822&cid=142; and Sayyid Hasan Nasrallah, speech in support of Arab revolutions, March 19, 2011, at www.moqawama.org/ essaydetails.php?eid=20205&cid=142.
3. Joseph Alagha, *Hizbullah's Documents: From the 1985 Open Letter to the 2009 Manifesto* (Amsterdam: Amsterdam University Press, 2011), 20.
4. Asef Bayat, "The Coming of a Post-Islamist Society," *Critique: Critical Middle East Studies* 9 (Fall 1996): 43–52.
5. Asef Bayat, *Islam and Democracy: What Is the Real Question?* (Amsterdam: Amsterdam University Press, 2007), 17–20.
6. Ibid., 20–21.
7. Some notable figures who framed such definitions include the following: Hajj Muhammad Ra'd, a member of the Hizbullah *shura* council and the head of the party's parliamentary bloc; Sayyid Abd Al-Halim Fadlallah, the head of the party's think tank, the Consultative Center for Studies and Documentation; Hajj Ghalib Abu Zaynab, a party officer for Muslim–Christian dialogue; Shaykh Shafiq Jaradi, the rector of Al-Ma'arif Al-Hikmiyya College; Shaykh 'Ali Daher, the head of Hizbullah's cultural unit; MP Hasan Fadlallah; MP 'Ali Fayyad; MP 'Ali Ammar; MP Sayyid Nawwaf al-Musawi; Shaykh Akram Barakat, the head of the Cultural Islamic Al-Ma'arif Association; and Shaykh Muhammad Kawtharani, a political council member responsible for the Iraqi file (interviews, Beirut, August and October 2009 and January and June 2010).
8. Peter Mandaville, *Global Political Islam* (New York: Routledge, 2007), 343–348.
9. Mahdi N. and 'Abdallah S., interviews by the author, Beirut, October 21 and 25, 2004, respectively.
10. *Al-'Ahd* 8 (21 Dhul-Qadah 1404/August 17, 1984): 6.
11. Minorities, such as Christians and Jews, were treated as residents holding limited rights and required to pay a poll tax in lieu of almsgiving (*zakat*).
12. Sayyid Hasan Nasrallah, National Broadcasting Network, July 21, 2002.
13. 'Ali al-Kurani, *Tariqat Hizbullah fi Al-'Amal Al-Islami* [Hizbullah's method of Islamic mobilization] (Tehran: Maktab Al-I'lam Al-Islami, Al-Mu'assa Al-'Alamiyya, 1985); Muhammad Z'aytir, *Nazra 'ala Tarh Al-Jumhuriyya Al-Islamiyya fi Lubnan* [A look at the proposal of the Islamic Republic in Lebanon] (Beirut: Al-Wikala Al-Sharqiyya lil-Tawzi', 1988).
14. Muhammad Z'aytir, *Al-Mashru' Al-Maruni fi Lubnan: Juzuruhu wa Tatawwuratuhu* [The Maronite project in Lebanon: Roots and development] (Beirut: Al-Wikala Al-'Alamiyya lil-Tawzi', 1986).
15. Joseph Alagha, *The Shifts in Hizbullah's Ideology* (Amsterdam: Amsterdam University Press, 2006), 38–42.

16. See Subhi al-Tufayli, interview by Tha'ir 'Abbas, *al-Sharq al-Awsat* 9067 (September 25, 2003).

17. Bayat, *Islam and Democracy*, 12–13.

18. Na'im Qasim, *Hizbullah: Al-Manhaj, Al-Tajriba, Al-Mustaqbal* [Hizbullah: The curriculum, the experience, the future], 7th rev. and updated ed. (Beirut: Dar Al-Mahajja Al-Bayda', 2010), 337–343.

19. Sayyid Hasan Nasrallah, National Broadcasting Network, August 4, 2002.

20. Al-Nabulsi argued that from a political standpoint there was a certain wisdom and interest (*maslaha*) that called upon Hizbullah to participate on the basis of the maxims of Islamic jurisprudence. He added that the political situation lifted any prohibition on Hizbullah's participation since it safeguards law and order in Lebanese society (National News Agency, August 10, 2005; and see Lebanese daily newspapers the next day).

21. Based on interviews I have conducted with high-ranking cadres, including members of the *shura* council.

22. Asef Bayat, "Islamism and Social Movement Theory," *Third World Quarterly* 26, no. 6 (2005): 891–908.

23. Sayyid Hasan Nasrallah, cited in Hasan 'Izzeddine, "How Is Hizbullah Looked Upon and How Does It Introduce Itself?" *Al-Safir*, November 12, 2001.

24. *Al-Intiqad* 1267 (May 30, 2008).

25. Sayyid Hasan Nasrallah, press conference, broadcast live on Al-Manar TV, November 30, 2009, at 1:30 p.m. gmt.

26. Alagha, *Hizbullah's Documents*, 32.

27. Nasrallah, press conference, November 30, 2009.

PART FOUR

Critique from Without

9

Post-Islamist Strands in Pakistan:

ISLAMIST SPIN-OFFS AND THEIR CONTRADICTORY TRAJECTORIES

Humeira Iqtidar

Even as scholarly research is settling into a definition of Islamism that demarcates it quite clearly from the other kinds of fundamentalisms and Islamic revivalisms in different parts of the world, popular media is increasingly expanding the purview of this term to include vastly different kinds of groups. Islamism as that particular strand of Islamic revivalism that focuses on taking over the state, as a movement guided by primarily college- and university-educated leadership and fuelled by the growth in literacy and urbanization in predominantly Muslim societies, and a phenomenon that owes much to U.S. support—military, economic, and political—against left-leaning movements during the 1960s and 1970s, is represented in popular media as involving vast unruly populations governed only by religious passions that defy logical and humane considerations. The paradoxical media construction of visions of small groups of highly dangerous and illogically influential men who are able to mobilize large segments of the population, creating a real challenge to secularism in states like Pakistan, remains at odds with the simultaneously repeated mantra that most people actually do not support the Islamists.

Pakistan emerges in this context as a particularly important testing ground for all kinds of theories about the place of religion in modern life, the scope of redemptive politics through development, and the expanse of the relationship between violence and religion. In the Pakistani context a wide variety of groups have been labeled Islamist. Starting from the quintessentially Islamist Jamaat-e-Islami (JI), newer and often much smaller groups such as Jamaat-ud-Dawa (JD), Tehreek Taliban Pakistan, Tehreek Nifaz Shari'a Mohammadi, Jaish-e-Mohammed, Lashkar-e-Tayyaba (LeT), Lashkar Jhangvi, Hizb ul Tahrir, and others are all being classified as

Islamist. Ulema groups like Jamiyat Ulema Pakistan and Jamiyat Ulema Islam have also been classified as Islamists by some. The wide range in the strategies and purported aims of these groups has not deterred easy and often misleading classification by mainstream media and some academics. More critically, the nuances in the responses of these groups to changes in the local and international context have been disregarded in building a case for continued military operations and air strikes in parts of Pakistan. In this fractured and exasperating context, Asef Bayat's detailed look at changes within Islamism makes available several productive avenues for thinking about the substantive changes in Pakistani Islamism and the political and conceptual implications of these transformations.[1]

In this chapter I look at the various spin-offs from one of the world's most prominent Islamist parties—the Jamaat-e-Islami—to highlight the diverse ways in which Islamism has been reconfigured and reworked beyond the party. One group of spin-offs has become quite expressly depoliticized, while another has become much more militant than the original. These different trajectories allow a rather dramatic window into the contradictions that Islamism carries within it and the conditions of possibilities that it holds forth for radically different kinds of politics. This may go some way toward explaining the continued impact of Islamism, in particular JI, even if it is expressed as disillusionment with JI's version of Islamism, with some of these spin-offs calling it not radical enough and others calling it too radical.

Classificatory Challenges

One way to cleave through the wide range of groups being categorized as Islamist is to emphasize the difference in their strategies as a rough guide. Groups like Jamaat-e-Islami may be classified as electoral Islamists. The JI supports jihad ideologically and also, during the 1980s, supported it quite actively in terms of providing the theological, organizational, and pedagogical context for jihad, but its mobilizations are centered around elections and electoral politics. Its members uphold militancy ideologically but are not militant themselves. The oft-cited acts of JI violence were limited primarily to university campuses and were carried out by the student wing of JI, called the Islami Jamiyat Tulba (IJT). These acts of violence may have afforded the student body some independence within the parent group and also allowed JI to use them as a strategic tool in the 1970s, but they lack the scale and scope of activities carried out by some other groups.

Therefore, despite these tendencies the electoral Islamists are by and large interested in gaining a share in the electoral pie; crumbs have sufficed in the past. As I have emphasized elsewhere, the JI has remained committed to electoral politics not because of easy successes but despite memorable failures.[2]

The Jamaat-e-Islami was founded by Abul A'la Maududi in 1941. Maududi had not been educated in a madrassa, but neither was he a product of the "modern" educational system in colonial India. He had been tutored at home primarily and had later learned some English in addition to the languages of the educated North Indian Muslim: Urdu, Arabic, and Persian. Maududi worked as a journalist and private tutor for many years prior to founding the JI. He accessed historical and philosophical texts in the Islamic tradition but was also familiar with Western history and political theory, and fusing the two he founded a party that was modeled on the Leninist party but was concerned primarily with Islamic revivalism. Before establishing the JI he had established himself as a writer and scholar through his popular writings. His style was distinctive, moving beyond the heavy style of the ulema—the religious scholars—while taking religious obligations and the Muslim identity very seriously. Maududi opposed the idea that modernity and religiosity could not coexist, and his party was committed to the idea of taking over the state to revitalize society. His writings have been translated into several languages and have been inspirational for Islamists around the world. The JI started as a small group of mostly middle-class men, the vast majority of whom were either journalists, teachers, or lower-level civil servants. They saw this as the party for educated Muslims, and unlike the ulema groups, JI did not establish a network of madrassas—religious schools—until quite recently. Instead, the organization relied upon attracting students in professional courses at universities and colleges.

Even though Maududi had opposed the formation of Pakistan, he chose to come to the newly formed country in the hope that a country founded on the basis of Muslim nationalism would afford him fertile ground for growth. In the first three decades after its formation, the party remained quite small, mostly because its appeal was limited and other nationalist and/or left-leaning groups presented it with stiff competition and partly due to the JI's cadre-based, Leninist party model. It took many years of committed service to be allowed to become a member of the party and many more to move up the hierarchy. The late 1960s and early 1970s were a transformative period for the party, as for Pakistan's political landscape generally. The encounter with leftist mobilizations galvanized the party into greater action due to the challenge that the Left presented to the JI at colleges and universities, highlighting its dependence upon the same.[3] In the 1980s JI became closely linked with the Zia regime, which used Islamization as a means to establishing its legitimacy. JI also provided moral, political, and logistical support for the mujahideen in Afghanistan, which meant some organizational alignment with Pakistani intelligence agencies and American interests. These antidemocratic alliances still haunt the JI, and its attempts at reinventing itself in the years after that decade of military rule have been hampered significantly by the memory of JI and IJT activities during that period.

This history has made the easy conflation of Islamism with militancy possible in popular imagination. However, a look at other groups such as LeT, Lashkar Jhangvi, Jaish-e-Mohammed, and Tehreek Taliban Pakistan is useful to establish the difference between those and the JI. These militant groups may claim to support the establishment of an Islamic state, but the contours of that state remain shadowy and undemarcated. The range of activities of such groups is also significantly limited compared with that of the electoral Islamists. The leadership of these militant groups is often not educated in schools, their support base is primarily rural, and their ideology is not clearly spelled out. Often they organize around particular issues rather than developing a deep and clearly defined ideology. For these reasons, the case for including them within the category of Islamists is quite a poor one. A more interesting classificatory challenge is provided by JD and Hizb ul Tahrir: both groups support the takeover of modern political structures for the establishment of a caliphate instead of a modern state and articulate a relatively sophisticated critique of modernity. However, in terms of membership class background and educational levels, the use of modern categories of analysis and organizational practices, and a sustained engagement with wider political structures, at least conceptually, these groups are much closer to the archetypal Islamist parties like Jamaat-e-Islami than militants like the Taliban.

To point out the differences between the various groups being called Islamist is not to render the term *Islamism* obsolete. Rather, it shows the diversity that has become integral to Islamism in Pakistan. The easy association of Islamism with religiosity in Pakistan has been facilitated by the production of a range of scholarly works that hint at a teleological move from the unresolved identity crisis of a precarious state for Muslims of India to a fragile country infested with Islamists.[4] Some new work is beginning to question this assumption of a linear move from Muslim nationalism to Islamism, highlighting the many alternative histories possible and contingent developments that facilitated the rise to prominence of Islamist parties.[5] A quick overview of the Jamaat-e-Islami in Pakistan is instructive in this respect. Its origins toward the end of colonial rule in India were a product of the many tensions brought to bear upon the relationship between state and religion as reified, abstracted entities. I have argued elsewhere that Islamism in North India is closely linked to colonial secularism, which created the possibility and framework of its existence.[6] The relationship is not one of straightforward negation but, rather, one of negotiation and creation. In any case, it is quite clear that the JI is not the product of intelligence agency funding and is, rather, an expression of a social, political, and intellectual turmoil introduced through colonial imposition, fractured and contested as that was.

When Maududi, the founder of JI, chose to move to Pakistan after the partition of India, his decision was motivated by tactical concerns such as the likelihood of establishing an Islamic state in a predominantly Muslim country, but the initial decades yielded little popular support for the JI. That the Islamists were catapulted to a more decisive role in influencing public discourse through U.S. support—monetary and political—is a well-known narrative within the Pakistani context. During the previous Afghan war, against Soviet occupation at the time, the United States provided economic, military, and political support to General Zia and his Islamization campaigns in Pakistan. General Zia had overthrown the popularly elected Zulfiqar Ali Bhutto and had allowed Pakistan to be used as a conduit for arms, funding, and training of the mujahideen who were, at that time, valorized as freedom fighters by the Americans. Within Pakistan, Zia used the Jamaat-e-Islami to articulate a vision of an Islamic state that could do without liberal democracy. Moreover, an intellectual and cultural climate of support for Islamist ideas, particularly regarding women's role in society, public displays of piety, and jihad, was created to provide legitimacy to Zia's regime as the enforcer of these values. The JI was a very useful ally to the general, particularly in the early years of his rule, for combating leftist influences at all these levels. However, what remain overlooked in this context are the changes that the fight against socialism in the 1960s and 1970s had created within Islamism and more particularly, the internal dissent that resulted due to the JI's support for General Zia-ul-Haq's U.S.-supported military dictatorship.[7]

Zia's appropriation of terminology and concepts used by the JI, not without the approval of most JI members, at least in the initial years of his rule, allowed Islamism a decided intervention at the discursive level, the actual manifestation of which in everyday urban life has been rather more haphazard and uneven than claimed by both the Islamists and their opponents. Practices that have a longer lineage than Zia's use of Islamization as a means to establish legitimacy were reframed using an Islamist language but did not originate at that particular historical juncture. The key impact has been the impulse to frame public debates and discussions within the Islamic paradigm even by those who wish to oppose Islamization. Islamism's rise in this context allowed for the public articulation of deeply embedded norms in contestation with a previously powerful discourse of modernization and secularism. So, for instance, certain ideas about the value of piety or about the correct behavior for women were already in circulation and practice within certain segments of the Pakistani population before they were legalized through Zia's Islamization. This is not to say that somehow Islamism is more authentic or popular than its competition but, rather, that it is important to realize that some practices and norms held particularly by the lower middle classes found an easier expression within Islamism.[8] The rise of Islamism to prominence within the Pakistani public sphere is, therefore, not just a product of U.S. or Saudi funding and support, however critical they may have been as catalysts.

The end of the Cold War and more particularly the war in Afghanistan against the Soviet presence there led to a decade of confusion for Islamists in Pakistan. Their previous sources of support no longer available, as American foreign policy began to be increasingly defined by its opposition to Muslim fundamentalism, and their own policies increasingly identified as the target of U.S. foreign policy, the Islamists had to carve a new role for themselves. Well-established electoral Islamist groups such as the JI moved to coalition politics under the leadership of Qazi Hussain Ahmed. The JI alliance with the socially conservative Mian Nawaz Sharif, who was also a protégé of Zia, allowed both a new lease of life beyond Zia.

Disavowing Politics: The Pietist Spin-Offs

Initial recognition of a serious change in Islamism is beginning in academic writings, and some attempts at grappling with the nature and extent of these alterations within Islamism are already under way. The most cogent of these by far is Asef Bayat's nuanced description of the phenomenon that he calls "post-Islamism."[9] His contention is that Islamism has lost much of its initial energy and is in the process of reconciling itself to notions and practices of democracy and pluralism. The debate about the validity of the term *post-Islamism* is linked intrinsically to the idea that Islamism has failed. Roy has proposed that Islamism has indeed failed;[10] Kepel and Ahmad sidestep the question of failure by emphasizing that Islamism has now morphed into post-Islamism, with a decentering of the focus on the state and greater acceptance of plurality within and outside the movement.[11] In responding to the widespread use of the term *post-Islamism*, Bayat points out that he understands the term to represent "both a condition and a project."[12] As a condition, it refers to the draining of energy from the initial sources of the legitimacy of Islamism. As a project, post-Islamism refers to a more explicit negotiation with democracy and liberalism. Bayat's arguments are compelling, and we can see parallels for Pakistani electoral Islamists in the experience of the revamped Muslim Brotherhood in Egypt. At the same time it is important to recognize the difference with the Iranian context because in Pakistan Islamism has not yet exhausted its potential as it has not been directly in power for long enough. Jamaat-e-Islami, one of the key Islamist parties in Pakistan, and indeed an influential one internationally, continues to be closely engaged in the electoral process, in claiming its continued ambition to influence and control the state.

Nevertheless, a subtle shift has occurred within the quintessential Islamists like JI. Elsewhere I have taken a detailed look at the changes within JI due to larger changes in the place of the state in the global political imagination.[13] It seems to me imperative to recognize that Islamism was one of a host of responses generated in the late nineteenth and early twentieth century to the rise of the bureaucratic, modern state. Like the vast majority of those ideologies—communism, socialism, fascism, liberal nationalism—that aimed to take over the government to transform society, Islamism was focused on taking over the state. It was part of a global intellectual and political moment that saw the state as the engine as well as the vehicle of societal transformation. Ongoing changes within Islamism are not divorced from changes in the place of the state in the political imagination. Islamism is often studied in terms that are either too global—an inherent push toward world domination within Islamism and/or Islam—or too local—the specific challenges of nation-states. It is important also to link changes within Islamism with the larger political and intellectual context in which they operate. The fall of the Soviet Union and an associated rise in neoliberalism that underplays the role of the state as a vehicle for societal transformation have had a profound impact on how Islamists organize their activities and manage their mobilizations.[14]

Here I want to think through the trajectories of the spin-offs from JI. A significant number of JI breakaway groups and individuals have had considerable influence in the Pakistani cultural and political sphere in recent years. JI spin-offs include a range of different groups and individuals: from the militant-linked Jamaat-ud-Dawa to Dr. Israr Ahmed's Tanzeem-e-Islami, which was vehemently opposed to JI's involvement in electoral politics; from Dr. Farhat Hashmi's Al-Huda to her sister Nighat Hashmi's Al-Noor, both of which cater to women; from Maulana Kausar Niazi, a minister in the populist government of Mustafa Bhutto, to the opportunistic politics of Hussein Haqqani, Pakistan's twenty-fourth ambassador to the United States; and from some within the current leadership of the pietist group Tablighi Jamaat to a purportedly anti-Islamist modernist, Javed Ahmed Ghamidi.

A significant segment of the spin-offs is opposed to the JI's focus on the state and on political engagement narrowly defined as electoral participation. Israr Ahmed (1932–2010) broke from the JI on the issue of engaging in the electoral process and on Maududi's decision to support the candidacy of Fatima Jinnah against the incumbent president at the time, General Ayub Khan, in 1965. He believed that JI had jumped into electoral politics too soon and without adequate preparation of the cadres. A particularly interesting example is that of Javed Ahmed Ghamidi, because of the manner in which Ghamidi treads a fine line between political engagement and public debate. Ghamidi's association with the JI ended in the 1970s, but his relationship with another JI dissident, Maulana Islahi, deepened after that. During General Musharraf's dictatorial regime (1999–2008), Javed Ahmed Ghamidi was associated "precipitously close" to Musharraf's program of enforcing secularization through Enlightened Moderation.[15] Many saw Ghamidi as opposing the Islamists' emphasis on direct political confrontation and their ideological support for armed struggle or jihad. Yet Aziz has persuasively argued that the internal logic of Ghamidi's methodological imperatives prevented an easy co-option by the state or the larger World Muslim Outreach,[16] a U.S. project of educating Muslims in the "right" kind of Islam, one more amenable to secularizing and historicizing. While Ghamidi does advocate a minimalist reading of Quran and shari'a, and his endeavor may be construed as substantiating human rights and democratic duties without recourse to the language of human rights tainted, for some, by its association with the West,[17] his framing accords more importance to Quranic fidelity than is assumed by the architects of Enlightened Moderation. Notwithstanding his points of tension with the state, it is interesting to note here the state's attempt at confronting Islamism in part at least, through recourse to its own discursive range.

A common feature of the Islamist spin-offs discussed above, and including Al-Huda, which is discussed in more detail below, is that they have disavowed the active engagement with politics that renders Islamism particularly problematic for state authorities and imperial projects today. The thread that connects them still with the Islamists is their reading of Islam and Islamic history, their attempts at eradicating contradictions found in popular practice, and their inclination to a scripturalist approach. Of these, Al-Huda represents a particularly interesting manifestation.

Al-Huda is a women-only group started in 1994 by Dr. Farhat Hashmi, who had been associated with the JI during her student years in college at Sargodha and at Punjab University, Lahore. She came from a family of JI activists, and her father had been a committed activist in the JI in the town of Sargodha. As a student leader of the IJT Hashmi gained some notoriety for her fiery and oppositional stances toward the university's management and other student unions. She met her husband, Idrees Zubair, at the university, and while they were both quite religious, her husband was a self-declared Wahabi, a fact often emphasized to me by members of the JI who had known Hashmi during this phase of her life. His Wahabism was a source of some contention within her family and also within the party, and eventually Hashmi left the party.

After her marriage, Farhat Hashmi and her husband taught at the Islamic University in Islamabad. Then both husband and wife moved to Glasgow, to complete doctorates from the University of Glasgow. Hashmi obtained hers in Islamic studies in 1989, and it is here that she also started organizing small study circles within her home. Upon her return to Pakistan, Hashmi started holding study circles where she delivered lectures that appealed to the cultural expectations of upper- and upper-middle-class women. She could switch between English and Urdu, pick references to everyday life appropriate to the class backgrounds of her audience, and explain her ideas by using examples from popular media both Western and local. There is some speculation about whether her access to the wives of the higher bracket of military officers was facilitated by the religiously minded officers who were now part of the military elite, but there can be little doubt that coming so soon after Zia's Islamization years, she was able to draw upon well-entrenched religiosity within the Pakistani army. Today the Al-Huda enterprise has developed into an international empire, with Al-Huda Pakistan (www.alhudapk.com), Al-Huda Canada (www.alhudainstitute.ca), and Al-Huda UK (www.alhuda.org.uk) being the most active chapters.[18] In addition to diploma courses and postdiploma courses, the Al-Huda enterprise generates CDs, booklets, Web casts, and other media material to spread its message. Courses include not just the diploma and certificate courses that last for a year but also "crash courses" during Ramadan.

The decade following the turn of the twenty-first century saw a dramatic rise in the influence of Al-Huda among upper-class, educated, and sometimes, professional women. The turn toward veiling or at least keeping the head covered using a *dupatta*, a loose piece of thin material previously used for ornamental reasons only by the women of this class, made the Al-Huda presence noticeable. Husbands complained publicly about the hold that Al-Huda had over "their" women. Some of these women refused to socialize at mixed-sex gatherings as they had previously and/or at gatherings where alcohol was on offer. All of this was sometimes a source of embarrassment for the husbands, and stories about marriages wrecked by the Al-Huda phenomenon circulated widely in this period. Some speculated that the women joining Al-Huda were elite women looking to fill the vacuum of meaninglessness in their lives. As one observer points out, "They have had their [share of] sleeveless blouses and coffee parties and are now ready for religion."[19] In response, Dr. Farhat Hashmi was quick to emphasize the rights of the husbands and the duties of wives to obey their husbands in public pronouncements at this point and in fact, drew considerable ire from secular liberals for her alleged support for polygamy.[20]

Academic studies of Al-Huda have emphasized pedagogical innovation as one of the reasons for its success.[21] They point not just toward Dr. Hashmi's use of technology, including PowerPoint, during her lectures, coupled with an emphasis on lived experiences, but also to the fact that she is one of the few women preachers who has achieved such a celebrity status. While her husband and daughter also assist in the running of Al-Huda, she quite clearly leads it. Hashmi distinguishes herself from the traditional ulema (scholars) and emphasizes her doctoral research as the basis of her knowledge. At the same time, her personal piety and charisma must go some way toward explaining her appeal as a role model. Mushtaq is right to point out that the Al-Huda phenomenon would have been impossible without the rise in women's literacy and a discursive importance attached to their educational qualifications.[22] Similarly, Ahmed's emphasis on widely shared cultural norms that value piousness among women and celebrate specific modes of comportment and public persona is useful to keep in mind when thinking about the phenomenal success of Al-Huda.[23]

What none of these studies look at in any detail is the emphasis away from active engagement in politics, which is a pronounced feature of Al-Huda's teachings. While Dr. Hashmi may draw attention to social and political problems in contemporary Pakistan, the route to salvation that she highlights is always through an increase in personal piety. The logic is that the sum of enough personal transformations will lead to a societal transformation. Given her family's and her own long-term association with JI and political Islam, Farhat Hashmi is not blind to the challenges facing any new social movement: "The expectations of Pakistanis have not been fulfilled in our 50-odd years of independence.... There is a feeling of betrayal and despair. Even political Islam has not been able to address people's grievances."[24] Her years of involvement with the JI may have taught Hashmi the value of organization, research for publication and dissemination, and most importantly, vanguardism. The JI founder, Maududi, saw it as a vanguard party, modeled on the Leninist party. He expected his party to attract the elite of the professional, educated Muslims of North India, who would then take over the state to transform society. JI was unable to attract the elite, although it did make significant inroads into the recently educated, socially conservative new arrivals in big cities who are today solidifying into a middle class.

Al-Huda also takes seriously this vanguardism, albeit with an apolitical twist. Its teachers and followers together emphasize the importance of women from the "educated classes" and the "elite" in setting examples for those socially and culturally "below them." In response to my question about the prominent absence of lower-middle-class and working-class women in Al-Huda, one of Al-Huda's long-term supporters and a key organizer in Lahore claimed that "Islam taat par bheth kar parhnay ka mazhab nahin hai" [Islam is not a religion to be studied while sitting on a torn mat].[25] She then proceeded to write off the vast majority of Pakistani women, who due to their illiteracy were incapable of appreciating the true nuances of Islam. Recently, however, Al-Huda has made some moves toward tapping the urban, educated, lower-middle-class constituency despite such views. Nevertheless, the main focus of the organization remains urban upper- and upper-middle-class women. Following the rise in immigration to Canada, Australia, and the United States within this class over the last two decades, Al-Huda too has gone global.

The focus on the elite within Al-Huda makes it unlike the other influential pietist movement, the Tablighi Jamaat. Al-Huda has retained JI's focus on educated, professional, and "elite" groups but has discarded the emphasis on political transformation that continues to inform JI today. This does not, however, move the organization close to the traditionalist ulema model, which had also opposed the political focus of JI. The gendered focus is only one reason why Al-Huda is not like the traditional ulema groups. Another important factor is the approach toward religious learning and authority that allows laypersons to develop as preachers. Certainly, Al-Huda has spread as far and as fast as it has because students in one year's course became teachers in their own localities and neighborhoods the next year. This is in stark contrast with the years of relatively structured study that are required to establish authority and legitimacy among the traditionalist ulema. Al-Huda's strategy of empowering lay preachers is, in fact, similar to that used by some evangelical and Pentecostal churches in Latin America.

As a spin-off of JI, Al-Huda's Farhat Hashmi is not unlike other figures such as Israr Ahmed (1932–2010) and Javed Ghamidi (b. 1951), who did not agree with the JI's increasing emphasis on electoral politics. Israr Ahmed had been active with the JI for at least a decade before he left the organization. He believed that the time was not right for JI to enter electoral politics when he broke with the group in 1957. He claimed that joining electoral politics at that point meant that the JI had lost its revolutionary potential and become one of the many jostling for power. In a similar vein, Javed Ghamidi questioned the emphasis on politics and in particular the aspiration to establish an Islamic state. He too worked with the JI for about nine years before leaving in 1977. Ghamidi then worked closely with Amin Islahi, a former JI member and scholar who had challenged Maududi's leadership but lost the political battle within JI.[26] In a style similar to other spin-offs from the JI, Ghamidi too has set up an institute. The Al Mawrid Institute of Islamic Science publishes his ideas and those of his followers in an English magazine titled *Renaissance* and an Urdu version called *Ishraq* and publishes books and pamphlets. Like Israr Ahmed before him, but perhaps more adroitly than Ahmed, Ghamidi has used television to spread his message. His television appearances have earned him a constituency among educated, urban professionals who are not motivated by the idea of a political revolution. Al-Huda falls within this spectrum of JI spin-offs: those who have disavowed direct political involvement, although their reasons may vary, but who have retained many of the organizational and mobilizational strategies of the JI. The use of in-house publications, study circles, think tanks, and media as well as the emphasis on attracting educated professionals and the dependence upon urban structures remain very much a hallmark of these spin-offs. They have a limited or no base within rural areas and among the working classes and are not geared to communicate with that large segment of Pakistan's population that is functionally illiterate.

Responding to the "War on Terror": Militant Spin-Offs

Notwithstanding the success of the pietist spin-offs, a radically different kind of JI spin-off, the militant Islamist group, has also gained importance in the last decade. The increased international attention on Islamic militancy after 9/11 and, in particular, the U.S. invasion of Afghanistan had a transformative effect on Pakistan and the militants among its Islamists. A prime example of that is the Lashkar-e-Tayyaba, the militant wing of Jamaat-ud-Dawa. Despite the role of ISI (the Pakistani intelligence agency), Saudi funding, and CIA interests in JD, it can be seen as a spin-off of the larger machinery of the JI. Like many other prominent Islamic—not just Islamist—leaders and figures of contemporary Pakistan, JD's founder, Hafiz Mohammed Saeed, was also introduced to the particularly Islamist fusing of religion and politics through his early association with the JI's student wing, the IJT. There is a significant overlap in the constituencies of the two groups, and as a socially conservative, religiously inclined new arrival in the big city of Lahore to pursue higher studies, Saeed was typical of the kind of person the JI attracted. After his initial involvement with the JI, Saeed went to Saudi Arabia and there came in closer contact with Ahl-e-Hadith or Wahabi thought. JD was formed toward the end of the previous Afghan war, as an Ahl-e-Hadith group that aimed to provide a steady supply of young men to fight the war in Afghanistan. Soon after its formation, however, the war in Afghanistan ended. ISI was careful in keeping LeT and JD alive but directed their activities outside of Pakistan. LeT focused its militant activities in Kashmir and India.

Unlike the pietists, JD has moved in a more complicated way as a JI spin-off. The increasing international pressure on jihadist groups transmitted through the Musharraf regime in Pakistan meant that the group was forced to disassociate itself, at least on paper, from its militant wing, the Lashkar-e-Tayyaba. At the initial stages of the current war in Afghanistan, U.S. pressure on the Musharraf regime to clamp down on *jihadi* organizations impelled a restructuring of the JD–LeT relationship. The official separation between JD and LeT in 2004 allowed JD to escape another round of Musharraf's attempts at banning militant organizations. While Sipah Sihaba Pakistan, Jeish-e-Mohammed and splinter group Jamaat-ul-Furqan, Harkat-ul-Mohajiroon, Hizbul Tehrir, and Tehreek-e-Jafria (a Shi'i group) were banned, JD remained legal. Although the separation between JD and LeT is largely cosmetic, it has meant that certain decisions by the latter are now out of the direct control of the JD emir, Saeed.

In any case, the JD had to look for an alternative raison d'être and expanded its social and political activities through the early 2000s. Over the last decade JD has expanded its services to include mobile clinics, schools, colleges, and computer centers. In keeping with its Islamist tendencies the JD has focused heavily on education. In 2007, there were roughly two hundred JD schools, mostly in Punjab but a few in Sind as well, with a total student population in the range of thirty-five thousand. The number of people treated by its free clinics is estimated at six thousand patients per year, and JD claims to have administered 800,000 hepatitis vaccinations in 2007.[27] The JD in-house printing press, Dar ul-Andulas, produces pamphlets, booklets, and six magazines, including the monthly *Al-Dawa*, with a reported circulation of 200,000.[28]

Jamaat-ud-Dawa, a more recent construction than the JI and very much a product of the war in Afghanistan, was tied to the Pakistani intelligence service ISI and retained a closer link to ISI concerns. Over the last decade a fundamental shift can be discerned in JD's relationship with its patron, the ISI. For the last four decades, ISI has been a key conduit of U.S. interests in Pakistan. This relationship was particularly intense during the regime of Zia-ul-Haq, when the ISI channeled CIA money, weapons, and training to support the jihad against the Soviets in Afghanistan. This much is well known but worth recounting to provide context for the situation today. It is possible to argue that the favored position accorded to JD, particularly in the last decade, has made it more dependent upon the ISI and, in turn, has made it accord the ISI greater control. However, given the new pressures both domestic and external, and the restructuring within ISI itself, more complex dynamics have been at play, and the JD was forced to expand its relationship with society.

The venture into social services, in particular the establishment of schools, free clinics, and emergency relief services, allowed JD some degree of autonomy but also came at the price of the flexibility of operations by the LeT. Certain kinds of activities, especially sectarian violence within Pakistan, could compromise the legitimacy that the JD derived from its expanded societal involvement. In this context, the focus on Kashmir took on a new salience. Jihad in Kashmir was a legitimate venture in Pakistan and had the added advantage, from the ISI's point of view, of occupying jihadis outside of Pakistan while also keeping the Pakistani army's overt confrontations with India to a minimum. The JD's need to (appear to) distinguish itself from the LeT, and the fact that the latter's activities in Kashmir had reached a level beyond which it was getting hard to expand because of resistance from local Kashmiris (on both sides of the border), meant that the organization faced a dilemma in redefining its mandate. There was an internal tussle within the organization about whether to continue with militancy or to move toward more of a sociopolitical role. A spectacular chance to display their social service capabilities was afforded the organizations when a devastating earthquake hit the Kashmir region in 2005. Thousands of people were left stranded and desperate in the mountainous region. While the Pakistani army waited for NATO-donated Chinook helicopters to arrive before starting rescue operations, JD and LeT activists rushed to the scene and carried injured people on their backs across the difficult terrain to medical help. In many cases, they were the first ones to reach the stranded locals. The JD's humanitarian arm, the Idara Khidmat-e-Khalq, maintained field hospitals in Muzaffarabad and Balakot, operated ambulance services and surgical camps, constructed one thousand shelters, and provided electricity through generators.[29]

In the post-9/11 international context, where militant Islam was increasingly used as the foil against which U.S. policy was defined, JD needed alternative options. The organization's increased social welfare, humanitarian relief, and community resourcing built on its original recruitment activities but soon expanded to draw in many different kinds of people and groups. However, the continued U.S. presence in Afghanistan, almost a decade long now, changed the dynamics once again and gave new impetus to militancy.

The U.S.-led war in Afghanistan and related American intervention in Pakistani politics have exacerbated problems that have plagued the country since its formation. Inequity, in such an already deeply unequal society, has increased significantly in the last decade, providing a catalyst for the

far-reaching militarization of society. To demonstrate a commitment to
the U.S. government, General Musharraf reduced basic state services as
resources were directed to the "War on Terror." At the same time, the massive infusion of U.S. aid provided immense benefits to a select few. For the
marginalized within Pakistan, options range between migration, crime,
organized resistance, and, of course, resignation. All of these options have
been tried in different ways. But increased violence and militancy are
gaining currency, as arms, drugs, and personnel for the Afghan war tran-
sit through the country and as direct U.S. attacks go unchallenged by the
government. The Pakistani army's strikes against civilians in the border
regions of Khyber Pakhtunkhwa and Baluchistan are an added dimension to these trends. The JD's vision of its role changed as the war in
Afghanistan began to spill over into Pakistan by the mid-2000s. The rise
of militancy in Khyber Pakhtunkhwa and Baluchistan cannot be explained
only as the retrenchment of members of the Afghan Taliban among their
tribal networks in Pakistan. The so-called Taliban in Pakistan comprises a
host of groups with different aims and strategies, some of whom reject the
Taliban label. Indeed, the politics of labeling these groups "Taliban" echoes
the discourse of Pentagon policy in Vietnam as the war was expanded in
Laos and Cambodia.[30]

The ongoing war in Afghanistan has given the option of militancy
renewed importance to an organization that only recently and very ten-
tatively had begun to think about its role beyond violence. While JD
social activities have continued, their growth has been curtailed due to
the renewed impetus for militant engagement within and outside of
Pakistan. Fighters from JD and LeT are suspected of training militants in
the Pashtun belt, an area where their reach was limited until very recently.
Further, it is alleged that LeT has become a "militancy consultant" available for hire to train others and to carry out operations beyond South Asia.
Indeed, there is some talk of LeT entering the fold of that vast and nebu-
lous network that is labeled al-Qaeda.[31]

The fate of LeT is also quite interesting because the transformation
of LeT from a local militant organization into an international terrorism
consultant tells us as much about the globalizing impulse in Islamism as
about the increasing impetus toward the privatization of warfare. In that
sense the LeT is very similar to the notorious private security company
Blackwater that the U.S. army has used in Iraq, Afghanistan, and now
Pakistan.[32] Indeed the similarities between the two are quite striking. Like
Blackwater, which acts as an extension of the U.S. army, but one that the

U.S. army can disavow in case of bad publicity or enforcement of Geneva conventions, the LeT operated as an extension of the Pakistani army in Kashmir. Both groups are mercenaries for hire that package their training within a religious, nationalist framework, and both provide a similar range of activities: training of local militias, "ground operations" including planting bombs, surveillance, and protection of other personnel. The key difference between Blackwater and LeT is the latter's continued relationship with a group with some political aspiration, the JD.

It has taken a decade of war, chaos, and senseless loss of life in Afghanistan for "Operation Enduring Freedom" to be acknowledged as a failure in Europe. In the United States, however, even the current low level of support for the war, polled at between 31 and 50 percent in 2012,[33] seems very high to those in the region who have to live with its consequences. Quite apart from the damage done directly to the people of Afghanistan and those U.S. soldiers who actually fight this war, the calculus of consequences must include the remilitarization of groups like JD. It seems increasingly likely that any calculation of the collateral damage of this war in Afghanistan will have to include the fragmentation of and increased militancy in Pakistan.

Conclusion

At the very least we can see that Islamism has facilitated the production of organic intellectuals in small towns and urban populations within the Pakistani context. Bayat may be correct to point out the draining of energies from the Islamist project of controlling the state, but it remains to be seen if the long-term influence of Islamism has exhausted its potential. The JI, under Qazi Hussain Ahmed, the third emir since Maududi, made significant moves to dilute the vanguard nature of the party. Rather than the cadre-based system in which becoming a member, *rukn*, of the JI was a long and arduous process, Ahmed opened up a separate category of party membership that allowed any who broadly sympathized with its electoral platform to become members. Democracy has certainly emerged as a central plank of the party's mobilizations over the last decade, and it has made overtures toward its erstwhile competitors such as the Left parties, small as they are in Pakistan today, to work together. This may be read as a weakening of Islamism's ideological program, but that would miss the diversity of issues that Islamists engage with in present-day Pakistan.

The transformations among and around the Islamists of Pakistan seem thus to be pulling in contradictory directions. On the one hand, the appeal of a broadly depoliticized life has gained much ground, and, on the other, the ongoing war in Afghanistan has forced sharp demarcations within Pakistani society; on the one hand, electoral Islamists are forced into a position of opposition to previous allies such as the Pakistani military, and, on the other, some militant Islamists are still being funded by various international and national agencies; on the one hand, there is official rhetoric against jihad, but, on the other, the continued war in Afghanistan provides too many opportunities and victims to forgo militancy. In the contradictory trajectories of Islamist spin-offs we may glimpse the internal contradiction of Islamism's ideology: its ready association with militancy but its malleability toward depoliticized pietism, its disavowal of elitism but its interest in managing the elite, its attempts at creating a modern Muslim subject but its reluctance to own modernity as its own project.

Notes

1. Asef Bayat, *Making Islam Democratic: Social Movements and the Post-Islamist Turn* (Stanford: Stanford University Press, 2007).
2. For instance, in the historic 1970s elections, JI fielded the highest number of candidates in West Pakistan. This was partly because a decade of martial rule had left all political parties unsure of their actual strength and partly because JI's ability to mobilize protests had led the leadership to assume a wider base of support than it actually had. Its dismal performance came as a shock within the organization and led to significant internal criticism (see Humeira Iqtidar, *Secularising Islamists? Jamaat-e-Islami and Jamaat-ud-Dawa in Pakistan* [Chicago: University of Chicago Press, 2011], 83–85).
3. Humeira Iqtidar, "Jamaat-e-Islami Pakistan: Learning from the Left," in *Crisis and Beyond: A Critical Second Look at Pakistan*, ed. Naveeda Khan (Delhi: Routledge, 2010), 245–273.
4. Farzana Shaikh, *Making Sense of Pakistan* (New York: Columbia University Press, 2009); Iftikhar Malik, *Islam, Nationalism and the West: Issues of Identity in Pakistan* (Oxford: Macmillan, 1999); Khalid Bin Sayeed, *Pakistan: The Formative Years, 1857–1948* (Oxford: Oxford University Press, 1968).
5. See various contributions to Humeira Iqtidar and David Gilmartin, eds., "State Management of Religion in Pakistan," theme issue, *Modern Asian Studies* 45, no. 3 (2011).
6. Humeira Iqtidar, "Colonial Secularism and Islamism in North India: A Relationship of Creativity," in *Religion and the Political Imagination*, ed. Gareth Stedman Jones and Ira Katznelson (Cambridge: Cambridge University Press, 2010).

7. See Iqtidar, "Jamaat-e-Islami Pakistan," for changes in JI as a result of its confrontation with the Left in Pakistan.

8. This remains valid today as well. Based on a survey of men and women in refugee camps displaced by the Pakistan army's offensive against the Tehreek Nifaz Shari'a Mohammadi in Swat, Farzana Bari, in "Gendered Perceptions and Impact of Terrorism in Pakistan" (paper presented at the Shirkat Gah Conference, Lahore, May 22, 2010), shows that many of the stipulations of the rebel group were favored by both men and women in Swat because of their closer alignment with local norms compared with state-supported initiatives.

9. Asef Bayat, "What Is Post-Islamism?" *ISIM Review* 16 (2005): 5; Bayat, *Making Islam Democratic.*

10. Olivier Roy, *The Failure of Political Islam* (Cambridge: Harvard University Press, 1994).

11. Gilles Kepel, *Jihad: The Trail of Political Islam* (London: I. B. Tauris, 2002); Irfan Ahmad, *Islamism and Democracy in India: The Transformation of Jamaat-e-Islami* (Princeton: Princeton University Press, 2009).

12. Bayat, "What Is Post-Islamism?" 5.

13. Humeira Iqtidar, "Secularism beyond the State: The 'State' and the 'Market' in Islamist Imagination," *Modern Asian Studies* 45, no. 3 (2011): 535–564.

14. Ibid.

15. For more details, see Sadaf Aziz, "Making a Sovereign State: Javed Ghamidi and 'Enlightened Moderation,'" *Modern Asian Studies* 45, no. 3 (2011): 597–629.

16. Ibid.

17. M. K. Masud, "Rethinking Sharia: Javed Ahmed Ghamidi on Hudud," *Die Welt des Islams* 47, nos. 3–4 (2007): 356–375.

18. Canada has emerged as an important center for Al-Huda because Dr. Hashmi and her family spend part of the year there. There is also a large Pakistani upper-class diaspora in Canada. The transnational aspect of the Al-Huda phenomenon has attracted academic attention. See, for instance, Khanum Shaikh, "New Expressions of Religiosity: A Transnational Study of Al-Huda International" (Ph.D. diss., Women's Studies, University of California, Los Angeles, 2010); Aneela Babar, "New Social Imaginaries: The Al Huda Phenomenon," *South Asia: Journal of South Asian Studies* 31, no. 2 (2008): 348–368.

19. Sahar Ali, "Pakistan Women Socialites Embrace Islam," *BBC News*, November 2, 2003, http://news.bbc.co.uk/1/hi/world/south_asia/3211131.stm.

20. Faiza Mushtaq, "A Controversial Role Model for Pakistani Women," in "Modern Achievers: Role Models in South Asia," theme issue, *South Asia Multidisciplinary Academic Journal* 4 (2010), http://samaj.revues.org/index3030.html.

21. In terms of numbers Al-Huda membership may not seem striking at first glance. Mushtaq (ibid.) estimates the number of women who have undergone Al-Huda year-long courses since its beginning to be around fifteen thousand. However, their class background and the high visibility of their transformation

particularly with regards to veiling lend the organization greater publicity. Sadaf Ahmed, *Transforming Faith: The Story of Al-Huda and Islamic Revivalism among Urban Pakistani Women* (Syracuse: Syracuse University Press, 2009).

22. Mushtaq, "Controversial Role Model for Pakistani Women."

23. Ahmed, *Transforming Faith.*

24. Quoted in Ali, "Pakistan Women Socialites Embrace Islam."

25. Samina Rafique, Gurmani House, Al-Huda Centre Gulber, interview by the author, Lahore, April 2005.

26. Syed Vali Reza Nasr, *The Vanguard of the Islamic Revolution: Jama'at-i-Islami of Pakistan* (Berkeley: University of California Press, 1994), 31–41.

27. Graham Usher, "Dangerous Liaisons: Pakistan, India and Lashkar-e-Tayyaba," *Middle East Report Online*, December 31, 2008, www.merip.org/mero/mero123108a.html.

28. Humeira Iqtidar, "Collateral Damage from the Afghanistan War: Jamaat ud Dawa and Lashkar-e-Tayyaba Militancy," *Middle East Report* 251 (Summer 2009): 28–30.

29. See Jawad Hussain Qureshi, "Earthquake Jihad: The Role of Jihadis and Islamist Groups after the October 2005 Earthquake," International Crisis Group, July 24, 2006, at www.crisisgroup.org/en/regions/asia/south-asia/pakistan/earthquake-jihad-the-role-of-jihadis-and-islamist-groups-after-the-october-2005-earthquake.aspx (accessed January 15, 2013).

30. See Humeira Iqtidar, "Who Are the 'Taliban' in Swat?" *OpenDemocracy*, April 30, 2009, www.opendemocracy.net/article/email/who-are-the-taliban-in-swat.

31. See Stephen Tankel, "Lashkar-e-Taiba: From 9/11 to Mumbai" (London: International Centre for the Study of Radicalisation and Political Violence, King's College, London, April 19, 2009).

32. Humeira Iqtidar, "Conspiracy Theory as Social Imaginary: The Case of Blackwater in Pakistan" (paper presented at the Post-nationalist Narratives Conference, University of Witwatersrand, Johannesburg, November 2010).

33. "Support in U.S. for Afghan War Falls Sharply, Poll Finds," *New York Times*, March 26, 2012, www.nytimes.com/2012/03/27/world/asia/support-for-afghan-war-falls-in-us-poll-finds.html?_r=0 (accessed January 15, 2013).

10

Saudi Arabia and the Limits of Post-Islamism

Stéphane Lacroix

The last decade has witnessed remarkable evolutions within the "mainstream" Saudi Islamist movement known as the Sahwa (from "al-Sahwa al-Islamiyya," the Islamic Awakening), leading to the increasing prominence of a group of reformers calling for democracy and human rights using the language and references of Islam. The rise of these "Islamo-liberals," along with other concomitant evolutions in Saudi politics, arguably corresponds to what several scholars have described as a "post-Islamist" turn.[1] Yet, while the discourse and early activism of this group have been the object of several studies,[2] the fate of the mobilization it spearheaded has never been properly examined. This is especially interesting since, despite the optimism it first inspired, it may be said in retrospect that the mobilization has failed. How can this be accounted for? And what does it tell us of the limits of post-Islamism?

The Sahwa emerged in Saudi Arabia in the late 1960s as a result of the increasing influence exerted within key Saudi institutions, especially the education system, of thousands of exiles from the Muslim Brotherhood. The Sahwa's ideology represented a blend between the "local" religious culture known as Wahabism and the political ideas of the Muslim Brotherhood. Throughout the 1970s, thanks to the central position its initiators occupied in the Saudi system, the Sahwa expanded its influence and soon acquired a quasi-monopoly on Islamic activism in the Kingdom. At the time, however, the Sahwa did all it could to neutralize its oppositional potential: the Muslim Brotherhood's worldview, according to which modern states were illegitimate and had to be replaced with "Islamic states," was applied to the whole of the Muslim world—except Saudi Arabia. This started to change in the late 1980s, as a result of several developments described elsewhere.[3] In this context, King Fahd's call for Western troops to come to Saudi Arabia to protect the Kingdom from the threat of an Iraqi invasion was the last straw: Sahwis spearheaded a broad movement of protest, which exerted unprecedented pressure on the regime. Fiery sermons were delivered in the country's mosques in front of huge crowds, and petitions asking for radical changes in the sociopolitical system were distributed and presented to the king. By late 1994, however, the movement had been crushed by the authorities. Hundreds of individuals, including the Islamist intellectuals and ulema who had been most heavily involved in the protest, were sent to jail, where most remained for several years.

The repression prompted ideological and strategical splits within the Sahwa: Some Islamists argued that peaceful protest was no longer an option, and they soon started supporting Osama bin Laden's calls for a "global jihad" directed not only at the Saudi regime but also at its American protector. Other Islamists, including most of the ulema who had led the protest in the early 1990s, preferred to return to a politically quiescent position toward the regime and to concentrate their energies on social and religious activism, as practiced by the Sahwa until the late 1980s. Members of a third group remained politically active, but they started calling for democratic change within an Islamic framework while formulating unprecedented criticisms of Wahabism. To achieve their goal, they advocated building alliances with other Saudi political forces. Those "Islamo-liberals" are the subject of this chapter.

The Islamo-liberal Movement

The debates that led to these splits began while the Islamist activists were still in jail. As soon as the first Islamo-liberals were released, they took advantage of the relative intellectual *infitah* (opening) that Crown Prince Abdullah was promoting to bring those debates out to the incipient public sphere. Soon, Islamo-liberal activists became active on the Internet forums (*muntadayat*). Also, some of them started writing articles in the press. Finally, prominent Islamo-liberal figures organized weekly salons (*salunat*) in Burayda, Riyadh, and Jeddah. Among the early sympathizers of Islamo-liberalism who participated in those efforts were Abdallah al-Hamid, a Sahwi professor of literature who had been one of the founders of the Committee for the Defense of Legitimate Rights in 1993; Abd al-Aziz al-Qasim, a Sahwi judge from a family of major Wahabi scholars, who had played an essential, yet mostly unacknowledged, role in the protest movement of the early 1990s; Sulayman al-Dahayyan, a Sahwi intellectual who had, among other things, been one of the organizers of the "intifada of Burayda" (a large demonstration that took place in 1994); and Mansur al-Nuqaydan, who had been close to rejectionist circles in the early 1990s, although he had also in the later stages come to support the Sahwi protest. Around them were others, too numerous to be named.[4]

It would be an exaggeration to claim that those individuals shared a common ideology. Yet their debates led them to agree on a certain number of ideas, which constantly came up in their discussions. They called for a more pluralistic political system in Saudi Arabia, which would resemble Western democracy in many ways. At the same time, they continued to see themselves as Islamists: This system, they argued, should be defined within the framework of Islam, and its mechanisms should be based on Islamic principles. This would only be possible after reforming the local religious culture of Saudi Arabia, that is, Wahabism, which they saw as partly responsible for the country's "political backwardness" and for some of its social problems.

By the turn of the twenty-first century, this group had become a genuine phenomenon in the public sphere, and its ideas had started to attract attention outside the circles of the Sahwa. The first contacts would soon be established with liberal activists such as Muhammad Sa'id Tayyib, a former Nasserite in Djedda; Matruk al-Falih, a former Arab nationalist in Riyadh; and Ali al-Dumayni, a former communist from the Eastern Province, among many others. Prominent Shiite Islamist activists from Qatif, such as Ja'far al-Shayib and Muhammad Mahfuz, also became partners of the Islamo-liberals. They were especially sympathetic to the Islamo-liberals' efforts since they had, themselves, gone through a relatively similar intellectual process in the 1990s when they abandoned the idea of an "Islamic Revolution in the Arabian Peninsula" (as in the name of the movement to which they had belonged in the 1980s)[5] and decided to subscribe to the discourse of democracy and human rights within a "pluralistic" Saudi nation.[6] Hejazi intellectuals with a "regionalist" orientation, such as Abdallah Faraj al-Sharif, a journalist and advocate of Sufism, and Jamil Farsi, a jeweler by profession, joined the loosely knit network that was taking shape. Sunni "regionalists" from the Ahsa' province soon did the same. Among them were Muhanna al-Hubayyil, a local activist who had been socialized within the Saudi Muslim Brotherhood, and Abd al-Hamid al-Mubarak, a local professor of Maliki *fiqh*. In August 2004, in parallel with his reformist activities, al-Hubayyil founded the "Patriotic Islamic Encounter for the Ahsa' Region" (al-Liqa' al-islami al-watani li-iqlim al-ahsa'), which, beyond promoting reform, aimed at "coordinat-ing efforts to restore the cultural and economic rights of the inhabitants of the Ahsa' region" and at "reviving the region's identity."[7]

The first collective action emanating from members of this improbable coalition was the publication in April 2002 of a manifesto entitled "How We Can Coexist" ("'ala Ayy asas nata'ayish"), which was drafted by Abd al-Aziz al-Qasim and Abdallah al-Subayh. It came at a crucial moment for the Kingdom: the attacks of 9/11 eight months before had prompted a crisis of conscience in Saudi Arabia, after the country had been accused by Western media and government officials of being a bastion of intol-erance and extremism. In their statement, the authors reaffirmed their commitment to peaceful coexistence with the West while stressing their attachment to their cultural and religious specificities. The document was signed by 153 individuals, and the list included not only the Islamo-liberals but also some of the major figures of the 1990s Sahwi protest movement, including Salman al-'Awda, Safar al-Hawali, and Nasir al-'Umar. The lat-ter three, however, subsequently withdrew their signatures after being submitted to harsh criticism from many of their followers as well from neo-*jihadi* sheikhs who accused them of having betrayed their cause. They would, in the future, be extremely reluctant to associate themselves with the activities of the Islamo-liberal movement.

On January 30, 2003, the movement took on a new dimension when the Islamo-liberals and their allies issued their first public manifesto addressing the issue of domestic reform, which they entitled "Vision for the Present and Future of the Homeland" ("Ru'ya li-hadir al-watan wa mus-taqbalihi"). In it, the 104 signatories—which included the Islamo-liberals and their above-mentioned partners—advocated the adoption of a consti-tution, the separation of powers, and the creation of an elected parliament (*majlis al-shura*), as well as total freedom of expression, organization, and assembly in order to give birth to a veritable civil society. Also, they called for a fairer repartition of wealth and an end to all discrimination in Saudi society. On December 20, 2003, came another "Islamo-liberal" petition called "National Call to the People and the Rulers Together: Constitutional Reform First" ("Nida' watani ila-l-sha'b wa-l-qiyada ma'an: al-Islah al-dusturi awwalan"), which comprised similar demands, but framed in bolder terms and containing more explicit Islamic references. This time, the 116 signatories called for the transformation of the Saudi political sys-tem into an Islamic constitutional monarchy within three years. In the next couple of months, two new projects started to be discussed: the first was called Sadad (inverted acronym of Da'wat al-islah al-dusturi al-sa'udiyya, "Saudi call for constitutional reform") and involved the creation in all cities of the Kingdom of reformist "secretariats" in charge of spreading the culture of reform to the people, notably by organizing political salons (*diwaniyyat*) everywhere. The second was that of an independent human rights organization.

None of those projects would see the light because, in March 2004, the regime decided to take action. Thirteen of the leaders of the movement were interrogated, and three of them—Abdallah al-Hamid, Matruk al-Falih, and Ali al-Dumayni—remained in jail. Arguably to show a sign of openness after Western officials, including Condoleezza Rice, denounced the arrests, the regime decided to put them on trial and to make the sessions public. Yet al-Hamid and al-Falih were quick to transform the courthouse into a political forum, demonstrating that their imprisonment had not deterred them from their commitment to political activism. They even took advantage of the trial to circulate several documents, including "Vision to Reinforce the Independence of Justice"[8] and "Toward an Islamic Constitution to Implement the Concept of the Just Rule of *Shura* in the Modern Islamic State—The Kingdom of Saudi Arabia as a Case Study."[9] The regime, which had been used to co-opting its opponents with relative ease, understood that it had a problem; the trial continued behind closed doors, and the three defendants were sentenced to seven, six, and nine years in prison, respectively. In a gesture of goodwill, Crown Prince Abdullah ordered their release on the day he was crowned king on August 1, 2005.

As soon as they were free, they resumed their reformist activities, and al-Hamid revived his weekly "civil society" salon. In February 2007, a new petition called "Milestones on the Way to the Constitutional Monarchy" ("Ma'alim fi tariq al-malikiyya al-dusturiyya") and signed by ninety-nine individuals (among a core group of thirty-one founding signatories) reiterated the group's previous demands.[10] Again, the authorities reacted with repression: nine of the movement's supporters, including respected Islamist figures such as Sulayman al-Rashudi, Musa al-Qarni, and Sa'ud Mukhtar al-Hashimi, were arrested. In order to neutralize any criticism from the West, the detainees were accused of "support for terrorism." They had, the government argued, "collected donations in order to enroll young Saudis, provide them with weapons and send them to the neighboring countries."[11] It is indeed possible that, in addition to their reformist activities, these activists had financially supported "jihad" in Iraq, a popular cause among Saudi Islamists.[12] If this was the case, they certainly were far from being alone in doing so in the Kingdom—but the government found the perfect pretext, and no Western official came to the detainees' defense.

Following the arrests of February 2007, more petitions were drafted and sent to the authorities, asking for the detainees' release.[13] Later that year, in September, Abdallah al-Hamid was indicted after being accused of inciting the wives of men detained without trial on charges of terrorism to demonstrate in Burayda. Consequently, he spent six months in custody from March to August 2008.[14] In May 2008, Matruk al-Falih, after having visited al-Hamid in jail, wrote a text denouncing the conditions of his detention. He was subsequently himself detained, and he remained in jail until January 2009.[15] That same month, it was the turn of Khalid al-'Umayr, a young former Islamist turned "Islamo-liberal" who had acquired some prominence in the movement, to be detained, after he tried to organize a demonstration denouncing the actions of Israel in Gaza.

A significant move was the creation in October 2009 by a group of eleven Islamo-liberal activists, including Abdallah al-Hamid, of the Saudi Civil and Political Rights Association (Jam'iyyat al-huquq al-madaniyya wa-l-siyasiyya fi-l-mamlaka al-'arabiyya al-sa'udiyya).[16] The creation of "civil society" institutions had been one of their core demands from the beginning, and they had tried on several occasions to organize themselves, generally prompting angry reactions from the regime. Yet what was surprising here was the silence of the authorities: No arrests followed the announcement, and the association has been able to exist through its Web site,[17] where it has regularly published statements and communiqués. For the regime, it seems, the reformist movement represented by those activists had become so marginal that it could almost be tolerated.

In the wake of the revolutions in Tunisia and Egypt, in early 2011, the Islamo-liberals tried to seize the opportunity to revive their activism. They published several communiqués, including one threatening the regime with revolution if no change took place, and they signed a couple of petitions. Most significantly, a number of individuals connected to the group proclaimed the creation of the Kingdom's first political party, the Islamic Umma Party (Hizb al-Umma al-Islami).[18] This party was among the groups that called for demonstrations in Saudi Arabia on March 11, 2011. Those demonstrations, however, turned out to be a complete failure on the ground, with only one protester—the now famous Khalid al-Juhani—showing up.

It appears therefore that the regime has very largely regained control of the situation. But had it ever lost control? It is true that, at some point in 2003, the Islamo-liberal reformist movement seemed to enjoy significant momentum. And the announcement, in June 2003, of the National Dialogue (al-Hiwar al-watani),[19] as well as that, in October 2003, of the organization of municipal elections, both of which echoed key demands formulated by the activists, indicated that the regime was taking them seriously. In March 2004, however, the reformist movement was crushed. More importantly, the repression provoked very little reaction on the ground,[20] demonstrating that the movement was much weaker than many had expected. The Islamo-liberal reformists had been unable to mobilize Saudi society beyond a core group of, at the most, a few hundred supporters.[21] Since 2005, the most committed activists, led by Abdallah al-Hamid and Matruk al-Falih, seem to have been struggling to remobilize this core group—but have mostly failed to do so.

The following paragraphs will explore the structural weaknesses of the Islamo-liberal reform movement. This is certainly not meant to minimize the effects of the regime's "carrot and stick" policies. In the weeks around the planned demonstrations of March 11, 2011, for instance, the regime distributed about $134 billion in aid packages to different sectors of Saudi society, while the security apparatus was ordered to step up the pressure on potential opponents. There is no doubt that, in the end, those policies are what prevented any significant protest from taking shape. But my contention is that those policies would certainly not have worked so effectively had the movement not been weakened beforehand.

Conflicts and Distrust within the Saudi Political Sphere

The Islamo-liberal reform movement was first made weaker by a series of splits that occurred in 2002 and 2003. The first of those splits opposed some of the former Islamists who had been at the root of the Islamo-liberal initiative. As mentioned previously, all Islamo-liberals agreed on the fact that political reform had to go hand in hand with—and, to some extent, had to be based on—socioreligious reform, that is, a revision of Wahabism and some of its social prescriptions. Soon, however, they disagreed on which of the two should get priority. In particular, a group of activists, which included Mansur al-Nuqaydan, Mishari al-Dhayidi, and Abdallah bin Bijad al-'Utaybi, all of whom had formerly belonged to the rejectionist fringe that existed on the margins of the Sahwa, argued more and more openly that political reform would have no, or negative, effects if it was not preceded by an all-encompassing redefinition of the local religious discourse.[22] They wrote articles in the press in which they criticized Wahabism in an unprecedentedly harsh way, going so far as to accuse it of being responsible for global jihadi terrorism.[23] This was unacceptable to the Islamo-liberals who were indeed dear proponents of religious reform but were certainly not ready to express their views in such provocative ways, which, they knew, would have no effect but to alienate many of the Saudi Islamists whose support they were hoping to gain. From mid-2002 onward, al-Nuqaydan and his companions started drifting away from the Islamo-liberal movement, with which they would end up breaking all relations.

The second split occurred with some of the liberals who had first supported the Islamo-liberal initiative. The term *liberal* is relatively new in the Saudi political lexicon. It started being used in the 1990s to designate the loosely connected group of activists of diverse secular political backgrounds—former Nasserites, Arab nationalists, communists, or even proponents of Western democracy—who opposed the Sahwa's social and political project. In December 1990, some of those activists had even presented to the royal family their own reformist manifesto, which was quickly overshadowed by the Sahwa's own political petitions.[24] In the Saudi political context, the Islamists and the liberals were archnemeses. The Islamo-liberal project of uniting the two groups was therefore extremely daring, given the amount of distrust that had traditionally existed between them. Despite this, the Islamo-liberals were initially relatively successful: the January 2003 petition was signed by most of the major Saudi liberal voices, including former communists Ali al-Dumayni and Najib al-Khunayzi and former Nasserites Muhammad Sa'id Tayyib and 'Abid Khazindar. Some of those liberals even actively contributed to drafting the text.

Such an alliance, however, would not last for long, since the liberals would gradually be split over the question of whether or not to support the Islamo-liberal movement. The bones of contention were several: first, the Islamo-liberals, now led by Abdallah al-Hamid, were willing to make Islam more visible in their political discourse. Indeed, while the demands presented in the January 2003 petition had been framed in relatively general Islamic terms, there was no particular emphasis on the role of Islam, and the document contained no Quranic verse or hadith. For al-Hamid, however, the only way to obtain broader support from the Islamists—and especially from the ulema—and, partly through them, from the people was to put more emphasis on Islam. This would be the case in the December 2003 petition, which contained numerous explicit religious references. This apparent "Islamicization" of the Islamo-liberals' discourse had significant effects on Islamist support for the movement: quite a number of relatively prominent Islamist intellectuals who had not backed the January 2003 move signed the December 2003 document. Among them were Muhsin al-ʿAwaji, Muhammad al-Hudayf, and Abd al-Aziz al-Wuhaybi, who had all been important figures on the Committee for the Defense of Legitimate Rights, the first Islamist organization created in 1993.

At the same time, al-Hamid argued that the demands had to be expressed in plain and uncompromising terms. In the January 2003 petition, the term *constitutional monarchy* had been dropped at the last minute, because of some of the signatories' preference for a softer formulation.[25] It would now—from the December 2003 petition onward—appear prominently in all the movement's demands, becoming, together with its other motto, "Civil society," the rallying cry of the Islamo-liberal reformists, who would from then on sign their manifestos as "the proponents of civil society and constitutional reform" (*duʿat al-mujtamaʿ al-madani wa-l-islah al-dusturi*).

In this context of infighting, the May 2003 bombings carried out by al-Qaeda in the Arabian Peninsula (Tanzim al-qaʿida fi jazirat al-ʿarab) radicalized each group's position: for al-Hamid and his companions, those attacks were above all the consequence of authoritarianism and the absence of political participation in the Kingdom. To designate what had happened, they used the word *ʿunf* (violence) and refused to talk about *irhab* (terrorism), arguing that this would be playing the regime's game. For their liberal critics, however, the perpetrators of those attacks had to be unequivocally denounced and branded as "terrorists." Doing otherwise would simply equal justifying their actions.[26]

Interestingly, many of those liberals who withdrew their support from the Islamo-liberals had a communist background. This was the case, for instance, for Ali al-Dumayni and Najib al-Khunayzi. For them, secularism was nonnegotiable. In contrast, many of those liberals who remained within the Islamo-liberal coalition had an Arab nationalist background. Although they were largely secular, they did consider Islam to be a central part of their identity and were not terribly shocked by the prominence it had acquired in Islamo-liberal discourse. This was also, somehow, the continuation of a historic rivalry that dated back to the late 1970s, when there were in Saudi Arabia two main secular parties, which strongly distrusted each other, as Ali al-Dumayni recalls in his memoirs:[27] the Communist Party (al-Hizb al-shiyu'i) and the Socialist Action Party (Hizb al-'amal al-ishtiraki), which comprised many of the remaining Saudi Nasserites, Ba'thists, and Arab nationalists. Hence, when one former communist interviewee was asked about who those liberals who continued to cooperate with al-Hamid were, he responded with a despising tone: "They are those fools from the Socialist Action Party!"[28]

However, those liberal "dissidents" were not just content with seceding from the Islamo-liberal movement. They also tried to organize their own reformist faction, claiming the legacy of the January 2003 manifesto and accusing the Islamo-liberals of having perverted its veritable meaning. To do so, they started issuing their own petitions. The first, which appeared in September 2003, was called "In Defense of the Homeland" ("Difa'an 'an al-watan") and was signed by 305 individuals, including Ali al-Dumayni, Najib al-Khunayzi, and the writer Turki al-Hamad, who was arguably behind the initiative. While it was intended above all to denounce global jihadi terrorism in the Kingdom, it also implicitly attacked the Islamo-liberals for their willingness to compromise with the Sahwa, described, again in implicit terms, as a movement "incapable by nature of debating with the other,...which contributed to the emergence of a terrorist and *takfiri* ideology from which our country continues to suffer attacks."[29] Around the same time, in June 2003, Turki al-Hamad declared in an interview: "Those Islamists who pretend to be liberals are nothing but little Khomeinis; if they get to power, they'll build a religious state."[30] In February 2004, another petition was drafted and made public by the liberal dissidents. It was called "Together on the Road to Reform" ("Ma'an fi tariq al-islah"). This time, the Islamist orientation taken by the Islamo-liberals was denounced along with their intransigence toward the regime, especially then– crown prince Abdullah, whom the signatories assured of "their understanding and esteem for his desire to implement reform" and to whom they offered "their support and assistance in this project."[31] In an obvious bidding game with the Islamo-liberals, al-Hamad and al-Dumayni managed to gather 880 signatures. Muhsin al-'Awaji, a supporter of the Islamo-liberal movement, would, however, be quick to point out that most of those were simply regular Saudis, while the Islamo-liberals had from the outset striven to obtain the support of public figures.[32] This would prompt, in return, accusations against the Islamo-liberals for being "elitists."[33]

Despite these splits, it is notable that among the three individuals who remained in jail after March 2004, two had a liberal background: Matruk al-Falih, a former Arab nationalist who had remained a committed Islamo-liberal and was very close to Abdallah al-Hamid; and Ali al-Dumayni, a leading figure among the liberal "dissidents" who opposed the Islamo-liberals after mid-2003. By arresting al-Dumayni as well, it seems therefore that the regime was willing to show that it would not tolerate any activism, even that expressed in softer terms. After 2005 and the release of the reformers, very few liberals—except for Matruk al-Falih and a few others—would remain part of the Islamo-liberal coalition.

This divorce with a large part of the liberal establishment had important consequences for the Islamo-liberal movement. Indeed, in Saudi Arabia, liberals have traditionally been very powerful in the media. Some of those liberal journalists had first used their positions to support, more or less explicitly, the Islamo-liberal initiative. They would now do all they could to undermine it.

Rivalries within the Royal Family

While the tensions and rivalries previously described did indeed correspond to well-defined ideological cleavages, they were also fuelled and, sometimes, instrumentalized by factions within the royal family. Since 1995, when King Fahd suffered a stroke and the state became headless, the royal family had been split between two factions that competed for resources and influence. On the one side was Crown Prince Abdullah, who had de facto inherited most of Fahd's prerogatives, allied with a plethora of other relatively minor princes, including his half brothers Mish'al and Mit'ab, as well as the sons of the late King Faysal, Turki, Khalid, and Sa'ud. On the other side were the so-called Sudayris (i.e., the sons of Hussa al-Sudayri), especially Nayif, Salman, and Sultan,[34] who had occupied some of the state's key ministries for decades and who, despite the fact that they could not count on the support of their full brother Fahd anymore, still retained a considerable share of political power. While Abdullah started as an outsider, he gradually consolidated his authority, to the extent that, by 1999–2000, one can deem that a perfect equilibrium of forces existed between the two competing factions. This is the moment when, in an attempt to make a difference and impose its supremacy, each of them started looking for allies in society, in what a Saudi interviewee once described as a veritable "electoral campaign."[35]

In this context, Crown Prince Abdullah and his allies began, from 1999 onward, to provide support to all groups and individuals calling for social and political liberalization. *Al-Watan*, which had been founded in 1998 by Prince Khalid al-Faysal, even became one of the principal forums in which liberals and Islamo-liberals expressed their ideas. After 9/11, Abdullah's involvement became more direct: a series of meetings between him and groups of liberal and Islamo-liberal activists was held. According to certain sources, the drafting and publication of the January 2003 petition were even implicitly encouraged by Abdullah, some of whose close advisers had been in contact with the petitioners. This is also what the timing of the petition suggests: two weeks before, on January 15, Abdullah had announced the launching of a "project to reform the state of the Arab world," which he said he would officially present at the forthcoming Arab summit in Bahrain in March and which aimed at "domestic reform and the development of popular participation in the Arab states."[36] The January 2003 petition therefore seemed to echo Abdullah's own plans. A few days after the manifesto was published, Abdullah received a delegation of forty of its signatories, to whom he declared: "Your vision is my project."[37]

In contrast, the Sudayris were from the outset opposed to the Islamo-liberals. Prince Salman, for instance, encouraged the secession of those Islamo-liberals who gave priority to socioreligious reform over political reform by offering them attractive positions in the media he controlled, especially *al-Sharq al-Awsat*, where Mishari al-Dhayidi would become a senior journalist, and al-'Arabiyya TV, where Abdallah bin Bijad al-'Utaybi would become a senior consultant. Prince Nayif also expressed his annoyance at the Islamo-liberals' increasing visibility and at the support they received from his brother Abdullah. To counterbalance this, he reinforced his relationship with the Wahabi religious establishment as well as with the former religious leaders of the Sahwa, especially Salman al-'Awda, Safar al-Hawali, and Nasir al-'Umar, with whom he had enjoyed a relatively trusting relationship since he had taken the credit for releasing them in June 1999.

The radicalization of the Islamo-liberals' demands put Abdullah in an increasingly awkward position. The crown prince seemed indeed ready to promote reform, but he was disturbed by the growing boldness of his allies. Above all, he believed that, now that "civil society" had expressed "its" views through the January 2003 petition, there was no need for more activism and it was up to the government to implement reform according to its own agenda. This explains why Abdullah's camp now supported the attempts of the liberal critics of Islamo-liberalism to "hijack" (as their foes would say) the reformist movement by publishing the two petitions "In Defense of the Homeland" and "Together on the Road to Reform" in 2004. This can especially be seen through the fact that one of the main promoters of these two petitions was Turki al-Hamad, known for being close to the crown prince. The May 2003 bombings also contributed to changing the situation. First, the Islamo-liberals' stance that the government was responsible for jihadi "violence" because it had failed to reform itself properly was extremely controversial in official circles. Second, the events enhanced the position of Prince Nayif, the minister of the interior, who was credited with the first successes in the fight against al-Qaeda in the Arabia Peninsula from mid-2003 onward. At the end of the year, he had become the government's strongman.

Abdullah's change of position and Nayif's rise to power both explain why the official reaction to the December 2003 petition was very different from the one that had followed the January 2003 petition. This time, Abdullah remained silent. Nayif, in contrast, summoned the first twenty signatories of the text and called them "terrorists" and "secularists" before threatening to send them to jail if they persisted in their activism. This did not deter the reformists from pursuing their activities. A few days after the meeting with Nayif, an anonymous text circulated in reformist circles and on the Internet, which contained a detailed account of the meeting and proclaimed that "we have reached a dead end with the rulers."[38] The activists continued to hold meetings, and on March 16, 2004, Nayif ordered the arrest of thirteen of the movement's leading figures, as mentioned previously. Again, Abdullah would do nothing to help his former allies.

On August 1, 2005, the day Abdullah officially became king, he decided to pardon the three activists.[39] Since then, they have striven to re-create the rift between Abdullah and Nayif that had contributed to the momentum they had gained before mid-2003. All their petitions, starting with "Milestones on the Way to the Constitutional Monarchy," were now addressed exclusively to King Abdullah, whom they praised for his reformist intentions while reminding him of his previous commitments. In contrast, Nayif became the target of many of their attacks. In April 2007, Abdallah al-Hamid, his brothers 'Isa and Abd al-Rahman, and Khalid al-'Umayr went so far as to call for the Ministry of the Interior to be put on trial for violating human rights. Later, Matruk al-Falih wrote a statement accusing the Ministry of the Interior of trying to assassinate him.[40] And in May 2008, Khalid al-'Umayr, again, wrote that the "tyranny

of the Ministry of the Interior is the country's biggest enemy."[41] More
recently, several activists have managed to raise a case against the Ministry
of the Interior at the Board of Grievances for violation of procedures in
its arrest in February 2007 and imprisonment without trial of Sulayman
al-Rashudi.[42]

Despite those efforts, never has King Abdullah sided with the reformists.
It is not so much that the royal family has re-created its unity—there are
still conflicts, although they are less visible than before 2005—but it now
seems that the Islamo-liberal movement is so weak and uncontrollable
that Abdullah's camp does not see what it could gain by supporting it.

Intellectuals versus Ulema

The essence of the Islamo-liberal project had been to bring together on
a common reformist platform individuals and groups belonging to all
spheres of Saudi society. Beyond striving to unify the political field by gaining support from both Islamists and liberals, the reformers also at first
tried to bridge the gap that exists between the ulema and the intellectuals,
be they of an Islamist bend or not. In fact, most of the early Islamo-liberals
were Islamist intellectuals. Abdallah al-Hamid, for instance, was a professor of literature at Imam University. The only exception was Abd al-Aziz
al-Qasim, who was trained as a judge and belongs to family that has produced important ulema. Yet his relatively young age and the fact that he
has never really performed the core functions of the ulema (i.e., sermons,
fatwas, etc.), preferring to concentrate on his work as a lawyer, have made
him a very atypical 'alim.

Getting the ulema on board was especially important because, in a traditional Islamic society like Saudi Arabia, they are, in theory, the only widely
accepted source of legitimacy. Without their support, no social movement
can hope to succeed. However, this was not an easy challenge: The ulema
tend to constitute a separate caste in Saudi society, with its own specific
signs of distinction, and they give themselves unmatched social importance by claiming to be the "heirs of the Prophet" (wurathat al-anbiya').
For this reason, they tend to look down on their main counterparts in
the cultural field, the intellectuals, whose primary field of specialization
is not religion. It is therefore, in principle, quite unlikely that they would
collaborate with them on an equal footing in any social or political project.
An exception is the post–Gulf War "Sahwa insurrection," which associated
Islamist intellectuals and Islamist ulema. Following French sociologist

Michel Dobry, one may argue that this was made possible by the political crisis the Kingdom was going through. In such circumstances, Dobry argues, the barriers that divide society tend to collapse, and individuals of different social backgrounds and located in distinct "sectors" may start working together.[43] This is what happened in May 1968 when workers, students, and intellectuals demonstrated hand in hand in the streets of Paris. The post–Gulf War political crisis came to an end in the mid-1990s, however, and there has been no real new political crisis ever since. In these circumstances, it has been extremely difficult for the Islamo-liberals to mobilize in the religious field.

This is not to say that the Islamo-liberals did not try to mobilize the ulema. In April 2002, they were even initially apparently successful when al-Qasim and others managed to convince tens of ulema connected to the Sahwa, including the three main figures of the early 1990s protest, Salman al-'Awda, Safar al-Hawali, and Nasir al-'Umar, to sign the "How We Can Coexist" manifesto. Arguably, the three sheikhs signed because they saw the manifesto as a timely opportunity to show concrete signs that they had become "moderates," as their new motto, "Wasatiyya" ("Moderation" or "Centrism"), proclaimed. A couple of weeks later, however, the three withdrew their support from the manifesto: in the meantime, they had faced a veritable rebellion from their base and had suffered constant verbal attacks by the neo-jihadi ulema. Interestingly, one of the reproaches was precisely their collaboration with intellectuals, and because of this, some of the neo-jihadis now referred to the three sheikhs as "intellectuals" in order to discredit them.[44] The withdrawal of the three sheikhs was a shock for the Islamo-liberals involved in the project. As one of them put it, they understood that "the ulema were not reliable and [that] we shouldn't count on their support in the future."[45] The prediction was right: all subsequent Islamo-liberal petitions would receive very little backing from the ulema. A few isolated sheikhs, including Sulayman al-Rashudi, a lawyer, and Musa al-Qarni, Abdallah al-Zayid, and Hamza Hafiz, all professors at the Islamic University in Medina, signed the December 2003 and/or February 2007 petitions, but they carried very little weight, especially in comparison with such figures as al-'Awda and al-'Umar. It is worth noting that the regime, aware of the peril that even these relatively minor ulema figures represented, targeted them in priority when it decided to launch a new wave of repression against the movement in February 2007: both al-Rashudi and al-Qarni were among the detainees.

Understanding this predicament from the outset, the Islamo-liberals—in particular Abdallah al-Hamid—decided to assume that their movement would be one of intellectuals and strove to turn this limitation into an advantage. First, they tried to make the fact of being an "intellectual" (a *muthaqqaf*) a principle for mobilization in itself. For that purpose, the Islamo-liberals had to redefine the nature and raison d'être of the intellectual, through what amounted to a veritable symbolic hijacking of the term. In their rhetoric, they made pains to present the intellectual as possessing a fundamental political dimension. He ought to be deeply concerned with the affairs of the country while maintaining complete independence from the regime.[46] It was therefore not surprising that, in November 2003, the Islamo-liberals were among the first signatories of a manifesto of support for the Egyptian writer Sun' Allah Ibrahim, who, in the name of the "independence of the intellectual" and "his refusal to be used to enhance the prestige of the ruling powers," had just refused to accept the "Arab novel prize" presented by President Mubarak of Egypt.[47] By taking such a stand, Ibrahim had embodied the model of the intellectual the Islamo-liberals hoped to promote in Saudi Arabia.

But the "true" Islamo-liberal intellectual was meant to be more than a "regular" intellectual, for he also possessed religious competence. As al-Hamid proclaimed, only he is able to go beyond the existing dichotomy between the religious sheikh "who knows nothing of the things of the world" and the secular intellectual "who knows those things but does not know how to draw from religion human rights or the idea of civil society." To do so, he has to combine *ijtihad* (religious interpretation) and what al-Hamid calls civil jihad (*jihad madani*).[48] As a representative of this model, al-Hamid allowed himself in his writings to offer new interpretations of Islam, which served as religious justifications for the Islamo-liberal project. Such a move would not be surprising coming from an Egyptian or Syrian Islamist intellectual. However, in Saudi Arabia, where the ulema had preserved their historic monopoly of the interpretation of the Islamic corpus, what al-Hamid and, through him, the Islamo-liberals as a whole were doing was practically unprecedented.[49] The new Islamo-liberal intellectual was thus presented as a "total intellectual" (almost in the manner of Jean-Paul Sartre), endowed with every competence and located above the divisions splitting the social arena. This supposedly allowed him to fulfill a socially and culturally legitimating function, to a large extent supplanting the religious sheikh.

Despite the fact that this was a very seductive theoretical construction, it largely remained an abstraction. While a nonnegligible, and indeed very diverse, segment of the elite was attracted by al-Hamid's arguments, those arguments carried little weight with ordinary Saudis. What al-Hamid was attempting was, in the end, a veritable transformation of the existing political culture—something much too ambitious for a group that remained socially marginal and with so few resources. Consequently, for the bulk of Saudi society, the legitimacy of the Islamo-liberals, who had been rejected by the ulema, remained subject to doubt. And no one, beyond their core supporters, seemed ready to mobilize in their favor.

Conclusion

Despite the initial momentum they gained, the Islamo-liberals have thus largely failed to establish any strong presence in Saudi society. Today, they remain an elite group with no more than tens of active members—as far as can be from a mass movement. Some expected the "Arab Spring" of early 2011 to be a golden opportunity for them to regain strength, but they have failed to seize it. It is undeniable that repression played a major role in this situation. But my contention is that, in March 2004, the movement already showed several structural weaknesses, which facilitated its repression and explain why there was so little reaction to the arrests beyond the core group of the movement's supporters.

The Saudi case points to some of the limits of post-Islamism. First, post-Islamist movements, which aim at transcending dominant political cleavages, suffer from the extremely strong distrust that exists between Islamist and non-Islamist actors. In historically very polarized political fields like Saudi Arabia's, bringing the two groups together can represent a real headache. Second, post-Islamist actors have problems establishing their legitimacy in the eyes of the societies they address. One key weakness in the Saudi case has been the difficulty of gaining the support of ulema, because the conservative nature of the latter makes them unlikely to support a "post-Islamist" project and because of the ulema's almost "corporatist" hostility to the intellectuals at the root of the post-Islamist initiative. To overcome this difficulty, Saudi post-Islamist intellectuals have had to try and promote an "alternative" form of legitimacy for themselves—but making this effective would have meant transforming the local political culture and its dominant legitimacy repertoires. In an authoritarian context where no real societal debate can take place because the public sphere is heavily constrained, this is an extremely difficult operation. In such a context, what appears most likely to give "post-Islamists" an impulse is thus their instrumentalization by some part of the ruling elite, as happened when Abdullah offered his support in early 2003—an irony for activists willing to challenge the existing political order.

Things, however, may be starting to change with the rise of a new generation of activists who have been socialized in a context much different from that of their elders. Being the children of globalization, they are Internet-savvy and make extensive use of social networks such as Facebook and Twitter. There, even more than on the "forums," they can debate freely and organize, not just among themselves but also with similar-minded youth from the rest of the world. Their political culture evolves quickly, borrowing from schemes that used to be totally foreign to Saudi Arabia. They blend Saudi religious conservatism with Western pro-democracy ideals, but there is a key difference between them and the Islamo-liberals: while for the latter, the blend was based on ideological and strategic considerations, for the young activists, this is a spontaneous operation that does not require the lengthy justifications provided by the Islamo-liberals. They are, in a way, "instinctive" post-Islamists. In Saudi Arabia as opposed to other countries in the region, they still remain a small—although ever-growing—group. And yet, if there is a post-Islamist future for Saudi Arabia, it is in many ways more likely to come from them than from their intellectual elders.

Notes

1. On the "post-Islamist turn," see Asef Bayat, *Making Islam Democratic: Social Movements and the Post-Islamist Turn* (Stanford: Stanford University Press, 2007). On post-Islamism, see also Asef Bayat, "What Is Post-Islamism?" *ISIM Newsletter* 16 (Autumn 2005): 5; Olivier Roy, "Pourquoi le 'post-islamisme'?" *Revue du Mondes musulmans et de la Méditerrannée* 85/86 (1999): 9–10; Gilles Kepel, "Islamism Reconsidered," *Harvard International Review* 22, no. 2 (2000): 22–28.
2. For instance, Stéphane Lacroix, "Between Islamists and Liberals: Saudi Arabia's New Islamo-liberal Reformists," *Middle East Journal* 58, no. 3 (Summer 2004): 345–365; R. Hrair Dekemjian, "The Liberal Impulse in Saudi Arabia," *Middle East Journal* 57, no. 3 (Summer 2003): 400–413.
3. See Stéphane Lacroix, *Awakening Islam: The Politics of Religious Dissent in Saudi Arabia* (Cambridge: Harvard University Press, 2011), chap. 2.
4. See ibid., chap. 7.
5. The "Organization for the Islamic Revolution in the Arabian Peninsula" (Munazzamat al-thawra al-islamiyya fi-l-jazira al-'arabiyya).
6. See Lacroix, "Between Islamists and Liberals."

7. "Nass al-bayan al-ta'sisi li-l-liqa' al-islami al-watani li-iqlim al-Ahsa'" [Text of the founding manifesto of the Islamic patriotic encounter for the Ahsa' region], at www.rasid.com/artc.php?id=3079. As a result of this move, al-Hubayyil was arrested on October 6, 2004. He spent five months in jail (see "I'tiqal al-shaykh Muhanna al-Hubayyil" [Arrest of Sheikh Muhanna al-Hubayyil], at www.rasid. com/artc.php?id=3146); Muhanna al-Hubayyil, interview by the author.

8. "Ru'ya li-ta'ziz istiqlal al-qada'," document in the author's possession.

9. "Nahwa dustur islami li-tatbiq mafhum al-hukm al-shuri al-'adil fi-l-dawla al-islamiyya al-haditha—al-Mamlaka al-'arabiyya al-sa'udiyya namudhajan," document in the author's possession.

10. "Ma'alim fi tariq al-malikiyya al-dusturiyya," document in the author's possession.

11. Communiqué of the Ministry of Interior on the day of the arrests, document in the author's possession.

12. However, it is much more doubtful that they would have encouraged young Saudis to go fight, as most Saudi Islamist leaders have argued against this.

13. See, for instance, "Munashada li-l-ifraj 'an rumuz al-islah al-mu'taqalin" [Call to release the imprisoned reformist figures], at http://sada.pagesperso-orange.fr/ alonyWEB2007/advertises/saudi4.htm.

14. "Al-sulutat al-sa'udiyya tufrij 'an 'Abdallah al-Hamid ba'd tawqif amtadd 6 ashur" [Saudi authorities release Abdallah al-Hamid after six months of detention], at www.saudiyoon.com/news-action-show-id-1957.htm.

15. "Al-ifraj 'an al-duktur Matruk al-Falih," at www.achr.nu/art546.htm.

16. "Al-i'lan al-ta'sisi" [Founding statement], at www.acpra-rights.org/news. php?action=view&id=1.

17. See www.acpra-rights.org.

18. See www.islamicommaparty.com. Most of the party's members were subsequently arrested, political parties being banned in Saudi Arabia.

19. Lacroix, "Between Islamists and Liberals."

20. There were, for instance, surprisingly few reactions on the Internet forums most commonly used by Saudis, including al-Sahat and Dar al-Nadwa.

21. Among the few responses were a petition by 105 of the Islamo-liberals and their supporters asking for the detainees' release ("Bayan al-tadamun ma' al-qiyadat al-islahiyya al-mu'taqala" [Statement in support of the detained reformist leaders], at www.metransparent.com/texts/bayan_tadamun_saudi. htm)—and twelve of the signatories later withdrew their support ("12 muth-aqqafan yu'linun bara'tahum min 'bayan al-tadamun'" [Twelve intellectuals withdraw their support from 'the statement of support'"], March 22, 2004, at www.elaph.com); a petition by ninety-five inhabitants of the Jawf region from which Matruk al-Falih originates ("Ahali al-Jawf yad'amun al-qiyadi al-Falih" [Ninety-five Jawf inhabitants support the leader al-Falih], at http://arabianews. org/section.cfm?sid=4&iid=1); and a meeting between thirteen Islamo-liberal

figures, including Abd al-Aziz al-Qasim and Ja'far al-Shayib, and Prince Nayif, without any significant result ("Al-amir Nayif yushaddid 'ala-l-hiwar wa yuhad-hdhir min istighlal khariji li-bayanat al-islahiyyin" [Prince Nayif insists on dia-logue and warns of foreign instrumentalization of the reformists' statements], *Al-Hayat*, March 24, 2004).

22. On this distinction, see Stéphane Lacroix and Thomas Hegghammer, "Saudi Arabia Backgrounder: Who Are the Islamists?" *ICG Middle East Report*, September 2004.

23. See, for instance, Mansur al-Nuqaydan, "Al-fikr al-jihadi al-takfiri...wafid am asil darib bi-judhurihi" [Jihadi *takfiri* thought...coming from abroad or home-grown?], *Al-Riyad*, May 11, 2003; 'Abdallah bin Bijad al-'Utaybi, "Al-tatarruf sina'a mahalliyya am mustawrada?" [Is extremism a domestic or an imported product?], *Al-Riyad*, June 24, 2003.

24. The text of the petition is found in *Al-jazira al-'arabiyya* 1 (January 1991).

25. "Mahdar al-tahqiq ma' al-duktur 'Abdallah al-Hamid" [Statements of Abdallah al-Hamid during his interrogation], in *Rabi' al-sa'udiyya wa mukhrajat al-qam'* (Beirut: Dar al-kunuz al-adabiyya, 2004), 298.

26. For examples of liberal criticism toward the December 2003 petition, see Jasir al-Jasir, *Mudhakkirat al-malakiyya al-dusturiyya tusib al-islah fi maqtal wa tu'id al-raya ila-l-islamiyyin* [The memorandum of constitutional monarchy kills reform and gives the lead back to the Islamists], December 22, 2003, at www.elaph.com; 'Ali al-'Umaym, "Shakliyyat libaraliyya wa madmun usuli" [Liberal form and fundamentalist content], *Al-Sharq al-Awsat*, January 7, 2004.

27. 'Ali al-Dumayni, *Zaman li-l-sijn...Azmina li-l-hurriyya—al-Juz' al-awwal* [A time for prison...a time for freedom—First part] (Beirut: Dar al-kunuz al-adabiyya, 2005), 108–109.

28. Former Saudi communist, interview by the author.

29. "Difa'an 'an al-watan," at http://bb.tuwaa.com/printthread.php?s=6138fc389b9 19ef2f84497f3e85f452f&threadid=25104&perpage=41.

30. Turki al-Hamad, interview by the author.

31. "Ma'an 'ala tariq al-islah," at www.arabrenewal.com/index. php?rd=AI&AIo=3307.

32. "Al-'Awaji: Khitab ma'an fi tariq al-islah intihazi" [al-'Awaji: "Together on the road to reform"—an opportunistic statement], February 25, 2004, at www.elaph.com.

33. See, for instance, Ahmad al-'Uways, "Al-Faqih wa-l-'Awaji...madha yuridan?" [Al-Faqih and al-'Awaji...what do they want?], February 28, 2004, at www.elaph.com.

34. Although, as Madawi al-Rasheed has rightly shown, it would be an exaggeration to say that the three constituted a coherent bloc, they did share certain goals and interests that objectively put them in the same camp, especially against the "out-sider" Abdullah. See Madawi al-Rasheed, "Circles of Power in Saudi Arabia,"

in *Saudi Arabia in the Balance*, ed. Paul Aarts and Gerd Nonneman (London: Hurst/Colombia, 2005), 185–213.

35. Anonymous Saudi intellectual, interview by the author.

36. "'*Al-sharq al-awsat*' tahsul 'ala nass mashru' sa'udi li-l-qimma al-'arabiyya hawla islah al-wad' al-'arabi" [*Al-Sharq al-Awsat* obtains the text of the Saudi project to reform the state of the Arab world presented to the Arab summit], *Al-Sharq al-Awsat*, January 24, 2003.

37. Matruk al-Falih, interview by the author.

38. "Bayan ila-l-sha'b al-sa'udi al-karim hawla ma'al al-da'wat al-islahiyya wa-l-mawqif al-rasmi minha" [Statement to the noble Saudi people regarding the results of the calls for reform and the official stance toward them], at www.cdhrap.net/text/tt-d/bayanat%20Mootafrqa/06/01.htm.

39. This should not necessarily be seen as a sign of support by Abdullah. It is common practice in Saudi Arabia for a new king to pardon prisoners. King Khalid had done the same in 1975 with many of the leftists and Arab nationalists arrested under Faysal.

40. "Matruk al-Falih—Wizarat al-dakhiliyya wa ajhizatuha al-amniyya tuhaddid hayati" [Matruk al-Falih—The Ministry of the Interior and its security apparatuses are threatening my life], at www.gulfissues.net.

41. "Bayan min al-Ustadh Khalid al-'Umayr" [Statement by Khalid al-'Umayr], at www.facebook.com/topic.php?uid=31172573408&topic=4484.

42. Accounts of the debates are available on the Saudi Civil and Political Rights Association's Web site: www.acpra-rights.org.

43. On applying Michel Dobry to the Saudi case, see Lacroix, *Awakening Islam*, chap. 1.

44. Nasir al-Fahad, "Al-tankil bima fi bayan al-muthaqqafin min al-abatil" [Condemning the errors found in the intellectuals' statement], at www.tawhed.ws.

45. Anonymous Saudi Islamo-liberal, interview by the author.

46. Abdallah al-Hamid and Matruk al-Falih, interviews by the author.

47. "Bi-tawqi' 115 baynahum 15 mar'a bayan li-muthaqqafin wa-mihaniyyin sa'udiyyin ta'yidan li-rafd Sun' Allah Ibrahim istilam ja'izat al-riwaya al-'arabiyya" [A statement signed by 115 intellectuals and professionals including fifteen women supports Sun' Allah Ibrahim's refusal to accept the Arab novel prize], November 7, 2003, at www.elaph.com.

48. Abdallah al-Hamid, *Li-l-islah hadaf wa-manhaj* [Reform has a goal and a method] (Beirut: al-Dar al-'arabiyya li-l-'ulum, 2004), 21.

49. Al-Hamid's writings and his claim to have a right to interpret Islam have prompted a number of refutations by Sahwa clerics, most notably by Sulayman al-Kharrashi. See, for instance, Sulayman al-Kharrashi, "Sa'alni sa'il 'an Abdallah al-Hamid" [Someone asked me about Abdallah al-Hamid], at http://saaid.net/Warathah/Alkharashy/m/38.htm; Sulayman al-Kharrashi, "Bayna 'Abdallah al-Qasimi...wa 'Abdallah al-Hamid" [Between Abdallah al-Qasimi...and Abdallah al-Hamid], at http://saaid.net/Warathah/Alkharashy/m/38.htm.

PART FIVE

Post-Islamism Always?

II

Islamism in Sudan:

BEFORE, AFTER, IN BETWEEN

Abdelwahab El-Affendi

In the year 1884, three years after the outbreak of the Mahdist uprising in Sudan and one year before the Mahdist takeover of Khartoum, a proclamation was issued by the Mahdi's right-hand man (and his eventual successor), the *khalifa* Abdullahi al-Ta'ayishi, reconfirming the ban on all Sufi *tariqas* (brotherhoods). In response to unnamed questioners belonging to the Tijaniyya tariqa, the khalifa chastised the petitioners for questioning the order to abandon their tariqa and confirmed to them that the Mahdi had indeed commanded such an abandonment of all sects and schools. "Had you reflected on this carefully the first time," the khalifa added, "you would have realized that you were not supposed to [hesitate in accepting this command], for this matter is as clear as daylight":

For since the Imam al-Mahdi is the successor of the Messenger of God, peace be upon him, and the seal of all saints in the eyes of both the followers of the *zahir* (manifest)[1] and *batin* (the esoteric), and since it is known to you, all people of insight, that he is endowed with divine light and support from the Messenger of God, peace be upon him, and has been foretold to abolish *madhahib*[2] and clear the earth of all dissent and work according to Sunna[3] so that only the pure religion is left, and so that even if the Messenger of God, peace be upon him, were to be here, he would have approved of all his actions. For the Messenger of God, peace be upon him, has said of him: "He follows my tracks without error." A person with these qualities, who is present and can be grasped by eyesight, how is it possible to turn away from him and rely on someone else who is not here, someone who even if he were present, would have had no recourse but to follow him? Can't you see that if the Messenger of God, peace be upon him, was present in such an immediate way,

would it be possible to follow someone else or someone opposed to
him, or to follow a path other than his?[4]

This intriguing line of theological reasoning (which for some reason
reminds me of the sophistry of Western Marxist debates) is of key importance to understanding the trials and tribulations of modern Islamism, and
not only in Sudan. Understanding the nature of religious authority is key to
grasping the modern role and function of Islamism. The Mahdist ban on Sufi
tariqas and legal schools, the dominant forms of organized religious life and
activism in premodern and traditional Islam, was a radical attempt at transforming the basis of religious authority. The Mahdi explained the matter to
his followers thus: the schools are like wells that travelers use in order to draw
water in the desert. If a mighty river then comes and submerges these wells,
there will be no point trying to look for them under the flood, since it would
be easier and more sensible to obtain water from the river. The Mahdist mission was just such a mighty river that makes all wells redundant.

On this understanding, tariqas and madhahib were (essentially fal-
lible) human attempts to understand and implement the divine message.
Moreover, historically, the madhahib emerged in the post–Righteous
Caliphate period, seen in turn as an extension of the Prophetic period.
During that era, there was no need for these collective interpretative (*ijtihad*) efforts, since a clear authority (divine or very close to it) existed to offer
guidance. For the Imami Shia, this situation persisted theoretically with
the imams, who could dispense unmediated divine guidance. However,
this privileged access to the divine was soon lost after the disappearance
of the last imam. The schools were the next best thing, since they represented an effort to come to grips with the absence of this direct guidance.
They were also a reaction to the decline in state legitimacy and an attempt
to compensate for it. In this sense, they attempted to capture and embody
the voice of religious authority, which the state could not. And it is precisely
in this capacity that the Mahdi declared them redundant. Now that divine
authority was manifest and directly accessible through him, there was no
longer any need for those alternative readings and approximations.

The Mahdist characterization of religious authority as immediately present, direct, and incontestable represents in many ways the ideal of many a
religious quest. However, as the Mahdist experience has itself demonstrated,
this ideal remains elusive. The majority of Sudanese Muslims did not subscribe to the Mahdist claims, and trust in its tenets declined even further
after the Mahdi's own demise before many of his predictions came to pass.

Neo-Mahdism as a Post-Islamist Experiment

The Mahdi's shocking death just six months after the conquest of Khartoum threw the movement into turmoil. However, the khalifa moved in quickly to save the day and reformulate the doctrine along lines already familiar from Christianity and Shiism. This was not too difficult, given that the khalifa had been playing a key leadership role during the Mahdi's own lifetime, and some reinterpretations were quickly made of the Mahdi's predictions of the conquest of the whole world. The khalifa continued to report visions of the Mahdi, saints, and prophets to bolster his own spiritual authority. However, aware that his credibility might be questionable, he also instituted a powerful military dictatorship in which he relied on his relatives and allied tribes. His rule deeply divided the Sudanese and was memorably repressive. In the end, the catastrophic defeat inflicted on the Mahdist armies by Kitchener's troops at Omdurman in September 1898 and the subsequent collapse of the Mahdist project were less easy to explain away.

However, the Mahdist movement emerged from that catastrophe, and the subsequent relentless campaign of persecution by the British authorities, as a powerful force in Sudanese politics and society. This was partly due to luck but also to the ingenuity of Sayyid Abd al-Rahman al-Mahdi, the Mahdi's posthumous and last surviving son. Luck came in the form of Turkey's entry into World War I on the side of Germany and Austria and the sultan's proclamation of jihad against the British. Wary of the dangerous potential of a renewed Mahdist uprising, the British authority decided to rehabilitate Sayyid Abd al-Rahman and task him with discouraging his followers from rebelling against the colonial authorities. This was not difficult to do, since there was no love lost between the Mahdists and Turks, against whom the original Mahdist uprising had erupted in the first place. Abd al-Rahman's luck did not stop there. For when an uprising against the British did take place in the 1920s, it was not by Mahdist jihadists but by the secularized civil and military elite, who were the product of the colonial educational and state institutions. Frightened by this new "danger," the British turned their back to the secular elite and sought a closer alliance with the traditional leaders, among whom Abd al-Rahman was a major figure. They had to overcome a deep animosity against the man and his movement and accept his protests of loyalty.[5]

But ingenuity was key to Sayyid Abd al-Rahman's rise from an impoverished fugitive, one of the few survivors of a massacre in which many of his elder brothers and family members perished, to a prominent figure in the urban religious and economic aristocracy. He did this via some gifted entrepreneurship in the realms of economics as well as in the political, intellectual, and ideological arenas. It was not easy to transform the revolutionary otherworldly ethos of Mahdism into a pacifist movement that would collaborate with the infidel colonial powers, but he managed to pull it off by adopting the Protestant way: harnessing the ascetic revolutionary drive into a combination of economic activity and inner-directed spirituality. Most crucial for success is that he established himself as the undisputed *religious* authority for his father's followers, thus making it feasible to lead them onto a "post-Islamist" path.[6] Neo-Mahdism, as the transformed movement came to be known, was the post-Islamist movement par excellence.

This was, in a sense, analogous to what his rival, Sayyid Ali al-Mirghani, leader of the Khatmiyya tariqa, did. The Khatmiyya, who were staunchly anti-Mahdist, made their peace with the British much earlier, and Sayyid Ali became a pillar of the pro-British social and political establishment. His hold over his followers was also absolute, and he did not have trouble selling to them the secular order established by the British or the postindependence system either. The Sufi sect he led was millenarian but not revolutionary or antiauthority. So it was not difficult to harness its tenets in the service of a new authority that could tolerate private religiosity.[7]

Between them, these two religious movements created a unique situation in Sudan, where religion appeared to have been "tamed" in a remarkable way in view of Sudan's Islamic revolutionary history under Mahdism and perhaps precisely because of that history and the disillusionment it has bred among wide sections of the population, including some adherents of Mahdism. And religion was not only tamed and harnessed in favor of a more quietist and inner-directed faith but even put in the service of a secular, foreign-dominated colonial authority.

Islamism, Traditionalism, and the Contest over "Spiritual Capital"

Appearances could be deceptive, however. The collaborationist tendency of the key religious leaders provoked anger and contempt from the emerging secular elite, who were ardently anticolonialist in spite of being the product of the secular educational system put in place by the colonial authority. In this, they were of course no exception to anticolonial elites elsewhere.

The resulting tension between the emerging modern educated elite and traditional leadership over the anticolonial struggle paved the way for the emergence of the modern Islamist movement in several ways. First, while the prominent religious leaders appeared to have cornered what Pierre Bourdieu calls "spiritual capital,"[8] maintaining a monopoly of religious authority over their followers, their *moral* authority came into question in view of their collaboration with the "infidel" colonialists. The rising secular nationalists used this anomaly very effectively against them, seeking to undermine their religious aura by deploying both religious and nationalist rhetoric and also through revolutionary action.[9] On the other hand, the prominence of religious leaders in the political arena meant that religion remained a central feature of political life and a focal point of political debate, even for the British authorities.

There was an irony here, as Islamists appeared on the face of it to have an uphill battle in the contest against entrenched leaders of vibrant religious movements. Habitually, modern Islamist movements found it very difficult to establish themselves in countries where the state enjoyed traditional religious legitimacy, as was the case with the monarchies in Morocco and Saudi Arabia, even when these authorities were stigmatized as "collaborationist." An Islamist movement worth the name must be able to put itself forward as a credible voice speaking for Islam. This is not easy when one has to wrestle this title from established and recognized authorities. To make matters worse, the modern Sudanese Islamists, with their antipathy toward the dominant Sufi brand of Islam in Sudan, were associated in popular perceptions with the hated Wahabi militants and faced strong initial rejection from the Muslim public.

Paradoxically, however, the fact that religious leaders in Sudan were branded as collaborationist tended to discredit religion itself among the modern elite. Sudan has thus one of the most powerful Communist movements in Africa. Islamists not only had to contend with entrenched religious interest but had to fight powerful secular rivals as well. However, Sudanese Islamists in the end managed to skillfully manipulate these adverse factors to their advantage. First, they sought to establish themselves among the modern elite, mainly in schools and colleges, where the traditional religious leaders lacked authority and where the secular Left and liberals dominated. In doing this, they appealed to the religious sentiment of students who came from devout backgrounds. In the second phase, they allied themselves with sections of the ulema and some minor Sufi sects, seeking to build broad alliances against what many saw as the menace of Westernization and secularization. They then used this alliance and the projected "Communist threat" to pressure, even intimidate, the traditional religious leaders into endorsing their agenda of Islamization.[10]

From its inception, Islamism was as much a challenge to traditional religious authority as it was to the established colonial or postcolonial secular orders. Hassan al-Banna, the founder of the Muslim Brotherhood in Egypt, began his mission by appealing to the ulema to make a stand against what he saw as the unstoppable secularizing tide. And when he received a lukewarm response, he proceeded to do it himself, starting with preaching at cafés and on the streets. He then began to organize the few individuals who responded to his call into an action-oriented group. It is a supreme irony that the first six members of the group were ordinary workers with almost nonexistent religious knowledge, to the extent that they had to be taught how to wash and perform prayers.[11] But the group would challenge everyone else in the community as the self-proclaimed advocate of the religious point of view and its authoritative exponent.

The pattern in Sudan was broadly similar: a group of young students and graduates from secular schools went on to challenge the religious leaders in the name of Islam, urging them to adopt a stance supportive of an "Islamic constitution." As such, the tiny Islamist groups became a destabilizing force for traditional religious authority. What is remarkable is not just the relative success of these groups in asserting their claims to religious authority but also the convergence in form and style between them. Whether in the Arab world, Africa, South Asia, Southeast Asia, or Central Asia, the phenomenon took the same form: secular educated intellectuals and activists organized themselves into politically active parties or pressure groups that managed to set themselves up as the voice of religion. Traditional religious establishments either acquiesced to this claim or were marginalized under the pressure of other (more "secular") forces of modernity.

No less remarkable is the response of the opponents of these groups, who appear to acknowledge the claims of the Islamists, sometimes even when they refuse to assert it. The Justice and Development Party in Turkey adamantly denies any Islamist credentials. But its opponents (and most observers) continue to describe it as an Islamist party and ascribe to it an Islamist agenda that is then projected from what these critics believe Islamism should entail. Similarly, when the new military regime that took power in Sudan in June 1989 strenuously denied any Islamist leanings, few believed it. By contrast, the Neo-Mahdist umma party, one of the two main political parties in Sudan, has been trying for decades to control the Islamist agenda, to the extent of calling itself the "Sudanese Islamic movement" during the 1980s. Its leader, who became prime minister of Sudan twice (in 1966–1967 and again in 1986–1989), has worked hard to project himself as a voice of Islamic moderation. However, at no point did either his international backers or his critics describe him or his party as Islamist.

The current Saudi regime has more title than any other entity to be regarded as Islamist. It pushes an agenda that even the most radical Islamist group would think too ambitious: implementing strict provisions of shari'a, allowing only a minimum of women's rights, uncompromisingly enforcing the strictest interpretation of religious morality in public space, and so on and so forth. But neither its allies, such as the United States, nor its critics among the Islamists seem to classify it in this category. Similarly, the Iraqi government is also made up of "Islamist" parties, some of which are very strict in their outlook, and relies heavily on legitimation by the Shi'i religious hierarchy in Iraq. It is also not condemned by the international community as Islamist, nor is it embraced by Islamist groups, even though the leading Sunni Islamist party is part of it. Meanwhile, the Iranian and Sudanese regimes, which are less strict on all these counts, are regarded as the epitome of Islamism. So are Hamas in Gaza and Hizbullah in Lebanon, even though both are much more lax with regard to enforcement in their respective fiefdoms. In all these cases, the "spiritual capital" is effortlessly cornered by, even foisted onto, a reluctant claimant.

It would appear that a certain measure of radicalism has come to be associated with the concept of Islamism, so that it is the degree of radicalism (and anti-Western stance and rhetoric) of a movement or regime that qualifies it to be described as Islamist, rather than its attitude to the public uses of religion. That is why traditionally legitimized "religious" governments or parties with moderate foreign policies are not categorized as Islamist.

The Worldliness of Islamism

If this tells us anything, it is that the populist side of Islamism is seen as its defining feature, rather than its insistence on the legal aspects of Islamic rule. In general, the modern Islamic movement is nothing if not the antithesis of Mahdism and other traditionalist expressions of religious activism. For whereas Mahdism is distinctly otherworldly, Islamism is stamped by the sign of our eminently disenchanted modern world. It is its decidedly this-worldly orientation that marks modern Islamism off from all premodern Islamic reform movements, which were spiritual and otherworldly in their focus.

In this, modern Islamism is in stark contrast not only with Mahdism, traditional Sufism, and traditionalist religious observance in general but also with modern Salafism of the type prevalent in Saudi Arabia. In all these models, including in the Saudi state, religion is effectively depoliticized and otherworldly oriented, while the pragmatism of the state and the political and economic elite takes a detached, effectively secular character. The division of labor between the political elite and the state mirrors the church–state relationship in early modern Western monarchies, where the church is firmly under state control. The same distinction between religion and politics was observed by the traditional religious elite in Sudan, who ruled the country as a secular democracy but led their followers as "holy men." This is precisely the approach that provokes Islamist anger in Sudan and why one of their tactics has been to bring this contradiction to a head by pressuring the traditional leaders into taking a stance on the public application of religious norms, hoping to embarrass them in front of their followers: "If one were to search for the defining characteristic of the modern Islamic movement, one would most probably find it in its acceptance (and in some sense, its embodiment) of man's estrangement from God."[12]

Islamism's grievances are of this world (the relative decline of the umma vis-à-vis its enemies, economic injustice, defeat and humiliation in wars, etc.), and so are its prescriptions. For these movements, the slogan "Islam is the solution" is supposed to recommend Islam as the vehicle that will bring prosperity, dignity, and worldly success to its adherents. While the Sudanese Mahdi was somewhat on the extreme side when he told his followers, "I have come to you with the destruction of this world and the refurbishment of the next," the spirit of his mission reflects to some extent the ethos of premodern Islamic reform (and religious reform in general), where worldly prosperity was not an objective and was often regarded as the problem. By contrast,

> the bulk of the arguments and writings of modern Islamic activists
> and thinkers are directed to people who do not believe in Islam or
> even religion as such.... [The] discourse is decidedly this-worldly in

its themes, thus implicitly accepting that we live in a world which understands only this kind of language, and that it is pointless to attempt to teach it a new one.[13]

Nowhere is this more evident than in the Sudanese Islamic movement under Hassan Turabi (b. 1932). From the beginning of his ascendancy in the mid-1960s, Turabi adopted a politically pragmatic approach that remains paradoxical from an Islamic standpoint. Pragmatism entails offering concessions on principles in order to obtain concrete gains in return. While this is inherent in all political action, Turabi pushed the limits by adopting a strategy that envisaged making huge sacrifices on the principles front in order to gain power and other material advantages. This approach is not only far removed from the original Mahdism but also anathema to radical idealists like Abu'l Ala Maududi and Sayyid Qutb, whose point is precisely that no such concessions should ever be made. You do not seek and gain power, these thinkers argue, by pragmatic means in order to implement Islamic principles later. Instead, society must be made to accept Islamic principles first and submit to them, before even the idea of Islamic rule can be contemplated.[14]

Turabi, by contrast, argues that Islamic activism must immerse itself into the reality of its times and become integral to it if it is to be effective. Rejecting the Maududi/Qutb argument that the "Islamic vanguard" must stand apart from, and above, society in order to guide it toward the Islamic path, he argues instead that the Islamic movement should be part of the society as it is, even assimilate some of its defects. In his writings, "Turabi hovers dangerously over the borderline which separates commitment and cynicism, although in most parts his work looks indistinguishable from apologetics."[15]

Methodologically, he offers the seemingly heretical view that the Islamic reformist should adopt the stance of the social scientist, not that of the theologian, jurist, or mystic. This means that the reformer is not supposed simply to engage in a philosophical defense of the creed against critics and skeptics or to be content with elaborating legal maxims derived from holy texts, or even to engage in a spiritual quest to fathom the inner and hidden truths of the faith as Sufi mystics are wont to do. For we are now in an era that questions the very relevance of religion for society. The answer to this challenge posed to religion can only come from a quest that employs the findings of modern social science to produce convincing arguments about the relevance, and even necessity, of religion to modern life.[16]

Needless to say, this is a rather risky undertaking, since putting the fate of religion in the hands of social scientists may not necessarily produce the proofs one is looking for. However, this whole approach confounds the categorization of Turabi as an Islamist. The distinction between an Islamist (or a fundamentalist) and a modernist is premised on the dogmatism of the first and the flexibility of the second when it comes to addressing the challenges posed by modernity. But Turabi appears to be a "pragmatic fundamentalist," or a "fundamentalist modernist."

Post-Islamism?

This aspect of Turabi's thought, combined with the practice of the Sudanese Islamist movement, prompted one commentator to question the adequacy of post-Islamism as a viable explanatory concept in the Sudanese case. There are two possible interpretations of Bayat's post-Islamism thesis, Salomon argues. The first and more emphatic one is in a sense a restatement of the secularization thesis: disillusionment with Islamist experimentation has caused many to support a dilution of the Islamist thesis to the extent of advocating resecularization. The weaker version assimilates post-Islamism to some form of Islamic liberalism. The Sudanese case challenges both:

> Thus, if a turn towards religious plurality in the face of a singular voice, a focus on rights instead of duties, and an orientation towards the future instead of the past denotes "post-Islamism" for Bayat, and such a state of affairs was *already* the case under the Sudanese Islamists of the early *inqaadh*,[17] we are forced to question not only the coherence of the analytical category of "post-Islamism," but perhaps of "Islamism" as well.[18]

According to this particular commentator, there are two senses of *Islamism* that are relevant to the Sudanese case. The first is descriptive, referring to the growth of a self-described and well-recognized local Islamist movement. The second is an analytical one denoting "a modern political ideology whose foundations are said to be partially, if not primarily, grounded in the Islamic tradition." It is difficult, if we take the descriptive category, to argue that Sudan is currently experiencing a post-Islamist phase. For in spite of splits, ideological shifts, and reshuffling of personnel, the Islamists remain firmly in control of the state almost twenty-five years after the launch of the *inqaadh* project through the 1989 coup. Using the analytical concept, Salomon adds that his own empirical research in the last few years indicates that the travails of the Sudanese Islamist project, far from signaling the failure of Islamism, have in fact enhanced it:

> Rather, it is my contention that the failure of the Islamic Movement to create a stable state and implement the projects it set out to accomplish, far from signaling the end of Islamism, has instead enhanced the political future of Islam in Sudan (and thus various forms of what we can clearly call Islamism, using the analytical definition) in often surprising directions.... What I observed in my time in Sudan is that it was precisely the Islamic Movement's failure to maintain hold of the steering wheel of the ship of Islamization on which they had embarked that was causing new Islamic actors to enter political debate. Thus while the debate occurred in the language of the Islamic Movement, they were not the only party to it.[19]

This can be seen in the emergence of a variety of new forms of Islamist discourse: Sufi-pluralist, Salafi antistate, even pro–Sudan People's Liberation Movement pluralists, not to mention a revival of "neo-Islamists" associated with the Republican movement of the late Mahmoud Mohamed Taha.[20]

The Sudanese experience does indeed call for a rethinking of the concept of "post-Islamism," and not only for the reasons cited by Salomon. The concept does in any case pose some serious problems of analysis and interpretation. As Bayat, who coined the term in the first place,[21] notes, the term's "poor conceptualization and misperception" has meant that its wide use, often without a clear definition, "seems to have confused more than it has clarified."[22]

As originally conceived, the term was devised to describe the dramatic "transformation in religious and political discourse in Iran during the 1990s,"[23] but it was later generalized to refer to a wide range of experiences where Islamism appears to have exhausted itself and started to engage in serious rethinking. In its final formulation, as Bayat puts it, the concept denotes both a condition and a project:

> In my formulation, post-Islamism represents both a *condition* and a *project*, which may be embodied in a master (or multidimensional) movement. In the first place, it refers to political and social conditions where, following a phase of experimentation, the appeal,

energy, and sources of legitimacy of Islamism are exhausted, even among its once-ardent supporters. Islamists become aware of their system's anomalies and inadequacies as they attempt to normalize and institutionalize their rule.... [As a consequence,] Islamism becomes compelled, both by its own internal contradictions and by societal pressure, to reinvent itself, but it does so at the cost of a qualitative shift.[24]

But "post-Islamism is also a project, a conscious attempt to conceptualize and strategize the rationale and modalities of transcending Islamism in social, political, and intellectual domains." In this sense,

> post-Islamism is neither anti-Islamic nor un-Islamic nor secular. Rather it represents an endeavor to fuse religiosity and rights, faith and freedom, Islam and liberty. It is an attempt to turn the underlying principles of Islamism on its head by emphasizing rights instead of duties, plurality in place of singular authoritative voice, historicity rather than fixed scripture, and the future instead of the past. It strives....to achieve....an "alternative modernity"....[and] is expressed in acknowledging secular exigencies, in freedom from rigidity, in breaking down the monopoly of religious truth. In short, whereas Islamism is defined by the fusion of religion and responsibility, post-Islamism emphasizes religiosity and rights.[25]

In the final instance, "the core spirit of the term referred to the metamorphosis of Islamism (in ideas, approaches, and practices) from within and without."[26] In this regard, defining exactly what is meant by *Islamism*, something Bayat omits to do, is crucial for pinning down the concept.[27] There are a few hints toward a definition, including suggestions that Islamism is an instance of "over-religiosity," that it denotes a "language of self-assertion" directed at the mobilization of those marginalized by modernity, and that it is a tendency opposed to "Western cultural domination."[28] Islamism is also said to imagine "Islam as a complete divine system with a superior political model, cultural code, legal structure, and economic arrangement." It is also an "interpretation of Islam" that is "accompanied by strong populist language and heavy-handed social control," which means that it "would inevitably marginalize and even criminalize those who remained outside its strictures": "At the core of the Islamist paradigm, then, lay a blend of piety and obligation, devotion and duty."[29]

For Olivier Roy, Islamist groups are those "activist groups who see in Islam as much a political ideology as a religion."[30] Bassam Tibi also emphasizes the political ideology of Islamism (he prefers the term *Islamic fundamentalism*), arguing that for these groups, and despite their "pragmatic use of religion," "the context is clearly more political than religious."[31] It is part of a global phenomenon that is both "an expression of....and a response to....the emerging world disorder."[32] Tibi further follows Martin E. Marty and R. Scott Appleby and the rest of the team of the Chicago Fundamentalism Project,[33] in arguing that fundamentalists, while appearing to reaffirm traditional doctrines, actually proceed to "subtly lift them of their original context" and use them *"as ideological weapons against a hostile world."* In this, fundamentalism demonstrates *"a closer affinity with modernism than with traditionalism."*[34]

This emphasis, repeated by many authors, on the politicization of religion and the mobilization of those marginalized by modernity, still does not account fully for the *religious* dimension of "religious fundamentalism." In particular, that aspect is pointed out in another of Tibi's quotes from Marty and Appleby, where "fundamentalists" are said to see themselves as "actors in an eschatological drama unfolding in the mind of God and directing the course of human history."[35] In this regard, religious "fundamentalism" is not just another "modern" political ideology.

This leads us back to the question of spiritual (and political) capital, which underlines the specific significance of Islamist groups. The groups become worthy of the name, and of being noticed, only if they manage to project some measure of religious authority. And this is what gives significance to the "post-Islamist turn," which has to be, as Bayat argues, a transformation *within* Islamism. Islamist groups have to be in control of this process to enable it to be effective, contrary to the connotations in most discussions about the subject, which appear to portray the process as a loss of Islamist influence and a fading away of Islamist groups.[36]

It is rather interesting that Iran appears to represent the primary locus of the presumed post-Islamist phenomenon, in the same way as it has been the primary locus of the rise of the phenomenon of Islamism (or "fundamentalism"). As Kramer has noted, the term *Islamic fundamentalism* came "into widespread usage, thanks in large measure to media coverage of Iran's revolution":

Journalists, ever on the lookout for a shorthand way to reference things new and unfamiliar, gravitated toward the term fundamentalism. It was American English; it was already in *Webster's Dictionary*, and it evoked the anti-modernism that Ayatollah Khomeini seemed to personify. The use of fundamentalism in connection with Islam spread rapidly—so much so that by 1990, the *Concise Oxford English Dictionary* defined it not only as "the strict maintenance of traditional Protestant beliefs," but also as "the strict maintenance of ancient or fundamental doctrines of any religion, especially Islam." By sheer dint of usage, Islamic fundamentalism had become *the* most cited fundamentalism of all.[37]

It is thus fitting that Iran, which gave rise to the concept (and the fears associated with it), should also be the place where the anticipation of transcending Islamism should also be at its most acute. But we have to remember that the contestations over religious authority are, in the final analysis, intra-Islamic affairs, even though it is mainly outsiders who are intent on leading this debate.

Lessons from Sudanese "Post-Islamisms"

In this regard, the Sudanese case is uniquely instructive in many ways. To start with, Sudan is probably the only country that entered the last century in "post-Islamist" mode. It experienced its own Islamic revolution a century before Iran and has gone through phases of conflict, disillusionment, and rethinking over many decades. As described above, secularizing, and even collaborationist, drives have been spearheaded by influential religious leaders and by politicians and intellectuals who grew up within the bosom of these religious movements. Neo-Mahdism represented an interesting rethinking and remolding of revolutionary Islamic ideology so as to keep up with the challenges posed by the colonial order and modernization.

The modern Islamist movement in Sudan thus emerged into an environment that has already been framed within a specific "post-Islamist condition." No less significant, however, is the emergence of a variety of post-Islamist "projects" simultaneously with the rise of the Islamist movement itself—and in some cases as a result of splits within it, which played an important role in shaping the way the movement evolved. One such "post-Islamist" movement emerged in 1953, when the Islamic Liberation Movement, the nucleus of the modern Islamist movement (founded 1949), suffered its first split as the more liberal and pragmatic wing reacted to its decision to identity with the Egyptian Muslim Brotherhood by forming a separate movement. The splinter group first called itself the "Islamic Group" but soon changed its name to the Islamic Socialist Party.[38] The new group did not have a large following, but key leaders in it played influential roles in various contexts, including shaping the ideology of the revolution in Libya, where some of its top leaders lived during the 1970s.

However, another slightly more influential and ideologically more coherent movement was spearheaded by the Republican Party (renamed the Republican Brothers after the ban on political parties in 1969), an intriguing movement described by some as "neo-Islamist," whose message consisted of a "fusion of Sufi principles and the notions of political freedoms, economic justice and social equality."[39] The movement's charismatic leader, Mahmoud Mohamed Taha, whose execution for apostasy in January 1985 caused an outcry and precipitated the fall of the regime of the former dictator Gaafar Nimeiri in April that year, was a man steeped in Sufi doctrine and exhibited liberal leanings. Taha's central thesis was to reverse the orthodox Muslim view on Islam as having evolved gradually toward its most perfect revelation just prior to the Prophet's death. For Taha, the reverse was true: Islam was revealed in its most perfect and lofty ideals in Mecca but was watered down because it was too much for the people of Arabia at the time to take. Twentieth-century humanity, by contrast, was ready to accept Islam's full message, which favors freedom, equality, and human rights.[40]

Needless to say, this message provoked a strong negative reaction from the traditionalists (including Sufis) and modern Islamists. In fact the Islamists and Republicans remain the bitterest of enemies. However, a small band of dedicated followers continued to support and propagate this message, and its leader earned the respect of most Sudanese leaders. The questions the movement provoked over the limits of Islamic shari'a and the boundaries of modernization were influential in shaping and directing the debate.

Within this broader context, the pragmatic and pro-modernist line propagated by the Islamist movement under Turabi had a mutually reinforcing relationship with a variety of trends within Sudanese Islam. While the repressive conduct of the Islamist regime after the June 1989 military coup appeared to contradict this ethos and even the language of the Islamist movement itself prior to the coup, disillusionment with the experiment, and the bitter internecine strife within the movement (which saw its leader Turabi ejected from power in 1999), appeared to give powerful support to a "post-Islamist" interpretation for events since then.[41]

As discussed above, these interpretations remain problematic for a number of reasons. The modern Islamist movement (e.g., Turabi and some of his critiques) in Sudan appears to have exhibited many of the tendencies associated with "post-Islamism" even before these recent developments. This turned out to be more of a problem than an opportunity. For, as I have explained at length elsewhere, Turabi's iconoclastic attitude toward orthodoxy provoked clashes with the forces of traditionalism and even precipitated splits within the movement. This in turn undermined the authority and religious legitimation of the movement, forcing Turabi on numerous occasions to recant his bold assertions.[42]

Ironically, if Turabi's project were to have succeeded, it would probably have paved the way for a more decisive post-Islamist transformation. Turabi is known for his stance against the ulema's monopoly over religious interpretation and his call for interpretation to be democratized and vested in representative institutions of which the ulema could form part, perhaps as "legal advisers" to the people's representatives. However, if this formula were to be adopted, then Islam would finally have something approaching church synods and other ruling bodies, which would in turn pave the way for all sorts of challenges to such an authority, perhaps leading to secularization.

Conclusion

The Sudanese experiment with Islamization and Islamism is a complex and multilayered phenomenon that sheds important light on the current debate on Islamism and post-Islamism. And the first thing this experiment teaches is the instability of post-Islamist orders. There is a sense in which all modern secular systems in the postcolonial Muslim world were "post-Islamist," in that they emerged as successors to premodern Islamic orders, in particular, traditional Islamic states. Some of these (in Kemalist Turkey and Pahlavi Iran) were more conscious of this orientation than others. However, Sudan is unique in having witnessed an Islamic revolution on the threshold of modernity and then proceeding to unravel its consequences as it labored to make its peace with modernity.

But then, all these orders have faced destabilization from the rise of Islamist movements. The central question with regard to the potency and influence of Islamist movements refers us to the structure of Muslim societies, which render the discourse of these movements effective and endow them with influence. Religious revivalist movements exist everywhere, but they have not been as influential as they have been in Muslim regions.[43] In this regard, the transformations associated with "post-Islamism" cannot be restricted to internal evolution within Islamist movements but, rather, must be accompanied by radical structural social change.

One has also to question the generally positive characterization of post-Islamism among the bulk of commentators who have taken up the issue. This stems from the fact that most of these commentators start from the premise that Islamism is a problem and post-Islamism is the solution. A post-Islamist order is therefore seen as having been "immunized" against the destabilizing impact of Islamism after having received a high dose of it, which bred rejection and aversion. The Sudanese case indicates that this "immunization" is not absolute. The Mahdist experience had indeed created an aversion to extremism among the majority of the Sudanese, including Mahdist loyalists. The Mahdist period continues to be remembered as an era of instability, conflict, repression, and massive famine. The recent Islamist experiment from the 1980s has also been associated with repression, famines, instability, and destructive conflicts. However, as many observers have noted, this did not result in a mass aversion to Islamism.

True, there is disillusionment among the majority, including many loyal Islamists, with the experiment. Violent splits and vociferous self-criticism resulted. Islamism has much less mass appeal today than would have been the case two decades earlier. However, at the same time, and as was the case with Mahdism, a mass of hard-core Islamist supporters still exists and continues to expand. Three decades of Islamist experimentation, which involved the use of the media, a reorientation of the educational system, and the reconfiguring of public space, have also resulted in a much higher level of religious observance and general support for a broader Islamic orientation. While many oppose the practices of the present regime, broad sections of public opinion couch their opposition in Islamist terms. Some, like the Salafis, some traditionalists, and the splinter "Muslim Brotherhood," adopt an even more hard-line stance than the regime, which they regard as having compromised its Islamist credentials.

Indeed the regime has made many compromises, including the signing of a peace agreement in January 2005 with a predominantly non-Muslim southern rebel movement, the Sudan People's Liberation Army, which entailed sharing power with that movement. This, and the general toning down of Islamist rhetoric and hard-line policies in the wake of the ejection of Turabi from power in 1999, prompted many to argue that the regime itself has become post-Islamist in its "Second Republic."[44] This could suggest that post-Islamism is not always a good thing, for the "post-Islamist" regime is more a reminder of other authoritarian "post-Islamist" (if the term is appropriate) regimes that continue to populate the Muslim world and are more preoccupied with survival than with any positive project, whether Islamist or secular. As we can see in Iran as well, the decline of the appeal of Islamism without the evolution of an alternative value system could leave a dangerous ethical vacuum in which all sorts of unprincipled conduct can flourish, without the benefit of the restraining influence of an overarching value system, Islamic or secular—a reminder, if any was needed, that the excesses associated with Islamism are only one aspect of a much more fundamental pathology inflicting Muslim politics.

Notes

1. The phrase "followers of the *zahir*," i.e., people who rely on "appearance," is often used to describe the majority of orthodox Muslims who accept the apparent or literal meanings of religious texts, in contrast to mystics and others who seek the esoteric or hidden meanings.
2. Traditional religious schools of thought.
3. Example of the Prophet.
4. Muhammad Ibrahim Abu-Salim, ed., *Manshurat al-Mahdiyya* (Khartoum?: n.p., 1969), 61–62; my translation.
5. Hassan Ahmed Ibrahim, "Imperialism and Neo-Mahdism in the Sudan: A Study of British Policy towards Neo-Mahdism, 1924–1927," *International Journal of African Historical Studies* 13, no. 2 (1980): 214–239; Gabriel Warburg, "From Mahdism to Neo-Mahdism in the Sudan: The Role of the Sudanese Graduates in Paving the Way to Independence, 1881–1956," *Middle Eastern Studies* 41, no. 6 (2005): 975–995.
6. See Abdelwahab El-Affendi, *Turabi's Revolution: Islam and Power in Sudan* (London: Grey Seal Books, 1991), 30–32.
7. Warburg, "From Mahdism to Neo-Mahdism in the Sudan," 985–986.
8. Bradford Verter, "Theorizing Religion with Bourdieu against Bourdieu," *Sociological Theory* 21, no. 2 (June 2003): 150–174.
9. Mohamed Omer Beshir, *Revolution and Nationalism in Sudan* (London: Rex Collings, 1974).
10. El-Affendi, *Turabi's Revolution*, 46–68.
11. Hassan al-Banna, *Mudhakkirat al-Da'wa wa'l-Da'iya* (Cairo: Al-Maktab al-Islami, 1983).

12. Abdelwahab El-Affendi, "The Long March from Lahore to Khartoum: Beyond the 'Muslim Reformation,'" *Bulletin (British Society of Middle Eastern Studies)* 17, no. 2 (1990): 137.

13. Ibid.

14. Abu'l Ala Maududi, *Minhaj al-Inqlab al-Islami* (Beirut: Muassasat al-Risala, 1979); cf. Sayyid Qutb, *Ma'alim fi'l-Tariq* (Kuwait: IIFSO, 1978).

15. Abdelwahab El-Affendi, "Hassan Turabi and the Limits of Modern Islamic Reformism," in *The Blackwell Companion to Contemporary Islamic Thought*, ed. Ibrahim Abu-Rabiʿ (Oxford: Blackwell, 2006), 144.

16. See Hassan Turabi, *The Islamic Movement in Sudan: Its Development, Approach and Achievements*, trans. Abdelwahab El-Affendi (Damascus: Arab Scientific Publishers, 2009).

17. "Salvation," in reference to the National Salvation Revolution, as the post-1989 regime in Sudan called itself.

18. Noah Salomon, "Post Islamism? Questioning the Question (Part 1)," *SSRC Blogs Islamism, Making Sense of Darfur*, Thursday, June 26, 2008 (8:56 a.m.), at http://africanarguments.org/2008/06/26/post-islamism-questioning-the-q uestion/ (accessed September 12, 2008).

19. Noah Salomon, "Post Islamism? Questioning the Question (Part 2)," *SSRC Blogs Islamism, Making Sense of Darfur*, Friday, June 27, 2008 (6:52 a.m.), at http://africanarguments.org/2008/06/27/post-islamism-questioning-the-question-part-2/ (accessed September 14, 2008).

20. Ibid.

21. Asef Bayat, "The Coming of a Post-Islamist Society," *Critique: Critical Middle East Studies* 5, no. 9 (Fall 1996): 43–52.

22. Asef Bayat, *Making Islam Democratic: Social Movements and the Post-Islamist Turn* (Stanford: Stanford University Press, 2007), 10.

23. Ibid., 11.

24. Ibid., 10–11.

25. Ibid., 11.

26. Ibid., 10.

27. Abdelwahab El-Affendi, "Review of: *Making Islam Democratic: Social Movements and the Post-Islamist Turn*, by Asef Bayat (Stanford: Stanford University Press, 2007)," *Journal of Islamic Studies* 19, no. 2 (2008): 297–299.

28. Bayat, *Making Islam Democratic*, 1, 6–7.

29. Ibid., 7.

30. Olivier Roy, *The Failure of Political Islam*, trans. Carol Volk (Cambridge: Harvard University Press, 1994), vii.

31. Bassam Tibi, *The Challenge of Fundamentalism: Political Islam and the New World Disorder* (Berkeley: University of California Press, 2002), 13.

32. Ibid., 2.

33. Martin E. Marty and R. Scott Appleby, eds., *Fundamentalisms Observed* (Chicago: University of Chicago Press, 1991).

34. Tibi, *Challenge of Fundamentalism*, 13; emphases in original.

35. Ibid.

36. Roy, *Failure of Political Islam*, ix–x; also S. Sayyid, *A Fundamental Fear: Eurocentrism and the Emergence of Islamism* (London: Zed Books, 2003), vii.

37. Martin Kramer, "Coming to Terms: Fundamentalists or Islamists?" *Middle East Quarterly*, Spring 2003: 65–77, www.meforum.org/541/coming-to-terms-fundamentalists-or-islamists (accessed July 31, 2010).

38. El-Affendi, *Turabi's Revolution*, 49–56, 153–156.

39. Muhammad Mahmud, "Sufism and Islamism in the Sudan," in *African Islam and Islam in Africa: Encounters between Sufis and Islamists*, ed. Eva Evers Rosander and David Westerlund (London: C. Hurst and Co. Publishers, 1997), 182.

40. Mahmoud Mohamed Taha, *The Second Message of Islam*, trans. and intro. by A. Ahmed An-Na'im (Syracuse: Syracuse University Press, 1987). Cf. Abdullahi Ahmed An-Na'im, *Toward an Islamic Reformation: Civil Liberties, Human Rights, and International Law* (Syracuse: Syracuse University Press, 1996).

41. Abdullahi Gallab, *The First Islamic Republic: Development and Disintegration of Islamism in the Sudan* (Aldershot: Ashgate, 2008). See also the debate on "post-Islamism" in Sudan on the ssrc.org blog *Making Sense of Sudan*. In particular, see the contributions of Abdullahi Gallab, Carolyn Fleur-Lobban, and Noah Salomon (see Turabi, *Islamic Movement in Sudan*): Carolyn Fluehr-Lobban, "Is Sudan Transitioning to a Post-Islamist State?" *African Arguments*, June 5, 2008, at http://africanarguments.org/2008/06/05/is-sudan-transitioning-to-a-post-islamist-state/ (accessed January 19, 2013); Salomon, "Post Islamism? Questioning the Question"; Abdullahi Gallab, "The Islamism Debate— Abdullahi Gallab Responds," *African Arguments*, June 18, 2008, http://africa-narguments.org/2008/06/18/the-islamism-debate-abdullahi-gallab-responds (accessed January 19, 2013).

42. El-Affendi, "Hassan Turabi and the Limits of Modern Islamic Reformism," 145–160.

43. Abdelwahab El-Affendi, "Democracy and the Islamist Paradox," in *Understanding Democratic Politics: Concepts, Institutions, Movements*, ed. Roland Axtmann (London: Sage Publications, 2003), 311–320. Cf. Ghassan Salamé, *Democracy without Democrats? The Renewal of Politics in the Muslim World* (London: I. B. Tauris, 1994).

44. Gallab, *First Islamic Republic*.

Syria's Unusual "Islamic Trend":

POLITICAL REFORMISTS, THE ULEMA,
AND DEMOCRACY

Thomas Pierret

Syria's Islamic trend constitutes a variant of the "Egyptian model" described by Asef Bayat.[1] The bloody repression of the 1979–1982 Islamic uprising, which came very close to replicating the Iranian Revolution, was counterbalanced by a powerful social movement that considerably increased the visibility of religion in everyday life. By the 1990s, mosques were packed with men and, for the first time in history, women; veiling had become the rule; Quran classes were mushrooming; and a growing number of families were organizing "Islamic" (that is, sexually segregated) marriage ceremonies. The Ba'thist regime was also "socialized" in the course of this process, since it had to progressively give up its aggressive secularist stance and show more tolerance toward nonpolitical religious activities.[2]

As in Egypt, most of the Syrian Islamic trend displays a conservative posture and fiercely opposes any doctrinal innovation. Of course, the country might appear as a relatively exceptional case because of the long-standing commitment of its Muslim Brotherhood (MB) to some form of political liberalism. However, that organization was completely uprooted following the uprising and is now a mere network of a few dozen gray-haired activists living in exile between Western Europe and the Middle East.

Although innovative religious figures will be presented in the following pages, the aim of this chapter is not to assess the—meager—signs of a coming post-Islamist turn in early twenty-first-century Syria. Instead, its main purpose is to underline the fact that envisioning the evolution of the local religious scene through such a lens might entail two major analytical problems: first, a temptation to oversimplify the ideological stance of the "old" Islamists (on issues such as democracy, human rights, or the political status of non-Muslim minorities) in order to contrast it more clearly with the aggiornamento carried out by the post-Islamists; second, a tendency to depict "Islamists"—that is, those who advocate the establishment of an Islamic state—in monolithic terms, since (marginal actors set aside) only a relatively coherent trend can undergo a paradigmatic shift. This danger is not peculiar to Bayat's conceptualization of post-Islamism: it is a potential corollary of all the attempts to identify a paradigmatic shift in the recent transformations of Islamism.[3]

I insist that I am not dismissing the different conceptualizations of post-Islamism, which have helped our understanding of important trends. Neither am I denying the claim that a paradigmatic shift did occur within Turkish Islamism at the turn of the last millennium or that such a shift has (temporarily?) aborted in Iran due to the implacable opposition of the conservatives. What I want to stress here is, rather, the fact that in my case study at least, the very idea of looking for a paradigmatic shift—or for its absence—might lead to a distortion of reality in order to make it fit a preconceived narrative.

The chapter addresses the first of the aforementioned analytical problems by showing that the Syrian MB's acceptance of such "post-Islamist" ideas as parliamentary rule, political pluralism, and the citizenship of non-Muslims is not the result of a recent shift but, rather, a long-standing feature that goes back to the very first years of the movement. My second criticism of the approaches in terms of a "paradigmatic shift" stresses the fact that they possibly entail the risk of ascribing excessive cohesion to Islamism. By implying that the latter is heterogeneous, I am not referring to such well-known distinctions as the one that separates the "moderates" from the "radicals." I am, rather, pointing to what appears to me as a structural factor of internal differentiation, that is, daily social practice. The vast majority of Islamic actors, whom I call "clerics," are specialized in the management of the goods of salvation (or what religion is primarily about, that is, showing the way of Heaven to the faithful and providing them with the means to reach it), whereas others are experts on political activism (that is, struggling to exert or share a monopoly on legitimate physical violence).[4] For those who prefer Pierre Bourdieu's terms to Max Weber's, the former category primarily belongs to the religious field, whereas the latter is part of the political field.[5] As I will explain in the second part of the chapter, both of these categories of actors are "Islamist" in the sense that they voice support for an Islamic order, but their distinct vocations entail fundamentally contrasting political behaviors and result in postures that often conflict with each other on the issue of political reform.

Building on the assumption made in the second section that clerics are the foremost conservative force within the Syrian Islamic trend, the third part of the chapter illustrates the fact that, albeit relatively secular by regional standards, Ba'thist authoritarianism is fundamentally detrimental to religious innovation. Indeed, it favors conservative clergymen while hindering the development of reformist trends, which mainly recruit among political-minded people. Therefore, I conclude by arguing that political reform is a precondition to religious reform, not the opposite.

The Syrian Muslim Brothers: Democrats by Birth?

On December 16, 2004, that is, at a time when the Syrian regime was facing growing Western pressure because of its policy in Lebanon, the London-based Muslim Brothers released *The Political Project for Future Syria*.[6] A follow-up of several initiatives taken by the Islamist movement in order to revive the Syrian opposition after the presidential succession of 2000, this 117-page-long document was the first detailed political program published by the organization since the uprising and more precisely, since the 1980 *Manifesto and Program of the Islamic Revolution in Syria*.[7]

The *Political Project* was well received among Syrian secular opponents because of its clear commitment to the establishment of a "modern democratic state."[8] The characteristics of the latter were avowedly inspired from the models provided by the "long-standing democratic countries": "rule of law," protection of "human rights," "separation of powers," "responsibility" of the executive authority vis-à-vis parliament, limitation of the length and renewals of executive mandates, and "free and multipartite" elections. The MB's new program also recognized the equality of all Syrians, regardless of their religion, on the basis of the principle of "citizenship."

At the same time, the *Political Project* retained distinctly Islamist overtones by calling for the "gradual Islamization of law." It also stated that non-Islamic parties should be authorized provided that they do not oppose what "has been clearly established by the shari'a," a principle that could be used to justify severe limitations on political pluralism. From this point of view the Muslim Brothers have remained "old Islamists" by comparison with more "post-Islamist" groups like the Movement for Justice and Development (Harakat al-'adāla wa-l-binā'), a small party founded in 2006 by London-based Syrian opponents. Avowedly modeled on the Turkish Justice and Development Party (Adalet ve Kalkınma Partisi, AKP), the Movement for Justice and Development considers Islam merely as a source of identity and moral values rather than as a set of legal and political rules.[9]

In any case, whatever its limits, the political liberalism of the MB is not the product of a recent ideological shift but, rather, the continuation of a decades-old political discourse. Indeed, most of the liberal elements contained in its 2004 *Political Project* were already present in the *Manifesto* published in 1980, that is, at a time when its member were engaged in an armed struggle against the regime—and were at times resorting to sectarian, anti-'Alawi propaganda.[10] In the *Manifesto*, the Muslim Brothers stated that they would respect "equality between the citizens," "separation of powers," and "freedom to form political parties," as well as "freedom of thought and expression" within the limits set up by the constitution and the "faith of the nation."[11] Later in the decade, a leader of the organization stated that the latter would accept a freely elected 'Alawi communist as president—admittedly a highly improbable eventuality.[12]

One might suggest, as would also be the case for the 2004 *Political Project*, that such moderate positions aimed to reassure the secular opposition, with whom the MB eventually allied within the National Alliance for the Liberation of Syria in 1982 and the Damascus Declaration for Democratic Change in 2005.[13] In fact, however, the program released in 1980 came within the scope of an already old political tradition that—in the worst possible conditions—had survived the rising influence of Sayyid Qutb's radical ideas within the movement during the second half of the 1970s.[14]

This is what the Muslim Brothers were referring to when they argued that their "political project" was a "return to basics." Between the French withdrawal of 1946 and the Ba'thist coup of 1963, Syria witnessed several phases of liberal rule. Members of the MB, which was officially founded a couple of weeks after the end of colonial occupation, sat in all of that period's elected parliaments, and several of them were appointed as ministers in 1949 and 1962. The rest of the time, the Islamists behaved as a loyal opposition: They were the only ideological party not to be directly involved in attempts at taking power through military coups, and they never radically challenged the legitimacy of the parliamentary system. In 1949, their political program stressed the necessity to abide by the "limits of the constitution" in order to preserve the "republican system," the "equilibrium between the powers," and "civil rights." The same document stated that the people had to choose their representatives "through free elections" and should be recognized as the "supreme authority."[15]

In 1950, during the parliamentary debate over the new constitution, the MB's proposal that Islam be declared the "religion of the state" was met with the fierce opposition of secular parties and Christian churches, even though the draft constitution presented by the Islamists also stipulated that there would be "no discrimination between the citizens of the state on the basis of religion."[16] MB deputies were forced to backtrack and eventually agreed to vote for a constitution that only stipulated that "the religion of the president is Islam" and that "*fiqh* is the main source of the legislation."[17] Mustafa al-Siba'i (1915–1964), the leader of the movement, justified his decision to support the text by describing it as "a model constitution for Muslim states."[18]

The ideological flexibility of the pre-1963 Syrian Muslim Brothers also manifested itself through their vocal embrace of one of the most fashionable ideologies of that time, that is, socialism. The movement named its political arm "Islamic Socialist Front" as early as 1949, and al-Siba'i released his famous *Socialism of Islam* ten years later.[19]

Why did the early Syrian MB share so many characteristics with today's "post-Islamists"? One might argue that the Muslim Brothers always remained a modest political force during that period: in 1961, the movement and its allies had their best electoral result ever by obtaining 8.7 percent of parliamentary seats.[20] However, being a minority is not in itself a factor of moderation. Another, more convincing element of explanation is the fact that whereas in mid-twentieth-century Egypt, for instance, the parliament was bereft of any legitimacy because it was seen as a tool of British colonialism, in Syria, on the contrary, it was perceived as a bastion of nationalist resistance to the French.[21]

Even more important was the MB's fear of military regimes after the bitter experiences of the rules of Husni al-Za'im and Adib al-Shishakli (1949–1954). As in most other Middle Eastern countries, secularism was deeply entrenched within the military, and during the 1950s, the Islamists' influence among the officers proved markedly weaker than that of other new ideological forces such as the Greater Syrian nationalists, Ba'thists, communists, and later Nasserites.[22]

Actually, although they were critical of the notables who dominated the political scene until the 1950s, the Muslim Brothers were structurally tied to the bourgeois order that would eventually disappear after 1963. Indeed, they mainly recruited among the educated sons of the old urban middle class and were almost completely nonexistent in the countryside, which clearly put them on the "conservative" side of the social conflict whose outcome would determine the fate of Syria for the decades to come, that is, the peasants' struggle against urban power.

The proximity of the Islamists to the bourgeois parties was well illustrated by the figure of Ma'ruf al-Dawalibi (1909–2003), who was at the same time a leading member of the People's Party (the political arm of Aleppo's notables) and a reformist Islamist intellectual closely associated with the MB.[23] During the 1950s, the sophisticated, "three-piece-suit Salafi" leaders of the Islamist movement were even privileged religious partners of the state, representing Syria in international congresses and being put in charge of establishing the Shari'a Faculty at the University of Damascus in 1954.[24]

A last explanatory factor for the Muslim Brothers' flexibility was their situation of professional politicians, which required giving priority to the demands of parliamentary games. In 1950, they eventually consented to supporting a more secular constitution than the one they had initially proposed because of their will to avoid a political crisis followed by new elections, the result of which would have been unfavorable.[25] Likewise, their claim to be "socialist" was tantamount to endorsing an ideology that was extremely popular among their main potential audience, that is, the urban educated middle class.

As illustrated in the previous paragraph, the main other component of the Syrian Islamic trend, that is, the ulema, have often displayed very different political behavior than that of the MB. By analyzing this contrast, I will show that the Syrian Islamist trend is not a coherent entity that could (or could not) undergo a paradigmatic turn. Indeed, the acceptance and rejection of post-Islamist-like values are perhaps less characteristics of particular historical periods than respective features of the two main components that coexist within the Islamic trend.

Duties versus Rights: Clerics and Political Activists

The ulema were unmistakably the most influential actors regarding social Islamization in twentieth-century Syria.[26] From the 1920s on, they have reacted to the spread of secular values by setting up Islamic schools and benevolent associations, modernizing and massifying the training of young clerics in order to reinforce the religious supervision of society, and setting up informal mosque-based networks aimed at edifying laypeople, in particular students and graduates of modern secular schools. Compared with that of the ulema, the MB's role in grassroots proselytizing pales into insignificance: at first a relatively elitist movement mainly concerned with high politics and sophisticated intellectual debates, it was forced to operate in secret after 1963 and was annihilated in the early 1980s. Therefore, the Islamic "awakening" that was witnessed from the late 1960s on was a distinctly ulema-led phenomenon.

The ulema's focus on bottom-up Islamization logically encouraged them to use politics as a means to promote moral and religious demands. During the liberal era, that is, at a time when the MB was involved in every major debate of political life, from foreign policy to land reform, the League of the Ulema—the political arm of the clergy during the liberal era—devoted most of its energy to asking for bans on "heresies," prostitution, beauty contests, cinemas, pictorials, and fun fairs.

One should not conclude, however, that clerics have been less "Islamist" than the MB. Indeed, they have also been openly calling for an Islamic state and the implementation of shari'a. Having no stake in parliamentary games, they even proved more inflexible than the MB during the 1950 debate on the constitution by castigating al-Siba'i's retreat regarding the provision stating that "Islam is the religion of the state." The ulema later reiterated their demand for the inclusion of this provision in the constitution in a petition released in 1973 and, more recently, through individual statements. For instance, during a formal interview held in his office, Second Mufti of Aleppo Mahmud 'Akkam (b. 1952) told me: "We want an Islamic state; we do not work for it directly in the political arena, but we think it will be the natural outcome of our efforts in the realm of *da'wa* [Islamic call]."[27]

Although both the MB and the ulema suffered from the Ba'th's authoritarianism and militant secularism, differences in political strategies persisted after 1963. In February 1973, for instance, the country's leading clerics signed an MB-organized petition rejecting a secular draft constitution and demanding that Islam be declared the religion of the state, but they de facto accepted the compromise imposed by Hafiz al-Assad, who ordered the reintroduction of the clause stating that Islam is the religion of the president. Meanwhile, the Hama branch of the MB went on organizing protest actions, given that the authoritarian nature of the constitution, which established a quasi–single-party system, also provided the Islamist movement with an occasion to exploit the secular opposition's discontent in order to destabilize the regime.

Three decades later, the weakening of the regime as a result of Western pressure in the context of the assassination of Lebanese prime minister Rafiq al-Hariri resulted in a similar outcome. Whereas the exiled MB and the Syria-based Independent Islamic Current (al-Tayyar al-islami al-mustaqill), a small network of lay activists, were echoing the secular opposition's demands for civil and political rights, the grand ulema, including those notoriously unsympathetic to the regime such as Sheikh Usama al-Rifa'i (b. 1944), consistently ignored this liberal agenda. In some cases, they even denounced the opposition's pro-democracy stance as a form of complicity with the Western–Israeli axis.

Leading sheikhs chose, instead, to promote distinctly religious demands by inviting the authorities to repress women's rights activists, defending Islamic schools, and pushing for the resurrection of the 1963-banned League of the Ulema. A short-lived avatar of the latter organization was created in April 2006 with the support of the state, an initiative that Sa'id Ramadan al-Buti (b. 1929)—Syria's most prominent Muslim scholar— presented as a way to fight nonorthodox trends, in particular those that are inspired by the "obsession of modernity."[28]

Of course, the exiled Muslim Brothers have been freer to express themselves than the ulema who live in Syria. However, state repression has not deterred the members of the Independent Islamic Current from asking for democracy, despite the fact that these laymen do not enjoy the relative protection provided to clerics by the sanctity of their persona—and in many cases ended up in jail. It is also interesting to note that the Independent League of the Ulema of Syria, which was founded in Jordan in 2006 by exiled ulema closely linked to the MB, almost completely avoided tackling domestic political issues at that time.

Institutional positions and economic dependence on the state are not particularly relevant variables either, since senior Syrian ulema are little integrated into the state administration and most of them rely on the resources of the private sector.[29] Neither is the ulema's reluctance to promote political change rooted in a fundamentally different conception of the desired political system. As far as principles are concerned, clerics agree with the MB and the independent Islamists on the fact that the ideal political system is one where the government is elected. Although a long-standing supporter of the regime, the aforementioned Sheikh al-Buti has written that "democracy defined as the freedom of the people to choose its rulers, and as the freedom of individuals to express their ideas...is a sacred demand of Islam."[30] At the same time, however, he departed from the Islamists by stating that *in the present context*, a democratic transition would be used by "the West's despotic forces" to "corrupt our values and turn the brotherly relations that characterize our societies into war and dissent."[31] To sum up, the difference between al-Buti and pro-democracy

Islamists is grounded not in opposite political theologies but in contrasting assessments of the *appropriateness* of democratic demands *here and now*. Of course, al-Buti and his colleagues' "assessment" of this appropriateness during the last decade had much to do with their choice to exchange loyalty to the regime for sectoral benefits.

In other words, the respective postures of the ulema and political activists are best explained by their respective daily practice. Because they are socially defined by their expertise on the management of the goods of salvation, clerics are a *sectoral* elite like, for instance, businesspeople but unlike the political activists, who claim to be an alternative *political* elite, that is, potential rulers for the country. These respective qualities entail different ways to deal with an authoritarian regime. Clerics usually promote the Islamization of society and state while not challenging the structure of the political system, since secularism, not authoritarianism, is the main obstacle to the achievement of their goals. Therefore, unless the state becomes overtly antireligious, like under the rule of the radical left-wing Neo-Ba'thists in the late 1960s, the ulema will generally favor negotiation over confrontation.

Political activists, for their part, face a radically different problem. Indeed, whatever the extent of the conservative measures taken by the regime to meet the demands of the clergy, lay Islamists remain excluded from the political game, which leads them to give priority to the structural transformation of the regime, that is, opposition in the strict sense.

It must be stressed that the rule expounded here is valid most of the time but that it knows exceptions *in times of crisis*. Indeed, as French political scientist Michel Dobry explains, one of the defining characteristics of political crises is the blurring of sectoral boundaries.[32] Typically, it is in such circumstances that sectoral elites no longer limit themselves to the defense of sectoral interests but also get involved in the public discussion of core political issues such as the nature of the existing regime.

Since the independence of Syria, only two crises were destabilizing enough to entail such a shift among the ulema. The first was the Islamic insurgency of the early 1980s, which in some places took the form of a quasi–civil war. In the northern cities of Hama and Aleppo, in particular, little space was left for neutrality, with the result that dozens of clerics who had refused to pledge allegiance to the regime were forced into exile. Many of them then joined the "Islamic Front" engineered by the MB in Saudi Arabia, which officially called for revolution against the Ba'th and for the establishment of the "liberal Islamic state" outlined in the political program of the MB.

The second of such instances was the popular uprising that started in March 2011 in the southern governorate of Deraa and then spread to large parts of the country. Like the case thirty years earlier, the ulema were split. Loyalists like al-Buti worked for deriving sectoral benefits from the crisis by offering their support to Assad in exchange for an Islamic satellite channel, a new institute for higher Islamic studies, the closure of the casino in Damascus, and the reversal of recent secularist measures such as the transfer of face-veiled schoolteachers to administrative positions.[33] Others, like Sheikh of the Quran Readers Krayyim Rajih (b. 1926), who had been known as an independent figure since the 1960s, refused to play the sectoral game and praised demonstrators who were risking their lives "in order to retrieve rights that were stolen from them forty years ago."[34] In secondary cities that were besieged by the army, such as Deraa and Banyas on the coast, local clerics openly echoed the protesters' revolutionary demands.

Regardless of these exceptional contexts of crisis, the conflicting political behaviors of the ulema and political activists seem to lie on opposite sides of the post-Islamist turn, which Bayat defines as the shift from a duties-oriented approach to a rights-oriented one. In normal circumstances, clerics mainly focus on *duties* (and sectoral privileges) because they wish to get the support of the state in the management of the goods of salvation. On the contrary, in a hostile authoritarian context, political activists logically concentrate on the claim for universal civil and political *rights*. Whether or not such statements reflect any sincerity (a rather unsound concept as far as social sciences are concerned), what matters here is the fact that political activists choose to *voice* different demands than clerics.

The preceding analysis leads me to critically address two kinds of academic perspectives on Islamism. The first is the widespread periodization that identifies a "political" phase of Islamic activism (from the early 1970s to the mid-1990s) whose failure resulted in a process of depoliticization.[35] There is no doubt that the political wing of the Islamic trend recorded little tangible success and that it no longer appeals to the Muslim youth as it did in the golden age of revolutionary Islamism. What I dismiss, however, is the novelty of apolitical (or, more exactly, non–primarily political) Islamic activism. In fact, the latter has been extremely influential from the start, not only in Syria, as shown above, but also, for instance, in Egypt, as illustrated by the case of al-Gam'iyya al-Shar'iyya, an organization that was founded in 1911 by an Azhari sheikh and remains the country's largest

Islamic association,[36] and by the immensely popular TV preacher Sheikh Metwalli Sha'rawi.[37]

Quietist Islamic activism is thus not new: it has only been overlooked by early research on the Islamic revival, which was understandably concerned with the most visible dimension of this phenomenon, that is, political movements. Therefore, the growing interest of Western researchers in the nonpolitical aspects of modern Islam is maybe less a result of the decline of Islamism than a consequence of the development and internal differentiation of the specialized academic field.

My second criticism concerns the conceptualizations of the "Islamic movement" that give the latter excessive coherence through the overpoliticization of religion, that is, by postulating a considerable overlapping of the "political" and "religious" realms. One of the most sophisticated of such approaches, which is inspired by the thought of Antonio Gramsci, sees apparently apolitical proselytizing as part of an overall Islamist project aimed at achieving ideological hegemony over society as a preliminary step to the takeover of the state.[38] Indisputably, both Islamist political activists and clerics aspire to the Islamization of society as well as to that of the state, and both categories see the former objective as favorable to the latter. Yet excessive focus on this similarity might obscure important differences between the two groups' respective conceptions of Islamic activism.

Gramscian readings tend to ascribe an instrumental character to the struggle for society since, as Bayat puts it, the state remains "the real target of change."[39] Such a state-centered perspective is indubitably relevant in the case of political activists, but it is less convincing as far as clerics are concerned. The reason for this is not that the latter are less "Islamist" than political activists, as has been made clear earlier, but, rather, that for them, elevating personal piety and morality is not merely a means to reach a supposedly higher political objective but, indeed, an end in itself, a goal that is no less important than the implementation of shari'a by the state.

The reason for this is that management of the goods of salvation, not political activism, is what defines the social identity of clerics: That is what they wake up for in the morning, and that is the domain in which their expertise is recognized. In other words, clerics prioritize a society-centered approach to Islamic activism not only out of political cautiousness but first and foremost because they are liable to play a much more prominent role in the process of social, rather than political, Islamization.

The Gramscian analysis of the "Islamic movement" also blurs an important difference in the ways political activists and clerics envision the advent of the Islamic state. Marxian tradition, to which Gramsci belongs, postulates a necessary relation between the nature of the political leadership and the content of its policies: only a government dominated by the proletariat can implement a genuine socialist program in the long term. Mutatis mutandis, such a model accurately describes the approach of the political wing of the Islamic trend. Indeed, like all other political activists in the world, the MB and the like are convinced that the best way to achieve the desired social and political order is to replace the current rulers with themselves. Clerics, as noted above, are characterized by a more "lobbyist" conception of political change: as a sectoral rather than political elite, they are much less concerned about the identity of the ruler than about the content of his policies. Whatever his background, any political leader can be pressured into implementing more "Islamic" policies. As the case of Egypt under Sadat and Mubarak shows, there is no need to replace him physically in order to achieve such a goal.

In the previous pages of this chapter, I have argued that duties and rights, which Bayat sees as the respective focuses of Islamism and post-Islamism, are relatively permanent centers of interest of two categories of Syrian Islamic actors *throughout the last decades*. By saying that, I do not rule out the very concept of post-Islamism, but I aim to specify the conditions that could lead to such a turn. In my view, the latter will not come from the spontaneous rise of a post-Islamist trend out of disappointment at the failure of the Islamist utopia. Indeed, clerics—the main factor of political stasis—are precisely the religious actors who have been the most immune to the naive belief that the Islamic state will provide a solution to all of the Muslim's problems—the reason for that being that their defining social practice (the management of the goods of salvation) has always led them to privilege a society-centered approach.

Therefore, a necessary condition for the emergence of a strong reformist trend seems to be the weakening of the clergy as a result of either secularization or the strengthening of political-minded Islamic actors thanks to liberalization, as is presently the case in Turkey. As I will show in the following section, the persistence of authoritarianism in Syria has resulted in the opposite outcome: Conservative clerics are stronger than ever, and reformist voices are hardly audible.

Syria's Reformists

Authoritarian regimes tend to favor conservative clerics who, for the reasons explained above, generally choose to promote Islamization without challenging the core principles of the political order. Syria's leadership is no different, since it does not select its religious partners according to their proximity to the "progressive" ideology of the Ba'th but, rather, according to their loyalty and, preferably, their credibility. Such is the rationale for the close partnership established in the early 1980s by Hafiz al-Assad with Sheikh al-Buti, a very popular writer who had openly condemned both nationalism and socialism—the two main components of Ba'thism—in his publications.[40]

Syrian authoritarianism not only provides a favorable context for religious conservatism: it is also fundamentally detrimental to reformist ideas. Indeed, reformists face a double constraint: If they promote political change, they inevitably bring down the regime's wrath; if they follow the path of theological reform, they expose themselves to the attacks of the religious establishment. As a consequence, they often have to give up one of these two options in order to secure the support of either the state or the clergy. In other words, they must choose between playing the game of an authoritarian regime or abiding by the grand ulema's doctrinal conservatism.

Syria's reformist spectrum ranges from theoreticians concerned with theology and law to activists focusing on political change. The first category chiefly includes Muhammad Shahrur (b. 1938), an engineer who sold thousands of his *The Book and the Koran: A Contemporary Reading* during the 1990s. Shahrur's reformism is of the most radical kind, since it promotes a positivist theism where truth is to be looked for not in Islam's foundational texts but in the progress of human reason. The laws contained in the Quran are never constraining because they are inherently in accordance with the rules established at each historical stage by the consensus and reason of men.[41] Unsurprisingly, Shahrur's arguments have been fiercely rejected by the whole Syrian Islamic trend, which probably helps explain why Shahrur not only refrained from supporting the Syrian pro-democracy movement in the 2000s but even criticized both its secular and its Islamist component for prioritizing political reform over religious reform.[42]

As for Member of Parliament Muhammad Habash (b. 1962), he is primarily concerned with the theological status of non-Muslims. He dismisses Islam's monopoly on salvation, a position that underlies his numerous initiatives for interreligious dialogue.[43] His attack on a core principle of Sunni theology has earned the young ecumenist the enmity of the grand ulema, with Sheikh al-Buti even accusing him of "heresy."[44]

Isolation within the clergy made Habash extremely dependent on the security apparatus, which engineered his election to parliament in 2003. In return, the Islamic MP played the role of an unofficial public relations officer in the international media.

Habash had greater ambitions, however: from 2004 on, he exploited the combined pressure of Western states and domestic opposition to present himself as a reassuring alternative to the Muslim Brothers in the realm of political Islam. This was a perilous game: Habash soon emerged as the most vocal proponent of democratization within the Syrian-based Islamic trend, which the regime tolerated for a while before progressively silencing him from 2007 on.

Other Islamic actors have tried to combine doctrinal and political reform without compromising themselves with the regime. Quite logically, they have faced even more acute difficulties than Habash. Such was the case, for instance, for a group founded in the 1990s in Dariya, a conservative suburb of Damascus, by a local preacher called 'Abd al-Akram al-Saqqa (b. 1946). Of all of al-Saqqa's views, the most controversial among the ulema were those that pertained to women. He gave popular lessons where members of both sexes were sitting in the same hall, encouraged girls to choose their husband, and, when the veil was still forbidden at school in the 1990s, stressed the fact that acquiring knowledge was more important than covering one's hair. On three occasions, Usama al-Rifa'i, one of the capital's most respected scholars, went to al-Saqqa's mosque and warned the faithful against his "deviant" ideas.

Needless to say, senior clergymen had no reason to support Dariya's preacher when the regime turned against him because of his political stance. In 2000, al-Saqqa had refused to invoke God in favor of Bashar al-Assad after the latter succeeded his father. Three years later, his group took advantage of the fall of Bagdad to mobilize Dariya's inhabitants against both the Western invasion of Iraq and the Syrian government's negligence and corruption. Following a peaceful demonstration, citizens were invited to refuse to pay baksheesh to functionaries as well as to organize themselves in order to make up for the authorities' poor performance at collecting trash. In the following weeks, al-Saqqa was arrested with twenty-five of his students, and he remained in jail until 2005.[45]

Starting from the mid-1990s, too, a former student of al-Saqqa, dentist Radwan Ziadeh (b. 1976) had joined forces with graduates of the Faculty of Shari'a to launch a more strictly intellectual initiative, al-Multaqa al-Fikri li-l-Ibda' (the Intellectual Encounter for Innovation). The members of this group were united by a similar project to "renew Islamic discourse" and claimed the influence of reformist thinkers such as Iranian 'Abd al-Karim Soroush and Moroccan Taha 'Abd al-Rahman. For example, they applied modern theories of linguistics to Quranic exegesis, and, although praising the reformist orientation of the early Syrian Muslim Brothers, they deconstructed such crucial Islamist concepts as the "Islamic state" and the "Islamization of knowledge." The Web site they created in 1999 attracted considerable interest and published dozens of articles, some of them written by prominent contributors such as Lebanese Ridwan al-Sayyid and Tunisian Ahmidat al-Nayfir.[46] Moreover, members of al-Multaqa frequently published articles in the leading regional newspaper, *al-Hayat*. Unsurprisingly again, senior ulema fiercely condemned their innovative ideas.

Although the goals of the group were initially defined as purely intellectual, Radwan Ziadeh and another member, 'Abd al-Rahman al-Haj Ibrahim (b. 1970), showed a growing interest in politics during the "Damascus Spring" that followed the death of Hafiz al-Assad in 2000. Both of them became very close to conservative industrialist and MP Riyad al-Sayf, who would spend most of the decade in prison after his first arrest in 2001.

In the following years, the two intellectuals established ties with human rights associations and oppositional parties. Ziadeh explained this shift by saying that "no religious reform is possible without political reform." Interestingly, a reform he deemed particularly important was to "keep clerics out of politics." Ziadeh and al-Haj Ibrahim described themselves as "liberal Muslims" or "liberal conservatives" rather than as "Islamists" and displayed a strong admiration for the Turkish AKP.

The gradual calming of the regional crisis that put the regime in trouble in the mid-2000s brought an end to the two intellectuals' relative freedom of action: in 2007, both of them were forced to leave Syria and have not been allowed to come back since then.[47] During the 2011 uprising, the Washington-based Ziadeh became one of the main voices of the exiled Syrian opposition in the Western media.

Other political reformists have been more cautious by seeking the protection of senior ulema, which in return encouraged them to downplay doctrinal innovation. The best illustration of such a strategy is probably 'Imad al-Din al-Rashid (b. 1965), a professor on the Shari'a Faculty of the University of Damascus. Another avowed admirer of the AKP, he had well-known political ambitions since the late 1990s and advocated the establishment of a "Muslim homeland" (*al-watan al-muslim*) that would grant all inhabitants full citizenship regardless of their religion.[48] Although initially despised by his senior colleague al-Buti because of his close ties with al-Multaqa and "exaggeratedly" rationalist views, al-Rashid eventually succeeded in obtaining the support of the "pope" of Syrian Islam by making an effort to appear as an "orthodox" scholar. As a result, he was described by a member of al-Multaqa as "moderate inside but conservative outside."[49]

However, al-Buti's support did not prevent al-Rashid's dismissal from the faculty in 2010.[50] This measure was part of a larger move against pro-democracy Islamists that had started in early 2008 with the arrest of several members of the Independent Islamic Current. That same year, Mu'adh al-Khatib (b. 1960), an engineer and former (outspoken) preacher at the Umayyad mosque, had been forced to resign from the chairmanship of al-Tamaddun al-Islami (the Islamic Civilization), an Islamic-modernist association from the 1930s he had tried to revive.[51] The state's offensive against Islamic dissent intensified the following year: Habash's think tank was closed, and his column in the official newspaper *al-Thawra* was suppressed; Salah al-Din Kaftaro, the son of the late Grand Mufti and the director of the private academy that was named after him, was arrested as a result of his general lack of discipline, which included, among other things, repeated praises for the "Turkish experience"; a similar fate soon befell Haytham al-Malih, an almost eighty-year independent Islamist and the most senior human rights activist in the country.

This onslaught on political reformists was paralleled by an unprecedented rise of the archconservative Sheikh al-Buti within the country's religious institutions: in 2008, the scholar, who had never occupied any prominent official position, was successively appointed as the preacher and director of the Umayyad mosque—one of Islam's most sacred worship places—as the head of the committee put in charge of reforming the programs of religious schools, and as the supervisor of the two higher institutes recently set up by the state in order to train future clerics.[52] More than ever, Syrian authoritarianism was proving more favorable to obedient and conservative ulema than to reformist dissenters.

Conclusion: What Makes Islam Democratic?

By looking for a post-Islamist turn in the discourse of the Syrian MB, one risks missing the fact that this discourse has never radically changed since the movement's inception in the 1940s: not because Syrian Islamists have remained inflexible "old" Islamists but because they have always been characterized by the acceptance of core features of the modern liberal state such as free multipartite elections and the citizenship of non-Muslims. The Syrian Muslim Brothers' political flexibility was the result of their early socialization within a democratic system: as professional politicians, they had to cope with demands such as seducing potential electors and forming alliances with secular parties. Moreover, given the strong influence exerted over the army by secular parties, the Muslim Brothers were convinced that they had everything to lose in the replacement of the parliamentary regime with a military dictatorship.

Envisioning the Syrian Islamic trend from the angle of a coming post-Islamist turn might also lead one to overemphasize the cohesion of this trend while neglecting internal structural differences. Indeed, contrarily to the MB, the ulema, who constituted the backbone of Syria's movement for social Islamization during the second half of the twentieth century, have shown unfailing conservatism and doctrinal rigidity. The reason for this is that they are clerics rather than political activists, which means that they do not have to bow to the demands of the political game and can more rigidly stick to doctrinal principles.

Under Ba'thist authoritarianism, the MB focused on the struggle for its *right* to return to the political game, thus challenging the single-party model. Clergymen, on their part, have generally worked for improving their position *within* the existing order, except in those exceptional moments when this order was overtly antireligious, as under the Neo-Ba'th in the 1960s, or when it was shaken by a major crisis, like in 1979–1982 and 2011. Being consequently perceived by the regime as a lesser threat than political activists, the ulema have always been treated more leniently despite their outright rejection of Ba'thist ideology.

What precedes lends much credence to the idea that in the Syrian context, democratization is the condition for Islamic reform to take root, not the opposite. If the ulema constitute a major hindrance to political change, it is less because of their ideology—although they would certainly not describe themselves as "democrats," they nevertheless support the idea of an elected government—than because of their status as a sectoral elite, which makes them reluctant to challenge state power.

Since what prevents the clergy from pushing for political change is not its ideology but its sectoral nature, there is little reason to believe that the spread of "post-Islamist" ideas among the ulema would entail significant change. On the contrary, a transition to democracy similar to what happened in Turkey is liable to bolster reformist voices by weakening the clergy, whose hegemony over the religious field would be challenged by activists deriving legitimacy from their political successes. To sum up, what will "make Islam democratic" in Syria will not be the victory of the "post-Islamists" over the "old guard Islamists" but, rather, the advent of a context that will allow for the rise of rights-oriented political activists to the detriment of duties-oriented clerics.

Notes

1. Asef Bayat, *Making Islam Democratic: Social Movements and the Post-Islamist Turn* (Stanford: Stanford University Press, 2007), 136–187.

2. See Annabelle Böttcher, *Syrische Religionspolitik Unter Asad* (Freiburg im Breisgau: Arnold-Bergstraesser-Institut, 1998); Eyal Ziser, "Syria, the Ba'th Regime and the Islamic Movement: Stepping on a New Path?" *Muslim World* 95 (2005): 43–65.

3. For a survey of the different conceptualizations of post-Islamism, see Bayat, *Making Islam Democratic*, 10.

4. Being a cleric or a political activist is a matter not of formal education (in Syria at least, the former category includes engineers and physicians, and the latter comprises shari'a graduates) but of *vocation* and actual social activity.

5. I am indebted for this conceptualization to Stéphane Lacroix's analysis of Saudi Islamists. See Stéphane Lacroix, *Awakening Islam. Religious Dissent in Contemporary Saudi Arabia* (Cambridge: Harvard University Press, 2011).

6. Society of the Muslim Brothers in Syria, *Al-mashrū' al-siyāsī li-Suriyya al-mustaqbal* [The political project for future Syria], June 1, 2007, at www.ikhwansyria.com.

7. See the appendix in Umar Abd-Allah, *The Islamic Struggle in Syria* (Berkeley: Mizan Press, 1983), 201–267.

8. All quotations in this paragraph are taken from the *Political Project*. For a more detailed analysis of this text, see Thomas Pierret, "Le 'Projet politique pour la Syrie de l'avenir' des Frères Musulmans," in *La Syrie au present*, ed. Youssef Courbage, Baudouin Dupret, Zouhair Ghazal, and Mohammed Al-Dbiyat (Paris: Actes Sud, 2007), 729–738.

9. Movement for Justice and Development, "Barnamij al-haraka" [Program of the movement], at http://forsyria.org/arab/programme.asp#_Toc1 (accessed August 2, 2009).

10. Most of the military operations were carried out not by the MB but by a radical split organization called the Fighting Vanguard (al-Tali'a al-muqatila). See the account of this period by a former member of this group: 'Umar 'Abd al-Hakim (aka Abu Mus'ab al-Suri), *Al-thawra al-islamiyya al-jihadiyya fi Suriyya* [The Islamic *jihadi* revolution in Syria] (n.p., n.d.).

11. See Abd-Allah, *Islamic Struggle in Syria*, 213–219; Hans Günter Lobmeyer, "Islamic Ideology and Secular Discourse: The Islamists of Syria," *Orient* 32 (1991): 395–418.

12. Hans Günter Lobmeyer, "Al-dimuqratiyya hiyya al-hall? The Syrian Opposition at the End of the Asad Era," in *Contemporary Syria. Liberalization between Cold War and Cold Peace*, ed. Eberhard Kienle (London: British Academic Press, 1994), 90.

13. Ibid., 87; Joshua Landis and Joe Pace, "The Syrian Opposition," *Washington Quarterly* 30 (2006): 55–56.

14. For instance, whereas in 1973 the Aleppo branch of the movement had indirectly taken part in the legislative elections by supporting Islamic-leaning independent candidates, four years later, it decided to boycott the polls. According to an MB leader who unsuccessfully advocated participation in the elections at that time, this decision partly resulted from an "erroneous" interpretation of Qutb's writings. See Zuhayr Salim, "Safha min tarikh al-ikhwan al-muslimin fi Suriyya" [A page in the history of the Muslim Brothers in Syria], September 19, 2010, at www.levantnews.com.

15. See appendix 3 in Johannes Reissner, *Ideologie und Politik Der Muslimbrüder Syriens. Von Den Wahlen 1947 Bis Zum Verbot Unter Adîb Ash-Shîshaklî* (Freiburg im Breisgau: Klaus Shwarz, 1980), 417. For a more detailed analysis of the views of the early Syrian MB on democracy, see Itzchak Weismann, "Democratic Fundamentalism? The Practice and Discourse of the Muslim Brothers Movement in Syria," *Muslim World* 100 (2010): 1–16.

16. Joshua Teitelbaum, "The Muslim Brotherhood and the 'Struggle for Syria,' 1947–1958. Between Accommodation and Ideology," *Middle Eastern Studies* 40 (2004): 144.

17. Reissner, *Ideologie und Politik*, 338–354; Teitelbaum, "Muslim Brotherhood and the 'Struggle for Syria,'" 142–144.

18. Jamal Barut, "Suriyya. Usul wa ta'arrujat al-sira' bayn al-madrasatayn al-taqlidiyya wa-l-radikaliyya" [Syria. Origins and aspects of the conflict between the traditional and radical trends], in *Al-ahzab wa-l-harakat wa-l-jama'at al-islamiyya* [Islamic parties, movements, and societies], ed. Jamal Barut and Faysal Darraj (Damascus: Arab Center for Strategic Studies, 2000), 258.

19. On the socialism of the MB, see Reissner, *Ideologie Und Politik*, 300–315.

20. Shakir As'id, *Al-barlaman al-suri fi tatawwurihi al-tarikhi* [The Syrian parliament in historical development] (Damascus: al-Mada, 2002), 377–383.

21. Reissner, *Ideologie Und Politik*, 10.

22. Ghada Hashem Talhami, "Syria: Islam, Arab Nationalism and the Military," *Middle East Policy* 8 (2001): 110–127.

23. See Ma'ruf al-Dawalibi, *Mudhakkirat* [Memoirs] (Riyadh: 'Ubaykan, 2006). For a conservative refutation of al-Dawalibi's modernist views on various issues, see 'Ala al-Din Kharufa, *Muhakama ara' al-Dawalibi fi al-qawmiyya wa-l-'ilmaniyya*

wa-l-ridda wa-l-fa'ida al-rabawiyya [Trial of the views of al-Dawalibi on nationalism, secularism, apostasy, and usurious interest] (Tripoli, Lebanon: Maktabat
al-Madina, 1992).

24. Bernard Botiveau, "La formation des oulémas en Syrie. La faculté de shari'a
de'université de Damas," in *Les intellectuels et le pouvoir: Syrie, Égypte, Tunisie,
Algérie*, ed. Gilbert Delanoue (Cairo: CEDEJ, 1986), 67–91.

25. Reissner, *Ideologie Und Politik*, 351–354.

26. This section is based on my *Baas et Islam en Syrie. La dynastie Assad face aux
oulémas* (Paris: Presses Universitaires de France, 2011).

27. Mahmud 'Akkam, interview by the author, Aleppo, November 20, 2006.

28. *Al-Ra'y* (Amman), April 28, 2006.

29. Thomas Pierret and Kjetil Selvik, "Limits of 'Authoritarian Upgrading' in Syria.
Welfare Privatization, Islamic Charities and the Rise of the Zayd Movement,"
International Journal of Middle East Studies 41 (2009): 599.

30. Sa'id Ramadan al-Buti, "Alladhina yakiduna li-l-dimuqratiyya bi-ismiha" [Those
who conspire for democracy and in its name], February 2000, at www.bouti.
com.

31. Ibid.

32. Michel Dobry, *Sociologie des crises politiques* (Paris: FNSP, 1986).

33. See http://all4syria.info/web/archives/2210, April 6, 2011.

34. Sheikh of the Quran Readers Krayyim Rajih, Friday sermon, April 22, 2011, at
www.youtube.com/watch?v=T8RS1FaVvik.

35. Bayat, *Making Islam Democratic*, 149. See also Olivier Roy's linking between
post-Islamism and the rise of neo-fundamentalism: Olivier Roy, *The Failure of
Political Islam* (Cambridge: Harvard University Press, 1994), 75–88.

36. Sarah Ben Nefissa, "Citoyenneté morale en Égypte. Une association entre État
et Frères Musulmans," in *Pouvoirs et associations dans le monde arabe*, ed. Sarah
Ben Nefissa (Paris: CNRS, 2002), 147–179.

37. Hava Lazarus-Yafeh, "Muhammad Mutawalli Al-Sha'rawi—A Portrait of a
Contemporary *'Alim* in Egypt," in *Islam, Nationalism and Radicalism in Egypt
and the Sudan*, ed. Gabriel Warburg and Uri Kupferschmidt (New York: Praeger,
1983), 281–297.

38. Bayat, *Making Islam Democratic*, 12, 42. For more strictly theoretical attempts
at applying Gramsci's theories to the Islamist phenomenon, see Armando
Salvatore and Mark LeVine, *Religion, Social Practice, and Contested Hegemonies:
Reconstructing the Public Sphere in Muslim Majority Societies* (Houndmills,
England: Palgrave Macmillan, 2005); Cihan Tuğal, "Transforming Everyday
Life: Islamism and Social Movement Theory," *Theory and Society* 38 (2009):
423–458.

39. Bayat, *Making Islam Democratic*, 12.

40. See, for instance, Sa'id Ramadan al-Buti, "Hakadha nasha'at al-qawmiyya"
[This is how nationalism was born], in *Shawqi Abu Khalil. Buhūth wa maqālāt*

muhaddāt ilayhi [Festschrift in honor of Shawqi Abu Khalil] (Damascus: Dar al-Fikr, 2004), 169–182; Sa'id Ramadan al-Buti, *Naqd awham al-jadaliyya al-maddiyya: al-Diyaliktikiyya (Réfutation des illusions du matérialisme dialectique)* (Damascus: Dar al-Fikr, 1986).

41. Muhammad Shahrur, Andreas Christmann, and Dale F. Eickelman, *The Qur'an, Morality and Critical Reason: The Essential Muhammad Shahrur* (Leiden: Brill, 2009).

42. Andreas Christmann, "Religious Reform before Political Reform: Muhammad Shahrur's Contribution to the Current Islah Debate in Syria" (unpublished paper, 2010).

43. Paul Heck, "Religious Renewal in Syria: The Case of Muhammad Al-Habash," *Islam and Christian–Muslim Relations* 15 (2004): 185–207.

44. Anwar Warda, *Hiwār…Lā shajār* [A dialogue…not a fight] (Damascus: Mu'assasat al-Iman, 2003), 15–16.

45. A relative of al-Saqqa, interview by the author, Damascus, March 2007; Radwan Ziadeh, interview by the author, New York, March 12, 2010.

46. See www.almultaka.net/index.php.

47. 'Abd al-Rahman al-Haj Ibrahim, interviews by the author, Damascus, 2005–2007; Radwan Ziadeh, interview by the author, New York, March 12, 2010.

48. 'Imad al-Din al-Rashid, interview by the author, Damascus, July 29, 2007.

49. Anonymous source, electronic communication, February 2010.

50. See http://all4syria.info/content/view/33817/113/, October 21, 2010.

51. Ahmad Mouaz al-Khatib, "Al-Tamaddun al-Islami: Passé et présent d'une association réformiste damascène," *Maghreb-Machrek* 198 (2008): 79–92.

52. Minister of Religious Endowments Muhammad al-Sayyid, interview in *Tishrin*, September 1, 2009.

Index